Individual Differences in the Classroom

Individual Differences
in the
Classroom

by

R. MURRAY THOMAS

UNIVERSITY OF CALIFORNIA, SANTA BARBARA

and

SHIRLEY M. THOMAS

SCHOOL PSYCHOLOGIST

DAVID McKAY COMPANY, INC.
New York

PREFACE

There are many books about the very exceptional child—the child who is so hard of hearing or lame or mentally retarded that he needs the help of an expert. Such volumes are excellent guides for that relatively small percentage of teachers who study to become experts in caring for the unique needs of these special children.

However, the great majority of children and youth are not so exceptional. They are taught by regular teachers in regular classrooms along with thirty or more agemates.

But to say they are in *regular* classrooms and are *not so exceptional* does not mean they are not different from each other in many ways. The typical classroom may seldom contain deaf students, but it often has children who hear with varied degrees of accuracy. It may not contain the exceedingly crippled, but it will have students with a variety of lesser physical handicaps that greatly affect their lives. It may not include the very lowest mentalities, but it often encompasses a range of intellectual ability that extends from the depressingly limited to the brilliant.

Besides these kinds of differences, the typical class exhibits decided variations in reading skill, musical and artistic ability, socioeconomic level, individual personality traits, and the like.

The regular classroom teacher is asked to accept this potpourri of talents and liabilities and to teach in such a way that each pupil makes the greatest progress that his unique abilities will allow. This is indeed a great expectation.

The most persistent, discouraging problems faced daily by teachers are usually caused by the fact that pupils differ from each other in so many ways. Despite teachers' great needs for suiting learning to individual differences, there seems to be no single modern textbook designed to aid them adequately with their problems in this realm. The purpose of *Individual Differences in the Classroom* is to help fill this gap.

We have chosen to focus on (1) intellectual differences, (2) differences in specialized abilities, like those affecting success in music, art, and motor activities, and (3) psychophysical differences, such as variations in hearing, seeing, and speaking. (Although such inter-group differences as race, religion, and social class are also important, they are not treated as central topics here but will be presented in a subsequent volume.)

For each of the foregoing aspects of students' personalities, we have tried to answer the questions that appear most vital to class-room instructors:

1. What is the nature or definition of this facet of the child's or youth's life?

2. What range of differences will teachers be likely to find in a typical classroom?

3. How can educators recognize or measure the differences?

4. What kinds of classroom organization and, in some instances, school-wide organization can best care for these differences?

5. What specific methods and materials should a teacher use to help students who have these differences learn at their optimum level?

In seeking answers to these questions, the writers have been aided by numerous teachers, school psychologists, and administrators. The assistance of Carl Morgensen, Dr. Robert Barry, Naomi Finnigsmier, and Thomas Hord was particularly appreciated.

Throughout the text the references in parentheses, such as (Magnifico, 1958:62–66), refer to the name of the first author of a reading source that is listed at the end of the chapter, the publication year of the article or book, and the pertinent pages in the reference.

R. MURRAY THOMAS
SHIRLEY M. THOMAS

CONTENTS

PREFACE

PART I: THE PROBLEM OF DIFFERENCES

PART II: INTELLECTUAL DIFFERENCES

PART III: ARTISTIC AND MOTOR DIFFERENCES

PART IV: PSYCHOPHYSICAL DIFFERENCES

PART I

The Problem of Differences

The initial questions to which this volume directs itself are: Which differences among children and youth are most important to teachers and school administrators? What attitude should a teacher take toward trying to alter or adjust to these differences? Part I, consisting of two chapters, poses answers to these questions.

CHAPTER 1

The Rule of Inequality

Children are not created equal, nor do they become more alike as they grow older. Rather, by the time they enter school the inequalities among them—intellectually, physically, and in social behavior—have increased manyfold. As they move upward through the grades, the differences increase even further.

This rule of inequality is no surprise to either prospective or in-service teachers. But not so obvious are the extent and importance of individual differences. Thus in Chapter 1 we shall try to cast some light on their extent and importance, and we shall foreshadow the contents of the rest of the book by inspecting three types of variability found among students in representative schools. We shall first inspect one elementary classroom in some detail, then turn our attention to certain characteristics of individual differences in junior and senior high schools.

Throughout the chapter, our discussion focuses on two questions: What is the range of significant differences? Why are these differences considered important?

A FIFTH–GRADE CLASSROOM

In viewing the students of this class, our attention will center on (1) intellectual talents, (2) artistic and motor skills, and (3) psychophysical characteristics.

When we label this classroom "representative" or "typical," we must qualify our statement by adding that it is typical of those found in city areas populated by families of lower socioeconomic

3

status. It is not a slum, but a section dominated by small houses and by larger, older ones that have been converted into apartments for families of laborers. In addition to these residences, the district contains lumberyards, commercial laundries, building-supply warehouses, and electronic-equipment plants. Obviously the socioeconomic and ethnic differences (with "ethnic" meaning both racial and national-origin characteristics) here are not the same as those found in more affluent parts of the city, where the price of homes and the attitudes of their owners tend to restrict the neighborhoods to middle-class and upper-class white Americans.

The fifth-grade class contains a mixture of children from Mexican, Negro, Italian, and Anglo-European ethnic backgrounds. The ethnic groups within the class accept each other, displaying friendship choices which do not reflect any apparent distinctions because of color or creed.

Intellectual Talents

Because most of the school's objectives focus on mental skills rather than physical or social ones, the area of intellectual talents is the one of greatest importance for most teachers.

In the fifth grade, as in many classrooms throughout the nation, the teacher's greatest interest at the beginning of the school year is in learning what range of intellectual talents he will face among his pupils. Report-card marks from last year's fourth-grade teacher provide some of this information, but a more comprehensive estimate is furnished by the two batteries of standardized tests which are administered during the first two weeks of school.

The first battery consists of a verbal test intended to predict a child's talent for understanding word meanings and verbal relationships and a quantitative test intended to predict a child's talent for working with mathematical relationships. Figure 1–1 shows the range of scores, expressed in terms of grade levels, for the fifth-grade class. In verbal ability, the tested pupils range from Grade 3 through Grade 8. In quantitative ability, they range from Grade 4 through Grade 9. We should note that Figure 1–1 refers only to *tested* pupils rather than to the entire class. This is because four of the twenty-seven students did not take the examination. One was Harry, a blind boy, who was given an entirely oral test by the school system's special-education department (and on which he earned an estimated intelligence quotient above 150). Another was Carmelita, who neither spoke nor read English at the time of the testing. Miguel and Ramon were absent.

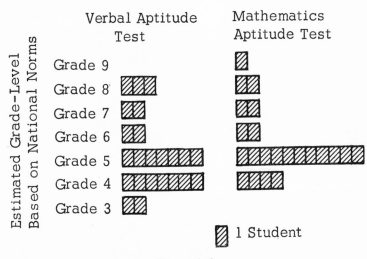

Figure 1–1

Grade-Level Standing of Fifth-Graders on Aptitude Tests

The second battery focuses not so much on aptitude as on past success with school learning as reflected by current knowledge of reading, mathematics, social studies, science, and the English usage needed in writing. (Though the aptitude and current-achievement tests are separate examinations, it is apparent that verbal aptitude will overlap a student's success in reading and writing and quantitative aptitude will overlap his skill in mathematics.)

Figure 1–2 shows an even greater range of skill in these school subjects than was found on the two parts of the aptitude tests. The most remarkable spread of scores is in reading: abilities range at least from Grade 3 through Grade 12. We say "at least" because on this set of tests there are no published national standards below Grade 3, so all the lowest scores are placed in the Grade 3 category.

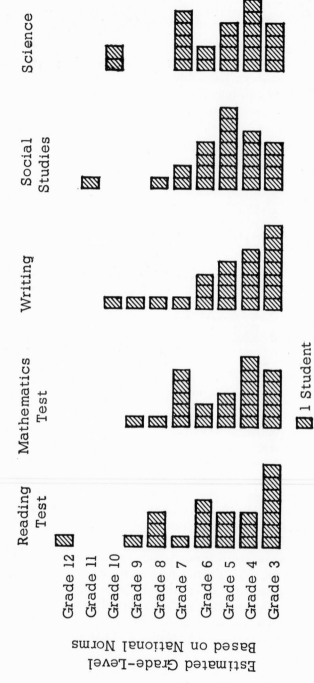

Figure 1–2

Grade-Level Standing of Fifth-Graders on Achievement Tests

It is likely that among the seven children whose reading scores fell in this lowest division, one or two actually read no better than an average second-grader. Therefore, the fifth-grade teacher this year faces the challenge of providing appropriate reading experiences that span a range of ten or eleven grades.

The spread of talent in mathematics, social studies, science, and writing is less than in reading, but in each instance it still encompasses between seven and nine grade levels.

If the teacher is to meet students' individual intellectual needs effectively, it is obviously important that he first recognize that such a wide range of skills exists. But equally important, though sometimes ignored, is the way these skills are patterned differently in each child's life. We can illustrate this by inspecting score profiles of four of the fifth-grade pupils.

Figure 1–3 shows the pattern of aptitude and school-progress scores of the most scholarly girl, Pat, and of the least scholarly, Lois. The score patterns are charted as percentiles. For example, on the reading test Pat scored at the 95th percentile, which means she reads better than 95 per cent of the several thousand fifth-graders throughout the nation on whom the test was standardized. On the other hand, Lois' position at the 9th percentile means that she reads better than only 9 per cent of the fifth-graders who were used in establishing the national norms.

The profile of Pat's scores indicates that she is very high in all areas with the exception of social studies, in which she ranked at only a moderately high level (71st percentile). Lois' profile shows very low scores on all tests except the quantitative, on which she was above average (69th percentile), and the science, on which she more closely approached the average for her grade.

Figure 1–4 pictures the score patterns of Don, who is an over-all average student, and Mario, who is the most capable scholar in the class. Don's test profile illustrates again the fact that even when most of a student's scores hit a given level, he may be more or less capable in one or two specific fields. On the other hand, Mario's scores indicate that it is also possible for an individual to achieve almost equally well across the board. Mario is the fifth-grader who ranked at high-school levels on all the school-progress tests.

Although these standardized test scores are valuable in suggesting

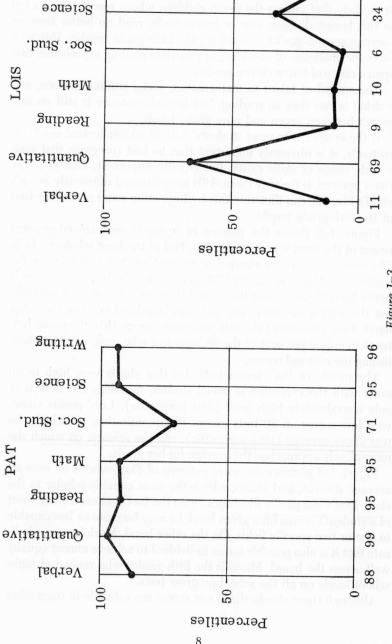

Figure 1–3

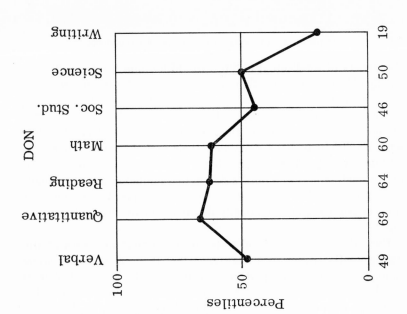

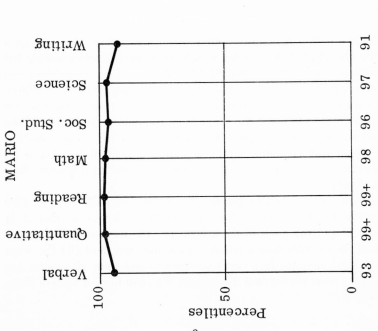

Figure 1–4

the variety of intellectual abilities the fifth-grade teacher will face, we should also recognize that such scores must be interpreted with some caution. For instance, at least some of the children from Spanish-speaking homes probably earned aptitude-test scores that are not accurate measures of their true potential. The lack of facility with English may have depressed their verbal-aptitude marks. In addition, we should recognize that a score on a single test reflects only a small sample of a pupil's skill in that limited area. Occasionally this sample of skill is inaccurate because the pupil was unusually tired or confused or emotionally distressed at the time of the testing.

Even though standardized tests are not perfect measures of student potential, experience has shown that they are rather accurate estimates of the school performance that can be expected of *most* pupils. Tests furnish the teacher an initial expectation—a set of hypotheses—with which to start planning his work. Then, as daily class sessions progress, he can revise and refine his original estimates by using the techniques described in Chapter 3.

Before proceeding to our analysis of the importance of intellectual differences, we should point out that the range of intellectual abilities in our illustrative fifth grade is not at all unique. Fifth grades all over the nation contain a similar breadth of talent. Nor is such a wide spread of ability limited to schools of lower socioeconomic circumstances or of mixed ethnic origins. It is true that in wealthier and more highly educated neighborhoods the proportion of children scoring below their grade level will usually be smaller than in our sample fifth grade. But the range from the bottom to the top of the class will be about the same. Whether pupils are from lower, middle, or upper socioeconomic strata, a similar spread of talent can be expected. Usually it is only the proportion found at different levels that varies.

We may now ask: Of what significance are these differences? This question can be answered from at least three viewpoints, that is, in terms of (1) the goals of the school, (2) the ways such differences affect the interpersonal relations within the class, and (3) the ways individual students feel about themselves and their classmates because of these intellectual differences. We shall inspect each of these viewpoints.

Goals of the School

The great significance that intellectual differences hold for the schools is shown by the extent of the administrative and classroom teaching efforts exerted to adjust the school's fare to varied mental abilities. The administrative devices, discussed in detail in Chapter 4, include placing children of similar ability in the same classroom, retaining the failing student another year in the same grade, allowing the very bright student to skip a grade ahead, providing special classes or tutors for slow learners and for the gifted, and eliminating grade levels. The teaching techniques, presented in Chapters 5 through 9, include furnishing individualized assignments, dividing pupils into groups of similar ability, permitting some to move ahead faster than others, using teaching machines, and marking students according to their own abilities rather than comparing them to their classmates.

The school in which our fifth grade is located makes several administrative provisions for intellectual differences. First, it provides special small-group or individual instruction for remedial-reading problems. A child who is obviously reading more than two grades below his grade level is considered in need of special help one period a day. Miguel is the only fifth-grade student now receiving remedial work. Second, the school provides each classroom with a wide variety of reading materials at various levels of difficulty rather than restricting materials to textbooks that are supposedly designed for average fifth-graders. Third, it allows the most apt and socially mature students to be accelerated an extra grade ahead if they attend a summer-school session to make up arithmetic, social-studies, and science material they would otherwise have missed if they had simply skipped over the next grade.

The school does not group children homogeneously according to their academic ability. That is, one fifth-grade teacher is not assigned the most apt students and another teacher the least apt. The two main reasons for not using ability grouping are: (1) when the children are homogeneously grouped for one characteristic, such as verbal ability, they are found to be heterogeneously grouped for other characteristics, like mathematical skills, art ability, and physical ability; and (2) since none of the classes contains more than thirty-two children and some contain as few as twenty-three, the principal believes the teachers can organize work within their classrooms to fit individual pupils' needs and abilities.

The fifth-grade teacher uses several techniques for adapting work to the varied intellectual levels. For reading instruction, he has divided the class into three groups. The four least-skilled readers are in one group, the thirteen pupils of average abilities are in a second group, and the eight most-skilled readers are in the third. The blind boy attends the special Braille class, which the school conducts, at the time his classmates are reading. While the teacher aids the four slowest readers, the second group of students read a textbook assignment silently and the members of the most-skilled group read books of their own choosing. After the teacher has worked with the slow group a while, he turns to the average readers. Later in the day, when all class members are writing compositions and completing workbook exercises, the instructor has individual conferences with the eight best readers.

For arithmetic the class is also divided into three groups. On a typical day the seven best mathematics students work on algebra and geometry problems for twenty minutes under the teacher's guidance while the rest of the class complete arithmetic assignments at their desks. For the next fifteen minutes the twelve pupils in the middle group work with the teacher on multiplying and dividing fractions and decimals. When they return to their desks to complete their written assignments, a group consisting of the five least-skilled mathematicians work with the teacher on reviewing the addition of simple fractions.

In science and social studies the teacher has the class work as a unit. However, he adjusts the work to individual talents in two principal ways: by assigning different pupils to read in books best suited to their abilities and by holding higher expectations for the most capable students' performance when they give their reports on social-studies and science topics.

All students take the same spelling test each week. In addition, each pupil keeps a "spelling demon" section in his notebook where he is obligated to list the words he has misspelled on his compositions. Periodically the students pair up to drill each other on their spelling-demon lists.

In summary, the school recognizes that of all the kinds of differences among students, the intellectual ones are the most significant. At the same time they are undesirable, in that the teachers and principal would be delighted if all students could be brought up to a common high level of excellence. But that happy ideal is obviously unrealistic, for the biological and sociological forces that produce intellectual variability are inevitable, at least in the foreseeable future. So the solution to the problems created by differences lies in frankly recognizing the variations and adjusting the school program as much as feasible to help each pupil attain his individual potential, whether it be high, moderate, or low.

The Class as a Social Unit

From time to time in the fifth grade the teacher asks the pupils to respond to a question which will reflect something about the social acceptability of the members of the class. On one occasion he asks whom they consider their best friends in the class, and each student writes this information on a piece of paper, which the teacher later consults as he constructs a chart of personal-social relations (a sociogram).

If we can trust the pupils' best-friend choices (collected in late April) as adequate measures of social acceptance, we may conclude that there is some relationship, though far from perfect, between intellectual ability and social desirability in this fifth grade. There is a tendency for the academically apt pupils to be selected as best friends more often than pupils who are academically least successful. This tendency is made evident when we compare the five most popular pupils with the five least popular on whom test scores are available. (Table 1-1.) The test mark used here is a combined verbal-quantitative aptitude score.

It is seen that the average aptitude-test score for the five most popular pupils is ten points higher than the average for the five least popular. If we were to compare the eight most popular pupils with the eight least popular, we would find that the relationship is somewhat more pronounced, though still far from perfect. The average score for the eight most popular is 60.8 and for the eight least popular 47.8.

This tendency is not unique to our sample fifth grade but seems to be a general one found in most classrooms. The relationship probably results from several causes. In the first place, the pupils are well aware of which classmates are the best and poorest scholars, and it is daily demonstrated that good scholarship is highly valued by such important adults as teachers, principals, and usually parents.

TABLE 1-1

ACADEMIC APTITUDE SCORES OF MOST AND LEAST
POPULAR PUPILS

	Five Most Popular			Five Least Popular	
Name	Chosen by how many classmates?	Aptitude test score	Name	Chosen by how many classmates?	Aptitude test score
Betty	13	60	Linda	1	48
Anne	11	54	Lois	3	49
Bruce	11	53	Jack	3	47
Mario	11	77	Manuel	5	46
Ralph	10	49	Leslie	5	50
Average	11.2	58.6	Average	3.4	48.0

Since pupils so often adopt the value systems of the influential adults around them, they, too, come to admire scholarship, and they accord prestige to those who exhibit it. In the second place, the more apt children are not only better at schoolwork but frequently have a greater fund of ideas for interesting games, and they can often create jokes and riddles that amuse their agemates. On the other hand, the least able pupils not only lack the academic skills valued by adults, but they are less likely to demonstrate active imaginations and may often display a lack of confidence. To some extent their lack of confidence is a result of the adults' and older students' negative reactions to the children's academic inadequacies.

Although the foregoing positive relationship exists between academic aptitude and social desirability, we should stress that it is only a tendency, not an inevitability. In the fifth-grade class, Ralph is a notable exception to the basic relationship. Not only is his over-all aptitude score low (49), but he is also one of the poorest in reading, mathematics, social studies, science, and writing. Yet he is one of the five most popular. (Table 1–2.) When the teacher charted each child's first three choices of best friends on a sociogram, no one was

TABLE 1–2

SOCIOMETRIC CHOICES OF A FIFTH–GRADE CLASS *

Sex	Name	Chosen by how many classmates?	Chose how many classmates?	Major ethnic category **
Girl	Betty	13	6	Italian
Girl	Anne	11	13	Mexican
Boy	Bruce	11	5	Mexican
Boy	Mario	11	5	Italian
Boy	Ralph	10	5	Negro
Boy	Paul	9	3	Anglo-European
Girl	Pat	9	6	Negro
Boy	Del	9	7	Anglo-European
Girl	Janice	8	8	Anglo-European
Girl	Myra	8	11	Mexican
Boy	Harry	7	5	Anglo-European
Girl	Sandra	7	5	Mexican
Girl	Jean	7	5	Mexican
Girl	Rosa	7	0 ***	Mexican
Boy	Frank	7	6	Anglo-European
Girl	Margaret	7	9	Mexican
Boy	Eddie	7	10	Anglo-European
Girl	Molly	7	9	Anglo-European
Boy	Don	6	5	Mexican
Girl	Leslie	5	9	Anglo-European
Girl	Carmelita	5	9	Mexican
Boy	Manuel	5	15	Mexican
Boy	Miguel	3	4	Mexican
Boy	Jack	3	0 ***	Anglo-European
Girl	Lois	3	14	Negro
Girl	Linda	1	12	Mexican

* Question to which children responded: "Who are your best friends in this class?"

** Ethnic categories are those used in this school's neighborhood (but for charting purposes the teacher substituted term "Anglo-European" for the ethnic group called "White" or "American" by residents óf the neighborhood).

*** Absent on day of sociometric study.

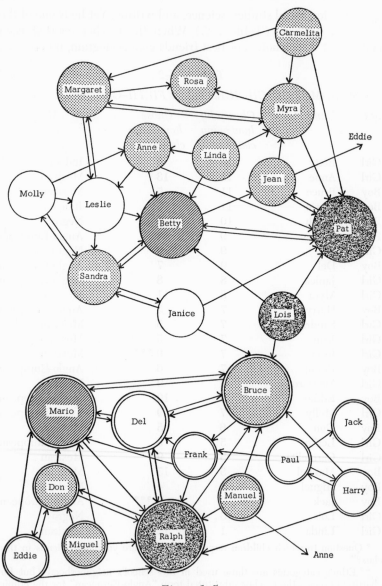

Figure 1–5
Sociogram of Fifth Grade

more popular than Ralph. (Figure 1–5.) The apparent reasons for his popularity can readily be observed by a visitor to the class. Though the boy is overweight and does not have a handsome face, he smiles a great deal, makes jokes (but not at the expense of his classmates), is helpful to classmates and the instructor, is an agile athlete despite his size, and is obviously well liked by the instructor, who frequently jokes with Ralph. Ralph is a child-size model of the friendly, jolly fat-man stereotype.

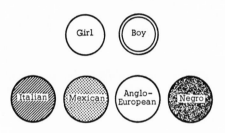

Key to Sociogram

When the social consequences of academic skill are discussed, a question frequently arises: Does the class split into social cliques based on levels of academic ability? That is, do several friendship clusters develop in the class, one cluster containing the most apt pupils, another containing the least apt, and other clusters composed of pupils of moderate mental skills? Although such a pattern does exist in some classrooms, an inspection of the sociogram for this fifth grade suggests that if such a tendency does exist, it is so slight that it is indiscernible. The least apt scholars do not often choose each other but tend to select the better students as best friends, and the most apt students choose from among their moderately skilled classmates as well as from their intellectual peers.

Individuals' Feelings about Themselves

There is little doubt that each school child's attitude toward himself is affected by his intellectual abilities, particularly as these abilities are reflected through school marks and comparisons made between him and his classmates.

In the fifth grade, Mario appears to have a quiet confidence in approaching new tasks. This confidence is probably due, at least partially, to the boy's recognizing that he is academically talented and stands a good chance of succeeding with whatever he attempts. Pat's habitual cockiness is also apparently fed by her realizing that other children do not find solutions to problems so readily as she does. Pat's mother suggests that the girl displays this same attitude at home: "There are two ways to do things: Pat's way and the wrong way."

The instructor believes that a discrepancy between Jack's intellectual abilities and his parents' ambitions for him has forced the boy into the habit of cheating in school situations. As the teacher explains it:

> Jack has low-average academic abilities, but his parents constantly talk about how he must do well in school so he can go to college. His mother shows her interest in his school success by coming to every affair we have. Jack's strongest point is nature study. He like to roam the hills to find rocks and small animals. But most of his classmates dislike him for his cheating. I think he sees cheating as the only way he can live up to what's expected of him. Last year the psychologist from the central school-district office studied him because he had so many nervous habits. It's the home pressure, I think.

At least one factor behind Miguel's reluctance to try hard on academic tasks appears to be his depreciation of his own ability. This is, in turn, a result of the low evaluation he has received from teachers and classmates during his first five years in school. It appears that children rather commonly consider marks on daily assignments and report cards to be mirrors of their own worth, at least to some degree. So when marks are constantly poor, the pupil can frequently be expected to hold himself in slight regard. It is true that an academic defeat will sometimes stimulate him to try harder next time. But a constant stream of low marks will more often cause him to try to escape the pain of scholastic defeats through the route of fantasy or truancy. Or he may strike out against classroom frustrations by acting sullen or aggressive. Educators' recognition of the negative effect that low marks often exert on pupils' self-esteem have caused teachers and administrators to experiment with the different approaches to marking described in Chapter 5.

Artistic and Motor Skills

Some school activities require a combination of intellectual and motor ability. These include the visual arts (drawing, carving, painting), musical pursuits (playing an instrument, singing), and such physical activities as athletics and typewriting.

Visual Arts

The fifth-grade teacher judges the range of artistic talent in his class by observing the pupils' drawings and paintings rather than by administering art tests. Students show individuality of several kinds in their art work. For instance, they exhibit different preferences for subject matter. Some girls are interested primarily in drawing horses and dogs. Others prefer portraits, flowers, or abstract designs. The boys' interests range from cars and planes to football games, war scenes, and rocketry. A second difference is in the degree to which drawings portray nature realistically. One boy is careful to include fine details of clothing, whereas another draws figures only in rough outline. One girl elongates human figures, whereas another draws people only in profile. A third area of difference is color-scheme preference, a fourth is preference of media (crayons, colored pencils, clay), and a fifth is formality or informality of design structure. These dimensions of difference, plus several others, result in marked individuality among the art products that pupils create.

Music

The classroom music program consists of two kinds of activities: singing and listening to recordings. The school offers special small-group lessons for students who wish to begin an instrument, and a school chorus and orchestra have been organized for the more apt and interested musicians.

Singing abilities in the fifth grade are quite varied. Some pupils sing in key, remember melodies accurately, and maintain correct rhythm. A few others easily slip off key, make mistakes in the melody, and skip beats every few measures. Between these extremes are those pupils who sing moderately well.

Not only do the students vary in singing skill, but they also vary in ability to recognize recorded musical selections. Furthermore they differ from one another in their preferences for kinds of music.

Motor Abilities

The motor skills that most obviously affect the fifth-graders' school performance are those governing handwriting and athletic achievement.

Some pupils' handwriting is so legible and attractive by the time they enter fifth grade that they need no instruction at that grade level. However, the illegibility of other pupils' writing requires the teacher's attention.

Physical abilities necessary for athletic success also vary widely. A few pupils are all-round athletes (Del, Janice, Paul). Others are adept at one activity but not so skilled at others. For instance, Ralph is a valued lineman on the touch-football team because he is both bulky and agile, but he has only average gymnastic skill. Bruce is not so talented in football but has proven to be the most capable tumbler in school. A few pupils, like Molly, are awkward in all sports.

Let us now consider how significant these motor-skill differences are from the viewpoints of the school's goals, the class as a social unit, and the individual children.

Goals of the School

Most schools include in their statement of goals a series of objectives related to art, music, and physical education. Therefore the individual differences that children display in these fields are of official importance to the staff.

In the fifth-grade class, the teacher regards the variations in pupils' art interests and drawing styles as desirable. He believes that art is a person's individualistic reaction to the world, so uniformity should not be expected. Thus he does not try to standardize either pupils' subject-matter choices or their drawing styles. He encourages them to express their own ideas in their own ways. Although he demonstrates the use of various media to them, he furnishes the pupils no direct instruction in drawing unless someone voices displeasure with what he has drawn. For instance, when Del was disturbed by the fact that "the road doesn't look like it's flat on the ground," the teacher taught him to suggest perspective by reducing the size of objects in the distance and by drawing the edges of the road so the lines converged in the background.

Children's differences in singing skill are not considered desirable by the teacher. He believes the pupils would all be happier if they could sing in tune and with good tone production and clearly understood lyrics. In contrast to his attitude toward art, in music he does not encourage much individuality of singing style. Instead, he tries to help each pupil sing according to the standard octave scale and the method of tone production usually considered desirable in Western cultures (as contrasted to the Oriental or African preference). However, in the area of musical tastes, he does encourage individuality. To promote music appreciation, he presents during the year a wide variety of phonograph records, and he tells the class:

Each person has the right to decide for himself what kinds of music he likes best and what kinds he will listen to in his own free time. So I don't think it is my business to tell you what types you should like. My responsibility is to show you many different kinds from which you can choose. And as I play records for you, I think you have two responsibilities: First, you should listen seriously to all the different recordings and to my explanations of why certain people like each kind. Second, you should not laugh at other people because they enjoy different kinds of music than you do.

The physical-education program in this school includes a variety of activities in regular classes as well as interscholastic sports for fifth- and sixth-graders. The success the school has enjoyed in competition with neighboring schools is reflected in the fact that the boys have not lost a touch-football or basketball game in three years. During the spring track meet in which twenty elementary schools participated, the school won thirty-two first places in the fifty scheduled events. The fifth-grade teacher explains:

The students try very hard in sports. Most of them aren't as gifted intellectually as pupils in some other parts of the city, so apparently our boys and girls try to compensate through athletics. I also think that physical prowess is valued more in their homes and neighborhoods than is true in the homes of children in other sections of the school district. This may be another reason they work hard at sports. We have a very effective physical-education teacher. The pupils are dedicated to him.

The Class as a Social Unit

Although the teacher has no formal measures of the effect that artistic and motor differences may exert on social relationships, he has concluded from casual observation that some effect exists. That is, class members often seem to enjoy the success in art, music, and athletics achieved by a student in their room. They brag to others in the school about Bruce's tumbling skill and Don's track and basketball exploits. When the school orchestra performs, they point to "my friend Pat" in the clarinet section. They direct other pupils' attention to Betty's and Linda's paintings that are exhibited in the main corridor. Consequently the teacher believes that this pride in the successes of classmates helps strengthen the bonds of respect and friendship which produce class cohesiveness.

At the same time, a counterforce which has a divisive effect is also operating. It is the jealousy that some students feel at seeing recognition, which they themselves would like, being accorded to a classmate for his artistic or athletic success. To diminish this jealousy, the teacher tries to find areas in which each pupil can do well and earn compliments. The instructor believes that pupils who have their needs for recognition satisfied will have less reason to be jealous of classmates. This ambition of the teacher—to praise everyone for achievements—is sometimes difficult to accomplish, because some pupils seem to do nothing very well. In these cases, the teacher is hard pressed to uncover an area in which to compliment them honestly.

Individuals' Feelings about Themselves

As mentioned earlier, it is usually difficult to judge how one factor, like artistic skill or a lack of it, affects the pupil's view of himself. However, occasionally it is possible to estimate with some degree of confidence the influence that artistic or motor skill is exerting. For instance, it was not until the middle of the school year that tumbling was taught in physical-education class. So it was at this time that Gary and his classmates first learned of his unusual gymnastic aptitude. The recognition which he received from pupils and teachers alike for this accomplishment added somewhat, the teacher believes, to the general air of confidence that Gary subsequently displayed. The teacher also believes that the confident friendliness shown toward peers and adults by Ralph (the corpulent Negro boy) is based partly on his knowing that his athletic skill is widely admired.

In contrast to Gary and Ralph, Manuel exemplifies a pupil whose ineptitude in athletics apparently diminishes his own self-regard. The fact that his peers criticize both his lack of skill and lack of courage in contact sports causes him to avoid athletics whenever possible. The physical-education instructor's attempts to help him gain skill appear wasted, for Manuel does not seem to try to learn even when given special help. When he cannot avoid activities, he will usually perform poorly and then glower and sulk, apparently angry with himself and the others.

On the other hand, Molly, who is noticeably clumsy in games, does not seem to be bothered psychologically by her lack of agility. When she misses the ball in a kickball game or does not jump rope well, she makes a joke about it and awaits her next turn with no show of embarrassment. Possibly she laughs and jokes only to mask disappointment. Or perhaps she does not consider athletic skill a necessary or even appropriate feminine trait, so she sees no reason to feel bad for not being an accomplished ball player or rope jumper. Apparently her feelings of adequacy are rooted in other fields.

We noted earlier that Pat, the best scholar among the girls, displays great confidence in her own abilities. It is likely that her apparent high self-appraisal is partially supported by her successes in the school chorus and orchestra.

The class's least successful scholar is Miguel, the fifth grade's most serious reading problem. However, in art he displays above-average ability. His consuming interest is drawing automobiles and, at home, making wooden auto models. Therefore it is in the area of art that he can honestly feel superior to some of his classmates. His teacher publicly compliments his work and puts it on display in order to increase Miguel's self-respect and his status in the eyes of his classmates.

In summary, we note that differences in artistic, musical, and athletic skills affect pupils' self-concepts and feelings of worth. Some students who suffer socioeconomic, ethnic, academic, or psychophysical disabilities may find in the realms of artistic and motor abilities their only opportunities to earn success and self-respect in the school setting.

Psychophysical Characteristics

In the category of psychophysical characteristics we include sight, hearing, speech, and physical handicaps like lameness and heart disease.

Sight

Within the fifth-grade class, the most obvious vision deviant is Harry. Because medical personnel administered too much oxygen to him directly after birth, Harry has been blind all his life. He is seated in the front row of the class so he can readily hear the teacher's instructions. On his desk is a Braille writer, a machine something like a typewriter. He uses it for writing, in the bumpy dot patterns of Braille, the answers to arithmetic problems and to questions about social-studies and reading assignments. The reason Harry is in a regular classroom rather than a special school for the blind is that this school system follows the somewhat recent trend of placing blind children as frequently as possible with their normal-sighted age-mates. The rationale behind such placement is that the child with a vision handicap is *like* other children in more ways than he is unlike them. Hence he should be with them as often as feasible so he can learn to grow up in a broad, normal society rather than in a restricted society of the blind. Because of their handicap, blind children obviously cannot lead a completely natural school life, so a compromise is made. In this city, as in many others, the blind or almost-blind from all neighborhoods attend one elementary school. A blind teacher is employed to teach them Braille reading and writing and other skills useful to the nonsighted. The special teacher also corrects their Braille compositions and arithmetic test papers. For two hours each afternoon, Harry and the other blind children of the upper elementary grades meet with this instructor for their specialized lessons. During the rest of the school day they are spread among the various classes of normal-sighted students.

A visitor to the fifth-grade classroom notices that three other pupils have vision problems, as attested by their glasses. The teacher suspects that a fourth child is farsighted, because the boy holds his book at arm's length when he reads. There may also be other minor vision problems as yet undiscovered.

Hearing

According to the hearing tests made early in the year, there are no pupils with marked hearing loss in both ears, although there are differences in auditory acuity among the class members. One girl has a noticeable but not serious loss in the left ear.

Speech

The most conspicuous speech problem is that of Carmelita, who arrived from Mexico early in the school year, unable to speak or understand English. By the end of the year in the fifth grade she understands much of what is said in English, but she is hesitant to try speaking it.

Because almost half of the children come from homes in which a mixture of Spanish and English is spoken, several of them speak English with a Spanish accent. The Negro boy's accent is reminiscent of Oklahoma, the home state of his parents.

Several minor speech problems are evident. Jack McVey has difficulty talking before a group. As the teacher describes it, "He has trouble getting the words out. He looks at his feet, makes false starts, blocks on certain words. When he talks informally to me or to the other children, he seems to be all right. But if he gets excited during a game, he repeats some syllables. It's almost stuttering."

Another boy, Paul Carlson, has a slight lisp. When reminded, he will be careful to say his *s* sounds clearly. But when he is not thinking about it he lets his tongue slip between his teeth on *s* sounds so that they become *th*. He has some other lazy-tongue and lazy-lip habits, such as saying "I'ne" for "I'm" and "fron" for "from." When reminded, he makes these sounds correctly.

A third student who has come to the teacher's attention is Anne Garcia, who accompanies *s* sounds with a slight whistle or hiss.

Other Disorders

No cases of lameness, malformation of bones, stunted growth, heart or kidney disease, cerebral palsy, or epilepsy have been discovered in the class.

As with the intellectual and artistic-motor differences discussed earlier, we ask: Of what significance are these psychophysical deviations from the standpoints of the school's objectives, the class as a social organization, and individual pupils' adjustment?

Goals of the School

Underlying the school's attitude toward the foregoing psychophysical handicaps is a general democratic ideal to which most Americans appear to subscribe, at least in theory. This is the belief that each child has the right to become all that he is capable of being. Such a belief is basic to the American citizen's willingness to support public education, contribute to muscular dystrophy and tuberculosis drives, finance research in polio, and aid the mentally retarded.

This general sentiment to help the handicapped gain a more equal chance in life is, in many states and communities, formalized by laws and policies to which legislatures and school boards subscribe in order to bring the sentiment to reality in a systematic way. Because of these laws and policies, the blind pupils are given a special teacher who instructs them in Braille on a Braille-writing machine furnished by public funds. The school's routine eye tests revealed Mario's need for glasses when he was in first grade. Last year, at the fourth-grade teacher's suggestion, Jack was observed and interviewed by a speech therapist from the city's special-education office. The therapist made suggestions to the teacher about how best to aid Jack's speech development. By such means the school systematically tries to equalize the psychophysically handicapped child's opportunities to learn.

The individual teacher's awareness of psychophysical differences and his attitude about them are just as important as the school system's formal techniques for aiding the handicapped. Most classroom teachers seem to accept the responsibility to make whatever classroom adjustments are feasible to give the handicapped child a fair chance to learn. The girl with hearing loss in the left ear is seated in the farthest row to the left and near the front of the classroom so that her better ear is toward her classmates and the teacher. The blind boy is in the front row so he can easily receive special instructions or explanations from the teacher when visual teaching materials are being used, such as charts or pictures. The teacher has asked the principal for a more thorough eye test of the boy who holds his book at arm's length.

In summary, the school believes that psychophysical handicaps are significant individual differences because they usually affect the efficiency with which children learn. Hence, the school system not only provides special facilities to ameliorate the harmful effects of handicaps but urges teachers to be aware of individual difficulties and make whatever adjustments in daily classwork seem reasonable to give the handicapped a fair chance to progress.

The Class as a Social Unit

Although it is not stated as a formal objective of the school, another humanitarian ideal accepted by the teaching staff relates to the attitudes our society wishes us to exhibit toward the handicapped. The ideal can be expressed in these terms: "We should be helpful to the handicapped. Since they are less capable of competing in life than the rest of us, it is our responsibility to aid them. The help should be not only in terms of physical facilities but also in terms of respect, friendliness, and an acceptance of them as worthwhile people."

In the fifth-grade classroom the teacher tries to pursue this goal of developing desirable social attitudes through (1) his own example of treating the handicapped children in a friendly, respectful manner, (2) occasionally pointing out to the class the way the handicap may affect the child's chances to succeed in life, so his classmates will understand him better, and (3) emphasizing appropriate attitudes toward handicaps illustrated in stories that pupils read or in current events they discuss.

The most obvious illustration of helping pupils understand and accept a handicapped child is the case of the blind boy, Harry. On the first day of school the teacher announced to the class that this year they had an unusual opportunity: the chance to have a blind pupil as a classmate. He introduced Harry and explained the purpose of the Braille machine on the desk. Within a week it became evident that Harry had an especially fine sense of direction, finer even than most blind people who become accustomed to using sound, touch, and body position to move about a room. As a kind of relaxing game after the class had finished an hour or so of concentrated study, the teacher occasionally blindfolded a girl or boy to see how well he would move about the room if he were blind. The instructor would lead the blindfolded pupil in a circuitous route about the room, then ask him to find his way to his own place. The stumbling and false moves that resulted delighted the class. The teacher then asked Harry to show how it should be done. Harry would be led by a twisting route around the desks, spun around a few times, then turned loose. He strode directly to his desk, accompanied by the admiring remarks of his classmates.

As the year progressed, the teacher concluded that Harry was a confident, well-adjusted boy, accepted by both adults and his peers. Thus the instructor judged that it would be all right to conspire with some of the pupils to play a joke on Harry, such as moving the Braille writer off his desk during recess. When Harry entered the room, his classmates watched as he moved straight to his desk, reached for the Braille writer, sat puzzling for a moment, and then announced, "You don't fool me. Who took it?" On other occasions Harry would conspire with classmates and the teacher to play a joke on some other student who the teacher felt was able to accept a trick in good humor.

Through such devices, the instructor tries to promote Harry's acceptance by his classmates and his feeling of being considered a normal pupil, able to give and take along with the rest. If Harry were the type of handicapped child who shows such feelings of inferiority that he suffers from the least criticism or laughter at his expense, the instructor would not permit jokes to be played. But Harry's parents and former teachers have helped him feel confident about his abilities, so the classroom humor in which he takes part seems to promote his social acceptance and feelings of worth rather than damage them.

On some occasions the students consider people with handicaps whom they meet in their reading. For instance, after completing a story about a boy who tried to recover his ability to walk after having his legs burned in a fire, the pupils were asked to discuss these questions: What things did the boy think were important in life after he burned his legs compared to what he had thought important before his accident? How might an accident like this change your own life? Which of the people in the story acted best toward the boy? Was anyone too helpful for the boy's own good?

Through the foregoing types of activities the instructor attempts to help students toward the goal of accepting and aiding the handicapped.

Individuals' Feelings about Themselves

Of all the subtle influences that affect a child's personality, it is difficult, if not impossible, for a teacher to estimate accurately the role that has been played by a handicap. For example, Miguel is a large boy in the class who might be expected to succeed well in athletics. But he does not. The fact that he wears thick glasses to correct very poor eyesight may be an important reason why he is not interested in sports. His lack of interest perhaps leads to lack of practice, and this induces lack of skill. The lack of skill affects his social acceptance among the boys, for they choose him as the last player for their teams and remark about his ineptness and his disinclination even to try hard. But whether it is the poor eyesight or a more general lack of self-confidence that underlies Miguel's difficulties with sports is unknown. And to what extent the poor eyesight affects his reading disability is also unknown. But it does seem fair to conclude that the boy's feelings about himself would probably be more positive if he did not suffer such a handicap which could cause him to feel improperly different from other children.

In some cases a physical handicap spurs the child to achievement. He tries to compensate for his defect by succeeding especially well in some other area of life. In the fifth grade the teacher suspects that this may be a factor causing the partially hard-of-hearing pupil to apply herself in such a dedicated manner to her schoolwork and to speaking well. But he cannot be sure.

Conclusion

The fifth-grade class which we have used to illustrate individual differences can be regarded as both typical and unique. It is typical because the kinds of differences found in it and the importance of these differences to the teacher are the same as those found in thousands of classrooms throughout the nation. It is unique because no two children, no two teachers, and no two neighborhoods are exactly alike, so the pattern of personalities and talents found in this fifth grade is not duplicated in any other classroom.

THE SIGNIFICANCE OF DIFFERENCES IN SECONDARY SCHOOLS

The kinds of differences that are important in junior and senior high schools are basically the same as those seen in the fifth grade. Only the range of variability and some of the implications for the school have changed. Therefore, rather than viewing the differences again in detail, we shall confine ourselves in the remainder of the chapter to illustrating the most important change that has occurred since the elementary grades and to mentioning some of the ways schools cope with pupil variability.

Increased Variability among Students

The most striking change since elementary school has been the continued increase in the range of variability. This is true of all the types of differences discussed for the fifth grade. Hence, if a high-school instructor has a classroom of randomly selected students, he can usually expect to find a greater spread of reading and mathematics talent, a wider range of knowledge of science and social studies, more variations in artistic and musical accomplishment, an increased range of motor skills,[1] and a greater variety of religious, social-class, and ethnic backgrounds than he would find in elementary grades.

To illustrate briefly this trend toward increased variability, we shall inspect the test scores in reading and mathematics of eighty ninth-graders who attend the junior high school in which the fifth-graders will enroll in two more years.

Figure 1–6 suggests the spread of reading and mathematics skills which may be found in a ninth grade. Two points illustrated in the

---

[1] The data on reaction time in Chapter 12 suggest that a few abilities may be more variable among primary-grade pupils than among secondary-school students. But in general, differences in both intellectual and motor skills increase as children progress through the grades.

graphs are particularly important. First, the ranges of reading talent (from Grade 4 through the sophomore year in college) and mathematics skill (Grade 3 through the junior year in college) are strikingly broad. Second, there are clusters of pupils at all levels of the ladder. It is not simply one student (like Mario in the fifth grade)

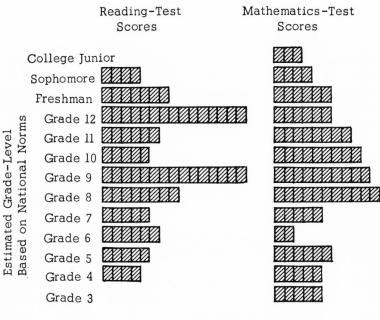

♦ 1 Student

Figure 1–6

Grade-Level Standing of Ninth-Graders on Reading and Mathematics Tests

who scores at one of the extreme ends of the distribution and thereby attenuates the range. Rather, there are at least several pupils at every level. It would hardly seem possible that one literature textbook or one mathematics class designed for the "average ninthgrader" could suit the needs of this typical collection of students.

Techniques for Meeting Individual Differences

As in the elementary school, the staff in the secondary school provides both administrative and classroom devices to meet the individual differences among students.

To care for academic, artistic, and physical differences, most secondary schools utilize some form of ability grouping.[2] That is, on the basis of test scores and the recommendations of teachers who had the student the previous year, each pupil is assigned to a section containing other students of similar ability.

In addition to ability grouping, schools also provide (1) different curricular tracks for various vocational goals (college-preparatory, business, general, industrial-arts), (2) special classes for retarded, gifted, or handicapped students, (3) opportunities for talented students to skip simpler courses and enroll directly in more advanced ones, (4) provisions for teachers to fail students and thus provide them a second opportunity to master a course by taking it again, (5) opportunities for gifted pupils to take classes in nearby colleges or through broadcast television, and (6) tutors for students who need more individualized attention.

Within the classroom, the high-school teacher may utilize many of the same approaches as those described for the elementary school. He may individualize instruction by (1) differentiating homework assignments so they fit the pupil's needs, (2) dividing the class into subgroups, each of which studies its own topic, (3) providing additional activities for students who complete the regular work ahead of time, (4) furnishing teaching machines and programed textbooks, and (5) holding higher expectations for the more able students. Specific descriptions of these and other classroom procedures are offered in Chapters 5 through 9.

SUMMARY

The purpose of Chapter 1 has been to introduce the major types of individual differences among students that are treated in this

---

[2] A survey of grouping practices in California high schools conducted by the writers in 1963 showed that 99 per cent of the high schools practiced ability grouping in at least one subject-matter area.

volume. We have inspected a typical fifth-grade class and a ninth grade in order to illustrate the range of differences a teacher may expect in his classroom. We have suggested that these differences are significant in relation to the school's and the teacher's goals, the class as a social unit, and the individual pupils' feelings about themselves.

SUGGESTED READING

CUTTS, NORMA E., and MOSELEY, NICHOLAS. *Providing for Individual Differences in the Elementary School.* Englewood Cliffs: Prentice-Hall, 1960.

HENRY, NELSON B. (ed.). *Individualizing Instruction* (Sixty-first Yearbook, Part I). Chicago: National Society for the Study of Education, 1962.

CHAPTER 2

The Foundation for Decisions

A teacher's beliefs about individual differences influence his decisions each time he assigns homework, gives a test, chooses members for an athletic team, corrects creative-writing assignments, criticizes a girl's handwriting, commends a boy for his singing, selects a textbook for a class, allows a girl extra time to complete a composition, reprimands a boy for using improper language, or carries out a score of other daily tasks.

The foundation for each of these decisions is the teacher's set of values or philosophical principles. Some of his principles he has adopted after careful thought. Others, however, have accrued over an extended period without his realizing it; these are principles which have developed from the thousands of small experiences that mold one's attitudes since the time of childhood. As a result, the typical teacher's set of values is a cluster of beliefs, some of them systematized and some not, some consistent and others contradictory, some conscious and others still below the threshold of recognition.

The first purpose of this chapter is to stimulate teachers to examine the beliefs they hold about individual differences so that they may form their values into a conscious, consistent system. The second purpose is to introduce the philosophical orientation toward individual differences on which subsequent chapters are based.

THE NATURE OF VALUES

At the outset, it is appropriate to clarify what we mean by "facts" and by "values." A fact is a statement of what *is*. A value is a statement of what *should be*. Facts are established by means of careful observation and measurement. Values, on the other hand, are beliefs not proven by observation or measurement but adopted because they appear to be self-evident or reasonable or because they are opinions passed on to us by people whom we trust. An example of a statement of fact from Chapter 1 is: "Reading skills among the fifth-graders ranged from Grade 3 through Grade 12." A statement of value is: "Teachers should provide a variety of reading materials to suit pupils' individual reading abilities."

There are four characteristics of teachers and their value systems which we shall examine in some detail. (1) Often a teacher is not aware of the exact nature of his philosophical principles until he is challenged to examine them. (2) The values which an individual says he holds may not always be the values which actually guide his decisions. (3) When he examines his values, a teacher may discover that some of them conflict with others. (4) Certain values may be unfeasible, that is, impossible to bring to realization because they are inconsistent with some of the facts in life.

Developing an Awareness of Values

There are several ways to help a teacher discover the values he holds concerning individual differences.

Perhaps the most obvious one is simply to ask that he write a statement of what he thinks are the rights and privileges of students who deviate from the average and what responsibility he thinks the school has for adjusting to these deviations. But the difficulty of this approach is that the assignment is phrased in such a general way that the teacher may inadvertently neglect certain areas of differences which he otherwise would have recognized as important if they had been brought specifically to his attention. For instance, when individual differences are mentioned, some teachers are accustomed to think only of pupils' intellectual abilities. But if these teachers were asked specifically about the roles that sight and hearing play in pupils' school success, they would readily admit that these psychophysical differences are also significant.

Another approach to discovering teachers' values will better ensure that no important areas of differences are ignored. It consists of posing for the teacher a list of questions or statements. The list is designed to cover the entire range of differences usually considered significant in school. The Inventory of Values included among the suggested learning activities at the end of this chapter is one such list. By examining the statements in the inventory and noting those with which he agrees, a teacher can better define the values he holds.

A third approach involves asking the educator to suggest solutions to a series of classroom problems that are presented to him. After he has stated his decision in all the hypothetical cases, he is asked to analyze the philosophical principles on which his decisions have been based. Perhaps this analysis is most profitably accomplished in the company of a group of colleagues who, through discussion, can aid him in discovering the details of his value system. Several classroom incidents which might serve as stimuli for this type of analysis are suggested in the learning activities at the close of the chapter.

A fourth approach can be used only by a person who currently has daily classes to teach. As he recalls decisions which he has made during the past week involving individual differences, he attempts to determine what principles apparently caused him to arrive at such decisions.

Stated Values versus Actual Ones

When a person's statement of beliefs is compared with the decisions he actually makes in the classroom, sometimes it becomes apparent that a discrepancy exists between what he claims to believe and the way he acts toward students. For instance, there are teachers who say that "a pupil should not be expected to accomplish tasks beyond his ability level"; yet in their classrooms they expect a single high level of accomplishment from pupils who have varied levels of talent. There are also those who will agree that "all pupils do not read equally well"; yet they will continually assign the entire class to read identical material.

To discover inconsistencies that may exist between his verbalized and actual principles, a teacher may compare his statements of values (such as his responses on an inventory of values) with the daily decisions he makes about pupils. Then, for the sake of consistency, a realignment of either the stated values or classroom actions appears to be called for.

Conflicts between Stated Values

Not only may inconsistencies exist between verbalized values and behavior but they are also found among an individual's stated principles. Following are six examples of pairs of value statements. In each example, the first statement of the pair is incompatible with the second; yet a teacher may subscribe to both at the same time without recognizing the conflict between them. Many of the doubts he experiences in making decisions about students may be rooted in the unrecognized conflict between these beliefs.

Example 1. All pupils have the right to equal treatment in school.

But all students vary in ability, in socioeconomic opportunities, and in energy, so that if the less well endowed children are to thrive, they must receive special, not equal, opportunities in school.

Example 2. Each social-class level has a right to its own standards of conduct and its own attitudes. The school should not require that children from one social-class level adopt the subculture patterns of a different level.

But if the school permits the ungrammatical speech, sexual freedom, and physical aggression that are characteristic of certain lower-class subcultures, chaos may result in classrooms and the children from lower-class homes will not learn the kinds of behavior that will enable them to better their lot in life. The middle-class patterns of behavior serve as the most appropriate standards for all children.

Example 3. A student's progress in school should be evaluated in terms of how much ability he has. The slow-learning pupil who works hard and achieves rather well for his meager potential should receive an appropriately high evaluation for doing the best he can. He should not be measured according to the high achievement level—impossible for him ever to reach—which is suitable for the most gifted student in the class.

But in life outside of school a person must compete with others of varied levels of talent. Each person must come to recognize and accept his own limitations as well as his own strengths. He also must expect to be rewarded in relation to his achievement, so that the worker who is less well endowed must learn to receive fewer rewards in terms of income, power, and prestige than his better-endowed, more energetic rivals. Therefore the school should prepare the child and his parents for the real-life situation by grading him in relation to the quality of his achievements as compared with those of his classmates, despite the level of his basic talents or energy.

Example 4. In a system of public, tax-supported schools, a high-school education is the birthright of every youth, except for the ones who are markedly feeble-minded.

But, since students are so varied in ability and in the diligence with which they apply themselves to school tasks, the high school cannot hope to establish any kind of sensible standards of work if each pupil knows he will pass automatically, whether he learns anything or not. A high-school diploma must represent the actual achievement of substantial learning. It should symbolize a measure of actual success. Therefore, a diploma should not be simply handed out to everyone who has spent twelve years in classrooms. The inept and indolent cannot expect the same recognition as that accorded the bright and studious.

Example 5. In America, the individual does not exist for the good of the state. The state exists to provide opportunities for the individual. Hence the school is obligated to ensure each student the chance to develop his unique talents and to express his individuality in his own manner. The school should not be an unyielding mold into which each student is pressed with the intention that all pupils should emerge in identical form.

But if people are to live compatibly and profitably together, they cannot differ from one another in all ways. In some ways they must be quite alike. They must share the same standards of conduct, speak and write the same language, understand the operations of the scientific world, and respect literature and the arts. It is the school's obligation to require each pupil to achieve these common learnings so that all people within the society may understand one another.

Example 6. It is each person's right to prepare for the vocation of his own choice and to pursue whatever education he desires.

But American society cannot operate efficiently if inept people are permitted to enter vocations for which they are not well suited. A surgeon whose hands quiver, a lawyer who cannot understand the nuances of regulations, a teacher who can neither master subject matter nor inspire students to learn, are liabilities to the society and should therefore be routed into other work. Furthermore, young people should not be encouraged to enter educational programs in which they will be frustrated by their inadequacies and waste time that should be used for learning a more suitable vocation. Therefore the school should appraise each student's abilities in order to direct him into classes appropriate to his talents and to his proper vocational goals.

When the foregoing statements are placed in such contrasting pairs, the conflict between them may at first appear irreconcilable. However, careful analysis shows that a logically sound position may often be constructed which incorporates aspects of each of the statements in the pair. For instance, the conflict between individuality and conformity posed in Example 5 may be resolved through defining more specifically those areas of life in which conformity is needed and those in which individuality should be encouraged. Here is one such resolution.

The properly organized society is the one which furnishes each person maximum opportunities to fulfill his own needs and to express his own individuality. But because most people live among others (hermits and recluses are rare), the individuals in a society must have certain patterns of behavior in common. In many ways they must agree to become alike, not different. To communicate with each other efficiently, they must use the identical written and spoken language and the same system of computation. They require a common knowledge of science, technology, and social organization. They need to agree upon fair ways to settle conflicts. With such similarity of rules and customs, one individual may not have his own particular way all the time, but in the long run the majority of people fulfill their needs a large part of the time. Hence, in methods of communication and in social intercourse the school should attempt to standardize behavior. But beyond these areas, individuality, not standardization, should be stressed. The school can stimulate individuality through (1) orienting all students to the wealth of opportunities for learning and for personal expression in literature, the natural and social sciences, the arts, and physical activities, and (2) encouraging students to offer their own unique interpretations of things they see and hear, create their own literature and art, and express their individual ideals—as long as their individual expression does not violate the rights of others.

On such a philosophical base as this an educator can support such diverse classroom practices as (1) insisting that all students use identical punctuation and spelling as well as a common polite respect for others' opinions, (2) providing survey science lessons that explore the variety of theories men have developed to account for the earth's beginnings or for the nature of light, and providing art lessons which explore the variety of media artists may use to interpret life, (3) encouraging students to create unique forms of poetry and song, adopt unusual hobbies, and propose inventions that might solve old problems.

As the foregoing example suggests, the teacher who discovers inconsistencies among his statements of values may profit from investigating these beliefs in greater depth. The investigation may reveal that when the beliefs are cast in a more complex relationship, they no longer conflict but furnish a proper rationale for classroom practice.

Conflicts of Values and Facts

Communist doctrine has contended that the distribution of the good things of this world should be accomplished in this manner: *From each according to his ability, to each according to his need.* Critics of this value statement have often said that, noble as the sentiment may be, it is unworkable because it conflicts with the facts of human motivation. By this they mean that it is not human nature for the diligent and apt person in the society to be willing to furnish his unapt and slothful neighbors exactly the same rewards of food, clothing, prestige, and power that he himself will possess. Therefore, they label the above-mentioned value statement unwise. They think that it should be recast in some such form as the following to bring it into harmony with what they conceive to be the facts about human motivation.

Each person in the society deserves a minimum level of physical well-being and psychological satisfaction. The society is responsible for providing at a minimally respectable level for the physical needs (food, clothing, shelter, medical care) and opportunities for psychological satisfactions (right to worship, opportunities to gain friendship and affection, opportunities for intellectual pursuits, polite treatment on the part of others). The minimal provision should be made regardless of the level of ability of an individual who needs it. However, beyond the minimal provision, the individual is expected to produce for himself and his own family. People who through skill and industriousness contribute much to the society deserve to receive greater rewards of worldly goods, prestige, and power than those who contribute little.

Which of the foregoing statements of value better fits the facts of human behavior has not been completely settled. But the evidence presently available, within and without Communist nations, appears to favor the second.

There are also other philosophical and ethical schemes whose feasibility has undergone scrutiny for some time. The practicability of using Christian ethics as the basis for all human conduct has been assailed and has elicited various answers from defenders who claim that Christian ethics *are* well suited to the facts of human nature. One defender has said, "How can you say Christianity won't work? No one has really tried it yet." For almost two hundred years, Americans have experimented with the belief that the most satisfactory government results when the governed people all wield equal power, through the vote, in determining how they will be ruled. So far, the experiment appears to have prospered, though there are doubters who question the ability of the populace to make wise choices and so predict that the system will fail. They believe that the values on which the system is built do not fit the facts of human nature.

When we move from these more general value systems to statements treating individual differences as related to education, we find similar questions about the suitability of certain statements in the face of the facts. Perhaps the most obvious example of a statement about individual differences (or lack of them) which has disturbed educators is, "All men are created equal." The naïve person extracts this phrase from its political setting and tries to regard it as a factual statement about human beings in general. On the contrary, it is a value statement which might be more precisely phrased as: "Although it is clear that people differ from each other physically, intellectually, and socially, all men deserve equal rights before the law." Observation and measurement furnish overwhelming evidence to support the first part of the sentence, that is, the factual part. But only personal convictions support the last part, that is, the value portion about equal rights. Americans in general appear to believe that the value portion of this sentence can be realized; they believe it is in agreement with the facts.

As this discussion has implied, teachers may profitably inspect their stated values to determine whether they are impracticable visions or are ideals that fit the facts of the world.

Summary

We conclude that an educator can form his beliefs into a more consistent, conscious, and useful value system if he attempts to (1) state his beliefs about individual differences in specific terms, applicable to the classroom, (2) compare his verbalized beliefs with the actual ones that motivate his behavior toward students, (3) resolve the conflicts that may appear between inconsistent values to which he subscribes, and (4) determine whether his values are realistic, that is, whether they are goals which can be realized in the light of the facts.

THE VIEWPOINT OF THIS BOOK

This volume is composed of both factual and value statements. The factual statements describe the kinds and degrees of individual differences among pupils as well as the techniques teachers use for identifying, measuring, or treating these differences. The value statements describe what the authors believe should be done about the differences.

Specific value judgments, mostly in the form of recommendations, appear in each chapter. However, it appears desirable at the outset to suggest to the reader the general viewpoint or value system on which most of these specific recommendations are founded. This viewpoint is perhaps best reflected in the following propositions, to which the writers, along with many people throughout America and other parts of the world, subscribe. These things we believe:

The Right to Be Educated. Each child and youth, so long as he is educable, has the right to an education suited to his capacities and learning pace, whatever his level of intellectual endowment. Hence the school is obligated to provide an administrative organization appropriate to the variety of intellectual abilities represented among students. Furthermore, teachers are responsible for suiting their teaching methods and materials as much as possible to the varied abilities found in their classes. The most apt should not be slowed to the pace of the average but should constantly be challenged to his best effort. Likewise, the least apt should not be overwhelmed by material which he cannot master or by a pace that is too rapid.

The Right to Equal Opportunities. There are marked differences among students in their opportunities to profit from schooling. Some of these differences, such as that of genetic intellectual endowment, apparently cannot be altered. Others, however, that serve as handicaps to learning (poor eyesight, malnutrition, stuttering, emotional disturbances, a lack of books in a socioeconomically depressed home) can often be ameliorated so the child's opportunities to learn are improved. It is basically the responsibility of parents to ensure that their children have optimum learning opportunities. However, when parents cannot or will not attempt to correct a child's handicaps to learning, it is the school's responsibility to take whatever measures are feasible to improve the pupil's chances for gaining an education. This means that children may need to be treated differentially, rather than identically, in order better to ensure them equal opportunities to learn.

The Right to Individualistic Self-Realization. Throughout his life, each person strives for self-respect and for feelings of accomplishment and success. Everyone possesses a unique patterning of intellectual, physical, and social skills. In addition, the environment in which he must utilize these skills is somewhat different from the environment of everyone else. Consequently, we can expect that the manner in which one individual realizes his potential and gains his satisfactions will vary from the manner in which another person achieves his. Society, therefore, should respect and encourage a wide variety of patterns for achieving self-identity and success so that as many individuals as possible can live satisfying lives. The school should stimulate these individualized approaches to self-realization through (1) orienting students to the rich diversity of ideas and ways of life with which people have experimented at different times and in different places and (2) encouraging youth to experiment with new ideas and modes of self-expression, so long as these attempts do not violate other people's rights.

The Responsibility to Respect Others' Rights. If individuals are to pursue with confidence their unique routes to self-realization, they require a social climate that is tolerant of variations in thought patterns, ideals, daily living habits, and methods of self-expression. A pupil who deviates in ways that do not violate others' rights should not be coerced, ridiculed, or rejected by the majority. It is probably natural for naïve people to regard different ways of living as wrong or as inferior to their own. Thus children cannot be expected "naturally" to be tolerant. Attitudes of tolerance must be taught. The school, therefore, is obligated to teach pupils to respect kinds of behavior and viewpoints which differ from their own but which do not harm other people.

The Responsibility to Acquire Skills and Knowledge Necessary for a Democratic Society. An assumption undergirding a democratic form of government is that each voting citizen is a literate and well-informed individual who considers others' rights as well as his own whenever he makes decisions. If he is to be literate and well informed, he is responsible for acquiring skills of communication and knowledge of the scientific and social world. He is also obligated to practice the techniques of social intercourse (participation in elections, respect for laws and for others' rights) congruent with democracy. The school is responsible for seeing that students learn these kinds of skill and knowledge. Because students differ in aptitude for learning, the level of competence that one individual reaches will differ from that attained by another.

The Teacher's Role. The classroom teacher should strive to suit learning to the individual needs and ability levels of the students. However, the needs are so varied that the goal of suiting learning to them perfectly cannot be reached by even the most able and energetic educator. Therefore the teacher should seriously attempt to meet the individual differences, yet at the same time should recognize that he should not feel guilty and should not despair because his efforts fall short of perfection. Thus the recommendations made throughout this book should be regarded as a pool of possibilities from which an instructor may draw as he meets individual differences in the classroom. No one could put all the recommendations into practice, nor is anyone expected to. The rule of thumb should be: Do what you can within the limits of your time and energy, and do not worry about the unmet needs beyond that point.

A Recognition of the Varied Purposes of Educational Institutions. In a democracy, different schools perform different functions. The public elementary and secondary schools of America should bear the motto *Help each individual become all he is capable of being,* because these are the schools charged with educating all citizens.

Other schools, however, have a different responsibility: to select and educate individuals to perform special functions for the society. In this category are found professional institutions like colleges of medicine and law and education as well as vocational schools like police and fire-protection institutes. One of the marked distinctions between public schools and professional schools is found in their attitude toward individual differences in student abilities. Elementary and secondary schools are *inclusive*, obliged to accept almost all applicants and bound to adjust their curriculums, teaching methods, and standards of achievement to suit the varieties of talent found in the population. On the other hand, professional schools are *exclusive*, obliged to reject those who fail to give promise of performing special tasks for the society in a competent manner after a reasonable period of special education. Some people believe that the senior high school, which once appeared to have the exclusive role mentioned for professional schools above, should still perform this role, excluding students who do not reach a particular standard in traditional academic subjects. The present writers, however, agree with the major trend in America of considering the senior high school as an institution obliged to suit its offerings to the needs of all future citizens, whether they are college-bound or not.

SUMMARY

Underlying the decisions a teacher makes about his students are the teacher's beliefs concerning individual differences. In order to form these beliefs into a conscious, well ordered value system, the educator should state them clearly and analyze them for their consistency with his actions and with the facts of the world.

The values concerning individual differences on which this volume has been founded focus on (1) the rights of the individual to equal opportunities for education and for self-realization, (2) the responsibilities of the individual to respect other people's rights and to become a literate, well-informed citizen, and (3) the teacher's dual responsibility: to the students (attempt to meet their individual needs) and to himself (do not expect to meet the needs perfectly; it cannot be accomplished).

SUGGESTED LEARNING ACTIVITIES

The following list of statements forms an Inventory of Values regarding the relationship of individual differences to the schools. A teacher who wishes to understand his own value system more completely may find it profitable to complete the following inventory, then review all the statements he has marked *Agree;* the collection of *Agree* statements should represent an internally consistent summary of his point of view on the issues included here.

Inventory of Values

DIRECTIONS. In the blank at the left of each statement, write *A* if you agree with the statement and *D* if you disagree with it. If you agree with one portion of the statement and disagree with another portion, rewrite the statement in a manner that suits your point of view.

____1. Because elementary schools are financed with taxes paid by all parents, the school system is obligated to provide for at least six years an education appropriate for each child's ability level.

____2. If an elementary-school child has worked diligently, he deserves to pass to the next higher grade at the end of the year whether or not he has made much progress in such subjects as reading and arithmetic.

____3. The principal job of the high school is to promote excellence in academic subjects like science, literature, languages, and mathematics.

____4. In planning his methods of instruction, the teacher should emphasize those activities which will suit the needs of the majority of the class, even though this may mean neglecting the needs of one or two of the less able pupils.

____5. Teachers should devote extra time after school to aid pupils who have individual problems like reading disabilities or speech defects.

____6. A student's school marks should reflect where he stands academically in relation to his classmates' achievement rather than how he has succeeded in relation to his own apparent potential.

____7. Beyond the eighth grade, the schools should not be obliged to adjust educational offerings to the meager academic abilities of the less apt or less interested students.

____8. In the typical classroom, it is reasonable to expect the teacher to make the special adjustments necessary to accommodate for the needs of a handicapped child, such as a child with extremely poor eyesight, very defective hearing, or a heart condition.

____9. The fact that an academically weak elementary-school pupil and his parents want very much for him to pass to the next higher grade should not influence the decision about whether he should pass or not. Instead, the decision should be made on the basis of whether he has achieved the teacher's minimum academic standards.

___10. Elementary-school students should be passed from one grade to the next on the basis of their social and physical maturity, not on the basis of academic attainments.

___11. Since all parents pay taxes to support high schools, each American youth is entitled to a high-school diploma. All diplomas should be considered equal, with no distinction made between students who have completed college-preparatory programs and those who have completed business or vocational programs.

___12. A junior-high or senior-high student who lacks either the interest or ability to pass regular course work satisfactorily should be allowed to drop out of school to take a job.

___13. The student's personal-social adjustment is the concern of the home and church, not of the school.

___14. Since the students with the greatest ability will ultimately contribute the most to society, the teacher should give more time and thought to meeting their needs than to meeting the needs of the average or below-average pupils.

___15. High-school students should be passed from one grade to the next on the basis of their social and physical maturity, not on the basis of academic attainments.

___16. Separating students into different classes according to their abilities (so the most capable are in one room and the least capable in another) is undemocratic. It violates the ideal of equal educational opportunities for all.

___17. When a decision is made about whether an academically weak elementary-school student should pass to the next grade or not, the crucial question should be "What is best for this individual?" rather than "Has this student met the school's standards academically?"

___18. In a classroom of thirty or thirty-five pupils, a teacher should not be expected to deal with the special difficulties of a handicapped child in the room, such as one with extremely poor eyesight, very poor hearing, or some measure of cerebral palsy.

___19. The fact that an academically weak high-school pupil and his parents want very much for him to pass to the next higher grade should not influence the decision about his passing. Instead, the decision should be made on the basis of whether or not he has achieved the teacher's minimum academic standards.

___20. If the nation is to prosper, each student must reach a standard of achievement that is at least as high as the average for his grade level. If he does not reach this level by the end of the year, he should repeat the grade until he has achieved it.

___21. Both the academic progress and personal-social adjustment of elementary-school pupils are prime responsibilities of the school, so both should receive equal amounts of the teacher's attention.

___22. A student in senior high school who fails to show either the ability or interest required to pass the typical English, social-studies, and mathematics courses should be encouraged to leave school and enter a vocation.

___23. Since the average and above-average students can work on their own rather well, the teacher should spend a major portion of his time aiding the least able students because they are the ones in greatest need of help.

___24. A good way to give each pupil a fair opportunity to learn is to group him with others of like ability. Thus he competes with his intellectual peers and is not bored or overwhelmed by material too easy or too difficult for him. This ability grouping is democratic because it provides for each one according to his needs.

___25. The academic progress and personal-social adjustment of high-school students are both prime responsibilities of the school, so both should receive equal amounts of the teacher's attention.

___26. Although provision for students of all ability levels should be made by the high school, only those students who have succeeded in the usual academic courses should be awarded a regular diploma. Academically inadequate students should receive a "certificate of completion" at the end of their twelfth year in school.

___27. When a decision is made about whether an academically weak high-school student should pass to the next grade, the crucial question should be "What is best for this individual?" rather than "Has this student met the school's academic standards?"

___28. Students of all levels of ability and with all types of interests should be required to complete high school. Curricular offerings and achievement standards should be appropriately diverse so as to enable all kinds of students to reach this goal of completing a suitable twelve-year program.

___29. Although the school should not be responsible for the personal-social adjustment of pupils, it is often necessary to aid pupils in such adjustment because disturbances in this area negatively affect the students' ability to succeed with academic work.

___30. Any student who really tries can reasonably be expected to master the basic work required in most academic courses.

Now, having completed the Inventory of Values, hand to a colleague a list of the statements with which you agree and ask him to search for inconsistencies among the statements. If he locates any, try to defend your subscribing to the values which he has judged incompatible.

Finally, to determine how your philosophical position on individual differences might apply to classroom problems, read each of the following descriptions of problem situations and offer an answer to the task posed at the end of the description. Then ask a colleague to inspect your answers and compare them to the pattern of your responses on the Inventory of Values (see the first paragraph of these suggested learning activities) in order to estimate whether your recommended classroom practices are in concert with your expressed values.

Situation A. A junior-high teacher has a classroom of unselected students in a course titled Introduction to Mathematics. In past years he has been distressed by the fact that some of the students progress more rapidly than the average, whereas others drag behind the average. This year, in order to keep the class together and moving at the same pace, he will dispense with the usual textbooks. Instead, he plans to hand the students daily lessons and assignments on dittoed sheets. Since the faster workers have only the current lesson available, they cannot push on to new material and get ahead of the class, as they tended to do when they had textbooks. To ensure that the slower workers keep up, he will send home with each slower student a Parents' Guide Sheet that describes how parents can best aid their boys and girls to keep up with home assignments.

Your task: Give your opinion of the desirability of this plan and of the likelihood that it will ensure that all members of the class will progress at about the same pace throughout the year.

Situation B. A school's second-graders receive report-card marks in these subjects: oral reading, silent reading, arithmetic, social living, music, art, health education, writing, and physical education. In one classroom, a boy named Martin scored the lowest in the class in arithmetic. His performance by the end of the year was poorer than that of many first-graders. His reading performance, though not the lowest in his class, was also near the bottom. His marks in the other subjects fell in the average range. His teacher recommended that Martin repeat second grade because of his very low arithmetic scores. The principal of the school, however, said he believed children should not repeat a grade unless they were extremely low in two or more subjects.

Your task: Tell whether you agree with the teacher, the principal, or neither. How do you support your position philosophically and psychologically?

Situation C. At the time of graduation, the staff of a high school faced the problem of whether or not to award a regular diploma to a Chinese girl who, as a small child, had escaped with her parents from China and had lived in Hong Kong for some years before entering the United States. She spoke and understood some English when she entered the American high school as a junior. She tried very hard during her junior and senior years, received excellent marks in mathematics and science, but continued to make many mistakes on English compositions written in class. On objective-type examinations she succeeded well, but on essay tests she did poorly. Her written homework was good, apparently because her cousin (a native-born American) helped edit her home assignments. The high-school staff faces these alternatives: (1) to retain the girl in school until her written English is satisfactory enough to warrant giving her a regular diploma, (2) to award her a special school-completion certificate on which is written the annotation: "deficient in written English," or (3) to award her a regular diploma.

Your task: Indicate which solution you think is best, and tell why you support such a recommendation.

Situation D. A totally deaf high-school sophomore girl has transferred into the local high school. She is a capable lip reader. As the staff discusses her case, one of them suggests that the girl be sent to a nearby city where, with the aid of public funds, she can attend a state school that is exclusively for deaf and blind students. The girl would be able to live at the special school during the week and return home on week ends. Another teacher believes the girl should be retained in the local high school to attend regular classes along with her agemates, and each regular teacher would be expected to make whatever special classroom arrangements were needed to adapt classwork to the girl's handicap.

Your task: Decide which of the foregoing solutions you favor. Give the reasons for your decision. If you feel you would need more information in order to arrive at a decision, tell what kinds of information you would like and explain why such information would be useful in arriving at a decision.

Situation E. Following an accident that involved a blow on the head, a third-grade boy of a working-class family began having occasional epileptic seizures of mild but noticeable magnitude. The seizures consisted of facial distortions, rolling of the eyes, a slight shaking of the limbs, momentary body stiffness, and a momentary loss of consciousness. Otherwise the boy's behavior was normal.

Your task: From the standpoints of the rights and responsibilities of this boy, his parents, the school, the third-grade teacher, and the other third-grade children, tell which of the following solutions is the most appropriate: (1) continue the boy in the third-grade class, (2) keep him at home to be tutored by his mother and a visiting teacher hired by the school system to teach shut-in children, (3) send him to a private school that accommodates children who have various physical and emotional disorders. Give the reasoning which supports your decision.

SUGGESTED READINGS

BRAMELD, THEODORE B. H. *Philosophies of Education in Cultural Perspective.* New York: The Dryden Press, 1955.

HENRY, NELSON B. (ed.). *Modern Philosophies and Education* (Fifty-fourth Yearbook). Chicago: National Society for the Study of Education, 1955.

———. *The Dynamics of Instructional Groups* (Fifty-Ninth Yearbook). Chicago: National Society for the Study of Education, 1960.

SMITH, B. OTHANEL; STANLEY, WILLIAM O.; and SHORES, J. HARLAND *Fundamentals of Curriculum Development.* Yonkers-on-Hudson, N.Y.: World Book Co., 1957.

Intellectual Differences

Of all the differences exhibited by children and youth, the intellectual ones offer teachers their greatest problems. Therefore intellectual differences receive major consideration in this book. Eight chapters are dedicated to them.

At the outset, it is well to understand the way the term "intellectual" is used throughout Part II. By "intellectual skills" we mean those needed for dealing effectively with language, quantities, and abstract ideas. These are abilities students use in reading, in mathematical problem-solving, in explaining ideas logically in writing and speaking, in understanding scientific and social facts and relationships, and the like. They are often called "academic skills."

Without doubt the intellect is also involved in such artistic endeavors as drawing, painting, singing, playing instruments, and composing music. The same is true of such manual activities as assembling and operating machines, making a dress, and so forth. But these aptitudes also involve some elements other than those demanded by the "academic" subjects. So, for the purposes of this book, it is convenient to relegate a discussion of artistic and manual skills to a separate section, Part III.

Our treatment of intellectual abilities begins with an inspection of ways to appraise or measure them, followed by a view of the range of differences to be met by a typical teacher in his daily work (Chapter 3). Schools' administrative provisions to meet these differences are surveyed in Chapter 4. General classroom organization and methodology are explained in Chapter 5 and the role of teaching machines in Chapter 6. Ways to solve special problems met while working with gifted children (Chapter 7) and retarded children (Chapter 8) are followed by suggestions for teaching reading (Chapter 9).

Measuring Intellectual Abilities

One of the most important daily tasks of teachers is to estimate the intellectual abilities of their students. An instructor finds himself asking such questions as:

"Is Frank working up to his potential? Should I transfer Wally to the group that's moving at a slower pace? Would Helen be better off if she skipped to a higher grade? Will Anne succeed in college? Can I trust Talbot to be chairman of the committee? Should the class have more homework? Are the new library books too difficult? Should Karl major in science?"

In all these cases the teacher is estimating either the pupils' present intellectual abilities or future intellectual level. Such judgments are essential if an instructor hopes to suit work to each student's needs. But the question is: How can a teacher best decide whether a student is high, average, or below average in each intellectual ability?

There are several ways of deciding. The most common is to *watch the way the student solves the problems he faces in his daily life.* Obviously, when he comes to good solutions for a person of his age, he is considered bright. When he has much more trouble than his agemates—and even then his solutions are often poor ones—he may be called dull or below average. If he is about like his agemates in problem solving, he is labeled average or typical or normal.

Such daily observations of classwork have two advantages, compared to formal ability tests. They not only suggest the level of the student's ability but indicate how this may show up more favorably in one kind of life situation than another. A boy may be better at working alone than in a group. Perhaps he does well on homework but is upset in test situations. Possibly he reasons clearly in all situations, even when under social pressure.

But there are disadvantages to depending solely on daily samples of behavior for judging intellectual skills. First, a teacher typically must wait several weeks before collecting enough evidence on which to base a halfway accurate judgment. By that time it may be too late to adjust teaching methods to fit pupils' different ability levels. In a departmentalized high school, where an instructor may see 150 or more students a day, the task of getting to know each one well enough to judge his abilities is extremely difficult.

A second disadvantage is that the teacher often does not have the same kind of evidence about all students, so he finds it hard to compare one with another so as to rate their abilities. Furthermore, the problems that some instructors pose for pupils to solve are not always well phrased or carefully thought out.

Therefore, although it is important to collect observations, note results of teacher-made tests, and evaluate compositions from daily classwork, it is also desirable to get the estimate of aptitudes that standardized tests can yield.

Standardized intelligence or aptitude tests, like teachers' daily observations, are based on a series of problems the student is to solve. The difference is that the problems on the published test have been very carefully constructed to give as good and broad a sample of pupil ability as possible in an hour or two. They have been tried on thousands of other students of the same age and of similar background, and these students' scores form *norms* that aid the instructor in judging the abilities of pupils in his class.

Still another source of information about students is the set of cumulative records the school keeps to show their past achievement.

In estimating intellectual capabilities, the wise teacher takes advantage of not one but all three of these sources: test scores, the student's past school records, and observations of the way he solves problems faced in class. The purpose of the first portion of this chapter is to help teachers improve their skills in using these three sources of information. The purpose of the latter portion is to help teachers understand the range of intellectual abilities to be found in a typical classroom.

WAYS OF APPRAISING INTELLECTUAL ABILITIES

In pursuing our purpose, it is desirable first to inspect what *intelligence* and *aptitude* mean.

Is Intelligence a Single Ability?

Years ago most psychologists and educators appeared to think of intelligence as being one amount of brightness a person possessed. The amount was measured by an intelligence test. A person who scored high on the test was expected to be generally apt in all aspects of mental life: in reading, writing, speaking, remembering facts, thinking about history, working with higher mathematics, arriving at sound solutions to social problems, reasoning wisely in the fields of philosophy and religion, and displaying excellent judgment in matters artistic. He might be excused some social ineptness or some clumsiness on the athletic field, but he was certainly expected to be universally skilled on the mental level. This belief—that intelligence is a single trait or capacity that pervades all areas of a person's mental life and primarily determines the level of his performance in all these areas—has been termed the *single-factor* or *unitary-factor* theory of intelligence. It is a theory of *general* intelligence.

There are, however, many people whose combination of skills is not accounted for adequately by this theory. Take, for example, the young woman who is adept at learning foreign languages but despairs of making headway with advanced algebra. Or the boy who learned to read at an early age and surpasses all others in his grade in history and science but cannot sing in tune or read vocal music with any accuracy. In investigating such instances of irregular patterns of abilities, psychologists have administered many different kinds of tests to students, with such varied items as block counting, defining words, doing mathematical reasoning, judging spatial relations, seeing visual details, remembering a list of words or numbers, fitting jigsaw puzzles together, judging which of two designs is the better, and listening to a pair of tones and telling whether they are the same or different.

After administering such tests, researchers have computed the correlation between a person's score on one kind of test with his score on another. This mathematical process of determining relationships among an individual's test scores has enabled psychologists to identify clusters of abilities. A person may have high aptitude in one cluster, such as *verbal comprehension* (ability to define and understand words), but have lower ability in visualizing *spatial relationships*, as an architect must do in designing a house. These kinds of investigations have led to a different theory: that intelligence is not a single capacity which determines the level of ability in all aspects of a person's mental life. Rather, intelligence is composed of groups of abilities, and a person may be more apt in one group than in another. This has been called the *group-factor* or *multiple-factor* theory.

During the past three decades, several varieties of multiple-factor theories have been developed and tests suited to each of these varieties have been created. Some psychologists believe that there are perhaps seven or nine different basic mental abilities. In the most influential of the recent theories, Guilford (1959:469–479) has created a complex scheme which pictures the intellect as being composed of three facets or dimensions, each of which is divided into subcategories. In Guilford's scheme there are theoretically as many as 120 different mental abilities having varied degrees of relationship to each other.

Group and General Factors Combined

Then what is intelligence really, a single capacity or several clusters of abilities? The truth of the matter, from the standpoint of classroom applications, seems to be a combination of these two theories.

There does indeed seem to be a kind of single or general ability which people may possess in different amounts. This general factor seems to pervade much of the mental activity of the individual. An elementary-school child who is highly capable in understanding and using words will also *tend* to be higher in computing skills and drawing ability than will a person who has very little talent with words. We can expect the intellectually gifted person *usually* to be superior to the moron in all facets of life: verbal, numerical, mechanical, artistic, and social.

But despite the fact that a general ability apparently affects much of life, at least in defining very gross differences among people, there is still plenty of room left for variations among the clusters of different abilities. So as we look at two people of fairly average general ability, we note that one is more at home in remembering digits, such as telephone numbers, while the other is more adept in creating campaign slogans for an election. On the basis of a theory of combined general and group factors, this would not surprise us.

Intelligence or Aptitude?

As a result of these theories of human abilities, there is often confusion among teachers concerning the use of the term "intelligence." Just what does it mean when someone uses it? The truth is, we cannot be quite sure. It is usually best to ask him specifically what he means. But if the word is used by a professional educator or a psychologist, we can guess that he has in mind one of three somewhat precise applications.

First, many psychologists use the word "intelligence" when referring to the *general ability to do academic work* and to handle language, abstract ideas, and mathematical concepts. This, they feel, is the general factor that seems to pervade all aspects of a person's skills in dealing with ideas.

But these same psychologists recognize the group factors, as well, which tend to be less highly related to the cluster of verbal-mathematical talents. They use the term "aptitude" to refer to the more specialized abilities, and the adjective preceding it identifies the specific kind of skill they are considering, such as clerical aptitude, artistic aptitude, mechanical aptitude, and musical aptitude.

Second, other psychologists and educators believe the term "intelligence" carries with it too much of the older idea of a single factor without recognizing that a person may act intelligently when learning to typewrite but may not act very intelligently when trying to discover why the car has failed to start. They prefer not to use the word "intelligence" at all. They speak only of "aptitudes," because this latter term seems to imply more of a group theory than a belief in a single factor.

Third, another group of psychologists recognize the fact that there seems to be a higher relationship among a person's abilities when he is a child of preschool or elementary-school age than when he is a youth or adult. Thus they still speak of intelligence and general-intelligence tests when discussing children's abilities, but they refer to older people's skills more often as aptitudes.

To keep such terms clear in this volume, we use one of the following devices to identify more precisely the cluster of skills or potentials we are talking about: (1) we include an adjective, like *academic* intelligence or *spatial-relations* aptitude or (2) we mention the device used for measuring the characteristic we are discussing and we note what this particular device seems to measure best in life; for example, the Stanford-Binet Intelligence Scale seems to measure ability of children to succeed in academic subjects in school. Therefore, we shall be speaking of intelligence and aptitude rather synonymously, but at the same time we shall specify the types of skills being considered at the moment.

Testing Intellectual Differences

If the single-factor theory were completely true, our task of measuring intellectual differences would be relatively simple. A single general-intelligence test would show the level of a person's entire ability. But a person has groups of abilities, so that numbers of different aptitude tests are needed, each designed to measure a particular cluster of talents.

Throughout the following discussion, two different kinds of tests are considered.

1. Those constructed by experts, tried out on groups of people, analyzed statistically to determine what they actually measure, printed, and sold by a publisher. These are called standardized tests.

2. Those constructed by a teacher for use with his own class, called teacher-made tests.

Different sets of skills are needed to use these two kinds of tests effectively. In the case of the standardized ones, a teacher needs to know how to select those suited to his purpose. For teacher-made tests, he needs to know how to construct good items to measure for the goals he has in mind.

The characteristics of standardized tests are emphasized in this chapter. For detailed suggestions on ways to create effective teacher-made examinations, the reader may profitably inspect one of the following readings at the end of the chapter: Ahmann, Green, Stanley, Thomas, Thorndike.

Since there are many varieties of published tests, which vary considerably in quality, an instructor needs to seek several kinds of information about them if the most appropriate one is to be selected. The teacher may properly ask: (1) How valid is the test for my purposes? (2) What kinds of students was it standardized on? (3) What form is it in, and how is it administered? (4) How is it interpreted?

How Valid Is the Test?

The first step is to determine what the test is to measure. Do you wish to *predict* how well a junior-high student will succeed in mathematics in high school? Do you wish to decide where a first-grade child *stands now* in his ability to learn reading? Do you wish to find out how well students who have just finished a study of national government *have reached the learning goals?* Depending on which of these questions you are trying to answer, you seek different kinds of data.

This characteristic of a test—what it measures—is called test validity. There are several different adjectives that may be attached to the term "validity." Each adjective indicates whether you are focusing on the past, the present, or the future. An inspection of each variety of validity may explain why some tests are labeled achievement examinations, others intelligence tests, and still others aptitude tests.

Predictive Validity

In trying to care for individual differences, one of our greatest interests is in predicting a student's future. We try to estimate whether a boy will succeed if we skip him from third to fifth grade or whether a girl will benefit by being moved out of the regular class into the special slow-learning class. Both standardized tests and teacher-made tests will aid us in making these decisions.

Standardized tests that are used for prediction may go under a variety of names: intelligence, ability, aptitude, predictive, or prognostic. Often the test name is accompanied by an adjective supposed to tell what the test validly predicts: general academic ability, mathematics aptitude, engineering aptitude, or the like.

Just because a test name is allied to a teacher's predictive needs does not mean it will do the job well. Some published tests are well constructed for their stated purpose, and some are not. The best way to judge a test's predictive value is to find one which fulfills these qualifications: It was administered to large numbers of students. A considerable time after this initial testing, the test constructors measured the students' later success in the field they were trying to predict, such as engineering ability, mathematics skill, or reading speed; then they compared each student's original test score with his later success in the field. If students who scored highest on the original test also proved most skilled in the field, we can place great confidence in the test's efficiency in predicting the future.

The best guide to how much relationship exists between test scores and later performance is the correlation coefficient. The highest possible relationship (perfect correspondence between how well a student scored on the test and how well he performed later in the field) would be shown by a coefficient of 1.00. No relationship at all between test scores and later performance is shown by a coefficient of .00. Numbers between these extremes describe different degrees of relationship. For example, a correlation of .90 is very high. If the relation between the test and later performance is of this magnitude, we shall make very few errors when using the test scores to predict students' probable future success. Correlations of .80 and .75 are also considered rather high. As the coefficients diminish toward .10 and .05, they are almost useless.

Where, then, will a teacher find such statistics, and how should he interpret them in choosing a test for prediction purposes? He can look in at least three sources.

Source 1: The manual that accompanies the test itself. If the test has been tried out carefully beforehand and its purpose is to predict success in an area, the test constructors will have examined a large group of pupils, then have waited and measured their performance at a later date. So when you look in the manual, seek information about the kind of performance in life with which the test scores were correlated.

For example, perhaps a mathematics-aptitude test was given to sixth-graders and their scores were kept until the pupils finished ninth grade, at which time the original test scores were compared with the average mark in mathematics that the pupils earned during their junior-high years. This later performance, in terms of grade-point average, is called the "criterion" or the "criterion measure." If in the case of the mathematics test we find a high correlation (perhaps .87) between original test scores and later report-card marks, we conclude that this test is quite valid for predicting success in junior-high mathematics.

Or, to take another example, let us suppose we read in the manual that accompanies a college-aptitude test that the test scores of freshmen have been correlated with these same students' average marks at the end of their third year in social-science courses, in literature and language courses, and in physical-science courses (these are the criterion measures). Let us suppose that the reported correlation coefficients were:

College-aptitude test and social-science marks +.48
College-aptitude test and literature-language marks +.61
College-aptitude test and physical-science marks +.27

From these data we conclude that the aptitude test is most valid for predicting literature-language success and least valid for predicting physical-science success. The accuracy of predicting success in the social-science courses obviously falls between the other two. In none of these cases would the accuracy of prediction be as good as in the case of the junior-high mathematics test (+.87). But in each situation the test would be of some aid in estimating the future—better than predicting from pure guess.

In summary, it is important to look in the test manual for the criterion measure with which the test scores were correlated. The size of the correlation coefficient will suggest how valid the test is for predicting the life activity in question.

Some test makers do not bother to administer their test to a large group of students, and they do not hold the results of testing for a year or perhaps five years in order to correlate the scores with some criterion in life (school marks, success on the job, or success in finishing college). Instead, they take the easier route of giving their standardization group another already-standardized test in addition to the newly constructed one. This is sometimes called *congruent* validity. For instance, we might construct an academic-aptitude test for elementary-school children. We administer it to 200 first-graders and then also give each child the individual Stanford-Binet Intelligence Scale, which for some years has been recognized as a rather good predictor of children's academic success. If we find a high correlation (perhaps +.85) between children's scores on the two tests, we feel rather secure in concluding that our new test apparently predicts about the same kinds of things as the Stanford-Binet whose validity has already been recognized. But the lower the correlation, the less confidence we can place in the comparability of the two tests. Generally, this indirect method of establishing predictive validity is not as desirable as the direct method of correlating test scores with a real criterion established at a later date.

In short, we conclude that when we look in a test manual we should locate the specific criterion with which the test was correlated. If there are no data about what future performance the test correlates with, we cannot conclude with any confidence that this measuring instrument has predictive value.

Source 2: Journals. A second place to look for statistics on the predictive validity of a test is in educational and psychological journals. In a library the *Education Index* and *Psychological Abstracts* may guide a teacher to articles written about the test he has in mind.

Source 3: Yearbooks. The best single source of information about tests is the series of *Mental Measurements Yearbooks* which contain authoritative evaluations of tests written by experts who have no personal interest in selling the tests. If you do not find data about the test you are seeking in one volume of the yearbooks, turn to another, for different tests are reviewed in various volumes of the series.

Concurrent Validity

This type focuses not on the future but on the present. In seeking concurrent validity we are trying to answer the question: What does this test correlate with in the pupil's life today? Hence we compare the test with some other measure used at about the same time the test is given to the pupils.

Let us assume that we wish to construct a reading-readiness test for first-graders. We hope that children who pass the test at a given level are ready to begin reading preprimer books. To determine whether our test validly does what its name suggests, we need to administer it to children and at about the same time determine by other means (the criterion measure) whether the test really does distinguish between children who are ready and those who are not yet ready to read. Our criterion measure may, for instance, be based on the teacher's actually starting all the tested children in a reading program and then keeping careful records of their rate of progress. Then we compute the correlation between test scores and teacher ratings of pupils' performance in reading. If the coefficient is high (showing that children with the highest test scores were actually able to read and those with low scores were not yet ready), we have established concurrent validity for the reading-readiness scale.

Reports of concurrent validity are sometimes found in test manuals, journal articles, and *Mental Measurements Yearbook* evaluations.

From the standpoint of meeting individual differences, tests with established concurrent validity are most helpful when we wish a measure that will help us (1) determine whether a pupil seems ready for a new area of learning or for the next higher step in a learning sequence, (2) homogeneously group pupils who are at various stages of readiness for the new learning, and (3) determine which children are ready to enter a special class for either slow or fast learners.

Content Validity

Assume that we have been teaching geometry to high-school students for the past semester and now wish to determine how well they have learned. To measure their progress we shall use a test, either one we create ourselves, a published one, or one created by a fellow mathematics teacher. Before giving the test, we wish to determine whether it is valid. But in this case we do not look for statistical studies, even if the test is a formally published one. Instead, we need the specific goals or learnings which we planned for the students to reach this semester. We then inspect each item of the test and compare it with our list of goals. As we pursue this task, we ask ourselves such questions as: Is this item aimed at one of our goals? Is the balance among the numbers of items proper so that each objective is getting enough stress—that is, are there too many questions aimed at one of our goals and hardly any aimed at others? Are there any goals not measured at all by this test?

From the foregoing inspection we determine whether the test is a valid measure of the goals or content of the course we have taught. This is *content* validity. It is what we are interested in each time we construct or adopt an achievement test to determine how much the students have learned in the past.

Valid for What?

In summarizing this discussion of validity, we can conclude that whenever we are asked whether a test is valid, we should ask in turn: Valid for what? No test is a valid measure for everything. Each is focused on a particular facet of life, and its validity must be judged in relation to that facet.

If we wish to predict the future, we look for statistical evidence of the future performance or criterion with which the test scores correlate. If we are interested in what the test correlates with at present, we look for a coefficient of its relation to a current criterion. If we want to know how carefully a test will sample the specific learning objectives of a class or an area of knowledge, we compare our objectives with the test items.

But the question naturally arises: Cannot a single test be used in all these ways? The answer is yes. A single test may often serve for predicting future success, indicating present standing, and reflecting past achievement. At the end of the first semester of a ninth-grade algebra course, the teacher constructs an achievement test to sample the major learnings of the semester. He then uses these test results in several ways:

1. As one element entering into the computation of a semester mark for each pupil. In this case he has focused on past attainment.

2. As a basis for recommending how the school's four algebra classes should be reshuffled for the second semester so they will be grouped more homogeneously. In this case he is focusing on readiness for new work as well as predicting how pupils will probably succeed during the coming year.

3. As a basis for predicting pupils' success several years ahead. That is, the test scores are given to the guidance counselor who helps

students plan their high-school programs and estimate whether they should aim at college and, if so, in what fields they will most likely find the greatest success.

In the cases of these second and third uses of the test—prediction of the immediate and more distant future—the teacher has not standardized his classroom examination, nor has he correlated it with criteria that lie in the future, such as high-school mathematics marks or college grades. Instead, he has made the assumption that in a given field of study, such as algebra, if all students have had about the same opportunity to learn, the ones who have learned best are the most apt (and frequently the most diligent), and these same students will tend to succeed best in this area of learning in the future. Although we can find exceptions to this rule of thumb, in general it is sound. So, if we have no better statistical evidence and no standardized test with established predictive validity, we can still use the results of our own well-constructed classroom-achievement test to make useful predictions about a student's probable future success.

What Was the Standardization Sample?

If we are choosing a standardized test for science aptitude among ninth-graders, we want one that was originally administered to students as much like our own as possible. Otherwise we cannot have much faith that the standards or norms accompanying the test will enable us to interpret the success of our own students accurately.

To judge how much our own group is like the original standardization sample, we look in the test manual to discover the following facts.

Where the Normative Group Lived. A test whose standards are based on a sample of British students is probably less applicable to a Seattle school than would be a test based on a sample of pupils in the midwestern United States. This decision about the comparability of the original sample of students and our own must rest on our understanding of social-class factors and of the curriculum offerings and quality of education in different geographical areas.

The Ages and Grades Tested. If the test norms are to be useful, they must be based on students of the same ages and grades as ours.

The Size of the Sample. Generally the larger the number of students tested in setting the original norms, the more faith we can place in the published results. If we are choosing between two tests of about equal worth, the one based on an original sample of 10,000 pupils will yield a more stable basis for interpretation than one based on a sample of 500 pupils.

What Is the Form of the Test?

There are several ways tests can vary in form. Some are administered to individuals, some to groups. Some demand reading ability, others do not. Some can be used with children who do not speak English, some cannot. In the following discussion, the principal advantages and uses of these different forms of tests will be noted.

Individual and Group Tests

An *individual* test is one administered by one trained tester to one pupil at a time. The Stanford-Binet Intelligence Scale and the Wechsler Intelligence Scale for Children are two of this type. Most tests, however, can be administered to an entire class at one time. These are called *group* tests.

Individual tests usually yield more stable results because the trained tester gives his full attention to discovering what the one child knows, and he can adapt the approach somewhat to the individual child's characteristics. In addition, the tester learns something by observing carefully how the child attacks the test problems. That is, does the child respond quickly and with confidence? Is he shy and hesitant? Does he answer hurriedly and then change his mind? Is he afraid to try? All these observations can throw some light on the child's personality.

Group tests typically can be administered successfully by a careful teacher who follows the testing instructions precisely. The special training needed to administer individual tests is not needed for most group scales. There are hundreds of different group tests, so for any particular testing task we can usually find a variety of tests from which to choose.

Generally the diagnostic and prognostic work of the school are conducted with group tests. Such scales can be administered with the greatest saving of time, staff, and money. But for certain situations, the school turns to individual scales. For instance, when a special class for very slow learners is being formed, group intelligence tests (meaning academic-aptitude scales) will probably be administered to all pupils in the school in an initial screening process. The children scoring lowest will then receive further individual testing to establish more precisely which pupils apparently belong in the special class and which do not.

Verbal, Nonverbal, Nonlanguage Tests

Tests can differ in the way instructions are given and in the way pupils are expected to respond.

With some group tests, the administrator tells pupils what to do and the pupils write their answers on the answer sheet. In other cases, the administrator just gives the opening directions and the students do the rest of the test themselves, reading each item on the test sheet and attempting to fill in the correct answer. These types, in which the child must understand the administrator's oral directions and answer orally or read the item and answer it, are typically called *verbal* tests. They are the most common variety.

A *nonverbal* test typically demands that the child be able to understand oral directions, but he does not need to be able to read or write the language. Instead, his response may involve some action such as building a design with colored blocks or drawing the missing parts of a sketch of a man. The nonverbal variety is most useful with young children who do not yet read, with older illiterates, or with those having other handicaps such as muteness.

A *nonlanguage* test is one that can be administered to pupils who do not understand either the spoken or written language. The tester gives directions by examples and gestures. The child responds by perhaps tracing a path through a printed maze or by fitting various-shaped blocks into the appropriate spaces of a form board. Nonlanguage tests are most useful with children who speak only a foreign language, or with those who are deaf or mute or do not yet read or understand oral directions well.

How Is the Test Interpreted?

As suggested earlier, a standardized test is usually one that has been carefully constructed to measure a certain ability or achievement. It has been administered to a large group of people, and the results of their success on the test are published as *norms*. These norms give a basis for comparing the success of our own pupils with others of similar age and grade. Norms may be of several types. The kinds that teachers should recognize are those based on age or grade averages or those reported as quotients (such as intelligence or educational quotients), as percentiles, or as standard scores.

Mental Age, Educational Age

Let us assume that we have constructed a general-intelligence test which correlates highly with success in reading, arithmetic problem solving, and defining words. We try it out on 2,000 elementary-school children. By computing the children's scores, we discover that the average seven-year-old gets 45 items correct. The average eight-year-old gets 53 items correct. The average nine-year-old gets 63 items correct. Therefore, we conclude that a score of 45 is equivalent to a *mental age* of seven, 53 represents a mental age of eight, and 63 a mental age of nine. In this way we have established norms based on 2,000 children. Later, if a teacher gives our test to a child who scores 63, the teacher concludes the child has a mental age of nine because he has performed the mental tasks like an average nine-year-old of the standardization group.

If we constructed an arithmetic-computation and problem-solving test, we might use the same procedure to establish an *arithmetic age*. That is, by administering the test to a large number of children of different ages, we would determine the average score achieved by those at each age level. In like manner we could establish a *reading age*, a *spelling age*, and any other type we might desire on the basis of tests. When several of these different achievement ages are combined, they form an *educational age*, which is supposed to be an over-all reflection of the child's success compared with that of his agemates.

Results of standardized tests are sometimes reported in test manuals in the form of mental or educational ages.

Grade Norms

In a manner similar to the foregoing procedure, we might discover that the average score on a science-facts test is 82 for eighth-graders, 94 for ninth-graders, and so on. With these norms we can later estimate at what grade level our own students appear to be working, by comparing their scores with the grade norms.

Intelligence Quotient, Educational Quotient

By dividing a student's mental age by his chronological age and multiplying by 100, we arrive at an IQ or intelligence quotient. The IQ suggests something about the rate at which a child is progressing intellectually (in relation to the particular intellectual tasks that the specific test measures) compared with his chronological age. A six-year-old who gets the average test scores obtained by six-year-old children in the standardization sample has an IQ of 100.

$$IQ = \frac{CA}{MA}(100) = \frac{6}{6}(100) = 100$$

However, if John, at eight and one-half years, earns an intelligence-test score which the average ten-year-old achieved in the standardization sample, we conclude that John is advancing intellectually more rapidly than his average agemates. When we convert his mental and chronological ages from years to months to make computation easier, we discover that John's IQ (rounded out to the nearest unit) is 118.

$$\frac{120}{102}(100) = 118$$

The IQ has proved to be a very handy way of expressing a rate of intellectual growth. Some educators have found it useful to convert other kinds of "ages" into quotients; for instance, arithmetic age becomes an arithmetic quotient when divided by the child's chronological age. In like manner we can derive a reading quotient or an educational quotient.

Percentiles

Increasingly, percentile norms are being published as a basis for interpreting a student's test success. A percentile tells what percentage of a student's agemates received scores below the one he achieved. For example, a high-school senior on an English-usage test earns a raw score of 83. To determine how this score compares with those achieved by seniors in the original standardization group of 5,000 high-school students, we look at a table in the test manual that converts scores into percentiles. Here we see that our student's raw score of 83 corresponds with a percentile of 92. This means that 92 per cent of the high-school seniors in the standardization sample received scores below 83 and 8 per cent received scores at 83 or higher.

Percentile norms have several advantages. They are more useful than the IQ for interpreting aptitude-test scores at the high-school level, because during adolescence the growth curve for intellectual functions tends to flatten off, so it is more accurate to compare a student with his agemates' success than with a theoretically steady mental-growth curve. A second advantage is that percentiles are usually easily understood by teachers. And as shown in Figures 1–3 and 1–4 in Chapter 1, percentiles provide a convenient way for comparing a student's success on several different types of tests that have different numbers of items on each test.

Standard Scores

Sometimes test norms are in the form of standard scores. The standard-score technique enables us to convert results from a variety of different kinds of tests into one common type of score. Their use is similar to that of precentiles, but they are derived in a different manner. (See Stanley, Thomas, or Thorndike in the readings at the end of the chapter for a complete description of standard-score computation.)

Summary

The most accurate and quickest way to estimate a person's intellectual abilities is through the use of a test or a series of tests. Intellectual abilities cannot all be combined into a single aptitude that is measured by a single test. Thus a teacher who wishes to measure an intellectual aptitude should first define as specifically as possible the skill he has in mind. He then selects a test or a series of tests which, according to proper validity measures, accurately estimates that skill or ability.

Norms published for standardized tests enable the teacher to estimate how his students' success on the tests compares with that of a large number of students of the same age or grade level.

How to Appraise Intellectual Differences through Use of Students' School Records

Although the actions of people we think we know well occasionally surprise us, there is generally a consistency in an individual's behavior from one day to the next and year after year. So it is obvious that if we have observed a person carefully for a time, we can often make quite consistent and useful predictions about his future behavior. For this reason it is helpful for the teacher to consult school records about a student's past when he wishes to make decisions about the student's present and future intellectual capabilities.

There are two main types of records on students that are particularly useful. The first is called a *cumulative record*. It consists of data routinely collected about each student from year to year. The record follows the child through his school career. The other type is called a *case study*. It often contains much of the same information found in a cumulative record. But in addition it also draws upon more sources of information and describes the student's past and present behavior in considerably more detail. A case study is not kept routinely for each pupil. Rather, it is a special, more complete picture of the pupil developed only on those students who are facing especially difficult problems in adjusting to school.

By inspecting the characteristics of cumulative records and case studies, we can see how each is developed and used by teachers.

Cumulative Records

The quality of cumulative records varies considerably from one school to another. In some places they may consist of only the marks the student has received in his courses each year. In other places data about his family and health are kept in addition to course marks. In still others the cumulative record includes marks, health information, family data, personality- and aptitude-test scores, notes on social and personal characteristics, and lists of organizations and activities in which he has taken part.

The form of the record also varies from school to school. It may consist of a standard card on which the desired information is written each year, or it may be a folder or large envelope in which information about the student is inserted.

Sometimes every student's cumulative record is kept in the school's main office. Teachers who wish to consult their pupils' records may borrow the folders from the office. In other cases (usually at the elementary-school level) the records are in each teacher's classroom file for use throughout the year.

A teacher has two principal responsibilities for cumulative files. First, he is responsible for contributing significant material to the records, endeavoring to be as accurate and objective as possible. Second, he is responsible for making wise interpretations of data placed in the record by other teachers and school officials. By "wise" interpretations we mean that he should recognize the limitations of the data. For example, he should realize that a single IQ for a child which is derived from one paper-pencil academic-aptitude test is not invariably a true, everlasting measure of the pupil's potential. Instead, it is one sampling of the pupil's apparent aptitude in a particular area, and it is subject to some error or variation. Hence it should be considered an estimate only. Or, as a second example, a teacher who reads anecdotal records written by former teachers should be aware that their biases may be reflected in their notes. Teachers who contribute information to records are not always careful to supply only objective, factual observations.

Contributing Significant Material

Cumulative record forms are published commercially for schools which wish to adopt them. (The Educational Records Bureau, 21 Audubon Avenue, New York, N.Y. 10032, is a good source.) But perhaps the most usable kind is one developed by the school staff itself. Such a form will more likely be one that teachers agree with and will be willing to furnish material for. As noted earlier, records vary greatly in completeness from one school to another. Hence, as we inspect the following suggested list of contents of a complete cumulative file, we should recognize that not all these areas will seem practical in certain schools. A thoroughgoing cumulative record consists of the following kinds of data.

Identifying Information. The opening section of the card or the front sheet of the folder should contain such items as the student's name, sex, race or color, address, and place and date of birth.

Home Background. A section can be devoted to parents' or guardians' names, ages, addresses, birthplaces, education, occupations. Names, ages, and places of residence of brothers and sisters. Type of neighborhood in which the home is located and an estimate of the socioeconomic status of the family. Customs or cultural influences of importance, such as foreign language spoken in the home or religious customs followed. Attitudes of parents toward the student and toward his success in school. Significant information about family relationships, such as divorce in the family or the presence of a mentally retarded sibling in the home.

Health of the Student. General health data should be recorded by the physician or nurse who gives the school's regular physical examination. But the teacher can also record observations of importance, such as: Does the child seem to have enough energy, or does he tire notably before the school day is over? Does he seem to suffer from skin disorders? Does he have any apparent sight or hearing difficulties? Does he catch cold easily?

School History. This portion can contain a list of the schools previously attended and how long the pupil was in each school. Attendance records are also useful in showing whether the pupil has missed school frequently.

Scholastic Achievement. The most important key to scholastic achievement is usually the record of marks the pupil has received from year to year in each subject-matter area. Standardized test scores are also of some value here (that is, if the achievement tests truly focused on exactly the same objectives as those toward which the teachers have taught). A record of the rate of promotion and of acceleration or failure should be included. Brief summaries written by teachers about the student's achievement are also useful, as are notes about scholastic honors he has won.

Aptitude-Test Scores. In this section intelligence- and aptitude-test scores are recorded. Tests administered at different grade levels help provide a clear picture of the student's development and potential over the years.

Special Interests and Talents. Evidences of interest and skill in musical, artistic, athletic, literary, mechanical, scientific, mathematical, and group-leadership areas can be recorded as anecdotal records, as test scores, and as notes of special awards and honors. A record of hobbies is also useful.

Personal-Social Characteristics. Summaries of teachers' observations of the pupil's approach to tasks, his apparent attitude toward himself, and his relationship with others are useful in understanding him. The teacher's observations can be guided by such questions as: What does the pupil do when he faces a problem? What does he do when he is frustrated by not finding a solution to the problem? How does he react to criticism? How does he react to praise? Does he work well on his own? How do his classmates react to him? Is he shy, aggressive, talkative, reticent? Does he offer ideas to the group or only receive them? Is he usually interested in classwork? Is he easily distracted? Is he a daydreamer? Is he often bored?

Outside Work Experiences and Organizations. To collect useful contents for this portion of the record the teacher seeks to answer: How does the student spend his out-of-school hours? Has he held any jobs, or does he now hold a job? What kinds of work does his job involve? How long has he worked and with what success?

Plans for the Future. What are the student's vocational and educational goals? What vocational and educational plans do his parents hold for him?

As noted earlier, making such a complete record as suggested above is often beyond the manpower resources of schools in which the guidance staff is small or nonexistent and teachers already carry a substantial load of work. In such situations, if the records are to be realistically kept up and actively used by teachers, a more modest array of data should be collected on each child.

Using the Records

Although there are numerous ways that cumulative records can help us make decisions about caring for individual differences, at this point we shall confine our considerations to the problem of estimating present and future intellectual capabilities of a student by inspecting his cumulative folder. For this purpose the most useful sections of the record are obviously those concerning his past scholastic achievement and his aptitude-test scores.

When we discussed achievement tests earlier, we noted that the person who has done well in a subject-matter area in the past will probably do well in it in the future, and the one who has shown up poorly in the past will probably be below average in the future. There are, of course, exceptions to this tendency. Some students succeed well in academic areas in the elementary school but fall to an average or lower level in high school. Others appear to be slow starters in elementary school, or at least they are uninterested learners. The mediocre talent they demonstrated in the lower grades seems to change into real aptitude in the upper grades, and they move forward at a fast pace. But in general, a past record of achievement suggests that in the future the student's success will be quite similar in quality.

If we take past achievement as reflected in school marks and combine it with aptitude-test scores, our accuracy of predicting future success is increased even more. For instance, a student's college-aptitude test score combined with an average of his high-school marks provides a sounder prediction than one based on either of these factors alone.

As we inspect aptitude-test scores derived from tests given at various levels of the pupil's school career, it should not surprise us to see some discrepancies in the IQ or MA as reported at different ages. This can result from several causes. One is that tested aptitude or academic intelligence does not necessarily grow at a steady pace. There can be surges and plateaus in its growth. (Bayley, 1955.) In addition, as we saw earlier, some aptitude tests (even when they are called *general* intelligence tests) measure somewhat different abilities than others do. We would put more faith in estimating a person's future on the basis of the average IQ derived from several different testings of a pupil than we would in estimating it on the basis of only one IQ score.

While analyzing a pupil's past achievement, it is well also to look at other elements of the cumulative record that might have affected his learning. If an eighth-grader has a somewhat poor achievement record but has above-average aptitude-test scores, we may perhaps account for this discrepancy by the fact that he has often moved from one community to another so that his attendance has been erratic.

Or perhaps his health has been poor. Therefore, even though we pay primary attention to his academic marks and aptitude-test scores, we also find that social, physical, family, and emotional factors on the cumulative record are often helpful in filling out our understanding of the child's mental abilities.

Case Studies

In a broad sense, a rather complete cumulative record on a child serves as a kind of case study. It represents an attempt to collect data about many facets of the child's life to enable the teacher to understand him as a unique individual. But in our present discussion we are considering the case study in its more formal use. We are referring to the compiling of a quantity of data about a student whose particular, serious problems have motivated us to make a special, more complete study of his life. Sometimes the problems that precipitate our interest are primarily in the realm of intellectual ability, for a child who is failing much of his classwork warrants special study. At other times the problem shows up in personal-social conflicts, as in the case of the student who continually fights with his classmates or the one who is always the class scapegoat and butt of teasing. Again, it may be a physical difficulty, such as progressively poorer eyesight or a skin disorder. More often it is a combination of several of these areas.

Perhaps the way a formal case study is developed can best be understood if we outline the steps typically followed.

1. *The Precipitating Problem.* A series of incidents in a particular student's life causes a teacher to realize that this student is a serious problem to himself and/or to others. His problem obviously demands a solution, but the way to accomplish it is not at all clear to the teacher, who does not yet know enough about its causes.

The teacher probably discusses the matter with the principal or director of guidance and perhaps with other colleagues who have had the student in class.

2. *The Initial Case Conference.* The principal or director of guidance recognizes that the problem is indeed serious and warrants the attention of a team of staff members. He calls a meeting of those he feels can be of aid: one or two teachers, a counselor, perhaps a

social worker attached to the school system, possibly the school nurse. It becomes clear that the information about the pupil which they have at present is too meager to furnish a sound diagnosis of the factors causing his difficulties. The group decides to make a formal case study.

3. *The Assignment of Roles.* The person coordinating the study, possibly the guidance counselor or the teacher, discusses with the others what part of the information each person can best search for. Thus each staff member will be responsible for gathering certain data. (The individuals will seek information in the same areas outlined earlier as those important for a cumulative record, except that the case-study information should be more complete.) A deadline is set for the data to be handed in to the coordinator, and perhaps a date is determined for another case conference.

4. *The Gathering of Material about the Student.* The teacher or teachers who have the student in class will collect data on his achievement, write brief anecdotal records about significant incidents that occur in class, and perhaps make a sociometric study to determine the student's relationships to classmates.

If there is a social worker assigned to the case, she may visit the home and collect information from other outside sources, possibly from a club or church leader. If there is no social worker, a teacher or guidance counselor may contact the parents for information.

In some cases physical causes may appear to be related to the problem, so a medical examination can be called for. The school nurse or doctor will be responsible for this report. If special testing appears needed, a school psychologist can administer individual intelligence scales and personality tests. The psychologist, or in more severe cases a psychiatrist, can provide additional data through interviews with the pupil and perhaps with his parents.

5. *The Compiling of the Report.* There are several ways the data can be compiled into a report on the student.

For example, each person who has gathered information can submit a written report to the coordinator of the case study, who will reorganize these parts into one statement that gives a comprehensive picture of the student's environment and his personality. Then, as a next step, another case conference is called at which all concerned read or listen to the completed report. They discuss it, try to isolate the factors causing the problem, and seek the best corrective measures.

It sometimes happens that both these steps are carried out at the case conference. Each person does not first submit a written report that is integrated into one final report to be considered at the conference. Instead, each one gives his information orally at the case conference, during which the causes are sought and possible solutions suggested.

6. *The Tryout of Solutions.* The most likely measures for solving the problem are put into effect, and those people responsible for these measures watch carefully for signs that the student is improving in solving his problems. As needed, further case conferences are called, additional material is compiled, progress is evaluated, and new variations of solutions are attempted.

This re-evaluation process continues until the problem is well on its way toward a solution or until further conferences appear unprofitable.

Thus the case-study process consists of six kinds of steps. Sometimes the entire case study is completed by a single teacher, who makes as intensive an analysis of the pupil as possible within the limitations of time and facilities. In other cases the process is quite elaborate, as noted in the foregoing, with a number of different people contributing material and analyses of the final reports. The study may be carried out for a brief time or, in severe problem cases, for a period of months or even years.

Summary

Throughout the foregoing section we have noted that a study of the student's school records can help teachers estimate his intellectual capabilities. One very useful source of information is the cumulative record, which is composed of a growing collection of data routinely collected about each child as he progresses through the grades. For pupils suffering particularly distressing difficulties, a more intensive analysis can be made of their past and present condition. This is called a case study. As noted in other sections of this book, cumulative records and case studies throw light on other aspects of pupil growth as well as on intellectual development.

How to Appraise Intellectual Differences through Daily Observations

We suggested at the beginning of this chapter that the most common way of estimating a person's mental abilities was through observing him solving common problems of living. It is not necessary to dwell on this method at length, for we are well acquainted with it as a normal daily activity. But it may be useful to point up a few of the ways in which teachers sometimes err in observing pupils. Thus alerted, we may be more careful to make accurate daily estimates of pupils' abilities.

Among the factors in a child's daily school performance that are useful in estimating his ability are (1) the breadth and aptness of his vocabulary, (2) his success in applying school learning to solving problems, and (3) the contributions he makes to discussions as a result of his own firsthand experiences and his knowledge from television programs or reading.

Brueckner and Bond (1955:34) have suggested that in using such daily observations, the teacher runs the risk of overrating the ability of the aggressive or talkative child as well as the popular, social one. The unattractive, shy, or rejected type is likely to be underestimated and the average child overestimated.

In making such appraisals, teachers often err because most faculty members hold middle-class standards and thus tend to associate higher intellectual ability with (1) good looks, (2) neatness in dress, (3) neatness in handwriting and compositions, (4) frequent oral contributions, (5) politeness and friendliness, (6) smooth social relations with adults, (7) "good" family, that is, family connections among important people in the community, and (8) conformity to middle-class patterns of speech and conduct.

The opposites of these characteristics are associated by many teachers with lower intellectual ability. There is ample evidence that children with lower socioeconomic-class characteristics and good minds do not receive proper recognition for their intellectual ability in the typical school. (Hollingshead, 1949; Warner, 1944.)

So, as we attempt to gauge students' mental skills through daily observations, we need to:

1. Base our judgments on the way the student actually solves his problems and on the content of his answers to our questions, not by his pleasant smile and neat tie.

2. Give each student a fair chance to display his abilities. For instance, the shy young lady who does not volunteer the answer may actually know it and will offer it if the teacher bothers to call on her.

THE RANGE OF INTELLECTUAL ABILITIES IN CLASSROOMS

Armed with tests, students' past records, and careful daily observations, we are prepared to appraise the intellectual differences among our students. But what will these measures tell us about the range of intellectual abilities in our classes? Two of the most useful and easily comprehended kinds of answers to this question come from these sources: (1) results of studies of IQ distribution in the population and (2) results of standardized achievement tests. Let us look at each.

Distribution of IQ's

Intelligence quotients derived from administering individual general-intelligence tests such as the Stanford-Binet have been useful in dividing children into descriptive categories, such as feeble-minded, normal, and gifted. The approximate percentage of the general population that falls within each of these categories is shown in Figure 3-1.

A brief description of each category can help the teacher recognize the terms commonly used in educational literature to describe each IQ level. The descriptions may also help him recognize where in this scheme he will probably find the students he faces daily.

But before we survey the terms used to describe different levels of ability, it is well for us to note that the terms are not completely standardized. Some authors use one word, some another, for designating the same category of ability. In our discussion we feature the terms we believe are most useful for teachers. Alternative terms will be added at several points.

The following descriptions begin with the lowest IQ levels and proceed upward through the scale.

DESCRIPTIVE CATEGORIES

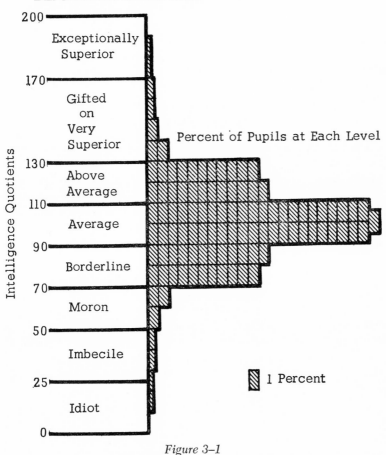

Figure 3–1

Percentage of Children in IQ Categories

IQ 0–50: Mentally Deficient, Feeble-Minded, or Mentally Defective

These three terms are used synonymously by many workers in the field of special education. Included in this category are children who (1) are so socially incompetent that they cannot manage their own affairs, (2) have been retarded mentally from birth or from a very early age, (3) will continue to be mentally retarded at maturity, and (4) are essentially incurable. These kinds of children need institutional care or the close supervision of a parent. Usually they are divided into two categories, idiot and imbecile.

Idiocy

A child with an IQ between 0 and about 20 or 25 on intelligence tests is typically classified as an idiot. He is so low intellectually that he does not learn to talk, or at most he learns only a few words. Usually he does not learn to care for his bodily needs. He must be fed and cleansed by others, for he does not develop ability to carry out even simple routines. He requires continual supervision.

Some idiots learn to walk. Others never learn and must lie in bed all their lives. On the average, idiots, even at their optimum stage of development, learn no more than a two-year-old baby. Frequently they die when rather young, for they not only are poorly endowed intellectually but their resistance to disease and accident is below normal.

Idiots are noneducable and nontrainable, so they will not be found in any type of school class, either special or regular. There is perhaps one idiot per 500 children in the population.[1]

Imbecility

Children with tested IQ's between about 25 and 50 are often categorized as imbeciles. They typically develop some language ability, can be taught to care for bodily needs, and sometimes can carry out such simple routines as washing dishes or dusting around the house. Because imbeciles, at least in the upper ranges, can be trained to perform very short-term tasks, they often are labeled the *trainable mentally deficient*. But throughout their lives they will always have to depend on others for support or supervision. There are an estimated four or five imbeciles per 500 or 600 children in the population.

In general, though they may be trained in simple routines, these mentally defective children cannot be *educated* in the usual sense of the word, so they do not warrant being called *educable*. They do not profit from either regular school classes or special classes for the

[1] A. F. Tredgold, *Mental Deficiency* (Baltimore: Wood, 1937).

mentally handicapped. In the lowest primary grades of some rural schools or crowded city schools which have ineffective screening processes, an occasional well-behaved high-grade imbecile will inadvertently land in a regular class, principally because of parental insistence that "all he needs is a chance" and because the school lacks other suggestions for the child's care. But these cases are fairly rare, and the child's unfitness for regular school is soon obvious.

Some leaders in the field of special education recommend that large public-school systems organize custodial classes for the care, training, and supervision of the trainable mentally deficient child (imbecile).

Such an organization would supervise the child for several hours during the day in a public school class. It would not be expected that such children could be educated to care for themselves at the adult level, but through training (not education as we usually conceive it) could be taught to function socially at a higher level around the home and neighborhood. This is a method sometimes preferred to commitment to a state institution since it assists those parents who wish to maintain responsibility for the child at home. The child's care and supervision in the home assisted by a public school class is not at present an established procedure. However, such a community organization will lessen the burden on those parents who wish to provide for their own children.[2]

IQ 50–70: Mentally Handicapped

Those with tested IQ's between about 50 and 70 are frequently labeled the *mentally handicapped, morons,* or sometimes *mentally retarded.* To some degree they can usually learn to read, write, and do simple computation. Many can learn to get along socially and develop some occupational competency, so they become partially or entirely self-supporting if they have had the proper kind of education and if they receive some supervision in their work. Many can take adequate charge of animals and learn to use some types of machinery. They cannot, however, plan ahead effectively. They are best suited for facing only problems for which they already have fairly routine, easily recognized solutions. An estimated 2 or 3 per cent of the child population fall into this moron category.

[2] Samuel A. Kirk and G. Orville Johnson, *Educating the Retarded Child* (Boston: Houghton Mifflin, 1951), pp. 9–10.

Many of these children are in institutions for the mentally deficient. Others live at home with their families and are enrolled in the public school's special classes for the mentally handicapped. In communities which have no such classes, children of moron status are found in the regular classrooms, despite the fact that their ability to learn is well below that of the majority of their classmates. If you are a teacher in an elementary school where no special slow-learner classes have been organized, you can expect to have an occasional mentally handicapped child in your class. In school systems which promote pupils regularly according to their increase in age rather than on performance in academic work, you may meet an occasional higher-grade moron in the secondary school.

Whether a mentally handicapped child is best placed in an institution or is able to adapt to a public-school program does not depend solely on his tested IQ. It depends partly on his parents' wishes and attitudes. In addition, such factors as his social adaptability, emotional stability, and diligence will help determine his placement and his success in fitting into a school program. Landis and Bolles draw the following distinctions between *stable* and *unstable* types of morons from the standpoint of the individual's potential effect on society.

Those who are stable are usually inoffensive, well behaved, fairly industrious persons who pursue their way of life comparatively unmoved by things going on around them. They are easily pleased and made happy by praise and by childish amusements. Neither their joy nor their sorrow is excessive or of long duration. They appreciate and return affection and have some conception of simple religious, moral, and social ideas; but their feelings regarding them are not very strong. Many of these stable morons, who are cheerful and obedient, get into difficulty because of their unthinking eagerness to do anything which is requested of them. They rush blithely into situations which intelligent individuals would hesitate to enter and, therefore, they become the causes and sometimes the victims of situations having serious consequences.

The threat to society which comes from the unstable moron is more direct and, of course, more severe. The combination of emotional instability and mental defect produces a class of maladjusted personalities which provides a seemingly inexhaustible reservoir of asocial and antisocial persons.[3]

[3] Carney Landis and M. Marjorie Bolles, *Textbook of Abnormal Psychology* (New York: Macmillan, 1947), pp. 133–134.

Cautions about IQ-Test-Determined Categories

Now that we have introduced mentally deficient and handicapped children, it is well to offer some cautions about these traditional categories which are based primarily on scores from general-intelligence tests. We have used the categories here because they are convenient, but it is proper now to stress their limitations.

Throughout the foregoing discussion you may have noticed many qualifying words among the descriptions of the children in the IQ ranges just discussed, such as "many can learn to" or "in general they may be trained" or "usually the mentally deficient." The necessity for such apparent hedging is caused by the fact that a single test score is only one measure of one aspect of the individual's personality. Even though children are classified together on the basis of an IQ test score, they will be found to differ from one another in many ways. Hence in each of these categories there are many different kinds of personalities. As Sarason has stressed:

> It cannot be emphasized too strongly that a low IQ score does not enable one to state in what ways a particular individual is different from others with an identical score, what his differential reactions are to a variety of situations, his attitudes toward himself and others, what effects he will produce on what kinds of people in what kinds of situations, and the relation of the foregoing not only to the presence or absence of central nervous system impairment but to the familial-cultural background in which he developed as well.[4]

Thus IQ categories serve as rough guides in helping us understand some of the capabilities of children at different levels. But to understand an individual child, we need also the kinds of material described earlier as parts of cumulative records and case studies.

Before we continue up the scale in describing general characteristics often possessed by children at different IQ levels, a second caution is in order. It should be clear that frequently it is impossible to determine precisely what category a given child belongs in because there is no real border line between one classification and another. The divisions merge gradually into each other. The categories are merely imposed descriptive classifications manufactured by psychol-

[4] Seymour B. Sarason, *Psychological Problems in Mental Deficiency* (New York: Harper and Brothers, 1953), p. 368.

ogists as aids in communicating about ability levels. Statements about the percentage of children we would find in each division represent estimates only.

IQ 70–90: Borderline or Slow Learner

Pupils who test between about IQ 70 and IQ 85 or 90 fall in the area between the mentally handicapped and the average-range children. In school these pupils have some difficulty adjusting because they cannot keep up with the regular classwork. An estimated 22 or 24 per cent of the child population is in this category.

Sometimes these children are said to be *dull* or to have *borderline intelligence.* In everyday school use, they are most commonly called *slow learners.* Because this last term is in such popular use among educators, we shall use it freely throughout this book in discussing children in the 70 to 90 IQ category. But we use the term with the following two reservations or cautions.

1. *The term may lack precision.* The label "slow learner" has a broader meaning for some educators than for others. Some use it loosely to mean all levels of ability below the average. But in a few schools the special slow-learner classes include children with IQ's ranging from about 70 to 85 only. In still others, the special classes enroll pupils whose IQ range extends from about 55 to 90 or so. Because the standards for placing a child in such classes vary considerably from one school district to another, it is difficult to avoid this elastic application of the term in everyday use among school personnel. But when you discuss the slow-learner category with another teacher, it is well to agree on what you both mean by it. Throughout the discussions in this book the label applies mainly to those with IQ's 70 to 90, but in a few instances it can include some educable mentally handicapped who have made good social adjustment.

2. *The slow learner is more precisely called a slow developer.* Tyler (1956) objects to the phrase "slow learner," charging that it is undesirable because too often it causes the teacher to misinterpret what the child's problem actually is. In the minds of many people the term designates a child who can learn to add or to analyze the causes of the American Revolution, but it will simply take him a longer time. The material "sinks in" at a slower rate. Tyler, however, takes exception to this belief and cites research indicating that the pupil, at least

at the elementary-school level, is a *slow developer*. If the nervous system of the child were sufficiently developed (as it may well be in a year or two more), he can learn to add just as well as his classmates with higher IQ. But the trouble with him now is that he is too immature to catch on to material so complex as this. He can learn only at a level of complexity commensurate with the present development of his nervous system. He grapples with but does not learn (either rapidly or slowly) skills or information beyond his level. Since the work in school does not stay at one level of complexity but climbs steadily into more complex areas, the slow-maturing child is always behind and is always struggling with ideas beyond his present capacity.

The importance of this distinction between slow learner and late developer from the teacher's standpoint is this: If the child is not learning current material or skills because his aptitude is less than average, the method of simply repeating the material over and over in the same pattern and at the same level of complexity is probably not going to work. He is not just learning slowly; he is not learning at all. As a teacher, you have two principal choices: (1) wait until the child is more mature before facing him with the tasks of this level of complexity or (2) break the task up into simpler components or present it with more concrete, everyday examples and less abstract reasoning. In these ways the material is adjusted to the pupil's level of comprehension.

We have suggested that in the elementary school the term "slow developer" more accurately describes the dull child's characteristics. This implies that he will reach the desired higher level of maturity, but it will take him longer. But at the high-school level, we must admit that the pupil with IQ 72 will never achieve the skill in abstract thinking that characterizes the IQ 100 or 130. Hence, by the time he is at high-school age and beyond, the student is not simply a slow developer who will some day "get there" but a person with definitely limited potential. He reaches a ceiling in ability to grasp more complex, abstract ideas and skills. No matter how long he lives or how steadily he grinds away at certain problems, he will never be able to master them, whereas his more apt agemates have mastered the necessary skills or concepts in their teens.

In every school and in almost every class there are some students with abilities at this slow-learner or slow-developer level. Usually the slow learner is in the regular class with pupils of average and above-average ability. But some larger schools have special sections for those of borderline intelligence.

Whether the child is in a regular or a special class, the methods and materials of teaching demand some modification if he is to progress at a pace in keeping with his potential.

IQ 90–110: Average or Normal Range

The 45 per cent or so of pupils in the population who receive IQ scores between 90 and 110 on intelligence tests are said to fall in the range of average or normal children. Because these students form such a large bulk of the pupils found in most classes, teachers often aim their lessons at about the understanding level of this middle mass of learners.

IQ 110–130: Above Average or Superior

An estimated 24 per cent of children have IQ's between 110 and 130. These are sometimes termed the *above-average* students. At other times they are called the *superior*, the *apt*, the *more able*, or the *rapid learners*. Because intelligence and school success go hand in hand to some degree, this group typically succeeds rather well in academic schoolwork.

Most often the above-average pupil is in the regular class with students of average ability and lower. The class leaders often come from this group. These students frequently provide their classmates with interesting ideas for activities, and they can often furnish solutions to problems more rapidly than can their more average agemates. They are not so far above the average IQ that they are out of intellectual and social contact with the bulk of the class. Their interests tend to be somewhat similar to those of their agemates.

In some schools the pupils in this category, or at least pupils in the upper ranges of it (above 120 or 125), are placed in special classes for rapid learners or *the gifted*.

IQ 130–170: The Gifted or Very Superior

Psychologists and educators do not agree on the IQ point at which we should begin to apply the label "gifted student." Some people say it refers only to those above 140 IQ. Some select 130 as the starting point. Still others use the term when referring to anyone above 125 or 115. In our present discussion, we shall limit the labels "gifted" and "very superior" to students in the IQ range of 130 to 170. In the population we can expect to find about three such pupils per hundred children.

Compared to the average child, gifted pupils typically are more apt readers, are better at numerical relationships, have better vocabularies, are quicker to understand abstract ideas, and are advanced in knowledge well beyond their grade level. In general, their health, strength, and physical agility are at least slightly above average.

In recent years the children and youth in this category have been receiving considerable attention from educators. During the 1950's there was a marked upsurge in conferences, publications, and new school programs aimed at satisfying the needs of the gifted.

Most schools place the gifted in regular classes along with their less apt agemates. In many places efforts have been made to enrich the high-IQ student's experiences within the regular class program. Other school systems have formed special classes for the gifted, designed to proceed at a pace and on an intellectual level commensurate with the very superior pupil's apparent potential.

IQ Above 170: The Genius or Exceptionally Superior

When we cut off the rare, exceptionally high-IQ students for special discussion in this manner, we are not following the most common practices. Usually these students are just considered to be the top of the gifted category. But at this place in our discussion we believe these few children who operate at the most rarefied intellectual heights deserve special focus. So we have arbitrarily set a cutting point at IQ 170. In this range there is an estimated one pupil per 500 children. Every few years you, as a teacher, may have one of these students in your class.

The term "genius" has not been used in any very standardized way in the past. Some people have thought that all pupils with IQ's above 140 should be so classified. Some have suggested a higher cutting point: 160 or 170. Still others have required some qualitative criteria in addition to, or instead of, a high score on an intelligence or general academic-aptitude test. For instance, outstanding creative ability in art, music, the drama, writing, or science is sometimes labeled of genius quality, whether or not the person's academic intelligence-test scores are high. Thus, when one hears the term "genius" it is well to inquire more precisely about what the speaker means.

In our present discussion we use the term for referring to those pupils with tested IQ's above 170 and/or those who have very exceptional ability and performance in a particular area of the arts or science. When we use the term this second way, we shall attach an adjective to describe the area we mean, such as genius in violin performance or genius in science.

Some pupils of this exceptional ability are in the advanced classes for the gifted, which enroll those of perhaps IQ 125 or 130 and above. The genius may find more stimulation in such a class than he would in a heterogeneous group, but still he is so far ahead of even the above-average classmates (with his IQ perhaps 190 and the bulk of his "gifted" classmates at 130 or 135) that he finds them quite slow in catching on to new ideas. Of course, if he is in a regular classroom with schoolmates whose IQ's range into the 90's or 80's, he is even more out of place intellectually.

The very brilliant student, therefore, may have a difficult time adjusting socially and getting schoolwork suited to his needs. He is a real challenge to the teacher.

Differences Shown on Achievement Tests

Although IQ's and mental ages as reflected by scores from general-intelligence tests give us some estimate of a child's academic potential, these measures yield only a single number and thus tend to hide the fact that a person is typically not equally capable in all areas of endeavor. As mentioned earlier, all of us can observe this fact of varied success in different tasks when we see children at their work in school. But the fact can also be illustrated through an inspection of the scores derived from the subtests of an achievement-test battery.

This matter of internal variation within the individual was illustrated with percentile charts of four fifth-graders in Chapter 1. But because this concept is so important, it will be illustrated again at this point, this time in a different form: that of grade-equivalent scores of two seventh-graders who took a standardized achievement-test battery consisting of the following subtests: reading, spelling, arithmetic, language usage, social studies, and science. The norms for the test are in the form of grade equivalents. Thus a student whose score yields a grade equivalent of 7.5 is said to have succeeded as well as the average pupil who is halfway through the seventh grade. A student with a 9.0 in social studies is said to have scored as well as an average beginning ninth-grader.

One of the most capable girls in this seventh grade, Jane Winters, had a Stanford-Binet IQ (based on testing three years earlier) of 135. On the achievement-test battery her grade-equivalent scores were:

			Arith-	Language	Social	
SUBJECT AREA:	Reading	Spelling	metic	usage	studies	Science
Jane was equal to grade	9.8	9.2	8.7	10.7	10.4	8.8

Although Jane was well above the other seventh-graders in all areas, her superiority was most marked in language and least in arithmetic and science. So by furnishing measures for several different kinds of schoolwork, the achievement-test battery gives a more individualized view of Jane's apparent skills than does the single IQ of 135.

Likewise, in the case of another seventh-grader, James Marks, we can see the individualized patterning of his success on the achievement battery.

			Arith-	Language	Social	
SUBJECT AREA:	Reading	Spelling	metic	usage	studies	Science
James was equal to grade:	4.3	3.6	5.4	1.9	5.6	3.7

As may be assumed, James, with a tested Stanford-Binet IQ of 89, was one of the least adequate scholars in the class. Compared with the children on whom the test was standardized, he showed up abysmally low in language usage but was fairly well informed in social studies, though still below the typical seventh-grader.

It may be of interest to note that in this particular seventh grade the average student (the median) had a Stanford-Binet IQ of 109 and grade-equivalent scores of:

Subject Area:	Reading	Spelling	Arith-metic	Language usage	Social studies	Science
Median grade equivalent:	7.2	6.5	7.9	7.0	8.2	8.2

Most students in the class ranged in performance somewhere between Jane and James, with the bulk of them clustered around the median. This class is not at all unusual. The range of talent is quite typical. Although the teacher is called a seventh-grade instructor, it is obvious that he must work with students whose understanding ranges over several grades. His job is to understand the unique patternings of different abilities *within* the personality of each student as well as understanding the differences *between* one student and another.

SUMMARY

Throughout this chapter we have inspected ways of appraising intellectual differences and we have surveyed the range of differences that can be expected in classes in terms of IQ's and achievement-test scores.

We have suggested that teachers can most effectively judge students' intellectual abilities through using standardized aptitude and achievement tests, teacher-made tests, school records, and daily observation.

SUGGESTED LEARNING ACTIVITIES

1. For a grade level of your choice, select one or more areas of learning in which you would like to try predicting pupils' future success. (Such areas of learning might be elementary-school reading, high-school algebra, foreign languages, and so forth.) Using Buros' *Mental Measurements Yearbooks* from a library, try to locate a test that will aid you in your prediction. List also other sources of information that will probably improve the accuracy of your prediction.

2. Visit a nearby school and interview a teacher or administrator to learn what kind of cumulative-record material is kept on each child. Ask the teacher what problems the school faces in collecting cumulative information. Ask also how often cumulative records are actually used by the staff.

3. Locate several standardized achievement and aptitude tests in an education-library test file. Inspect these tests to determine what kinds of items are included, what the tests purport to measure, and how the teacher administers the tests. Inspect the accompanying manuals to discover what criterion measures the tests were validated against.

SUGGESTED READINGS

Descriptions and Evaluations of a Variety of Standardized Tests

BUROS, OSCAR K. (ed.). *The 1938 Mental Measurements Yearbook.* New Brunswick: Rutgers University Press, 1938.

———. *The 1940 Mental Measurements Yearbook.* Highland Park, N.J.: The Mental Measurements Yearbook, 1941.

———. *The Third Mental Measurements Yearbook.* New Brunswick: Rutgers University Press, 1949.

———. *The Fourth Mental Measurements Yearbook.* Highland Park, N.J.: Gryphon Press, 1953.

———. *The Fifth Mental Measurements Yearbook.* Highland Park, N.J.: Gryphon Press, 1959.

Measuring Intellectual Differences

ANASTASI, ANNE. *Psychological Testing.* New York: Macmillan, 1954.

BRUECKNER, LEO J., and BOND, GUY L. *The Diagnosis and Treatment of Learning Difficulties.* New York: Appleton-Century-Crofts, 1955.

CRONBACH, LEE J. *Essentials of Psychological Testing.* New York: Harper and Brothers, 1959.

LYMAN, HOWARD BURBECK. *Test Scores and What They Mean.* Englewood Cliffs: Prentice-Hall, 1963.

STANLEY, JULIAN C. *Measurement in Today's Schools.* Englewood Cliffs: Prentice-Hall, 1964.

THORNDIKE, ROBERT L., and HAGEN, ELIZABETH. *Measurement and Evaluation in Psychology and Education.* New York: John Wiley and Sons, 1961.

TYLER, LEONA E. *The Psychology of Human Differences.* New York: Appleton-Century-Crofts, 1956.

Nature and Growth of Intelligence

BAYLEY, NANCY. "On the Growth of Intelligence," *American Psychologist*, December, 1955, pp. 805–818.

GUILFORD, J. P. "Three Faces of Intellect," *American Psychologist*, August, 1959, pp. 468–479.

Social-Class Influences on Judgments of Ability

DAVIS, ALLISON. *Social-Class Influences upon Learning*. Cambridge: Harvard University Press, 1951.

ESTES, B. W. "Influences of Socio-Economic Status on Wechsler Intelligence Scale for Children: An Exploratory Study," *Journal of Consulting Psychology*, 1953, pp. 58–62.

HOLLINGSHEAD, AUGUST B. *Elmstown's Youth*. New York: John Wiley and Sons, 1949, Chap. 8.

WARNER, W. LLOYD; HAVIGHURST, R. J.; and LOEB, MARTIN B. *Who Shall Be Educated?* New York: Harper and Brothers, 1944.

Teacher-Made Classroom Achievement Tests

AHMANN, J. STANLEY; GLOCK, MARVIN D.; and WARDEBERG, HELEN L. *Evaluating Elementary School Pupils.* Boston: Allyn and Bacon, 1960.

DUROST, WALTER NELSON, and PRESCOTT, GEORGE A. *Essentials of Measurement for Teachers*. New York: Harcourt, Brace and World, 1962.

GREEN, JOHN A. *Teacher-Made Tests*. New York: Harper and Row, 1963.

SCHWARTZ, ALFRED, and TIEDEMAN, STUART C. *Evaluating Student Progress in the Secondary School*. New York: Longmans, Green, 1957.

THOMAS, R. MURRAY. *Judging Student Progress*. New York: Longmans, Green, 1960.

WOOD, DOROTHY ADKINS. *Test Construction: Development and Interpretation of Achievement Tests*. Columbus: Charles E. Merrill, 1960.

CHAPTER 4

Meeting Intellectual Differences I:
Administrative Provisions

There are many ways in which schools can try to suit the work to each student's unique intellectual abilities. One is to hold him longer in the same grade if he has not mastered the work by the end of the year. Or if he has learned much faster than his classmates, he can be skipped ahead an extra grade. Another way is to place him in a class containing other children of about his own ability. Still another method is to place him in a class with children of varied abilities but to form within the class small groups of about equal ability; since pupils in each of these smaller groups have similar talents, schoolwork specially focused on their present learning needs can be designed for them.

As we consider these procedures for meeting intellectual differences, we see that they can be divided into two categories: (1) those involving *administrative adjustments* among the different grades and classes, such as school-wide promotion policies and ways of assigning students to particular classes when there are several class sections at each grade level; (2) those that involve organization and teaching methods *within the classroom* and are thus primarily the responsibility of the individual teacher.

Although these categories are closely interrelated, for the sake of analysis it is convenient to consider each separately. Hence, Chapter 4 focuses on school-wide administrative practices, and Chapter 5 concentrates on methods and materials most useful to the classroom teacher.

Administrative provisions to meet intellectual differences are analyzed under the following headings: (1) ability grouping, (2) special classes for slow learners, (3) special classes for the gifted, (4) other special classes, (5) ungraded classes, (6) retention and acceleration, (7) frequent promotion plans, (8) parallel-track plans, (9) contract and unit plans, and (10) team teaching. As our discussion develops, it will become obvious that these divisions are not at all mutually exclusive but involve much overlapping. Frequently a school follows practices under several of these categories.

In our analysis of each plan, first we define and describe it, next we consider its advantages and disadvantages, and then we suggest under what conditions the plan works best.

HOMOGENEOUS OR ABILITY GROUPING

Homogeneous grouping means putting together students who are like each other. The opposite of this, *heterogeneous grouping,* means putting together students who are unlike each other.

As simple as these distinctions appear, in actual practice much confusion often exists in the use of the terms because different schools use different bases for deciding how students are alike. When you hear that a school provides homogeneous grouping, it is well to ask what specific criteria or measures are used for forming the groups. Otherwise you cannot be sure you understand what the school's practice really involves.

It would be rare to find an American school today that does not have some form of homogeneous grouping. The most obvious type is the division of children into different grades, a practice that is said to have begun in the Quincy Grammar School of Boston in 1848 and spread so rapidly that almost all schools in the larger cities had adopted it by 1860. This formation of grades was a departure from having pupils of all ages in the same class in schools that were large enough to have several classes. Putting children of about the same age together in one room simplified the teacher's job considerably. This most widely practiced method of grouping is based primarily on chronological age or years of experience in school.

However, today, when educators speak of homogeneous grouping, usually they do not mean our familiar grade-level scheme. They are referring to something additional: the further division of pupils on the basis of some other characteristic. One common criterion in the 1920's was a pupil's intelligence quotient. In a school with ninety children to be divided among three fourth-grade classes, the thirty pupils with the highest intelligence-test scores were assigned to Class A, the next highest thirty to Class B, and the lowest thirty to Class C. The hope was that each teacher could better suit work to the particular level of the students. In addition, each pupil would be competing with classmates of like ability at a pace just about right for him. This has been called "ability grouping." Some schools call it "cluster grouping" because it involves clusters of students with similar talents.

But using intelligence-test scores for dividing up the pupils did not bring all the results hoped for. The scheme had two principal shortcomings.

First, as explained in Chapter 3, intelligence is not a single factor but is composed of groups of abilities, so that when pupils are grouped according to a single test score they will still be found to vary significantly in many other specific abilities, such as those relating to language use, social understandings, spacial relations, mechanical tasks, arithmetic computation, science problem solving, or physical agility. So children who have been homogeneously grouped for the factor or factors measured by the test end up being heterogeneously grouped for many other factors important in school.

Second, ability as judged by a test is not the only variable influencing success in school. Other variables include the strength of a student's motivation (some pupils constantly strive hard to work at peak efficiency, while others are lackadaisical), efficiency of work habits, interest in the subject matter, emotional adjustment, and the amount of other activities in his life that compete with schoolwork (such as football practice or a job in a store after school or dates with girl friends).

Because of these shortcomings, schools have turned to other measures besides intelligence-test scores, such as previous marks in school, ratings of social maturity, or physical size. In all, at least twenty-three different criteria have been tried out at one time or another. (Otto, 1954:200.) Schools have often combined several of these measures as the basis for grouping.

Advantages of Ability Grouping

Numbers of advantages have been claimed for homogeneous grouping. It is very difficult to draw valid generalizations about these claims because the research studies used to test them have been conducted under such a range of conditions. For example, we should be quite hesitant in using the results of a study of ability grouping in a high-school science department when we intend to make judgments about how wise such grouping would be for third-graders who spend all day with one teacher. Thus, even though there have been scores of studies made in the past (mainly in the 1920's and 1930's), the existence of so many variables affecting them complicates the task of drawing valid, broad conclusions about homogeneous groups. Such variables include school size, teacher skills, method of assigning teachers to different ability levels, teaching materials available, basis for grouping students, and socioeconomic level of the school district.

Therefore recognizing the possibility that all the following general conclusions may not be applicable to your own particular school situation, we present several generalizations that indicate at least the main tendencies found in the research on grouping.

Students grouped according to ability tend to make better progress than they would in ungrouped classes. This is especially true where the materials, standards, and teaching methods have really been adapted to the needs of the particular class the teacher faces.

Grouping limits the range of talent the teacher must deal with. However, ability grouping in the typical school does not reduce the range of talent in each class as much as we might expect. For instance, if there are three homogeneously grouped fifth-grade classes, we find considerable overlapping in the level of achievement between one class and another. The best students in the lowest class will, in many instances, achieve at a higher level than the poorest students in the top class. Otto reports:

The indications are that in general the variability in achievement (which is an index of difficulty of teaching and the need for instructional adjustments) in ability groups, in grades which have three groups each, is about 83 percent as great as in unselected groups. In grades having two groups each, the variability in achievement in ability groups is about 93 percent as great as in unselected groups. These percentages are reduced to about

74 and 84, respectively, if the plan of ability grouping is accompanied by a multiple track of promotion.[1]

Most teachers prefer to work with homogeneous groups rather than heterogeneous ones. There are several reasons for this. Many feel they can provide reading materials better suited to the level of each individual if students have been sectioned according to ability. Teachers feel they can give the same, or almost the same, work to each student without needing to differentiate assignments to suit a wide range of talent. In addition, some teachers prefer working only with slower learners, others prefer the average group, and still others are best attuned to the challenge offered by the bright pupil.

The majority of parents with children in ability-grouped schools are favorable to grouping and "believe that children are at least as happy, do better work in school, and are correctly sectioned according to ability." (Otto, 1954:202.)

It is unjust to hold back the fast learners and at the same time overwhelm the slow learners by conducting a heterogeneously grouped class at one average speed. This is not a research finding. It is a belief, a value judgment held by many American laymen and educators. If the teacher of a mixed class cannot care for a variety of levels of talent within the class by differentiating assignments and teaching methods to suit each level, then ability grouping will probably help each student live up to his potential learning speed.

Disadvantages of Ability Grouping

Critics of ability grouping cite its several limitations, some of which we have already touched upon.

Students grouped on the basis of one characteristic will be unlike in other characteristics important in school. This, as has been mentioned, is because each of us often has a different level of talent in the various areas of life's activities. In addition, the level of a person's achievement is not governed only by his innate talent; it is also affected by his diligence and his interest in the activity.

This first criticism of grouping is more serious at the elementary-school level than in the high school. That is, in the typical elementary

---

[1] Henry J. Otto, *Elementary School Organization and Administration* (New York: Appleton-Century-Crofts, 1954), p. 201.

school the children are with the same classmates for all studies in one room all day. In the typical larger high school, a student may easily be placed in a fast-moving social-studies class for one period but in a slow-moving mathematics class the next, the respective classes being suited to his abilities in social studies and mathematics.

Ability grouping may reduce somewhat the range of talent within a class but will not eliminate it. Therefore, a teacher who wishes to suit work to individual levels of talent still often needs to make some adjustments within the class, such as regrouping pupils within the room into more homogeneous small units, giving differentiated assignments for the various levels of talent, providing varied levels of reading materials, or using different teaching techniques with the rapid learners than with the slower ones.

Grouping is impractical in small schools. Despite the fact that more and more American children attend schools in cities and that many rural schools have consolidated into larger bus-fed units, there are still many thousands of schools which are relatively small. They have no more than one or two class sections at each grade level. Or, in the case of high schools, they have no more than one section of certain classes, such as plane geometry or first-year French. In these situations, it is either impossible or not worth the effort to group children.

Ability grouping makes it difficult in midsemester to move a pupil into a class that is more appropriate to his current achievement. Frequently, after pupils are divided into sections, some show up considerably better or worse than was expected. In these cases it is often difficult to move the deviants into sections better suited to their progress level because the other sections have been moving at a different pace and perhaps have been covering different materials. However, if the deviants are not moved to a more appropriate section, either they must try to adjust as best they can to the pace of their own class or the teacher must make special provisions for them within the class. In the latter case, the original purpose for the grouping has been defeated.

Homogeneous grouping is undemocratic and promotes personality problems. This complaint carries the two most common and perhaps the most powerful arguments against sectioning students according to ability. To support their charge, critics of grouping have marshaled a variety of arguments. The two chief ones are:

1. Children relegated to the slow sections develop feelings of inferiority with resultant symptoms of personal and social maladjustment. Some pupils become aggressive lawbreakers, while others isolate themselves and brood. On the other hand, children assigned to fast sections develop feelings of superiority, scorn children from lower sections, and in general turn obnoxiously snobbish.

2. Outside of school, the critics say, people in a democracy mix with fellow citizens of all walks of life, of all levels of talent. Should not the school, therefore, serve as a training ground for this melting-pot society? Should not pupils work together with classmates of all types and learn to get along with them, learn their characteristics, and learn to respect them despite their level of talent and socio-economic status?

In spite of the heated emotion and frequency with which these arguments have been uttered, they have, unfortunately, been supported by little, if any, clear research evidence that the present writers are aware of. It is true that from clinical evidence and teachers' observations we know that children who do poorly in school often develop undesirable personality traits. But there is no convincing evidence, as far as we know, that these symptoms occur more often in ability-grouped classes than in heterogeneous groups. Nor do we know whether superior pupils are more likely to become snobbish in ability-grouped classes than in mixed ones.

The charge that "students should be in mixed classes because that is lifelike" has been questioned by people who point out that in life outside of school each of us has some choice of companions, neighbors, workmates, and situations in which he will compete with others. Usually our chosen companions seem to have ability and interests similar to our own. Hence, there is room for doubt that the mixed class is truly more lifelike than the homogeneous one.

Our purpose here is not to say that the "undemocratic" and the "personality maladjustment" charges against homogeneous grouping are invalid. In fact, it is quite possible that they are valid in certain circumstances. Rather, we mean to point out that although many words have been spoken against ability grouping under the banner of these arguments, there is really a paucity of research evidence to support them as yet. Therefore, when we consider the whole range of student ability (the slow, the average, the superior), we do not actually know how ability grouping affects mental hygiene or preparation for democratic citizenship.

(Evidence concerning the social acceptability of the very slow learner in heterogeneously grouped classes will be presented in a later discussion of special classes for slow learners.)

Ability Grouping Works Best Where:

1. The school is rather large so that several sections of each grade (in elementary school) or of each course (in high school) can be formed.

2. There is a departmentalized high school where pupils can be readily assigned to separate classes each period of the day according to their varied levels of skill and interest in different subjects. Grouping is less appropriate for the self-contained classrooms of the elementary school, although even here it can be adopted with success if other favorable conditions exist.

3. Teachers have particular skills and preferences for working with pupils of one ability level—superior, average, or low.

4. Teachers are *not adept* at making adjustments to suit work to a variety of ability levels within the class, but they tend to teach the same way to the entire class.

5. There are some classes or activities that bring pupils of all ability and socioeconomic levels together. In these situations students can mix, learn to get along with each other, and understand the characteristics of other students of different talents. These opportunities for more heterogeneous groups occur in art, music, physical education, home room or orientation, and American-problems classes, and in extracurricular groups like clubs and committees.

SPECIAL CLASSES FOR SLOW LEARNERS

Many schools which in general do not practice ability grouping nevertheless make an exception of the very slow learners and place them together in a special class.

These classes are known by various names in different school systems: special rooms, opportunity classes, slow-learning sections, or mentally retarded sections.

Just as terminology is not standardized, neither are the criteria used for determining who is assigned to such sections. However, intelligence tests commonly figure importantly in establishing the standards, and certain IQ levels are used as at least rough guides to who belongs in special classes. In addition to a child's IQ as established by an individual test (such as the WISC or Stanford-Binet or Arthur Point Performance Scale), the school usually considers also his past school performance, social adjustment, self-reliance, apparent emotional reaction to a special class, and his parents' attitudes toward him and the school.

Standards for placing a child in a special room vary somewhat from place to place. Some districts have slow-learner classes for pupils with IQ's between 70 and 90. Such sections are intended for the borderline intelligences, the ones between the mentally handicapped and the normal. Other schools organize their special classes for a lower group, those with IQ's between 50 and about 75, the group often called the "educable mentally retarded." Still others enroll children from about 50 IQ to those in the upper 80 IQ range.

But despite the intelligence range a school system plans to use, it will usually be found in practice that no very strict IQ limits can be adhered to. This is not only because children have different levels of aptitude in different areas of life but also because some pupils with a "normal" tested IQ often perform in school at a low level because of emotional problems or because of such handicaps as a reading or speech disability. And at the lower levels of the intelligence scale, a child with an IQ apparently rather low for a slow-learner class may show unusually good social adjustment and may have, for him, such good work habits that he can profit by being in the special class rather than in an institution for mentally handicapped.

Some idea of the range of talent represented in typical special classes is gained from statistics collected in a study of the characteristics of 207 pupils assigned to slow-learner classes in eleven California secondary schools. When these students were tested on the Wechsler-Bellevue Intelligence Scale, their IQ average for the full scale was 74 (the lowest child scored 36, the highest 110). This full-scale score is made up of the two separate sections of the test: performance and verbal. The average performance IQ for the students was 81 and the average verbal IQ was 71, reflecting their greater disability in verbal skills. Further analysis of these test scores showed:

For 22 per cent, a full-scale IQ above 80.

For 53 per cent, a performance IQ above 80.

For 14 per cent, a verbal IQ above 80.

For 55 per cent, a verbal IQ below 70.

For 23 per cent, a performance IQ below 70.

Commenting on these statistics, Daly and Cain noted that

. . . at least 15 to 20 percent of the students had IQs as high as those of students who are considered of normal mental ability. The school problems encountered by the students in this group were probably caused by poor motivation, emotional blocking, or some factor affected by a substandard environment. Many conditions that directly affect school adjustment may make a person appear to be mentally retarded when he is not.

. . . on the basis of measured intelligence, only about 80 percent can be described as dull or retarded; and if the problems of the other 20 percent of the group had been studied more carefully, they might have been given more help in a regular class than they were offered in a special class for the mentally retarded.[2]

There are three major types of special classes.

1. *The homogeneous special class.* Twelve to eighteen children of a narrow range of chronological ages and mental abilities are in one class. That is, primary-age slow learners will be in one class, those of chronological age about eight to eleven in another, and so on. Obviously this kind of organization is most suitable to large school systems where there are enough slow learners sufficiently alike in age and ability to make up several different classes. This is usually the most satisfactory type of special class.

A reasonable expectation in large urban communities is a class at each of four levels (primary, intermediate, junior high, senior high) so the mentally handicapped child need not spend more than

[2] Flora M. Daly and Leo F. Cain, "Mentally Retarded Students in California Secondary Schools," *Bulletin of the California Department of Education,* October, 1953, p. 29.

two or three years in one room. He can have the social advantage of being alike in age with the children in his class and have the social prestige of moving physically upward through classrooms that represent the commonly followed graded progression of experiences of our school system. (Birch, 1949.)

2. *The ungraded special class,* encompassing all mentally handicapped children from six to sixteen years of age. "The ungraded class is not the ideal type of organization, but it is the only practical solution for a small school system which has within the school only twelve to eighteen children who require assignment to a special class." (Kirk, 1951:124–125.)

3. *The modified special class,* best suited to schools that are so small that they have too few students for either homogeneous or ungraded classes. As Kirk and Johnson (1951:124–125) have pointed out:

> The modified special class . . . takes a number of forms, some of which are: (1) the mentally handicapped children are assigned to a teacher for part of the day and placed in the regular grades the rest of the day; . . . (2) the mentally handicapped children are assigned to a teacher of a regular class who is interested in their problems; . . . (3) the mentally handicapped children are assigned to a regular grade but a special itinerant teacher is provided for tutoring purposes; . . . (4) the mentally handicapped children are sometimes placed in a special class with educationally-retarded children, or behavior-problem children, or other kinds of children who are not adjusting to the problem of the regular grade.

Advantages of Classes for Slow Learners

Advocates of such special classes list their main advantages as follows.

Classwork can focus on the unique learning goals, personal characteristics, and needs of this special group of pupils. The slow learner is usually different from his more gifted agemates in several important ways. He is less adept at abstract thinking, needs more drill to master simple intellectual functions, and finds more success dealing with such concrete things as handicrafts and in learning from models and pictures rather than words alone. He is usually poor in reading and computing. His attention span is short. His focus is on the immediate and nearby rather than on things distant in time and space. He needs more training in such fairly basic daily tasks as caring for his own health, getting along moderately well with others, and communicating his ideas and wants. He is less capable of working on his own, so he needs more supervision from the teacher.

When such a child is put into a special class with a relatively small number of others of the same caliber, he can work more successfully toward his set of rather limited goals and receive better guidance than he would usually have in a mixed class.

Special methods and materials can be provided for the class by a teacher who has had some training and experience handling slow learners. The special materials may involve more handwork, more concrete objects to learn from, and more reading materials with easy words and short sentences but focused on topics of interest to older pupils.

It is also probable that the teacher of this group will be more sympathetic and patient than would be the average classroom instructor of mixed groups who is more accustomed to attuning his methods and emotional reactions to average and superior students.

The slow learner can find satisfaction at his own work level and not always feel confused, inadequate, and overwhelmed as he would be when functioning as the poorest student of a heterogeneously grouped class.

Disadvantages of Classes for Slow Learners

A variety of disadvantages have been claimed for slow-learner classes, including:

They are undemocratic, for they segregate a minority and prevent the social interplay that all prospective citizens in a democracy have a right to expect. Critics of special classes state that even though a pupil may be limited intellectually, if he is placed in a mixed-ability group he can still profit by the warm friendships he develops with his more apt classmates.

Though this claim appears quite sound at first glance, experts in the area of the mentally handicapped have located a flaw in it. They note that when the slow learner is placed in a mixed class bodily, he still frequently finds himself rather completely segregated socially. This is especially true, they say, of the child whose mental retardation places him below about IQ 75 or so. The ostensible social satisfactions and warm friendships with more apt classmates seldom develop for the quite retarded.

Evidence to support this view that the very slow learner is often rejected by agemates has been provided in several studies, the best of which was conducted by Orville Johnson (1950) in twenty-five heterogeneously grouped elementary-school classes. Each class contained one or more children with tested IQ below 70. Sociometric results showed that the mentally handicapped were significantly more isolated and rejected socially than the typical children. The lower the IQ, the more the rejection. These very slow learners were seldom isolated because of low academic success but usually because of unacceptable social behavior like bullying, fighting, misbehaving, showing off, lying, cheating, and their apparent inability to conform to group standards of conduct.

Johnson's study showed further that the borderline group (those between IQ 70 and IQ 85 or 90) had a social position not different significantly from that of the remainder of the typical children in the class. This suggested that the regular elementary-school classes apparently met the borderline-IQ student's social-acceptance needs and that at least from a social standpoint it was unnecessary to put him in a special class. On the other hand, for the group below IQ 70, the special class apparently would be the best place for the pupils both socially and academically.

Therefore we conclude that segregation is not just a physical state but occurs psychologically in ostensibly unsegregated classes. Whether a slow learner will profit socially more by a special class or a mixed group is a judgment best made after study of the particular child's personality and of the group he might be placed in. But, generally, the lower his IQ, the better it is to put a very slow learner in a special class with children more like himself and with a specially trained teacher than to put him with typical pupils who will reject him.

The special class is too often a dumping ground for all problem children, not just for slow learners. The class for retarded learners can become the depository for delinquents, emotionally disturbed pupils, those with speech and hearing defects, pupils with foreign-language backgrounds in the home, and the like.

This multiplicity of problem personalities not only confounds the teacher and reduces his effectiveness with the actual slow-learner group, but it also gives the class a bad name among other pupils and their parents. True, the teacher of the slow learners will have to face an inordinate number of other social and physical handicaps among his charges because those poorly endowed intellectually also suffer from other handicaps more frequently than do their more apt agemates. But this does not mean that all children in the school who prove difficult to teach should be relegated to this one class. Unless the school administrators are careful, they load up the slow-learner class with pupils whose problems are basically different and require attention from other quarters (such as from the physician, psychiatrist, psychiatric social worker, and guidance counselors).

Parents object to special classes and do not like their children segregated and labeled "special." There is undoubtedly truth in this accusation. But according to numerous authorities in the special-education field, this negative attitude is not nearly so widespread as many educators fear. Bower, in commenting on the California program which provides special classes for all children who appear to need them, has concluded:

With perhaps one or two exceptions, all classes in California for mentally retarded children have been successful. Segregated classes once thought to be the bogey man in the program turned out to be a false alarm. While some parents have objected, the overwhelming majority have been eager for their children to profit from this special service.[3]

It is likely that parents of the borderline children (those in the upper 70 and 80 IQ ranges) object more to segregation than parents with children who are so markedly retarded that the parents themselves are painfully aware of the pupils' unusual inadequacies and their need for special aid.

Small schools cannot afford to set up special classes for slow learners. Schools in poorer communities cannot readily afford the teachers, special book collections, and equipment desired for these groups.

---

[3] Eli Bower, "California's Program for the Mentally Retarded," *American Journal of Mental Deficiency,* April, 1951, pp. 502–505.

Many teachers do not like to "get saddled" with a slow-learning group. It is often difficult to find well-trained, willing teachers for such classes.

Slow-Learner Classes Work Best Where:

1. A school system is large enough to provide a class for each of several narrow ranges of chronological age.

2. Class size is between about twelve and eighteen pupils.

3. An efficient testing and guidance system exists to determine which children are to enter the special classes.

4. School officials explain carefully to parents the advantages and disadvantages as well as the teaching methods used in the classes.

5. The teacher has had some special training in working with very slow learners.

6. There are opportunities for the slow learners to be with typical children at some time during the school day. This is probably more important for the borderline–normal group than for the lower mentally retarded.

7. The school supports the program with special materials, such as books of mature interest level but low vocabulary load, audio-visual facilities, and handicrafts.

SPECIAL CLASSES FOR THE GIFTED

The 1950's brought a great surge of interest in the gifted child. He was considered the lost American, the newly discovered under-privileged of the educational scene. The retarded had been receiving special attention for years, but it was apparent that in a great many schools the very talented members of the student body were left to care for their own needs pretty much by themselves.

One way to adapt schooling to the superior learner's talents is to put him in a special class for the gifted. For years such classes had been in operation in some school systems. During the 1950's these programs were newly publicized, and other cities which heretofore had organized special classes for the mentally retarded only now skimmed off the top IQ's in their schools and formed special classes for them as well.

As with slow learners, the standards for placing superior students in a special class are not the same the country over. Aptitude or intelligence tests figure prominently in the criteria used, along with teacher recommendations, past school performance as reflected in marks, and social adjustment. In some schools, pupils with IQ scores above 120 are placed in the fast-learner sections. Probably it is more common to have as a lower limit an IQ of 125 or 130. Others consider an IQ of 135 or 140 as the required level for a pupil entering a section for the gifted.

Classes for the fast learners take a variety of forms. At the high-school level, these gifted may sometimes be segregated with their intellectual peers for all studies. But this is a less flexible and less popular method than placing the superior pupil for just one or two periods a day in groups composed of other especially gifted classmates in special subject-matter areas where their superiority is marked. For other subjects in which their talents are not so different from their agemates, they may be in mixed groups. Departmentalization in the high school makes this possible. The bigger the school, the more flexibility there is.

Advanced-placement courses are one variety of special class. Advanced placement means that while still in high school, gifted students take some college-level courses, taught either at the high school or at the college. Often university credit is awarded for these classes. By the early 1960's, more than four hundred high schools were cooperating with universities in this effort.

Classes for the gifted in the elementary school are not so easy to arrange, particularly because elementary schools are usually smaller and the children commonly stay with the same teacher all day. However, gifted sections have been formed in larger school systems, most commonly at the upper elementary levels. Another procedure involves placing the gifted in a mixed class for part of the day but having them leave the regular group for an hour or two and attend a special smaller class that challenges them academically.

Advantages of the Class for Superior Learners

Supporters of classes for the very bright child cite such advantages as the following.

The superior student gets the opportunities and challenge commensurate with his abilities. The new inventions, the intellectual leadership, the solutions to complex problems must come from the nation's gifted minds. It is in society's interest to see that they are trained well and have the best opportunities in school. It is a marked loss to society when the bright person becomes lazy or does not have chances to develop his abilities.

In the special class, the gifted pupil does not have the daily invitation to become bored and careless, as so often happens when he is in a mixed group that always moves too slowly for him. Rather, he is stimulated by the lively ideas of his intellectual peers, who provide him with a healthy push of competition that urges him to make the most of his talents.

The teacher can do a better job in a better-equipped classroom. The characteristics of the slow learner and the gifted pupil are sufficiently different to make it desirable for the teacher to use different methods, materials, and subject matter with each of them. This is usually difficult to do in a mixed class with slow, average, and rapid learners together. In a segregated class of only superior learners, the teacher can spend less time on drill and more time on advanced intellectual activities. Projects can require greater pupil independence and creativity.

In addition, the school can more readily provide a teacher who gets along well with quick minds and is stimulated by them rather than puzzled or intimidated or angered. The gifted child in the regular class sometimes finds himself at odds with a less adept instructor who is uncomfortable when faced by the mental gyrations of the very apt.

Supplies for the class can also be more specialized. The fast learner typically is a fast and interested reader. He consumes books and magazines at a rapid rate. So the teacher of the special class can give particular attention to furnishing a large amount of reading material suited to advanced intellectual appetites.

The average child also gets more opportunities and satisfactions. When the gifted pupil is in a regular class, he shows up so much better than the average pupil on intellectual tasks that he sometimes comes to be resented by his more typical classmates. If the teacher tries to enrich the gifted student's program in the regular class, the average student often interprets this as giving special privileges to the supposed teacher's pet. But if the gifted students are placed in a segregated class, the more typical learners in the regular class have better chances for recognition and success that is not overshadowed by the efforts of very superior agemates.

Disadvantages of the Class for Superior Learners

Four criticisms of a class for the gifted have been:

1. *The segregated fast learner often becomes a snob. He makes poor social adjustment.* According to some educators, the gifted child in the special class has few chances to learn the characteristics of more average people. He does not learn to get along well with those of less ability. Because he is always segregated with his intellectual equals, he loses patience with the average child's lesser knowledge and his slower grasp of new ideas.

How accurate are these claims? There is no doubt that the fast learner can become conceited. But it is very likely that he develops snobbery as readily (or even more so) in a mixed class where his superiority is always evident as in a segregated class where he competes with those as capable as himself. In fact, some schools have reported that pupils who have entered a segregated class with attitudes of snobbery have, because of individual counseling, been able in the special class to develop a more amicable relationship with agemates. Thus we may recognize that the gifted child may become conceited and perhaps overbearing, but research studies indicate that the poor social adjustment and undesirable attitudes are not necessarily the outcome of separate classes for the gifted. (California Elementary School Administrators Association, 1958.)

Evidence about social adjustment suggests that being *somewhat* above average intellectually is an asset to a child. But as we go on up the IQ scale—to 140, 150, and above—we find that high-powered intellect can be a barrier to warm social relations. The greater the child's superiority, the more likely it is that his interests will be too advanced for his more average schoolmates, that his agemates will resent his brilliance, and that they will fail to understand and accept him. Being too different from the crowd, either at the upper or lower end of the scale, is a social liability. (Magnifico, 1958: 62–66.)

Thus the *very superior* student will often profit both academically and socially by entering a segregated class where he finds companions whose mental agility and interests match his own. The student who is above average but not highly superior (perhaps in the IQ range of 120 to 130 or so) often makes a very good social adjustment in the regular classroom and, at least from the social standpoint, does not need a special class. (Johnson, 1950; Jordan, 1951:35.)

2. *Small school systems cannot readily collect enough really gifted students to warrant starting special classes.* Retarded learners of several age levels are often grouped together to form a single class in a moderate-sized school. But with the gifted, it is more common to include not more than one or two grade levels in one room. This arrangement necessitates having a larger school system to draw pupils from if special classes are to be formed.

3. *It is sometimes hard to find teachers who understand the gifted, can stimulate their potential interests, and can keep up with their wide-ranging thoughts without becoming harried or intimidated.*

4. *Parents whose children do not get into the fast-learner class may resent it and charge the school authorities with providing special privilege for a favored few.*

Classes for Fast Learners Work Best Where:

1. The elementary school is large enough to warrant the formation of a class of really advanced pupils at each grade level or at least one special class for each pair of grades (such as one special class comprised of fifth- and sixth-graders).

2. The secondary school is departmentalized so that the student with advanced talent in one subject-matter area can be placed in the advanced class for that subject but in classes with more typical students for studies in which his abilities are more typical.

3. The class is directed by a teacher who likes and understands the fast learner and has the personal imagination and classroom facilities to furnish activities that greatly enrich school experiences.

4. The gifted have some opportunities to work with and understand their less apt agemates.

5. The activities of the special class include emphasis on the *responsibilities* and *rights* of people in a democracy. The gifted should recognize their own responsibilities as well as the right of each person to receive respect and fair treatment, regardless of his level of talent.

SUPPLEMENTARY CLASSES AND TUTORING

Sometimes a school does not practice regular homogeneous grouping, nor does it have special classes for the gifted, but it does provide a supplementary class or two which pupils with special needs enter for an hour or so a day. It is true that this category of supplementary classes overlaps those for slow and fast learners discussed above. But there are also some differences. A few examples will illustrate this.

The most common supplementary class is in remedial reading. In the elementary school, the child who is markedly retarded in reading skill may leave his regular classroom for a half-hour or an hour a day to receive special coaching either individually or, more commonly, with a few classmates who show the same disability. Remedial arithmetic and speech training are often provided in this same manner.

Extra classes or tutoring sessions are also made available in special-interest areas, particularly in instrumental music. These sessions may be substituted for some of the regular class periods or may be given during free periods (in lieu of study hall in high school) or after school.

Coaching sessions can be furnished the gifted child who, the school authorities feel, should soon be skipped ahead to the next grade. The tutoring helps bridge the gap between where his present classmates are now and where the next grade's pupils will be. Such coaching is usually needed primarily in subject-matter areas that involve a rather definite sequence of learning, such as arithmetic and mathematics, where the understanding of each new topic typically depends on a good understanding of every previous one. To a lesser extent, success in science and social studies depends on sequential learning.

Advantages of Supplementary Sessions

Supplementary classes and tutoring can:

Help the small school provide special opportunities for the very slow learner, the gifted, and the pupil with special interests. Where school enrollment is too small to warrant special all-day classes, individual needs can be met to some extent through teaching selected pupils outside their regular classes for a period a day or perhaps an hour or two a week. Because such coaching groups are smaller than regular classes, each pupil's unique needs can receive more special attention.

These sessions may often be given by a part-time teacher. Part-time teachers can be of different varieties. Some are specialists, as in remedial reading or speech, who are shared by several small schools. Some are half-time counselors and half-time special teachers. Others are parents or members of the community who supplement the school's offerings by tutoring or by conducting small extra classes, as in advanced science, business education, creative writing, music, or art.

Help the slower learner make a better adjustment to his regular class. This is especially true in a tool subject like reading. The special-reading teacher can emphasize the skills that enable the pupil to understand better his reading assignments in arithmetic or social studies and thus make more adequate progress in the regular class's academic pursuits.

Special coaching can often enable a slightly below-average learner to stay in the class with his agemates rather than have to remain behind when they are advanced to the next grade. In addition, if the pupil has a disability in just one area, such as arithmetic, his inadequate efforts are not displayed publicly to his classmates each day if he does arithmetic with a tutor.

Challenge the gifted to expand his knowledge beyond the confines of his regular class. The fast learner can move into new, more advanced fields through the special sessions, and when the sessions are designed to prepare him for skipping ahead a grade, he does not arrive in the next grade with gaps in learning that would hamper a smooth transition to the more advanced class.

Disadvantages of Supplementary Sessions

Such classes can:

Remove the student from his regular class at a time the group is doing something important which he should not miss. Especially in the nondepartmentalized elementary school, this is a problem. The teacher must always keep in mind the schedule of special students who are to withdraw and to try to see they do not miss worth-while class activities. This reduces the flexibility of the teacher's planning. The goal of making sure special students miss no important regular work is often impossible to attain. If there are numbers of different pupils to be tutored (music lessons, remedial reading, special coaching in speech), there is a continual parade of students in and out of the room, making the regular teacher's task frustrating indeed.

Emphasize the difference between the special child and his classmates. Probably this does not disturb the gifted child as much as the slow learner, whose periodic removal from class emphasizes to his agemates anew each day his "abnormality."

Necessitate the administration's hiring specialists. Not only are specialists difficult to find for a small school, but since they work with small groups or individuals, they are costly.

Supplementary Sessions Work Best Where:

1. There is a small school that cannot, in any more practical way, provide for students with markedly special needs.

2. The community contains parents with special talents who can be enlisted to enrich the regular school program.

3. The school wishes to aid a student who has special disabilities or abilities in one area, but it is considered best for the student to remain in a regular class with his more typical agemates for most of the school day.

NONGRADED SCHOOLS

The terms "nongraded school," "ungraded unit," and "continuous-promotion plan" refer to certain related innovations in school organization that rose to popularity in the late 1950's and have continued to gain adherents in the 1960's. Although such plans have been inaugurated in secondary as well as elementary schools, their greatest popularity continues to be at the primary-grade level where these types of programs originated.

It is incorrect to speak, as some educators do, of *the* nongraded plan or *the* continuous-promotion plan because there is no single type. There are various forms used by different schools. But there are two elements which all such plans share in common (at least theoretically). These are (1) the opportunity for the student to work at a level of difficulty commensurate with his abilities and (2) the desire of the school not to identify a student's work level by a grade number.

In elementary schools, nongraded plans tend to encompass only the kindergarten and first three grades. This block of four years' work is not divided into grades in the usual sense. Rather, the four grades are considered to be one unit. Within the unit, the work is divided into eight or ten smaller levels above the kindergarten. Children move from one level to the next at the speed suited to their individual talents. The same teacher can stay with a group of children for more than one year, thus coming to understand them more thoroughly. There is no passing from one grade to the next. There are no grades to fail at the end of the year. Pupils remain in the same classroom with the same teacher but move to the next block as soon as they have completed the work of the levels below. Thus the teacher of such a class is dealing with several different levels at the same time.

The typical time it takes a pupil to complete the work of the primary unit or primary block (kindergarten through Grade 3) is four years. Slower-maturing children will take five years. Although some of these nongraded programs have encouraged the fastest learners to complete the unit in three years, this procedure does not seem to be in general favor. A more common approach provides broader, enriched activities at each level for the gifted child rather than having him push directly through the entire block in three years or less.

In some schools, a nongraded intermediate unit (comprising the work of Grades 4, 5, and 6) is superimposed on the primary unit. Continuous promotion from one sublevel to the next within this block is practiced, as in the primary block.

At the junior and senior high-school levels, a variety of administrative arrangements have been labeled "nongraded." In some instances—perhaps most instances—the plan is simply a form of homogeneous grouping that provides for easy movement of students from one group to another as their progress warrants. That is, a student in an average-progress English class may demonstrate more writing and reading skill than his classmates, so he is moved into a higher group that works at an accelerated pace.

Other high schools have laid claim to the nongraded title by permitting a student to enter whatever classes are appropriate to his abilities, despite the length of time he has been in school. Thus a class labeled English Literature will not be designated as a course for sophomores, but it will contain some sophomores, some juniors, and some seniors whose abilities and interests are similar. Educators who are well acquainted with practices of high-school scheduling recognize that the practice of permitting pupils of various grade levels to enroll in the same class is not a revolutionary move. It has been a rather common custom, particularly in courses like geology or news-writing, which do not follow the kind of set sequence usually required in social studies and literature programs. Although the idea is not new, the extension of this scheduling pattern to encompass most or all courses in a school is a departure from tradition and does, indeed, make the classes nongraded.

In addition to the foregoing scheduling systems, other variations, such as independent study for gifted pupils, are being inaugurated under the title of nongraded or continuous-promotion education. (Brown, 1963.)

There is evidence to suggest that some (perhaps many) teachers working in nongraded elementary-school plans have changed neither their teaching methods nor their ways of talking about pupils' achievement ("He's doing second-grade work") to fit the real intention of the plan. They continue to think in grade-level terms and try to bring the slower learners "up to standard" by the end of the year. When the classroom teacher thus fails to alter his approach to suit the children's individual learning speeds, the school is following a traditional pattern. It does not deserve the nongraded title that it wears.

Advantages of Nongraded Plans

At the elementary-school level, supporters of the nongraded unit claim that it provides:

1. A unit span of years that is adaptable to the lags and spurts normally accompanying the development of a child.

2. Progress levels that permit a child to pick up after an absence from school at the point where he previously left off.

3. A time range that permits children of approximately the same chronological age to remain together while progressing at different academic rates suited to individual capacities. (Goodlad, 1955:171.)

At the high-school level, the principal advantage is that the apt student is not retained in a class simply because it is traditionally the type planned for his grade level, but he is able to enroll in more advanced classes containing students who are his intellectual peers.

Disadvantages of Nongraded Plans

Critics of nongraded units in elementary schools state that such systems:

Demand the skills of especially adept teachers who can adjust classwork effectively to a range of abilities in one room, and such teachers are often hard to find. The nongraded unit can end up being just a regular graded system, labeled nongraded, if teachers do not alter their methods to provide continuous progress for each child at his own speed.

Are not well accepted by the kind of parent who wants the security of the system he grew up with. Parents of a slower-developing child may not wish to recognize the fact that it will take their child five years to get through the primary block. The advantages of the system need to be explained carefully to such parents before it is attempted.

Badly cripple the learning opportunities of any child who gets stuck with one inferior teacher for four years.

At the secondary level, critics direct their barbs particularly at the administrative difficulties that the various forms of nongraded plans bring forth.

In the middle of a term a student cannot be moved conveniently to a class better suited to his current rate of progress.

Slower students cannot be retained conveniently in the school until they have mastered the material considered appropriate for graduation in most high schools. In the primary grades, it is possible to keep a slow-maturing child in the primary unit an extra year until he has better command of the skills assigned to the primary block. But in high school, the slower student must either be given credit for a course even though his success has been slight or be failed in the course and required to repeat it. If given credit, he has earned a unit toward graduation and deserves to graduate when he has accumulated enough units, despite the fact that the school considers him ill qualified to graduate or to enter the working world. If failed, he seldom wishes to spend an extra year or so to reach the school's standards of adequacy, so he drops out—a choice he did not have in the primary grades. Thus a program of gradual steps for continuous progress to a particular standard is difficult, if not impossible, to achieve in the traditional high school.

Where the Nongraded Plan Works Best:

1. In the primary grades.
2. In classes directed by teachers skilled in diagnosing pupils' needs and in carrying on a variety of activities at one time in the classroom. Each of these activities must be suited to the particular learning speed of a small segment of the class.

RETENTION AND ACCELERATION

Traditionally, the most popular way to care for the case of the slow learner has been to hold him back to repeat the grade when his classmates are promoted at the end of the term. This practice goes under a variety of names: retention, nonpromotion, retardation, retarded progress, failing, flunking, and repeating.

Likewise, the very fast learner's case has most often been treated by hastening him through the grades at a faster pace than his age-mates. There is a bit of confusion about the terms used for this practice. The general word is "acceleration." In most schools, this simply means the same as "skipping." The fast learner, usually at the regular promotion time, is moved an extra half-grade or whole grade ahead of his classmates. Other schools, however, make a distinction between skipping and acceleration. They use the term "skipping" in referring to the child's hurdling over the work of the next grade, but they reserve the term "acceleration" or "modified acceleration" for the practice of having the child proceed at a more rapid pace but not miss or skip any work.

We shall discuss retention and acceleration separately, since each is based on different assumptions and each is accompanied by different advantages and disadvantages.

Retention

In the past, retention has been practiced very widely. About 10 per cent of the public-school population can be classified as repeaters (students held back at least once). Studies show that in the typical school there is about four times as much retardation as acceleration, and there is much more retardation in rural than in city schools. (Jones, 1956; Monroe, 1950:1123.)

In the elementary school, by far the largest amount of failing occurs at the first-grade level. The number of pupils retained diminishes in the upper grades.

Where retention is practiced very consistently in a school, it is usually based on the assumption that there is a minimum standard of work for each grade level that must be met by a pupil before he should be allowed to pass to the next higher grade. If he does not meet the established standard, he remains behind to try again.

Advantages of Retention

When we inspect the advantages claimed for nonpromotion, we see that some of them relate to individual differences and some to other characteristics of the pupils or of the school program. Supporters of retention say that it:

Gives another chance to the slow learner to master material he did not grasp the first time through. This assumes that the slow learner was too immature to learn effectively the first year in the grade and that with more maturity and another repetition of the teaching he can master the material the second year.

Stimulates children to work hard by holding over them the threat of not passing.

Maintains the standards of the school. Where retention is widely practiced, one can always know the minimum skill of a sixth grader or know what level of mastery a tenth-grader has attained, for he would not have been allowed to pass to that level if he had not met standards set for each lower grade.

Simplifies the teacher's job in the higher grades by holding back slow learners and thus reducing the range of difference in ability within the group that passes.

Disadvantages of Retention

A significant amount of research has been conducted on the promotion-versus-retention problem. Summarizing studies focused on the elementary school, Otto (1954:268–269) has concluded:

It is now evident that practically all of the notions previously held about the value of nonpromotion or the motivating value of the threat of failure have been exploded. Out of a group of repeaters, about 20 percent will do better than they did the preceding term, about 40 percent will show no change, and about 40 percent will actually do worse. If doubtful cases are divided into two groups appropriately matched on essential items, and one group is promoted and the other group is held back to repeat the grade, several studies have shown that the achievement of the promoted group, as measured by standardized tests, is equal to or greater than the achievement of the group held back. If the objective of the school is to promote the optimum educational development of pupils, nonpromotion is not the way to get it. As far as personality adjustment is concerned, group studies show that the adjustment of pupils of low achievement is not more satisfactory when they are retained in grade groups more nearly representative of their levels of achievement. Numerous cases are on record which show the contribution which nonpromotion, especially repeated nonpromotion, has made to the personality maladjustment of individual cases.

Likewise, other supposed advantages of retention fail to stand up when judged against studies made of retention in practice. For instance, in the matter of school standards, research shows that the average levels of achievement actually tend to be a bit higher in schools that do not fail many students. In general, there seems to be little, if any, connection between a school's academic standards and its rate of promotion.

In regard to the range of talent within classes, research indicates that both in schools that have high rates and in those that have low rates of nonpromotion the range of talent within a class is about the same. Thus, retention does not appreciably reduce the spread of achievement levels or variation of mental ages which the teacher must work with.

Where Retention Works Best

Research suggests that the generally accepted tendency today is to allow students to progress with their classmates each year. The welfare of most students will be best served in this way. But when a student is outstandingly below the achievement of his classmates, his case should be carefully studied to determine whether he should be an exception to this practice, because a few children actually profit more by remaining in the same grade again.

To make this judgment about keeping a pupil to repeat a grade, it is wise to consider a variety of factors, not just academic standing. You need to investigate his social adjustment, mental maturity, chronological age, his size, his attitude toward being retained, his future goals, and the attitudes of his parents. Before it is finally decided that he should be held back, it is wisest to secure the consent of the pupil and his parents. The decision should finally rest on the answer to the question, Which solution will help this pupil make the most satisfactory adjustment: promotion or retention? The focus, then, is on the pupil's welfare rather than on what would be most convenient for the school authorities.

Some schools use trial promotion for doubtful cases. That is, when the authorities cannot decide whether to promote or retain a student, they promote him temporarily with the understanding that if he does not do well he will be put back. This attempt at a solution is usually a shaky, unsatisfactory one. Oftentimes the doubt which the teachers had in mind when they struck upon the trial promotion is still not completely resolved after the child has been in the upper grade awhile, so this measure has not really helped them make a decision but has only postponed it. Typically the trial promotion automatically becomes permanent because it is so awkward to have to demote the child again. Usually it would have been better to promote him unconditionally in the first place than to use the pretense of a trial.

Acceleration

Acceleration has been practiced for a long time to care for the fast learner's needs. About 4 per cent of elementary-school pupils have skipped ahead. More girls than boys are accelerated. Schools that promote pupils twice a year (January and June) have higher rates of skipping than schools that promote only once annually. (Otto, 1954:169.)

Usually acceleration takes the form of skipping, but there is some tendency in the elementary school to urge more use of a continuous acceleration system such as the ungraded primary and elementary blocks.

The practice of acceleration is generally based on the assumption that the child is mature enough socially, emotionally, and physically as well as academically to fit in well with the pupils in the next higher grade. It is also presumed that perhaps with a little coaching in the tool subjects the child will miss little or nothing essential by skipping a grade. It is assumed that he will do at least average or above-average work in the higher grade he skips to. (This assumption is usually valid, for the very superior child from the lower grade typically is also one of the better students when moved to the next higher grade.) It is believed that if the child stays in his present class he may be bored, lose interest, waste his time and talent, and possibly end up a maladjusted, lazy, or belligerent member of the group.

Advantages of Acceleration

The practice of speeding the fast learner through the grades is said to:

Provide more scope for his abilities through more advanced work. It furnishes him intellectual peers, thus stimulating him to work hard and not waste his talent in lackadaisically dragging along at the pace of his intellectually slower agemates.

Care for the gifted without necessitating the organization of special fast-moving classes or the hiring of tutors. Acceleration is the simplest of the administrative procedures and can be utilized by small and large schools alike.

Help reduce the range of talent the teacher must deal with in a class, for it moves the most advanced students into the next grade. This is true, but to a limited extent. When you skip the one or two best students ahead, you have reduced the over-all range of ability in the class by only a small amount.

Disadvantages of Acceleration

According to critics of skipping children ahead, the practice can cause problems because:

The very bright child's superiority is usually not so great in other aspects of his life as in the intellectual sphere. This discrepancy between mental maturity and physical or social maturity can, it is said, cause undesirable personality maladjustment. How much personality disturbance is actually likely to result from acceleration is not completely agreed upon by educators who have studied the problem closely. In discussing the plight of the very gifted, Hollingworth concluded:

If the child be accelerated in the regular classes to the point where he can function with real interest intellectually, he will be out of harmony with the classroom situation in other important respects. A child of eight years graded with twelve-year-olds is out of his depth socially and physically, though able to do intellectual work as well as they can. Classroom furniture will not be adapted to his size; he will always be regarded as a nuisance in athletic contests; it will be doubtful how to treat him at class parties; his handwriting will be poor and slow in contrast with that of his much older classmates; he will be emotionally immature in comparison with those about him.[4]

However, Terman and Oden (Witty, 1951:43) concluded from their extended studies of the gifted:

There is no doubt that maladjustment does result in individual cases, but our data indicate that in a majority of subjects it involves chiefly a temporary feeling of inferiority which is later overcome. The data on physical and mental health, both in childhood and the adult years, favor the accelerates. (Witty, 1951:43.)

In this case, the accelerates were contrasted with students usually in regular classes, not with those in classes especially for the gifted.

It is apparent that the chances for maladjustment are greater for the very gifted (IQ 170 or above) than for the ones not so different from their agemates (IQ 130 to 150).

[4] Leta S. Hollingworth, "Personality Development of Special Class Children," *University of Pennsylvania Bulletin, Eighteenth Annual Schoolmen's Week Proceedings,* XVIII (June 20, 1931), 443.

Most schools today seem to make some kind of compromise in accelerating the very talented student. That is, it is common to skip him not more than a grade or a grade and a half ahead and then try to care for his still advanced intellectual needs by enrichment of the program within the classroom. In this way, he is not placed too far in advance of children of his size.

In the opinion of Terman and Oden:

No universal rule can be laid down governing the amount of acceleration that is desirable. It is our opinion that nearly all children of 135 IQ or higher should be promoted sufficiently to permit college entrance by the age of 17 at latest, and that a majority in this group would be better off to enter at 16. . . . Although there are some children who could be made ready for ninth grade at 9 or 10 years, and for college at 13 or 14, such extreme instances of acceleration in our gifted group have usually had unfortunate results. (Witty, 1951:45–46.)

If a child is skipped without having first been aided in making up the necessary knowledge and skills he is leaping over, he is likely to be handicapped in the future and may never fill in these gaps successfully.

Acceleration Works Best Where:

1. Enrichment of studies in the regular class fails to challenge the gifted child at his optimum level of ability.

2. The child is advanced socially and physically as well as intellectually.

3. The child's social and physical skills are not greatly different from those of his new classmates. (Thus, skipping a child more than a grade or so ahead is often inadvisable.)

4. The child has been helped to fill in the gaps of knowledge that would result from his missing blocks of subject matter in the skipping process.

5. The teacher in the advanced grade aids the student in making a social adjustment to the new class.

FREQUENT PROMOTION PLANS

One attempt to adjust the school's pace to the child's abilities is the provision of more than one promotion period a year. Usually this involves a semester system and promotions in both January and June.

A much rarer variety is found in the St. Louis elementary schools, which have used a four-times-a-year promotion plan (every ten weeks) since 1862. In actual practice, the children do not pass to a new teacher at the end of the first (November) and third (April) terms. Rather, these represent reporting points when special promotions and demotions are possible.

Advantages of Twice-a-Year Promotions

From the standpoint of individual differences, the chief advantages of the semiannual promotion system are:

Children who come of school age in midyear can enter school without having to wait until the following September.

Twice-a-year special acceleration of rapid learners can be accomplished, and classes can be regrouped to provide more homogeneous groups if ability grouping is the school's practice. Schools with annual promotions only must usually wait till September to carry out these changes.

In a departmentalized high school, students can make more rapid progress or receive a broader education by taking an extra course for a semester or so. In addition, the student who has failed a course will often have the opportunity to make it up immediately the second semester and does not have to wait till the following year.

Disadvantages of Frequent Promotions

Promotion more often than once a year may cause too frequent change of students from one teacher to another so that *the teacher does not come to learn the students' needs and capacities well enough.* On the other hand, frequent promotion does occasionally furnish a student a welcome early escape from a teacher of little ability or understanding.

Frequent-Promotion Plans Work Best Where:

1. The school is large enough to have a class of new students entering every half-year.

2. There are several sections at each grade level so that, if some type of ability grouping is practiced, the groups can be reshuffled

twice a year to provide for shifting pupils that seem ill suited to their section.

PARALLEL-TRACK PLANS

One variety of ability grouping involves the establishment of two tracks, one designed for average or slower workers and the other for more rapid learners. The fast track enables the fast workers to complete the typical grade's work in a shorter time. Historically, the most notable of these plans were carried out in Portland, Oregon, and Cambridge, Massachusetts.

In the Portland Plan, introduced more than a half-century ago, the nine-grade elementary-school course of study was divided into fifty-four units. A child in the regular-progress track was expected to complete six of these a year. A child in the rapid-progress track (in a separate class) completed eight units a year (but only six the final year). In this particular form, the plan has been long since discontinued.

In Cambridge, beginning in 1893 and revised in 1910, all children had the same work for Grades 1 through 3, but from Grades 4 through 9 they were divided according to ability into two parallel courses. In its original form, the regular-progress track was completed in six years, the special track for fast learners in four. In its 1910 revision, the school was put on an eight-grade basis with all grades involved in the parallel-track system.

Both of these plans focused more on the needs of the average and bright pupil than on those of the slow learner.

Advantages of Parallel-Track Plans

The advantages claimed for the parallel-track systems are similar to those cited for other varieties of homogeneous grouping. Principally, *students are provided with material, methods, and speed of progress better suited to their abilities than would be true in a single-track system.*

Disadvantages of Parallel-Track Plans

Two-track systems are fraught with more difficulties than some other types of homogeneous grouping. Since the classwork is differentiated chiefly in the speed at which students proceed through the units rather than in the breadth of the program, *it is difficult to move a student out of one track into the other, once he has started.* Thus, when a student has been placed in the slow track for a year but shows good work habits and ability not recognized earlier, it is extremely difficult to get him through enough additional units to catch up with the fast track. So he is usually destined to his original track throughout the grades.

Children do not divide themselves into two neat ability groups that can be assigned to the two tracks. As noted in Chapter 3, they often have more talent in one area than another. In addition, children do not necessarily grow at an even pace intellectually, but they may experience spurts and plateaus in their achievement. Such characteristics of children upset the smooth operation of a two-track plan.

Parallel-Track Plans Work Best Where:

1. There is a very careful analysis of the intellectual, social, emotional, and physical capabilities of every student before he is definitely assigned a track.

2. The curriculum is differentiated more by greater enrichment in broader fields for the fast-working group than by having these students simply speed through the same assignments at a quicker pace.

Generally, a strict parallel-track system seems to have been found somewhat difficult to operate to the parents' and school's satisfaction.

CONTRACT AND UNIT PLANS

The two best-known of these plans for meeting individual needs are the Dalton (Massachusetts) Plan and the Winnetka (Illinois) Plan. Each attempts to divide the curriculum into two kinds of work: (1) academic work which is taught individually through contracts and (2) creative and group work which is taught to the whole class at once.

Each plan depends on specifically designed units or work contracts in academic subjects which each child works on by himself, with teacher guidance, at his own speed of development. The school day is divided so that some time is spent on the individual work units and some in group activities.

Both plans depend somewhat on individual initiative and self-guidance and self-discipline, so they are better suited to children above the primary grades.

Advantages of Unit Plans

The chief advantage of this kind of plan is that it *provides each student academic work suited to his achievement level and at the same time keeps the pupil with his agemates for social, physical-education, art, and music activities.* Extensive evaluations of the Winnetka Plan made in the 1920's when it was in full swing suggested that it succeeded rather well in suiting work to pupils' abilities and in raising the general level of school progress.

Disadvantages of Unit Plans

To succeed, the unit plan typically depends on several conditions which, for many school districts, are difficult to provide, such as:

Carefully prepared individual work units with clearly written explanations and techniques for student self-evaluation. The plan usually depends also on adequate reading ability on the student's part. Since the teacher must divide his attention among so many progressing at their own speeds, each child must spend much time working under his own guidance. Thus his great dependence on well-constructed units.

Children who can keep themselves at the task even when the teacher is not supervising them closely.

Teachers who are skilled in working with many children, each going at his own pace.

Good coordination of studies among the different grades, so that when a child passes from one teacher to the next he can continue smoothly with the next contract, even though some of his classmates have already completed it in the former grade.

In addition to these conditions, which are often difficult to meet, there are the problems of (1) the teacher who sticks to the individual contracts when some other teaching method, such as group work or class discussion, would be more suitable and (2) those students who are best able to learn through teacher examples given to the whole class or through seeing other students make errors and thus profiting by others' experiences.

Contract or Unit Plans Work Best Where There Are:

1. Carefully written, interesting units constructed which are continually revised to keep them up to date and make them easy to understand.

2. Skilled teachers who stay with the school system long enough to gain experience in teaching well in this manner.

3. Diligent students who can understand written directions and are interested in doing academic work under their own direction. (These are usually the brighter students in the school.)

4. Careful curriculum coordination so that the transition from one grade to another is smooth.

TEAM TEACHING AND TEACHER AIDES

An administrative arrangement that has been adopted widely and enthusiastically during the past decade is team teaching. Although it is found at all educational levels, its great impact seems to have been at those of the junior and senior high school.

Team teaching means basically that two or more teachers cooperate in instructing a group of students. Under this broad definition, many varieties of administrative organization may be instituted. Typical plans currently in operation are suggested by the following five examples.

1. In a community whose school staff and classroom space are being strained beyond their expected limits by a population influx, a fully qualified teacher with forty-five fourth-grade pupils has been assigned a teacher aide. The aide is a mother from the community who has completed only two years of college and thus is not a state-certified teacher. But, at a salary below that of a fully qualified teacher, she has been employed to help in the fourth grade by correcting papers, supervising reading and arithmetic subgroups, and assisting individual children who need special help.

2. Three United States history teachers in a suburban high school are together assigned ninety students. Since these instructors also have the same period free each day, they can meet conveniently to plan their class sessions cooperatively. Twice a week, all ninety students meet in the auditorium for a presentation by one of the

instructors. The presentation is an illustrated lecture, usually treating a topic on which that particular teacher has specialized. During the other three class periods each week, the students meet in groups of thirty in separate rooms for discussions and small-group work. With this arrangement, the instructors have time for more careful preparation of lectures, share ideas during cooperative planning sessions, and can assign pupils to subgroups which seem to fit their current needs and interests best.

3. In a newly built high school, two social-studies and two English teachers team up to teach economics, sociology, and English to eighty students in a two-hour-a-day block of time. Two-thirds of the class time is used for lectures, resource speakers, films, testing, and other comparable activities. These sessions are attended by the whole group in an over-large classroom designed for this purpose. During the other one-third of class time, small groups, ranging from three to fifteen students each, discuss current events, books, individual research reports, and issues presented in the lectures.

4. Kimball has described a plan used in Everett, Washington:

Two hundred fifty seventh-grade students with four teachers are involved in language arts, social studies, and mathematics. One half of the students are in the project the first three periods in the morning and the other half the last three periods in the afternoon. The teaching area consists of four regular classrooms, two of which can be opened to provide a seating area for 125 students. Teachers find they have from five to seven more hours each week for preparation and evaluation, have received much help from the rest of the group, are reaching the students' individual problems to a greater extent, are better prepared, and are more satisfied with teaching now than three years ago.[5]

5. Berry (Michael, 1963:58) has written of the Modesto, California, scheme:

All junior English classes, except a small class of Honor students, are involved with four credentialed teachers, a teacher-aide, a secretary, and several student helpers. Classes meet for large-group instruction approximately 40 per cent of the time and in conventional size classes for 60 per

[5] Lloyd Michael, "Team Teaching," *Bulletin of the National Association of Secondary-School Principals*, May, 1963, pp. 55–56. Reprinted by permission. Copyright: Washington, D.C.

cent of the time. Strengths of the program include: greater uses of specialized teacher talents; better teacher preparation; better student work habits; benefits to students from varied teacher viewpoints, varied ways of teaching, and more carefully structured lessons. Weaknesses at present include: not enough direct student-teacher relationship; some student objection to fast pacing and tight structuring of large-group sessions; student difficulties in readjusting to different teachers; need for more effective use of small-group sessions; physical facilities need improvement.

In addition to the social-studies and English programs illustrated above, team teaching has been reported for biological and physical sciences, mathematics, driver training, industrial arts, fine arts, music, and home economics. It is being used for junior-high core classes in which the students are instructed by specialists from such diverse fields as English, psychology, and art.

Schools that utilize closed-circuit television are necessarily involved in a team approach, with the team typically consisting of a studio teacher, three or four classroom instructors, a secretary or teaching aide or student teacher, and the studio technical staff. The small schools which do not have rich science facilities or highly trained instructors and thus use the John Baxter chemistry films or Harvey White physics films as the core of their instruction are, in a sense, using a team approach. That is, the film provides basic instruction and demonstrations, allowing the classroom teacher to devote more time to aiding individual students.

Advantages of Team Teaching

It is clear from the rapid adoption of team teaching in recent years that many administrators and teachers see it as highly advantageous. But it is equally clear that the chief concern of these staff members in endorsing a team approach is not always to care for the individual student's needs more adequately. Rather, some administrators view the teacher-aide plan or the use of student-teachers from the nearby college as a way to staff the classrooms at low cost. If the administrator hires a teacher aide and then assigns forty to sixty pupils to the class, he has not improved the teacher-pupil ratio enough to ensure more and better individual attention for pupils. Rather, the instruction under these conditions is usually going to be worse than if the children were divided into two groups and assigned to two smaller and less adequate rooms but under the direction of a fully qualified teacher in each room. In many other schools that have embraced team plans, the staff's chief interest has been to furnish teachers more chances to share ideas and more time to prepare high-quality lectures and demonstrations that a hundred students at a time, rather than thirty, could view. Although this improvement of instruction is most desirable, it has nothing to do with caring for individual differences among students. Rather, it is intended to make the most of the individual strengths of the teachers. So it is only when the team plan also provides for small-group instruction or for subgrouping pupils according to their specific talents that team teaching meets individual differences more efficiently.

Therefore, as we describe the advantages of team teaching, it is proper that we distinguish between (1) its advantages for the administrators, teachers, and large groups of students and (2) its advantages for the individually different student.

Advantages for administrators, teachers, and large student groups include: teachers grow professionally through cooperative planning; teachers have more time to prepare if they share responsibilities for lecturing to a large group of students several times a week; a teacher's special talents and interests can be utilized by a larger group of students; in-service education of new teachers results from the cooperative planning and sharing of class responsibilities; and uncertified team-teaching assistants can be used to lower the cost of staffing the school.

Advantages for individual students, if small-group instruction is frequently conducted or if individual conferences are frequent, include: more opportunities to express ideas and have the teacher and other students react to them; more suggestions by the teacher for individualized projects that the apt student can pursue; better teacher understanding of the individual's problems and progress; and more teacher time to correct compositions or reports and write individual comments on them or to discuss these compositions with the student.

Disadvantages of Team Teaching

From the standpoint of individual differences, team-teaching schemes are undesirable if:

Teachers eagerly accept the time off provided by sharing large-class lectures with colleagues but do not use at least part of this extra time for working with individual students or small groups.

Administrators hire relatively untrained teacher aides to reduce school finances but do not hire enough aides to reduce teacher-pupil ratio.

The teachers composing the team do not get along well together. This is possibly the greatest potential shortcoming of team-teaching plans. If one member of the team does not respect the others professionally or personally, if he believes they are not living up to their responsibilities, if he feels the students prefer another teacher to him and resents it, and if he thinks other members are trying to dictate the direction of classwork—then conflicts are bound to arise in the team and the effectiveness of the teaching may well diminish.

Team Teaching Works Best Where:

1. Team members share the same philosophy of education and are personally compatible.

2. The school plant is readily adaptable to both large- and small-group instruction.

3. Teacher aides who may be hired are not expected to substitute for regular teachers but are assigned more routine duties in order to free the certified teachers for work with individual pupils and for more adequate preparation of lessons.

4. Team members have a common free period during the day for cooperative planning.

5. Teachers diligently use their freed time for aiding individuals or small groups. That is, when one team member is instructing a group of a hundred, the other members who are free at this time should not simply consider this to mean shorter working hours or recess. Rather, they should be engaged in activities that will promote better learning for the students.

SUMMARY

A variety of administrative procedures can be used to suit the school program better to the needs and abilities of the pupils. The most popular of these procedures involve (1) ability grouping, (2) special classes for slow learners, (3) special classes for the gifted, (4) other special classes, such as in remedial reading or remedial arithmetic, (5) ungraded units, (6) retention and acceleration, (7) frequent promotion, (8) parallel tracks of study, (9) contract and unit plans, or (10) team teaching and teacher aides. Sometimes a school uses one of these procedures, sometimes several. By considering the advantages and disadvantages of each and by comparing them with the characteristics of the particular school system they have in mind, educators can estimate which ones may be applicable in their community.

SUGGESTED LEARNING ACTIVITIES

1. Interview an administrator or teacher of a local school system to discover what administrative procedures are used to suit this school better to the intellectual differences among pupils. From your knowledge of this school system, write an opinion regarding (a) how appropriate the administrative procedures it uses seem to be for meeting individual differences and (b) what other measures might be adopted to meet students' individual needs.

2. Interview a teacher to discover what criteria he (or she) uses in determining whether to retain or accelerate a child at the end of the term. Ask the teacher also what part parents play in such decisions. Write your opinion of the adequacy of this procedure from the standpoint of the teachers, the child, and the parents.

3. Interview a teacher or an administrator in a school that uses either ability grouping or special classes for slow learners and/or fast learners. Ask for (a) the criteria used and the procedure followed in assigning pupils to these classes, (b) problems that the school faces in using this system, and (c) methods tested in solving these problems. Report this interview, along with your own opinion of the adequacy of this plan.

4. Visit a school which conducts some classes on a team-teaching plan. By attending class sessions and interviewing teachers about their activities, try to determine (a) the amount of individual aid students receive under this team plan compared to the aid they would probably receive in a conventional classroom and (b) what small-group activities are carried on and how adequately these apparently suit individual needs and abilities of students. On the basis of your evaluation, give your opinion about whether this team plan meets individual differences more adequately or

less adequately than would a more traditional plan with one teacher in one room.

SUGGESTED READINGS

Acceleration and Retardation

GOODLAD, JOHN I. "Some Effects of Promotion and Non-Promotion Upon the Social and Personal Adjustment of Children," *Journal of Experimental Education*, June, 1954, pp. 301–328.

HARRIS, CHESTER W. (ed.). *Encyclopedia of Educational Research*, 3d ed. New York: Macmillan, 1960. Pp. 4–10.

JONES, JAMES I. "Recent Trends in Promotional Theory," *Progressive Education*, January, 1956, pp. 5–6.

MONROE, WALTER S. (ed.). *Encyclopedia of Educational Research*, 2d ed. New York: Macmillan, 1950. Pp. 1121–1125.

OTTO, HENRY J. *Elementary School Organization and Administration*. New York: Appleton-Century-Crofts, 1954. P. 201.

SHANNON, DAN C. "What Research Says About Acceleration," *Phi Delta Kappan*, November, 1957, p. 32.

Contract Plans

MONROE, WALTER S. (ed.). *Encyclopedia of Educational Research*, 2d ed. New York: Macmillan, 1950. Pp. 374–375.

Homogeneous Grouping

BAUSCHER, DOROTHY C. "Homogeneous Grouping Fosters Progress in Reading," *The English Journal*, January, 1950, pp. 34–36.

COOK, W. W. *Grouping and Promotion in the Elementary Schools*. Minneapolis: University of Minnesota Press, 1941.

NATIONAL SOCIETY FOR THE STUDY OF EDUCATION, *35th Yearbook, Part I: The Grouping of Pupils*. Bloomington, Ill.: Public School Publishing Co., 1936.

SEAGOE, MAY G. "Why Homogeneous Grouping," *California Journal of Secondary Education*, January, 1955, pp. 22–27.

Social Acceptance and Academic Success

BUSWELL, MARGARET M. "The Relationship Between the Social Structure of the Classroom and the Academic Success of the Pupils," *Journal of Experimental Education*, September, 1955, pp. 37–52.

JOHNSON, G. ORVILLE. "A Study of the Social Position of Mentally Handicapped Children in the Regular Grades," *American Journal of Mental Deficiency*, July, 1950, pp. 60–89.

JUSTMAN, JOSEPH. "Personal and Social Adjustment of Intellectually Gifted Accelerants and Non-Accelerants in Junior High School," *School Review*, May, 1953, pp. 468–478.

Special Classes for Retarded Learners and the Gifted

BIRCH, JACK W. "The Public School Approach to Mental Deficiency," *American Journal of Mental Deficiency*, April, 1949, pp. 574–576.

CALIFORNIA ELEMENTARY SCHOOL ADMINISTRATORS ASSOCIATION. *The Gifted Child: Another Look*. San Francisco: CESAA, 1958. Pp. 31–45.

GARRISON, KARL C., and FORCE, DEWEY G. *The Psychology of Exceptional Children*. New York: The Ronald Press Co., 1959. Part II.

GREER, WILLIAM C. "Education of Mentally Retarded Children Fourteen Years of Age and Beyond," *American Journal of Mental Deficiency*, January, 1952, pp. 560–569.

HECK, ARCH O. *The Education of Exceptional Children*. New York: McGraw-Hill, 1953. Chap. 3.

INGRAM, CHRISTINE PORTER. *Education of the Slow-Learning Child*. New York: The Ronald Press Co., 1953. Part II.

JORDAN, EDWARD T. "Segregation or Non-Segregation of the Educable Mentally Defective," *Teachers College Journal* (of Indiana State Teachers College, November, 1951, pp. 25–35.

KIRK, SAMUEL A., and JOHNSON, G. ORVILLE. *Educating the Retarded Child*. Boston: Houghton Mifflin, 1951. Part III.

MAGNIFICO, LEONARD X. *Education for the Exceptional Child*. New York: Longmans, Green, 1958.

WITTY, PAUL. *The Gifted Child*. Boston: D. C. Heath, 1951.

Team Teaching

BAIR, MEDILL, and WOODWARD, RICHARD G. *Team Teaching in Action*. Boston: Houghton Mifflin, 1964.

MICHAEL, LLOYD. "Team Teaching," *Bulletin of the National Association of Secondary-School Principals*, May, 1963, pp. 36–63.

Nongraded Units

BROWN, B. FRANK. "The Non-Graded School," *Bulletin of the National Association of Secondary-School Principals*, May, 1963, pp. 64–72.

GOODLAD, JOHN I. "Ungrading the Elementary Grades," *NEA Journal*, March, 1955, pp. 170–171.

———— and ANDERSON, ROBERT H. "Educational Practices in Non-Graded Schools: A Survey of Perceptions," *Elementary School Journal*, October, 1962, pp. 33–40.

———— and ————. *The Nongraded Elementary School*. New York: Harcourt, Brace, 1959.

CHAPTER 5

Meeting Intellectual Differences II: Classroom Methodology

No matter what administrative measures are taken in your school to care for individual differences, you still will find a marked range of intellectual talent in your classroom.

It is the purpose of this chapter to suggest ways of organizing classwork to suit varied levels of ability and interest. Throughout the discussion, we shall assume the typical situation of one teacher with a class of about twenty-five or thirty-five pupils.

There are three ways of looking at this problem of classroom methodology.

1. In terms of how you *differentiate objectives or subject matter* for the subgroups or individuals in the class. For example, you can have the fast workers in mathematics speed ahead to the next topic, or you can have them, instead, work in a different field, such as special art projects, to broaden their education.

2. In terms of how you *divide the class* to care for their differences. That is, you can split the class in two, divide it into small groups, or teach each child individually.

3. In terms of the *kinds of activities* you provide for students. For instance, you can give different homework assignments to various subgroups, or you can provide books of varied levels of difficulty for students to read in class.

The first, shorter section of the chapter will be dedicated to an analysis of item 1. The second, longer section treats items 2 and 3 together.

SECTION I: DIFFERENTIATING THE OBJECTIVES OR SUBJECT MATTER

The only way you could possibly have everyone at the same place in classwork would be to insist that all students move at the speed of the slowest. But if you tried this, you would find it could not be accomplished. Bright students cannot be restrained. They will find something of their own to do if you fail to provide adequately for them.

One of the decisions you must make as you plan how to care for these faster workers is: Should you have them go right on with the regular subject matter and thus get farther and farther ahead of the class? That is, should you *accelerate?* Or should you have them pause in their forward lunge and instead pursue learnings on the periphery of the subject-matter area to broaden their knowledge while the others catch up in the basic work? That is, should you *enrich?*

Your decision about which approach to adopt will be a wiser one if you recognize the advantages and disadvantages of each route. But before we consider them in detail, it is best that we come to an agreement about what *acceleration* and *enrichment* mean, for today there is some confusion about them in educational circles. For the purposes of this book, we shall use these terms as follows.

Acceleration. In classroom practice, acceleration is based on the same principle as the administrative acceleration discussed in Chapter 4. All pupils are expected to do the same work, but the brighter or more diligent ones move through it at a faster pace. For instance, in the first grade, by the time the slowest readers have finished the first preprimer, the fastest learners are three books ahead; they are already in the first reader of the same reading series. In the junior-high arithmetic class that operates on a contract system, the fastest workers are on Contract 10 by the time the slowest have reached Contract 5.

Enrichment. This means that the faster learners do not simply move ahead rapidly in the same track that the slower workers will follow later. Instead, the teacher provides new activities that broaden the bright pupil's education. These enrichment activities are in addition to the basic work, and the slower learners will not take part in them even later.

We can distinguish two kinds of enrichment which, for convenience's sake, we shall call "same area" and "other area" enrichment.

By "same area" enrichment we mean that the added activities are drawn from the same subject-matter field or problem area as the one in which the student has advanced beyond his slower classmates. For example, in sixth-grade arithmetic the teacher has the fastest workers periodically carry out special projects on the periphery of current topics, such as making a scale map of the school or searching out and creating number games. Or in a high-school history class, the teacher provides the more advanced students with extra historical novels about the American and French revolutions, which is the era being studied by the class.

By "other area" enrichment we mean that the added activities are drawn from a subject-matter area or topic not related to the one in which the student has advanced beyond the rest of the class. For the pupil in sixth-grade arithmetic who is ahead of his class, the teacher might not provide more arithmetic work but might, instead, encourage the pupil to make a booklet on current developments in space travel. Or in the high-school history class, the teacher might suggest that the advanced students read magazine accounts of current archaeological techniques and findings. Though related to history in general, this project is not connected at all to the American and French revolutions, which are topics pursued during regular classwork. Instead, the archaeological study is a different topic entirely.

As our discussion develops, it will become clear that in practice these kinds of enrichment and acceleration often overlap or merge. But by distinguishing among them at the outset, we can sharpen our analysis of the possibilities of each approach.

The Use of Acceleration

Acceleration finds its greatest usefulness in the following situations.

The course is not one in a sequence. This is more often the case in high schools. For example, in one large secondary school a one-semester course in geology is included in the curriculum. It is not related sequentially to any other course but stands by itself as a unit. Therefore, the teacher can accelerate the fast learners to more advanced topics without fearing that this practice will disrupt the learning pattern or the teacher's plan in any class that follows the next semester. Other nonsequential classes in this same school are: astronomy, economic geography, creative writing, news-writing, dress design, dramatics, oil painting, and business arithmetic.

The teacher wishes to help a child skip to a higher grade. During the early weeks that a very bright pupil is in fifth grade, the teacher decides it will be wisest at the end of the semester to skip him ahead half a year into sixth grade. To prepare him for this jump, the teacher wisely urges him to move ahead of the class, completing during the first semester the work the others will not meet until the second.

The teachers in each grade practice acceleration. If the third-grade teacher accelerates fast learners but the fourth-grade teacher does not, the third-grade teacher is very likely getting her bright pupils ready for a frustrating and boring year when they move into the fourth, because in the next grade they will repeat much of what they have already learned. This problem is especially acute in the elementary school, where reading and arithmetic are taught sequentially. It is also serious in two-semester courses in a large high school where a student may transfer from one physics teacher or history teacher to another at the end of the first semester.

In the elementary school, it is not enough that there be a consistent pattern from grade to grade—that is, if one class practices acceleration, they all should. Each teacher must also have sufficient communication with the teacher of the grade below to know where in the learning sequence every pupil stands when he leaves the lower grade. Or, even more important, at the beginning of the year each teacher, during the first few weeks, should evaluate where each pupil now stands in all the principal areas supposedly taught previous years. Only if the teacher possesses such information can she suit her teaching to the varied levels of achievement of the pupils she receives.

How well do teachers know the practices of the grade below them? To answer this, the writers made a study of elementary-school teachers working toward advanced degrees during summer sessions in a large university. The study focused on how much the teachers knew of (1) the specific subject matter taught by the teachers in the grade below them in their school and (2) the methods the teacher in the grade below used for meeting individual differences. As it turned out, it was the rare teacher who knew much about the techniques used by teachers who had previously taught the children who would enter his class in the fall. In addition, the evaluation techniques used at the beginning of the year by the teachers in the study were typically not thorough enough to yield a very clear picture of each pupil's present status.

Probably this sample of elementary-school teachers was quite typical of those throughout the nation. We could not expect an acceleration system to work very smoothly if there is so little coordination or communication between one level and another and when testing at the beginning of the year is no more complete than it often appears to be.

The Use of Enrichment

Most current writers on classroom methodology appear to favor enrichment over acceleration. They prefer to broaden the child's education rather than scoot him along the same track at an advanced speed. Compared to acceleration, enrichment does not depend heavily on what the pupils have done in the previous grade. A single teacher in the school can practice enrichment successfully without disrupting the pupils' transition into the next higher class.

Enrichment is most successful:

When the teacher plans activities really suited to the faster learners' needs and interests and does not simply give them tasks designed to keep them busy. Some teachers who claim to offer enriched experiences either do not understand fast learners or are too busy or lazy to make appropriate assignments. Too often in mathematics class, "enrichment" consists of assigning the fast learners twenty extra problems of the same kind they have just completed. The fact that they have finished the first assignment accurately and rapidly indicates that they have mastered the skill and now need something different to learn. They do not need more practice at the same task.

Too frequently in primary reading the teacher has the fast workers, who complete their workbook exercises rapidly, use their extra time coloring all the pictures on the page. Children often enjoy this. They learn to color carefully, not letting crayon strokes slip across the line that divides the pig from the house or the tree. But it is very questionable whether day after day of coloring workbook drawings is using the child's time to advantage and enriching his education. There is not enough opportunity in school to teach children everything it is well for them to know, so the school has no time to waste on mere busywork.

To avoid making these mistakes of choosing inappropriate activities as enrichment, you can be guided by two questions: (1) Are these activities aimed at important goals of the school? (2) Will these skills or subject matter be treated in the regular minimum program of the school a grade or two higher than mine?

To answer the first question, you need to know the general objectives of the school. These you can often find in the curriculum handbook or course of study. If not, you can ask the principal. If he can give no satisfactory answer, you may wish to turn to books on goals of American education to see what outcomes most modern schools of the United States aim at. Each enrichment activity should carry the student toward one or more of these goals. Activities which should receive priority are (a) ones in which your school program tends to be weakest and (b) ones which treat skills or knowledges that your particular students appear to need the most help with. For instance, if your school's program in creative activities is not strong, you may well emphasize enrichment activities in that direction. If your students' training in the use of scientific methods appears weak, they may well profit by emphasis in scientific methodology.

To answer the second question, it is well also to inspect the school's curriculum guide to see what skills and specific subject matter are assigned to different grade levels. This helps you decide which topics you should *not* use for enrichment at your grade level, because they are topics to be met by all students at a higher level in school. If all students study Robert Frost's and Carl Sandburg's poetry in eleventh-grade literature class, you would probably be unwise to focus your faster learners' attention on these writers as enrichment in ninth grade.

When the teacher knows a variety of good sources of enrichment activities. We would hope the teacher himself would be able to create many good projects by simply thinking frequently about what would be challenging and worth while for his faster learners. But in addition to these self-developed activities, all of us can profit from ideas of others. Such enrichment ideas can come from the following sources.

1. Other teachers. If you make it a habit to ask colleagues what they do to broaden education for their brighter students, you can collect useful ideas.

2. Professional journals. Frequently national and state educational publications carry articles explaining activities some teacher has found successful in caring for individual differences.

3. Textbooks about teaching in your subject-matter field. A book or pamphlet on teaching science in the elementary school will contain ideas for home assignments or projects students can carry out as enrichment activities. The same is true of teaching-methods books in mathematics and arithmetic, reading, social studies, the language arts, home economics, business education, industrial arts, physical education and recreation, and health education.

4. In-service programs organized by the school focusing on practical ways to care for individual differences.

When the school administration supports the enrichment program enthusiastically. This support can take several forms. The administration can furnish money to purchase supplementary books suited to different reading levels, educational games, and materials students need in carrying out projects. Some faculty meetings and in-service education sessions can focus on ways to enrich classwork. And when present buildings are being altered or new ones constructed, administrators can work with teachers to plan flexible classroom facilities: the kind that can be shifted quickly to adapt the room for work in large or small groups or for individual work.

SECTION II: DIVIDING THE CLASS FOR VARIOUS ACTIVITIES

Whether you accelerate or enrich or practice a combination of the two, you face the same kinds of class-organization problems. Suiting work to individual needs means that usually not every student is doing the same task. Some must be working in groups in class or working individually under their own direction. The teacher cannot be with all at once. Often students may be given differentiated homework assignments. Here, again, they need skills of self-direction. The success of the program to suit individual differences often depends heavily on the pupils' ability to work on their own.

The remainder of this chapter is directed at improving teachers' skills in choosing appropriate activities and in teaching students to work efficiently in groups and alone. But before launching into descriptions of ways to succeed with these tasks, it is well first to illustrate more concretely what we mean by group work and individual work. Following are nine descriptions of classes involved in a variety of acceleration and enrichment activities. With these introductory descriptions in mind, the reader is better equipped to understand the explanations that follow on how individualized assignments and group work can be carried out efficiently.

Examples of Group and Individualized Activities

1. In a primary grade, the pupils were divided for reading into three groups according to their varied levels of reading skill. Every day the teacher worked with each reading group for twenty minutes in the morning and twenty minutes in the afternoon. While she directed one group, the others completed tasks in their workbooks or finished arithmetic lessons or did art projects. To differentiate the reading lessons for the fastest and middle groups, the teacher drew on both acceleration and enrichment in the same area. For example, the most advanced pupils were not only ahead of their classmates in the basic reading-book series which formed the foundation for the entire class's work, but they also periodically read stories in other supplementary readers that the less mature pupils would never work on.

2. In a sixth-grade class, each spelling lesson contained two categories of words. The twenty words in Category 1 were studied by everyone, and at the end of the week every pupil was tested on them. The ten words in Category 2 were extra ones to be studied by the segment of the class that succeeded best in spelling. These were more advanced words, that is, ones not commonly used by all students in their writing but needed by those who wrote more sophisticated, complex material. During a brief private conversation near the beginning of the school year, each student agreed with the teacher on which plan he would follow: (*a*) just the

twenty Category 1 words or (b) all thirty words in both categories. As the year progressed, any changes in which plan, a or b, a pupil followed were decided on by the pupil and teacher together.

3. Every student in a high-school chemistry class was expected to write a report on some chemistry problem or topic as a home project. To aid class members in selecting a topic, the teacher offered a series of possibilities divided into three categories, each category representing a different level of difficulty or challenge. On the basis of a student's past performance, the teacher recommended to him the category in which he would find a topic commensurate with his ability. Sometimes the student himself proposed a topic, which he was allowed to pursue if the teacher agreed it was suitable to his level of skill.

4. Students of a high-school Spanish class were divided into conversation drill groups of four pupils each. On most days when they practiced conversing, groups were organized so that each contained students of about the same ability. In this way the more advanced pupils were not slowed up by the halting pace of the less advanced and the teacher could concentrate more on supervising the less able ones. The less advanced pupils, in turn, did not need to compete with classmates of much greater fluency—ones who usually dominated the conversation. Some days, however, the groups were organized differently. The best students in conversation were each put in charge of a group and functioned as assistant teachers to give more aid to classmates than could be provided by the one regular teacher.

5. To study the topic "Feeding the World," the teacher of a high-school class which focused on world affairs divided the students into six groups. Every group was expected to collect information about one phase of the food and clothing problems which had been defined during a general class discussion. These phases assigned to the groups included: What are present rates of population growth and what, if any, problems do these pose for each area of the world? What methods of population control have been used in the past and are being used today? What are the natural resources of different regions of the world? What are the eating habits in different regions, and how do these habits affect people's health? What farming methods are used in different regions? Who controls production and distribution of food and clothing? The most apt students were spread evenly among the groups, so that no committee was composed of members of only one level of ability. But within each committee, reading assignments were differentiated according to ability. That is, when the teacher recommended sources for a group's research, he suggested more advanced books and articles for the more capable students.

6. Pupils in the fifth-grade class who completed their regular tasks earlier than their classmates were free to choose reading material from a classroom library shelf containing books of varied levels of difficulty. Sometimes the teacher recommended to a pupil a book that might suit his interests and skills. At other times the pupil simply browsed and selected one that seemed right to him.

7. Arithmetic in a seventh grade is taught on a contract or unit basis, with each pupil receiving a series of lessons composing a unit. Each unit represents a contract between the student and teacher. The student completes it at his own speed. When he has finished a unit, the teacher gives him a test on the material and the pupil takes up the next unit. This is really an individual-progress plan, for few pupils are exactly at the same place in a unit at the same time. Most of the instruction consists of the teacher's aiding individuals in solving problems they cannot understand sufficiently by reading the written instructions accompanying each unit. Occasionally, when several pupils face a difficulty in common, the teacher calls them together in a small group and helps them solve it together. This system involves both acceleration and enrichment in the same area, because not only do the faster workers move through the regular series of units at advanced speed but from time to time the teacher adds a supplementary unit which broadens their knowledge in a related area of arithmetic.

8. In a history class, several of the faster workers were challenged by a special assignment to write a series of radio dramas based on historical events which the class had been studying. Characters were chosen for the parts, and after school and at noon the students tape-recorded the plays. Later the tapes were played back to other history classes.

9. Each year the junior high sponsors a science fair at which pupils exhibit special projects they have carried out in extra time at school or at home. Ideas and supervision are furnished by the science teachers.

In the foregoing examples, we have seen a variety of ways to divide the class. The sixth grade was divided into two parts for spelling. The second grade was divided into three parts for reading, each part representing a different level of reading skill. The chemistry class likewise was divided into three levels of skill, as represented by the three different groups of topics available for term papers. In the high-school social-studies class, mixed-ability committees of between four and seven pupils each were formed to work on the long-term project; sometimes this class worked as a whole, sometimes in committees; and sometimes pupils worked individually on special assignments they had received within their committees. The Spanish students conversed in groups of four. Although most of the time the history class worked as a unit, a small number of the most apt students formed a special group that wrote radio programs as an extra assignment. And in three of the illustrative situations (arithmetic contracts, free-reading opportunities, science-fair projects) each student had his own activity suited to his own ability level.

Sometimes a teacher tentatively tries one or two of the kinds of activities described above, only to find the students becoming confused, turning belligerent, acting silly, or failing to complete assignments. Naturally he rejects further attempts to differentiate classwork through individualized or group activities.

But in most cases the fault lies not with the students but with the teacher, who has not understood what steps to take to ensure the efficiency of such projects.

In the following discussion, the teacher who is yet a novice at individualizing work will find guidelines that should help him find success in this area. The discussion treats methods of (1) differentiating assignments that are to be done in school or at home; (2) assigning pupils to groups; (3) organizing groups to work efficiently; (4) keeping track of each group's or individual's progress; (5) ensuring that each pupil receives help when he or his group needs it; (6) giving marks to a class of students who have been working on assignments of varied levels of difficulty.

Giving Effective Assignments

One sure way to inject chaos into your classroom is to give vague assignments to different segments of the class and then turn the students loose to work them out under their own direction. To avoid such chaos, the successful teacher (1) creates assignments which he is confident are not beyond the students' ability to do on their own and (2) makes sure that the tasks are completely understood before the students launch into them. Though these two rules of thumb appear to be truisms, they are often violated in classroom practice.

Let us inspect several examples to see how such rules of thumb can be carried out in different ways for different teaching situations.

Giving Assignments for Reading Groups

Before school begins in the morning for the second-graders, their teacher, Miss Stott, writes on the chalkboard the assignments for each of the three reading groups. The assignments appear in some such form as this:

Caroline's group: (1) Read with Miss Stott "Little Toy Boat" in *Under the Apple Tree*. (2) Do work sheets at desks. (3) Do health charts.

Freddie's group: (1) Do pages 29 and 31 in workbook. (2) Read with Miss Stott "Zeke, the Raccoon" in *We Are Neighbors*. (3) Finish workbook and do health charts.

Madeline's group: (1) Do work sheets called *Word Keys*. (2) Work on health charts. (3) Look at storybooks from Reading Table. (4) Read with Miss Stott "Chris" in *Around the Corner*.

Caroline's group consists of the less apt readers, Freddie's (the largest group) of the average readers, and Madeline's of the most capable. They are identified by the name of one of the group members rather than a term like "slow-reading group," so as to reduce the stigma that such a label could bring.

Miss Stott explains the work by having a pupil from each group read aloud the assignment applying to him and his comrades. She adds comments or asks questions to ensure they know what they are to do. For example, after a pupil from Freddie's group reads the assignment, the teacher asks, "Have you all found the right page in your workbooks? Let's see. All right, remember that you read the story yesterday afternoon which these two pages talk about. Look at page 29, and we'll be sure you know what to do before you start." She questions the pupils briefly about what they are to do in the workbook, to make sure they understand. Then she has Madeline pass out the teacher-made mimeographed work sheets to her group, and Miss Stott asks one of them to explain briefly how they think they are to complete the task. At this point, Caroline's group members are asked to carry their chairs quietly to the front of the room, where they will meet in a semicircle around the teacher to read "Little Toy Boat."

As Miss Stott works in the front of the room with Caroline's group, she glances occasionally about to make sure the other pupils who are working individually at their seats are tending to their tasks. Any pupil at his seat who does not understand his task may ask another member of his group to aid, or he may go to the front of the room for a word of help from the teacher. At the times in the reading lesson that Caroline's group are reading a page or two of the story silently to themselves, Miss Stott may stroll briefly round the room to estimate how the children working alone at their seats are progressing.

After twenty minutes or so, Caroline's group have finished the story. Before they return to their seats, Miss Stott passes them the work sheets which will give them practice on phonics, and she explains to them how the sheets are completed. They all work the first problem together as an example before the pupils return to their desks to work individually, and Freddie's group is asked to come to the front of the room to read with Miss Stott.

This transition period, when the reading groups are changing, is a time when confusion can well arise if the pupils do not know what the next phase of their assignment is and if the teacher does not remind them to settle down to these tasks right away.

Through the general approach described here, the teacher makes sure the pupils understand exactly what they are to do. She writes the assignments on the board so that if a pupil forgets the next step he can glance up and find it out himself. Miss Stott estimates whether the tasks she asks them to do on their own are within their ability range by seeing how accurately they complete the tasks and by observing how smoothly they can work individually without asking many questions or appearing confused.

Assigning Term Reports

Homework assignments furnish upper elementary and secondary-school teachers one of their best opportunities for meeting individual needs. But too often teachers ignore this opportunity. Instead, the same assignment is given to all students in the class, despite their different abilities and interests. Even then, the assignment is often presented badly. Too frequently the assignment is something shouted at the students as the bell rings at the end of the period: "Remember to read pages 276 to 302 and be prepared to answer questions about it in class."

As we inspect the matter of the homework assignment, we need to remember a prime fact about learning. It is that education cannot be poured into a student. He is not an empty bucket to be filled at the teacher's will. Instead, the student is a very active organism trying to fulfill his needs. He pays attention and learns those things that he sees as helping him meet his needs, and he ignores or rejects those things for which he sees no personal use.

Therefore, if we agree that students work diligently only on those tasks which they are convinced will benefit them, the wise teacher is the one who takes time to make sure pupils see how the assignments they are given are really worth the effort. Although in class pupils receive stimulus to learn from their schoolmates and the teacher, some of the most important learning occurs when they work alone at home to solve problems they have accepted as being worth while.

Here is the way the high-school chemistry teacher attempted to (1) suit homework to individual abilities and interests, (2) make certain the assignment was understood, and (3) convince the students that the task was worth their effort so that they would pursue it with a will.

The day before the assignment was given, the teacher had prepared a duplicated instruction sheet which contained a space at the top for the student's name, three columns of suggested chemistry topics, an explanation of the criteria the teacher would use in evaluating the completed reports, and the date the reports were due. This was to ensure that every student would clearly understand what was expected of him.

The following day, the teacher did not simply hand out the assignment sheets and expect he had thus done his job. Instead, he dedicated a major portion of the class period to the assignment, for he considered this term report important and he wanted to make sure it had a good chance of succeeding. So he opened the period with what he considered a *pep talk* that he hoped would explain the purposes of the assignment and would stimulate student interest and a desire to do the job well. His remarks went something like this:

We've been studying chemistry together now for more than a semester, and you've learned many things. And we hope you'll learn much more by the end of the present semester. But there's so much to know about chemistry and the way it changes our lives that this one year isn't enough. And many of you will never be in a chemistry class again, because you won't be specializing in this area of science. So my problem as a teacher is to figure out how I can help you continue to learn about chemistry by yourselves after this school year is over. That is, how can you learn on your own the rest of your lives when I'm not around to help answer your chemical questions?

Well, I have a plan that I think will do the trick. It will take us three weeks to work it out together. But by the end of that time I'm pretty sure you can say to yourself, "I've tackled a problem in the field of chemistry by myself and I've done a good job of it. When I want to attack a similar problem in chemistry in the future, I can do it with confidence."

So with the individual projects you'll be carrying out during the next three weeks you will be growing up intellectually. You'll make some real progress—and on your own, too.

At this point, he passed them the instruction sheets, each with a student's name already written at the top. On some papers he had made a check mark at the top of the Column I list of suggested topics. On others he had checked Column II. On the rest he had checked Column III. These represented topics of three levels of difficulty, and on the basis of his knowledge of their past achievement, he had checked the column that he thought most appropriate to the particular student's abilities. He explained:

On your assignment sheet you see three columns of suggested topics you can study and write a report on. On each of your papers I've checked the column which I think contains topics that probably will best suit you individually. You'll have the next three days to think about your choice. And if you don't like the topics in your column and would prefer to suggest to me one of your own, you can talk to me about it personally and we'll come to some agreement. Let me know when you've made your choice and we'll list your name and topic on the blackboard so your classmates will know which ones have been spoken for. No more than two people can select the same topic. By following this rule we'll be sure to get good papers on a variety of subjects.

After answering several students' questions about this aspect of the assignment, the teacher drew their attention to the set of criteria he would use for judging the goodness of the final reports. The criteria (in the form of questions) included: (1) Was the problem or question posed by the topic answered satisfactorily? (2) Was information drawn from appropriate sources, and were these sources identified in footnotes and bibliography? (3) Was the explanation clear, that is, did it move from one logical step to the next? (4) Did the explanation stick to the main problem, or did it wander off? (5) Was the explanation illustrated as needed? (6) Was the paper in neat form and the English correct?

He explained each of these points, giving examples from former years to clarify what mistakes to avoid. He explained that some criteria (such as 1 and 2) would count more heavily than others (such as 5 and 6) toward the final mark.

To clarify the assignment further, the teacher passed to the class some of the better papers handed in to fulfill this assignment during the three previous years. This, he thought, would give them a clearer idea of what was expected and would enable them to try judging these sample papers according to the six criteria.

This process, and the students' questions that accompanied it, took up the major portion of the chemistry period. After class and after school, the teacher was available to give further advice to individuals who requested it.

Demonstrating the Assignment

To introduce the use of conversation groups in the high-school Spanish class, the teacher organized a demonstration which she felt might better ensure that each group in the class would understand the assignment and would flounder less in their first try at the technique.

She organized her demonstration by asking three of the moderately fluent students to meet her after school. She explained to them the purpose of the conversation groups and told them the hypothetical situation they should be prepared to face (that is, going to the store with a friend to buy food). They discussed briefly the kinds of things they might talk about in this situation, and the teacher told them they would have a chance the following day to try this out in class, with her as one of the participants in the demonstration.

The following day she explained to the students:

By signing up for this Spanish class, you've shown a desire to be able to speak and understand Spanish. But this takes practice, and with thirty-three in one class you don't have much chance to speak if we work only as one big group. So from now on, each day we shall spend some time in small groups, carrying on conversations suited to situations that might come up in everyday life if you lived in a Spanish-speaking country like Mexico or Spain or Argentina. Each day we'll agree on what the following day's topic will be, so you can think about it overnight and plan a few phrases you might be able to use. To show you how this can work, four of us will give a demonstration of a conversation group here in front of the class.

Following the demonstration, the students were able to make comments and ask questions. Then the teacher gave the entire class the task of thinking of appropriate phrases to use the following day when everyone would be assigned to a conversation group that would be playing out this same kind of situation: shopping for food.

Taking Advantage of Student Participation

So far, we have inspected assignments created only by the teacher. Many educators believe, however, that students themselves should take part in the creation of certain types of assignments. Through their participation, students learn desirable techniques of (1) entering an area involving problems, (2) clarifying what these problems really are, (3) deciding what kinds of data or efforts are needed to solve the problems, and (4) dividing up the responsibilities for work and assigning this work to members of their group.

Such was the case with the high-school class studying contemporary world affairs. The teacher planned to use general class discussion as the method for working through the four above-mentioned steps with the students. He estimated that the discussion would consume one or possibly two class periods. He prepared for it by bringing to class several recent news articles related to problems in the area of feeding the world. He would use these articles to trigger students' interest and to open the discussion. He opened the class session in this manner:

I've clipped five recent articles from newspapers or news magazines. They're about some problems the world is facing. I'd like to read portions of them to you and get your opinions about what might best be done to solve these. In a couple of these articles a solution is already mentioned, and I'd like to know what you think of this solution.

He then read short portions of the articles. They were concerned with: (1) methods Japan was currently using to curb its population growth, (2) food-surplus storage problems in the United States, (3) a famine in a province of China, (4) loss of work efficiency because of excessive wine drinking in France, and (5) failure of the plan to transmigrate large numbers of Indonesians from the overcrowded island of Java to underpopulated islands in that nation (Sumatra, Borneo, Celebes).

After reading each article, the teacher asked different students for their reactions. As the discussion developed, it became apparent that there were certain terms used in the articles that many of the students did not understand completely, such as population control, soil bank, level of intoxication, and transmigration. When one of these terms arose, and it was apparent there was some confusion in students' minds about it, the teacher wrote it on the blackboard. It was clear also that class members disagreed among themselves about which of the recommended solutions were the best. Each time one of these differences of opinion arose, the teacher noted it briefly on the board. In addition, questions of fact often came up, such as "Is the population in the United States growing faster now than during World War II?" or "How much absenteeism in America is caused by excessive drinking?" These were added to the blackboard, along with some questions the teacher himself posed that could not be answered satisfactorily by the students, such as "What is the official policy of the Republican and Democratic parties concerning the best solution to the food-surplus problem?" and "How is the crop fertilization problem in China related to health factors?"

By the time all five articles had been read and discussed, the blackboard was covered with questions and words that needed clearer definitions.

The teacher said that for the next few weeks they would concentrate on finding answers to these questions and to others that arose during their study of their central problem of feeding the world. He suggested that before they could study these matters efficiently, it would be well for them to take this conglomeration of scribblings on the blackboard and recast them into some clearer organization. Students then suggested that several of the questions or poorly understood terms would logically cluster together under a more general question that was rephrased by the teacher as: "What are present rates of population growth in different countries, and what, if any, problems do these rates pose for each nation?"

Likewise, other clusters were formed until every term or question had been subsumed under one of six major questions or headings.

The teacher then suggested that the most efficient method for answering these questions would probably be to divide the class into six groups, each of which would be responsible for investigating the issues falling within the realm of one of the major questions. Through discussion, they estimated how many students would probably be needed on each committee. For example, they felt more would be needed on the population-growth committee than on the farming-methods committee.

This teaching process so far had taken one class period and the beginning of a second one. They had arrived at the stage of dividing the class into subgroups. To do this, the instructor asked each student to write on a slip of paper (1) which major problem area he would like to work on, and (2) which two classmates he thought might also work well with him on that committee. (The advantages and disadvantages of this method of committee formation are considered in a later section of the chapter.)

It is obvious that up to this point the teaching procedure has not cared for individual differences but has been directed at the entire class. But in the next phase—the point at which individual committees begin work—the assignments of duties within a committee can be suited to the abilities of the individual members. For instance, after the teacher forms the groups on the basis of the papers handed in by the class, he provides reading materials on their topics, suggesting that certain students in the group concentrate on certain magazines or books or pamphlets. In making these suggestions, the teacher has kept in mind the reading skill and the ability to organize ideas of each group member, so the better readers face more complex materials than do the poorer readers.

In addition to differentiating reading materials, the teacher meets with the committee chairmen to offer suggestions on ways they can best direct their groups and best divide up the work or assignments among individual members. During this planning session with chairmen, the teacher emphasizes that the chairman is responsible for (1) dividing up the group's work so that each member has responsibility for a task commensurate with his apparent skill and (2) clearly defining what the assignment is, when it should be completed, and how it should be reported to the committee.

During the ensuing weeks, the teacher continually checks on the progress of the groups and of individuals in them to see whether each pupil is indeed working on tasks suited to his skill level.

Summary of Assignments

In the foregoing examples, we have seen several ways that assignments can be used to care for individual intellectual differences. Some differentiated assignments, such as for the primary-grade reading groups, are carried out during class time. Others, like the term projects in chemistry, are individual homework. Still others, like the compilation of materials on world food problems, may utilize both school and outside time.

Some assignments are short-term ones, like the workbook activities in the first grade or the short conversation groups in Spanish. Others involve long-term projects, as in chemistry or social studies.

Despite the specific nature of the assignment, the teacher will find it succeeds best if he makes sure that (1) the task is well suited to the student's ability level, (2) the student understands very clearly what is expected of him, and (3) the student understands why it is really worth while for him to work diligently to complete the assignment.

Assigning Pupils to Groups

When individual differences are to be met through small-group activities, the teacher has several choices of ways to form the groups. The selection can be made solely by the teacher, or it can be made by the teacher with consideration of pupil requests, or it can be made solely by the students. By inspecting these methods, we may be able to estimate more accurately the conditions under which each will probably be most appropriate.

Teacher Decision Alone

The most common way to assign pupils to groups is for the teacher himself to decide who should be in which group. When this approach is followed, it is usually based on one or more of the following assumptions: (1) that the teacher is the one who can best judge student abilities and thus knows which group is best suited to a given student's present level of skill, (2) that the teacher can best judge which students will profit most socially by the companionship of certain other classmates, (3) that students will work more willingly and diligently when assigned by the teacher than they would if they made their own choice of group mates.

These assumptions are sound in such classes as the second grade, where the pupils would not be expected by themselves to judge accurately what reading group was best suited to their abilities. Teacher selection is also defensible where pupils have not worked with each other before and thus might not take seriously the opportunity to make their own choices.

Obviously, how effective the teacher's choices will be depends on the accuracy of his information about the pupils' abilities and personalities. We might expect the elementary-school teacher who teaches the same children all day to have better information than the high-school instructor who deals with a different group each hour.

In the second-grade reading class, the teacher's judgments were based on two sources: (1) information given her by last year's first-grade teacher who had taught these same children and (2) hearing the children read in temporary groups which she formed on the basis of the first-grade teacher's recommendations. On the basis of this information, the second-grade teacher, after the first three weeks of school, divided the class into three more or less permanent reading groups, each group representing a different level of ability. As the year progressed, she occasionally moved a child from one group to another as his performance seemed to warrant.

In the Spanish class, the students were also assigned to conversation groups on the basis of the teacher's decision alone. She based her selections on the quality of the students' earlier reading and writing performance and test scores (since they had not yet had much chance at conversation) and on her estimate of how well a given student would probably work with certain classmates. After a couple of weeks of conversation practice, it became apparent that some of these initial judgments had been in error, so changes in group personnel were made.

Student Suggestions

Not all educators accept the assumptions noted above in favor of teacher selection as the best method of determining group membership, or at least these educators do not agree that the three assumptions are supportable under all class conditions. A number of studies in the formation of class groups have suggested strongly that better results are obtained, at least in certain circumstances, when the students themselves nominate the people they will work with. One of the most prominent workers in this area has concluded from her investigations that "better work in general is done when pupils are in close association with other pupils with whom they want to be and with whom they feel most comfortable. Moreover, many other outcomes of such grouping practice make the teacher's work easier and more enjoyable." (Jennings, 1950:203.)

The teacher who wishes to use such an approach is usually wise to introduce the process to the students with an explanation something like the following. (The wording of this introduction is suitable for a sixth-grade class. For other grade levels, obviously the phrasing should be readjusted to the pupils' maturity level.)

As planned, we shall spend the next week searching through science books for interesting experiments we might do. We've decided to work in committees, with each committee finding experiments about a different area of science—like fire, water, air, and so forth. Four pupils will work on each committee. Since you all know the people you like to work with most, we are going to have you choose the people you would like to be with in your group. On the slip of paper I passed to you, write your name at the top. Then on the first line write the name of the person who is your first choice to be on the committee with you. On the second line write the name of your second choice. On the third line write the name of your third choice. Remember, choose the people you want to work with in finding science experiments. They may be the same people you like to be with on ball teams or in party committees, or they may be different people. It doesn't matter. Just make the best choice to help your committee succeed. You may not all get your first choices, but we'll try to put everybody on a committee with one or more of the people he has selected or who have selected him.

Obviously this choosing process will not automatically yield compact, self-evident groups of four. Some pupils are very popular with their classmates, and others are not popular at all. Therefore the teacher must exercise judgment in dividing the pupils into committees. In making these judgments, she depends on her own knowledge of the pupils and their needs and abilities, in addition to considering the choices they have made. Here are some of the thoughts that passed through the mind of one teacher as she formed the committees.

Albert was not chosen at all. This was probably because he is so withdrawn and sullen. I think he needs the help of such a group as Michael's. Since Michael was his first choice and will be a good worker, I'll put Albert on that committee. I'll also include Larry, since he and Michael chose each other. Helen can be the fourth member. She chose Michael, and that will also include a girl in the group.

Carol and Diana chose each other. They're both excellent students and would work well on the committee. But for this project I think I should split them up since each is a leader, and a couple of the committees will end up without a capable organizer if Carol and Diana are together. I'll put Carol with one group and Diana with another for the good of the groups' progress.

Student Choices Only

The rarest way of forming groups is that of using student choices alone without adjustments suggested by the teacher. Except in the selection of teams for sports and classroom games, this technique is probably not very widely used. There are, however, certain instances in which teachers have reported success with this approach. One has been in the "buddy system" of students pairing up to work on reading or on arithmetic drill on number combinations. In such instances, several teachers have reported to the writers that when the children themselves select buddies or helpers, they are often likely to choose other children with whom they feel comfortable and who are not too different in ability from themselves. These choices can, therefore, be more appropriate than those the teacher may make.

However, if the pupils do not take the work seriously and do not base their selections on a desire to reach the learning goals, they may simply select companions with whom they expect to have a good time.

Summary of Assigning Pupils to Groups

Teachers are most successful in assigning pupils to groups when their judgments are based on sound information about pupils' abilities, their social and intellectual needs, observations of how well they get along together, and the probable effect various groupings will have on the quality of work each group can do. Evidence suggests that it is often desirable to allow the pupils to express preferences for group mates, and it is well for the teacher to consider these preferences seriously when forming the groups.

Organizing Groups to Work Efficiently

As a teacher contemplates group work for a new class, he should try to determine whether the pupils have already had similar experiences and how mature they are in supervising their own activities. In general, less mature and less experienced pupils have better success working in small, short-term groups. Older, more experienced students can carry out tasks in larger groups and can succeed with projects that take several weeks or months to complete.

Usually when the teacher initiates committee activities with a new class, it is wisest for him not to start any long-term committee work. Instead, he should begin with a very simple problem for the pupils to discuss or to solve in groups so that as they work he can judge how capable they are of taking responsibility and how well they work together. The topic or activity they are assigned should be one that interests them, one they will take seriously.

Committees of four or five students each are usually effective to begin with. The instructor may wish to have these initial groups organized geographically in the room to save time. That is, those sitting near each other form a group.

Before they begin their discussion, it is important for the instructor to outline their job. Failure to make the task clear invites confusion when the pupils meet together; consequently the groups may fail because of the teacher's lack of adequate instructions rather than the pupils' lack of efficiency. Here is a sample of directions given to a ninth-grade English class which was contemplating the publication of a mimeographed class newspaper.

Now we'll go over the plans again briefly so that everybody understands. You are to meet in the groups I've indicated. The topic you're to discuss is this: "What kinds of articles or news items and features should be put in our class paper?" As you give your suggestions, be ready to support them with reasons why you think the kind of article or feature you mention would be good. You'll meet for fifteen minutes. Then I'll call you back together again as a whole class and we'll hear what each group discussed and what you wish to suggest to the rest of us. All right, move into your discussion groups.

During the class period, the teacher circulates among the pupils, listening to their exchange of ideas. His main purpose is to judge how well they work together and progress toward the goal of answering the assigned questions.

His observation is directed by such questions as these:

Does some pupil, either voluntarily or by selection, become the leader to pose the problems? Does someone, either voluntarily or by selection, bother to write down the ideas presented? Do they stick to the topic or wander away from it? Do they spend time telling jokes or gossiping? Do they consider this activity nonsense or take it seriously? Are there certain pupils who are especially helpful group members? Are there some who dominate the discussion? Are there others who do not enter into the discussion? Are there some who tend to destroy the group work?

Through his observation, the teacher judges whether to proceed slowly with group work, using only short discussion sessions (sometimes nicknamed *buzz* sessions) and keeping close rein on them, or whether the pupils can accept more freedom and responsibility so that longer-term committee work is possible. Using this cautious beginning, the teacher can avoid the errors of allowing freedom that children cannot handle until they have been guided gradually into ways of taking responsibility.

The principle involved in the discussion above—beginning slowly with simple, short-term groups before expecting students to carry out more complex assignments—obviously should hold true for groups other than those involving only discussions. For instance, in the Spanish class the first sessions of conversation groups were kept quite short and were under close supervision by the teacher. Later, after the class had more experience, less precise directions could be given and longer conversation sessions were possible. In a junior-high industrial-arts class, various projects were carried out by the groups. An early project centered on bricklaying, for which the boys worked in threes for one class period at a time, with very detailed directions as to each step they should take. After working together on several activities of similar levels of difficulty, the boys were given opportunities to do more of the planning themselves and to attempt longer-term activities, such as building stage sets for the ninth-graders' annual play.

Often the purpose of the group work is not to carry out class projects but to divide the students into different ability levels so each one is working with classmates who are making progress similar to his own. This is the case with reading and arithmetic groups in the elementary school and with any subject-matter area in the secondary school where students are divided within the class according to their progress. In such instances, the teacher wishes to train the individual groups to carry out their own teaching-learning sessions at times when the teacher is working with other members of the class. In using such an approach to instruction, the teacher's problem is to develop a pupil-teacher in each group to conduct lessons. That is, a pupil in the group functions as a substitute for the regular instructor. This role of pupil-teacher may be passed from one student to another on different days so everyone who is capable of assuming such responsibility has a chance in the leadership position. Pupil-teacher procedures can be operated successfully at both elementary and secondary levels. As would be expected, this plan typically succeeds best with the most capable students in the class and can be handled much less successfully by the slower ones.

Detailed descriptions of how such self-taught ability groups can be developed are presented in Chapter 9.

Keeping Track of Individual and Group Progress

Whether the students are working on individual assignments or group projects, it is essential for the teacher to develop a habit of evaluating each step of the process. By having systematic methods of continually taking stock of *where we are now* and *where we should go next,* he can fulfill these important functions of good teaching:

1. Determine how far the students have progressed so as to know when they are ready for the next stage.

2. Diagnose weaknesses or misunderstandings or undesirable habits that are creeping into the students' learning.

3. Determine how well the teacher's methods and materials are working.

4. Train the students in self-evaluation.

In the case of group work, continuous evaluation in which the pupils take part also provides opportunities for training students in improving their group-work skills.

By inspecting a series of classroom examples, we may see more clearly these roles of evaluation as they serve to suit work to individual differences.

Evaluating Individuals' Progress

Careful evaluation of individual progress may well be the most important element in the entire scheme of designing schoolwork to fit the differences among pupils. Unless the teacher knows where the student stands now, he cannot confidently decide what materials and methods should be provided next. Therefore, we wish to place considerable stress on this evaluation aspect of the teacher's job.

As important as the actual testing and observation processes is the keeping of accurate records of how each pupil is getting along. In the following descriptions, we shall illustrate the variety of evaluation techniques that are applicable under different teaching situations as well as the ways different teachers keep records of each student's work.

Primary Reading

In the second-grade reading groups, the teacher originally established which children should be assigned to the three ability-level groups by hearing each child read aloud to her several times and by comparing this performance with the records the first-grade teacher had provided. The individual reading was done in the temporary groupings the teacher had organized during the first weeks of school. To standardize somewhat her observation of each child's oral-reading performance, she used the following kind of check list, or rating scale, which she put in each child's manila record folder after she evaluated his reading.

ORAL READING CHECK SCALE

Name _____ Date _____

Estimated Reading Level
from First Grade teacher:
   Preprimer _____
   Primer _____
   1st Reader _____
   Grade 2, book 1 _____
   Grade 2, book 2 _____
   Grade 3, book 1 _____
   Other _____

Difficulty Level of Material
used for today's testing:
   Primer _____ Page no. _____
   1st Reader ___ Page no. _____
   Book 2–1 ____ Page no. _____
   Book 2–2 ____ Page no. _____
   Book 3–1 ____ Page no. _____
   Other _____

ORAL READING COMPREHENSION: Correctly answered 5 questions on material read (circle number of questions correctly answered):
     5   4   3   2   1   0

MISTAKES (circle number of mistakes per page):
   Miscalled words: 0 1 2 3 4 5 6 7 8 more
   Couldn't make out words: 0 1 2 3 4 5 6 7 8 more
   Skipped words: 0 1 2 3 4 5 6 7 8 more
   Ignored punctuation: 0 1 2 3 4 5 6 7 8 more

FLUENCY (check terms that most aptly describe performance):
   ___Continual hesitation; very labored pace.
   ___Continually loses place and must stop.
   ___Steady pace but monotone; does not reflect meaning of passage with voice expression.
   ___Some hesitations, but mostly steady pace.
   ___Smooth, fluent pace; voice inflection reflects meaning of passage.

OTHER CHARACTERISTICS NOTED (write on back of sheet).

Although this check sheet is somewhat diagnostic, its main purpose is to establish with some accuracy the level of the child's reading so that he can be placed in a group with others of similar ability. By using a check sheet, not only does the teacher make a more standardized analysis of each child's reading than she would if she just took casual notes but she has automatically provided a record of the performance for later consultation.

After the ability groups have been established, the teacher's routine of teaching has built-in evaluation techniques. That is, in the small reading groups each pupil every day has a chance to answer at least one or two questions about the contents of the passages read silently. Every day or so, each child reads a short passage aloud, so the teacher can observe how much skipping and guessing of words he is doing and she can also check on pronunciation. Workbook and teacher-made mimeographed exercises which children usually complete alone at their desks provide a further picture of skills and comprehension.

Through this constant evaluation, the teacher always knows where each child stands at the moment, what his strengths and weaknesses are, and what new material he is ready to attempt. The teacher can determine whether to provide easier books, more phonics exercises, supplementary books for broader reading, or suggestions to parents concerning ways they can help their child at home.

Spelling

The task of determining where a child stood in spelling was a relatively simple one for the sixth-grade teacher. The regular spelling tests provided the basic evaluation. By inspecting the number and kinds of mistakes on the tests and in student written work, the teacher was able to determine what each pupil's strengths and weaknesses were.

Science Term Papers

The chemistry teacher who assigned term reports at three levels of difficulty based his initial judgments of students' abilities on three sources: (1) weekly quizzes, (2) class discussion, and (3) the quality of laboratory work.

He did not, however, simply present the students with the term-paper assignment and then await the final reports. Rather, he set up several subgoals or periodic deadlines for completing certain phases of the term-paper assignment. In this way he always knew whether each student was mastering each step of the process. For students whose work unwittingly strayed off on a tangent, the teacher was able to discover the problem before the pupils' deviations from the goal became disastrous. In addition, this plan of setting subdeadlines provided continuous motivation for pupils. They could not wait till near the end of the three-week period to do the paper in a rush but had to work on it steadily. The psychological pressure was low but constant—not a sudden urgency as the final deadline drew near.

Here are subgoals and deadlines set up for the papers.

Tuesday, February 10: Assignment given.

Friday, February 13: Topic selection made by each student. Suggested sources of information on topics given by teacher. Students begin finding books and magazines. Teacher outlines note-taking methods and gives bibliographical form.

Tuesday, February 17: Each student hands in bibliography he plans to use. Teacher discusses system for outlining final paper.

Friday, February 20: Each student hands in outline for report along with reading notes for teacher to inspect and comment on over weekend.

Monday, February 23: Students are handed back reading notes and outline with teacher's comments. They begin final writing of paper. Teacher reviews form that final paper should be in.

Monday, March 2: Final paper handed in.

Spanish Conversation

To keep a record of individual students' progress in Spanish conversation practice, the teacher visited one group after another each day and observed the part each pupil played. From time to time, she used the kind of rating scale shown below to record her impressions of a particular child's fluency. The scale was not filled out while she observed the group, for she was afraid that her writing on the scale while watching the participants would make them unduly nervous. Therefore she kept in mind the items on the scale, and after watching a particular group returned to her desk, where she quickly checked a given student's scale sheet.

CONVERSATION CHECK SCALE

Student _____ Date _____

Conversation Topic _____

DIRECTIONS: Check the point on each scale that best describes the student's performance.

Pronunciation is accurate:

Always	Usually	Much of the time	About half the time	Rarely

(Write common pronunciation errors here:)

COMPLEXITY OF EXPRESSIONS:

Uses shortest possible utterances:

Always	Usually	Sometimes	Rarely	Never

Confines comments to only a few stock phrases:

Always	Usually	Sometimes	Rarely	Never

Develops appropriate new phrases on his own:

Always	Usually	Sometimes	Rarely	Never

APPROPRIATENESS OF EXPRESSIONS:

Has apt statement, question, or reply ready:

Always	Usually	Sometimes	Rarely	Never

Uses wrong word or wrong phrase for intended meaning:

Always	Usually	Sometimes	Rarely	Never

FLUENCY

Hesitates between words:

Always	Usually	Sometimes	Rarely	Never

Makes false starts, changes mind, starts over:

Always	Usually	Sometimes	Rarely	Never

Blocks completely, cannot reply:

Always	Usually	Sometimes	Rarely	Never

Deliberate, slow but steady:

Always	Usually	Sometimes	Rarely	Never

Smooth-flowing conversational pace:

Always	Usually	Sometimes	Rarely	Never

PARTICIPATION (check the phrases that best describe the student's performance):
___Regularly takes his turn in carrying conversation.
___Avoids taking part in conversation.
___Dominates conversation group, aggressively overshadows others.
___Participates more than average but does not overdominate group.
___Participates, but somewhat less than average.
___Typically takes conversation work seriously.
___Typically does not take conversation practice seriously.
OTHER COMMENTS (write on back of sheet).

Recreational Reading

In the fifth-grade class which gave some free choice of reading materials to students, the teacher estimated the students' progress by asking each child, after he had finished a book or magazine, to write a brief opinion of the book on a half-sheet of paper, which was then inserted in a reading folder kept for each pupil. In addition, from time to time the teacher would ask a pupil questions about the book he was now reading or would ask him to describe the book briefly to his classmates.

Arithmetic Contract Plan

A series of carefully designed exercises and tests treating each step or contract in the seventh-grade individualized arithmetic program gave the teacher regular information about each pupil's progress. Thus the instructor always knew whether the student was ready to go on to the next step or needed additional explanation or experience with the present one.

Radio Dramas of More Advanced Students

To evaluate the progress of the faster-working students who were creating radio dramas based on historical events, the teacher asked them to set up deadlines for each phase of the work: the selection of the historical event, the decision about how many characters would be used, the outline of the script, the writing of the script, the selection of actors, the practice sessions, and the final recording. When a deadline came, the teacher asked for a report of group progress and of each person's role in the work. Therefore the work of the committee as a whole and each person's contribution were constantly evaluated.

Science Fair Projects

The science teachers made a sign-up sheet on which students who were entering projects in the science fair could write their names and a brief description of their proposed projects. Periodically during the weeks before the fair, the teachers went down the list and asked the pupils who had signed up to report briefly on the present state of the projects. In this way, problems that students were facing in developing their exhibits were brought to the teachers' attention at regular intervals and help could be offered.

Therefore, as seen in the foregoing examples, teachers in the illustrative classes tried to keep continual check on each student's progress through the use of a variety of evaluation techniques.

Evaluating Group Progress

Usually when students are working in groups the teacher is interested in fostering two kinds of learning. First is the learning of the subject matter or skill that the group work is focusing on, such as reading skill or the knowledge of ways to approach world population problems. Second is the learning of better ways to work together in groups. By periodic evaluation, the teacher can gather information about progress and problems met by the students in both these areas of learning.

By inspecting two classes carrying on committee projects, we can see that the evaluation process not only tells the teacher and pupils where they stand now but also provides the teacher with an opportunity to teach the students further skills of working well together and of analyzing ways their groups can improve. The first class is a sixth grade working on health projects, and the other one is the high-school group that studied the problem of feeding the world.

Post-Group-Meeting Discussions

The postmeeting general discussion is one useful technique for evaluating group progress and at the same time for stimulating better student insights into their own strengths and weaknesses in committee work. We see the way such a discussion can be conducted as we visit a sixth grade which has begun the study of health practices around the home and school. The pupils have just met in small groups to suggest ways they might study such health practices. They also plan to suggest activities they might carry out to improve undesirable conditions they may find. After the teacher has given them fifteen minutes for small-group discussions, they meet again as a full class and report the suggestions from each group. Then the teacher focuses the pupils' attention on the group-work process in such a manner as this.

TEACHER: Now we've listed on the board the main ideas your committees discussed. We have some really useful ones here. But for a moment, let's talk about these group meetings you've had. I noticed that when some of you told your ideas to the class, you apparently had forgotten some ideas you'd discussed in your committee. Later you seemed to remember them when another committee was reporting. Is there some way we might be more efficient next time we have small discussion groups like this?

BRENDA: In our group Phil wrote down the ideas. Then we didn't forget them.

TEACHER: That's a good way. Maybe we should all do that next time. Perhaps we should list some suggestions about ways we can work better in groups, like this suggestion about recording the ideas as they come up. We can put these suggestions on a chart so they'll be available when we have group work again. Let's write this first idea on the board. Later we can copy it onto a chart. How should we say it?

ROB: Why don't you just say, "Have somebody write down ideas"?

TEACHER: All right. But how do you decide who will write down the ideas within your group meeting? Do all the group members do it?

BRENDA: On our committee Phil just said he'd do it.

CATHY: Or you could choose somebody.

TEACHER: Yes, you could do it either way. Every time you work in groups you won't need a recorder or secretary. But when you're discussing things you want to remember, it's a good idea to pick somebody to write them down.

Such discussions as this of efficient group techniques would not always follow a group-work session. However, they should be sufficiently frequent to give pupils insights into the anatomy of group work. Too often adults, as well as children, do not understand the reasons why a group operates well or the reasons it fails. But through these discussions of their own committees, they gradually achieve insight and become better leaders and group members.

As seen above, during such discussions the teacher, through questions, draws ideas from the pupils and also inserts some of his own. These ideas are more meaningful if the students achieve their insights through analyzing the success of their own committees than if the teacher merely tells the class what good group work is. Here are some of the conclusions about committee work which were developed from the pupils' ideas over a period of time at various grade levels.

If we choose a chairman or leader to give us the topic and keep us working on it, we usually get more done than if we just get together and talk.

Just because a person isn't elected leader doesn't mean he doesn't work. Every person is as important as the rest.

If you want to be liked, it's a good idea to do your share of the work on the committee.

The leader shouldn't let just one or two people talk. He should ask everybody for ideas.

Everybody can't talk at once. You should raise your hand or ask the leader's permission.

Although to the adult these may appear to be simple or even trite generalizations, they are important insights when they come from the pupils' own experiences.

Periodic Progress Reports

Unless the students are unusually mature and experienced, the teacher cannot expect successful long-term group work (that is, groups that operate for more than a week or so) if he does not set up regular progress-report requirements. At the junior-high and high-school levels, the report may often be most efficient if it is written and then also summarized as an oral report which is heard by the entire class. To assure that these reports focus on important aspects of the committee work, it is well for the teacher, ahead of time, to outline clearly what items should be covered. Here is an example of such an assignment of progress reports given by the teacher of the class studying world food production and population problems. The early part of the example shows how the teacher first develops the assignment, which then leads to his requirement of progress reports.

TEACHER: You see the names of the members of each committee written on the board. The committees were based on your choices of committee partners as well as on my own judgments of which people might work well together.

Today we'll meet for the first time in these committees. On the side blackboard I've listed the steps I think might be best for your committee to take during its first meeting. Let's talk briefly about each step so we're sure you understand and so you can make suggestions about any changes that should be made. First, it would be well to select a chairman who'll be responsible for the general supervision of the group's work. What characteristics do you think he or she should have? What kind of chairman will you need? What would be one characteristic? Dan?

DAN: He ought to be able to get along well with the others.

TEACHER: Yes, that's important. Virginia?

VIRGINIA: Should be good in social studies.

TEACHER: Well, yes, it helps to have somebody who knows something about the subject.

CARL: Need somebody who works hard and takes responsibility.

TEACHER: That's true. Although we hope everybody on the committee will do that. All right, when you choose a chairman, think of these things. If you don't select a good leader, your group's work may not turn out well, and that will hurt everybody on the committee. Now to the next point on the list. You'll need somebody to take notes—a recorder. This may be the chairman or it may be somebody else. You'll have to decide that. But every day or so your group will have to report to me and to the rest of the class about the progress you've made and about the problems you have to solve next. So you'll need a recorder or secretary.

Next, I think it'll be best for you to try to list the specific questions—in addition to those we had on the blackboard yesterday—that your group is going to try to answer. You can get some of these questions just from talking among yourselves. But for others, you may have to learn something more about your topic. And to help you with this step of learning more about your topic I've made a suggested reading list for each committee. On this sheet that I'll hand to your committee you'll see a series of books and magazines I've brought from the library. On your list are the ones I think are most helpful for your group's topic. Beside each book or magazine is written the name of the student on your committee who I think can best collect ideas from this particular reading source. You can use these books in class today or you can check them out to work on at home tonight, whichever way your committee decides is more efficient.

Another thing your committee should do today is to come up with more ideas about sources of information on your topic. Then different students should be given responsibilities to gather materials from these sources. And you should discuss what will be the best way to gather the information together that you will need eventually for answering the questions.

Tomorrow in class we'll spend the first fifteen minutes of the period working in groups again. By the end of that time we'll expect each group to have ready a brief report, written in outline or summary form, telling these three things I've listed on the board: one, what progress you've made as a group; two, what individual assignments have been given to members of the group; three, what the next step in your planning will be. We'll have each committee at that time give a brief oral report to the entire class touching on some of the main points in this report. In this way one committee can profit from the ideas of the other ones, and we can discuss common problems you face.

All right, now, let's collect in our small groups. If you forget what your group is supposed to do, just consult this outline of your assignment written on the side blackboard.

Through this procedure the teacher gives an assignment which starts the groups on some fairly easy, well-defined tasks. This helps ensure their success in this early stage of group work. (As the week proceeds and the teacher sees how capably the groups are solving their problems, he can give to each committee more or less responsibility for planning its own future activities commensurate with its present progress and the amount of initiative its members are displaying.)

On the following day, the students in the social-studies class are allowed the first fifteen minutes for summarizing the progress they have made, including the work they have done individually at home. This summarizing is done in their committees. During this time they can also compile their brief committee reports of progress and of future plans.

The teacher has asked to have the report written so as to encourage the committee chairman or recorder to be more precise and also to provide for the teacher a record of the committee's current progress. The oral report to the entire class has several purposes. It is intended to:

1. Furnish the pupils of one committee an overview of the progress and working procedures of each other committee.

2. Furnish an opportunity for the entire class to discuss together common problems that several groups are facing (such as how best to keep reading notes and where to locate articles in out-of-date magazines).

3. Furnish the motivation that can be engendered by healthy competition among groups. By "healthy competition" we mean competition between groups which have about equal chances of succeeding in the assigned task. If one group is composed of the brightest pupils and another of only the dullest, the latter committee cannot hope to compete successfully, so we would consider this "unfair competition." But it is fair when pupils of varied ability are spread rather evenly among the committees so that the progress of one group can serve as a desirable stimulus to another group which has as much potential ability to succeed but which, perhaps, has not as yet tried as hard or has not used as efficient work methods as has the first committee. The oral progress reports can provide this stimulus.

The oral evaluation session also provides an opportunity for the teacher to give the pupils their assignment for the next step in their work. Or, if the committee has enough initiative, the teacher can ask them to suggest their own next steps.

The way such oral evaluation sessions, plus new assignments, can work in actual practice is suggested by the following excerpt of one committee's report to the social-studies class the following day and the teacher's reaction to it. Note that the teacher is not the only one who reacts to the report, but he frequently asks class members' opinions. His purpose here is to stimulate the students themselves to make judgments of their classmates' and their own progress. The purpose is to encourage self-evaluation habits which, it is hoped, will carry out of the classroom into other life activities.

JOE EMORY (Committee D chairman): Our committee is supposed to study the kinds of food people eat in different parts of the world. And we're supposed to find out what this food does to their health. Last night we all took some of the books and magazines home so we could get some idea of how to collect the information. And I don't think we've made much progress, because today our report is mostly about problems we're meeting in doing the job.

TEACHER: Well, that in itself can be progress. You'll find that in investigating a new area, one of the most important first steps is to define the problems you're facing so you can see how to solve them. Let's hear the problems.

JOE: The first one is that there are too many different countries in the world to cover them all, and besides, all the people in one country don't eat the same things exactly. Like the people in this class didn't all have the same things for breakfast today.

TEACHER: All right. Those are both important problems. Who has a suggestion about what the committee might do? (No one volunteers.) What about the problem of covering all the countries? Is there some simpler way to do it? Carol?

CAROL: Why not take just big ones? It might be easier to get information about them.

TEACHER: That's a possibility. Take some typical countries. Any others? (No one volunteers.) Frank, what's your opinion about it?

FRANK: I agree with Carol.

JOE: I think that's what we ought to do, but we'll be sure the countries are spread in different parts of the world.

TEACHER: Well, that gives your committee a start toward a possible solution. You can discuss it further in your group later. Now to the problem of people having a variety of diets or eating habits within one country. What about that? Who has a suggestion? Ralph?

RALPH: Take the most popular foods, the ones people usually eat. Rice is very popular in Asia but not in America.

MARGARET: We eat rice.

RALPH: But you wouldn't call it very popular. Americans eat more potatoes and meat and bread.

TEACHER: All right, there's a start toward a solution. Try to find the common foods.

JOE: That's going to be hard to decide. Would you call oranges common in America and lemons not common?

TEACHER: You're right. You'll have to make up some way of deciding what you'll include as popular foods. That's something for the committee to work on. Now, what other problems did you find?

JOE: About what the eating habits do to people's health. We think it's going to be hard to find that out.

TEACHER: Then let's think about some possible sources of that information. A few weeks ago when we were talking about the United Nations, we discussed one source. What was it? Carol?

CAROL: W-H-O.

TEACHER: That's right. You should ask the librarian about what materials she has available from the World Health Organization. And you can check with the city library, too.

JOE: We could write to W-H-O. They probably have free information.

TEACHER: That's a good idea. You'll have to do it very soon so the information has a chance to get here. What's another possibility?

In such a pattern the progress-report session continues until finally the Committee D report is brought to a close. As the chairman sits down, the teacher offers a last suggestion:

TEACHER: Try to get information also about the way food is prepared for eating in different lands. You should know what happens to the food value of rice when it's polished and the value of brown bread compared to white. You should know what happens to vegetables when they're boiled a long time.

In this brief excerpt, we have seen how the progress-report session serves to evaluate current work as well as to help students see methods of working efficiently and outlining their next steps. Note that the teacher has tried to give class members a chance to make suggestions and in doing so to practice solving problems. But the teacher has also taken an active part in supporting good ideas and in keeping the discussion moving along so that time is not wasted and so members of other committees are not unduly bored. The teacher has also offered ideas of his own when adequate suggestions have not arisen from the class members.

Summary of Evaluation Techniques

Constant evaluation of individual progress is an essential element of suiting schoolwork to pupils' individual differences. As seen in the sample classes, the teacher has a variety of evaluation techniques available for this task, including tests, rating scales and check lists, student reports, and progress charts.

When students are working in groups (either like-ability groups, as in the second-grade reading class, or mixed-ability groups, as in the high-school class studying world population problems), the wise instructor makes continual evaluations of group efficiency through the use of such techniques as observing committees while they work, asking them to write progress reports, and having them report orally to the class so their progress can be discussed.

In the following chapters, further useful approaches to evaluation are illustrated.

Providing Help When Students Need It

In a class where students are working on different tasks and at different speeds, the teacher faces the problem of furnishing each one with the help he needs at the moment he needs it. If Harry is working at his desk and is stuck on a problem, how can he receive aid when the teacher is handling a small group of students at the front of the room? There is no magic formula for accomplishing this. Each teacher must work out the techniques that best suit his style of instruction and the characteristics of the particular class. We can, however, suggest a few devices which some teachers have found useful.

In the first place, it is usually well, when giving differentiated assignments to different segments of the class, to tell the class members how they are to receive help when they need it. For instance, they may be told to look for instructions on the blackboard, to ask a neighbor, or to come to the teacher. Knowing at the beginning where they can find help will save class time and reduce confusion. These sources of aid may then function in the following ways.

Written Instructions

For certain kinds of classes, clearly written instructions can be offered for pupils to consult when they are puzzled about the next step. Classes that operate on contract plans, such as the arithmetic class mentioned earlier, must usually depend on such written illustrations and explanations. Here the student is given the explanation that goes with the contract or present unit, and if he has trouble with it, he may have to review the former one.

In other types of arithmetic classes, the teacher may write on the chalkboard the numbers of the pages in the textbook which will help the pupils review a given arithmetic process if they have forgotten it or if they become confused in solving the assigned problems. The same device may be useful in the English class, where pupils are working exercises treating usage or grammar.

When the teacher has noticed in the past that certain problems of understanding frequently crop up as students work on their own, he may himself create new written explanations of how to attack the problem, and he can have these mimeographed and available for the individuals who need them. For example, in a high-school news-writing class the teacher developed a *style sheet* explaining the rules governing punctuation, spelling, limits on length of sentences and paragraphs, and headline writing for the local school paper.

Sometimes the needed explanation itself is written out on the chalkboard. In a third grade, the teacher can list the steps to follow in studying a new spelling word, and the students can look to the board for the next step when they forget.

Student Helpers

Frequently pupils can aid each other. This arrangement is usually a simple agreement between the teacher and the class that anyone needing help when the teacher is not immediately available can turn to a neighbor for aid. This system usually works satisfactorily if the teacher keeps an eye open for signs that show abuse of the privilege. That is, he can watch out for students who are merely visiting with companions and can send them back to work.

In some classes, the teacher appoints one or two students as official helpers for the day or for the week, and they are the ones to be consulted when aid is needed.

Sometimes students are paired up to work on some task, such as practicing spelling words which each student, individually, has collected as being ones he commonly misspells. With this system, the partners practice drilling each other.

One of the problems with student helpers is that some teachers exploit the talented pupils. That is, they constantly use the most capable ones as assistant teachers. Although this aids the less capable by providing more individual help and may satisfy the talented student's ego, it robs him of chances to expand his own knowledge by preventing him from attempting more challenging activities. Such teachers need to be reminded that they have just as much responsibility toward the gifted as they do toward the slower pupils. The gifted, too, need to learn at a speed commensurate with their abilities.

Another problem is that some students do not know how to help classmates in the most profitable way. Sometimes the fast learner becomes disgusted and shows irritation with the slow student's inability to catch on. Thus, when student helpers are assigned, it is well for the teacher to give them some training in how best to aid classmates.

Teacher Consultation

The teacher himself is the main source of consultation. How he provides opportunities for students to talk with him depends primarily on the way he organizes class activities and the amount of time he is willing to give.

One way to save time in consultation is to notice which students are having the same kind of difficulty at the moment and to collect

them together for a discussion rather than giving the same explanation to each one individually.

A way to save student time is to tell pupils that when they need
teacher help which cannot be given at the moment, they should
turn to a different task or different problems and not simply wait
without doing anything until the teacher can aid.

Some teachers do all their paper correcting and marking of the
roll book while students work silently at their seats. But if these
routines can be cared for after school or during free periods, the
teacher is available to cruise about the room and give students individual aid.

Lunch periods and the hour before or after school offer good
times for individual help. Whether this outside time will be offered
to students depends, obviously, on the degree of teacher willingness to sacrifice it to help with individual problems.

Marking Individual Progress

Teachers inevitably face the problem of marking students. For
those educators who are acutely aware of individual differences
in ability, this problem is perhaps doubly puzzling. An inspection
of report cards from a variety of schools shows that there exists
today some confusion, or at least difference of opinion, concerning
the proper basis for students' marks. Part of this confusion has resulted from the increased concern in recent decades with the problem of individual differences.

Schools of a more traditional cast often mark a pupil on how
well he compares with a standard of excellence set up by the teacher
or administration. That is, the student receives a mark of 95 per
cent in arithmetic because during the semester he got 95 per cent
of the test questions correct.

Other schools compare the child with his classmates. The mark
of C is often defined as showing average performance, B as above
average, and so forth.

With each of these first two schemes, when a child receives a
higher mark it means he has displayed more knowledge or skill
than a child who has received a lower mark.

But this is not necessarily true with a third system, which has developed chiefly at the elementary-school level. With this plan, the pupil is marked in comparison with his own apparent potential ability. Therefore, it is possible for a less apt but diligent child to receive a higher mark than does a bright but lackadaisical child even though on objective measures the brighter child has reached a higher level of knowledge or skill. This approach to marking developed after educators recognized clearly that high-level performance is based not only on diligence but also on aptitudes. They felt that the more traditional marking systems were not fair because the slower learner, no matter how diligent, would always receive a low or failing mark. The brilliant student would almost always receive high marks when compared with his less apt agemates, even when he coasted along only half trying. But, it was reasoned, if each student is compared with his own potential (as determined by aptitude tests and past performance), the less able ones can be rewarded for their small but, for them, significant successes, while the gifted can be stimulated to work up to their potential.

When these marking schemes are discussed, voices and temperatures may be raised, but a solution satisfactory to all may not be forthcoming. Because of complex factors influencing it, we cannot hope to settle the controversy here. But we may profit from a brief inspection of several facets of the problem. By analyzing the uses to which marks are put in school, each of us may be able to determine more clearly which system—or combination—he prefers and how that system may affect his providing for individual differences. We shall consider both daily marks and final grades.

The Uses of Daily Marks

Daily marks on assignments and tests are used in one or more of the following ways by teachers: (1) to inform the pupils of their progress, (2) to motivate pupils, (3) to furnish a basis for planning the student's current schoolwork, (4) to furnish evidence that can be summarized at the marking period as a report to parents and to the school administration.

Inform the Student of His Progress

It is unnecessary to give a student a formal mark to inform him of his progress. In fact, he can understand his strengths and weaknesses more clearly if some kind of verbal comment is given by the teacher, either orally or as a note on his assignment or test. For instance, a teacher writes on an English composition: "This paper was quite interesting. Your topic sentences were much clearer this time. But the possessives are still giving you some trouble. See page 28 in the text for possessives." This comment should be a more helpful guide to learning than a simple mark of B— or 81 per cent.

Although it is true that the letter or number mark does convey the teacher's general impression of the quality of the work, the specific analytical comments are more helpful in explaining the student's strengths and weaknesses.

So, logically, specific comment, not a mark, is the sounder way to fulfill this progress-information function. But students are not always logical, and in the race for A's and B's to which their school career has conditioned them, they often feel uneasy—especially in the secondary school—if there is no formal mark on their returned assignments. Most students (or at least the more diligent ones) in secondary schools will probably much prefer receiving a mark as well as comments even when the teacher does not wish to use a mark as an indicator of progress.

Motivate Pupils to Work Hard

The mark apparently comes to symbolize slightly different things to different individuals. But it is likely that many students interpret it as signifying one or more of the following: (1) the extent of adult (symbolized by the teacher) approval and, when the mark is taken home, the extent of parental love and acceptance, (2) an objective measure of the pupil's worth, and (3) a promise of success or failure to reach desired goals that will require formal education.

Symbolizing such things as these, the grade can serve for some students as a strong motivator. But even as we admit this, we must also recognize that the grade is not a *necessary motivator*. That is, the things that the mark has come to symbolize can be provided in other ways. A teacher's comment of "well done" can as easily indicate adult approval and can be accepted by the student as a measure of his worth. Parental pleasure can arise when father reads the instructor's complimentary remarks written on a term paper, even though no mark is included.

So as a motivator the mark itself is not essential. In schools that have done away with traditional forms of marking, there is no evidence that the problems of motivating students are any greater than in schools which continue to stress periodic grades.

Planning Daily Work

Marks on daily tests and assignments have been used for determining whether the student has mastered the current task and is ready to go on with new ones or whether he needs more work on the current activity. So the teacher may decide that everyone with less than 70 per cent or less than a C on the English-usage test should restudy the material, whereas students with higher marks are ready for work in literature.

It is obvious, however, that daily work can easily be planned without the use of marks. A glance at each student's usage test enables the teacher to see what kinds of mistakes were made and, as a result, what types of relearning are needed for each individual.

Evidence for Final Reports

Which kinds of daily marks will be most useful for compiling a semester-end report depends primarily on the form of the final report card used. If the final report is to be in the form of "per cents," it is most convenient for daily evaluations to be in this same form. That is, daily marks of 95 per cent, 91 per cent, and 84 per cent are easily averaged to a final mark of 90. If the final report is to be a letter grade, such as a C or D, the teacher can keep daily marks as letters and try to average them at the end. Or daily marks can be kept as numbers and then totaled and converted to letters at the end of the marking period.

If, however, the final report is in the form of an interview with the parents or a letter written to the parents, as is true in some elementary schools, the teacher does not feel as obligated to keep daily marks in numerical form. Instead, verbal descriptions of the quality of the student's work are enough.

Elementary-school children are probably more easily satisfied with comments on their papers or their work and are less likely to demand a formal grade. Secondary-school students are more strongly conditioned to a marking system and, rather logically, wish to make continual estimates of what their eventual fate will be on report-card day.

In considering these possible functions of daily marks, we have not yet faced the problem posed earlier about the proper basis for the mark. Does the mark represent a comparison of the pupil with a set standard, with classmates, or with his own apparent potential? From the standpoint of being fair in recognizing individual differences, the comparison of the child with his own potential seems most logical. But there are some other considerations we must recognize—such as the realities of college-entrance requirements, of the school's regular reporting system, and of parent and student expectations—when we decide on the plan to follow with our class.

In addition, there should be no conflict between the kind of comparisons made in grading daily work and that required for the semester-end report. It seems desirable for the teacher to be honest with the students so they are not given marks comparing them with their apparent potential on daily work but with classmates on their report card. The diligent but slow ones should not need to complain, "He said I was doing fine all along and then gave me a *D* minus at the end."

To summarize our discussion of the uses of daily grades, we may conclude that marks in the form of letters or numbers are very often used but are not necessary for informing the student of his progress, motivating him to work hard, and planning his daily work. Teacher comments specifically suited to the individual student and the particular task at hand can carry out these functions more directly.

However, the function of providing evidence that can be summed up for a final report is often a different matter. The form that the final report is to assume usually determines, or at least strongly influences, the kinds of daily marks or evaluations that are used.

Teachers in the elementary school are in a freer position to suit marks or comments to the individual's ability level than are teachers in most high schools, where pupils and their parents have already become strongly conditioned to traditional grading schemes and where college entrance is so often based on traditional types of marks.

The Uses of Final Marks

Final marks, which appear as summary evaluations of the student's work at the end of grading periods, are designed to do one or more of the following: (1) determine which students are to be promoted to the next grade and which ones retained in the same grade, (2) motivate students to work hard, (3) provide records for the school authorities, and (4) provide reports of pupil progress for parents and the child.

Final Marks Determine Promotion and Retention

What is the purpose of the school? Is it (a) to set standards of achievement for each grade level with the intention of promoting only those students who meet the standards and of failing or eliminating those who do not? Or is it (b) to provide education for all, with the work adjusted as nearly as possible to each pupil's needs and with the promotion-retention system also adjusted to the individual's welfare?

If you select (a) as the proper purpose, the procedure of setting 65 per cent or D as the lowest passing mark is commensurate with your philosophy.

But if you select (b) as the proper purpose of the school, you cannot logically have marks function as the criterion for promotion. Rather, you need to adopt some such plan as the following.

When a student in your class is found to be considerably behind or ahead of the others, he is not automatically retained or accelerated, but you are alerted to look at his case more closely to:

1. Carefully evaluate his achievement in all areas of his work, his mental ability, chronological age, size, social adjustment, attitudes, and ambitions. On the basis of this study, make a recommendation about what will be best for the student's welfare.

2. Be sure you have the cooperation and sincere consent of the

student, his parents, and the school administration so that all of them feel that the recommendation—for promotion, retention, or acceleration—is for the pupil's benefit.

The point of view underlying (a) is more common at the high-school level, although as a high-school education is increasingly being regarded as each American's birthright, procedure (b) is becoming more acceptable. Plan (b) at the high-school level operates best where a good counseling and guidance system is available to analyze students' aptitudes and interests so that students can be routed into suitable courses, that is, courses in which they are less likely to experience failure.

Procedure (b) appears to be more workable in elementary schools. Of the two plans, it is the one better adapted to caring for individual differences.

Final Marks Motivate Students

The earlier comments concerning the motivating value of daily marks hold true for final grades. It should be recognized that grades have become motivators for pupils to work hard. But it should also be realized that grades are not *necessary* motivators. Other devices— such as teacher comments, recognition of pupil successes, and the student's seeing for himself that he is making progress toward important goals—can be sufficient stimulators.

Final Marks Provide Records for the School

The school needs records of pupils' work on which to base future educational plans, transfers from one school to another, and reports to outside agencies such as universities and prospective employers.

Despite the many shortcomings of the final grade, it often functions as a useful predictor of future success in school. In general, the person who has achieved high grades in a particular area of learning in the past can be expected to do relatively well in that area in the future. Likewise, if he has done poorly in the past, he may be expected to be poor in the subject when he meets it again.

These relationships are not invariably true, but they are consistent enough to make past school marks quite useful to counselors at the junior-high level where plans for a differentiated high-school education are being made. High-school grades are one of the most useful predictors of success in college. Of course, numbers of other factors need to be considered in the educational counseling situation, such as test scores and student interests, but school marks form one part of the useful data.

It should be recognized that the kinds of marks that compare the student with his classmates are more useful in predicting future success than are marks comparing the pupil's progress with his own apparent abilities. Such marks based on class-wide comparisons are also the ones typically requested by prospective employers and colleges. But for the purpose of having school records that permit a good understanding of the student, it is useful also to have a report of how the student's achievement compares to his apparent abilities.

Final Marks Are Progress Reports to Parent and Child

As implied earlier, various kinds of progress reports are used in different school systems. The most diverse are found at the elementary level, where the report may be in the form of a card, a letter written to the home, an interview, or a combination of these. The child may be compared with his own aptitudes, a set standard, or his classmates.

High schools usually depend solely on a report card which compares the student with an ostensibly set standard or with his age-mates.

Elementary report cards have tended to change in form more than have high-school cards in recent decades. Elementary reports frequently break down the student's performance into component elements and as a result are more diagnostic and provide a clearer picture for the parent.

Parents of elementary-school children often seem satisfied with information about how the child is progressing in relation only to his own ability. But many also ask, "How does he stack up against the others?" For this reason, educators who wish to adopt the kind of report that compares the student's work only with his potential are frequently requested by parents to furnish more traditional marks. Some schools solve this problem by reporting both kinds of comparisons. Others provide a regular report comparing the child only with his potential, then include the following note on the card: "If you also wish to know how your child's work compares with that of his classmates, you may receive this information during a consultation with the teacher concerned."

SUMMARY

Throughout this chapter, we have considered general classroom practices which enable teachers to care for intellectual differences through individualized and group work.

The uses of enrichment and acceleration have been inspected. Stress has been placed on giving clear assignments, dividing the class into efficient groups, training pupils in individual and group responsibilities, and continually evaluating their progress.

We have suggested that the kind of evaluation or mark best suited to individual differences is one comparing the student with his own apparent potential. But the requirements of school records, the difficulties met in trying to determine the student's real potential, and the realities of parent attitudes and tradition often make it desirable to add evaluations comparing the student with agemates.

SUGGESTED LEARNING ACTIVITIES

1. In a library, search through copies of educational journals and teaching-methods books related to your teaching specialty to collect reports of how other teachers have met individual differences.

2. Visit several classes in nearby schools to observe what techniques and materials teachers there are using to meet intellectual differences. Pay special attention to their methods of evaluation and of giving assignments. Write a brief report of your conclusions and compare them with those made by your classmates in other schools.

3. Interview two teachers to discover: (a) which children in their classes at the present time are posing the most difficult problems because of intellectual differences, (b) what measures the teachers are using to solve these problems. In your written report of these interviews, suggest any techniques you can think of which might help solve such problems.

4. Collect report cards from four different school systems. From the

standpoint of individual differences, give your opinion of the apparent adequacy of each card in suiting the marks to individual abilities and in making the student's specific strengths and weaknesses clear to the parents.

5. For a given grade level, prepare two lesson plans designed to reach goals in your subject-matter specialty or teaching field. If possible, design the plans for a specific class whose range of abilities you know. If this is not possible, prepare your plans for a hypothetical class that exhibits a typical range of talent. Make clear in these plans how you will care for the individual differences in ability among the students.

6. For your teaching specialty, develop one evaluation device (such as a test, a rating scale, a check list) which would enable you to estimate the strengths and weaknesses of students in regard to a particular set of objectives you wish them to reach.

SUGGESTED READINGS

BELL, J. W. "Individualizing Instruction at the High School Level," *The High School Journal*, April, 1959, pp. 252–254.

BERGMAN, F. L. "Individualization: Key to More Writing," *English Journal*, March, 1962, pp. 192–196.

BLAKE, H. E. "Studying Spelling Independently," *Elementary English*, January, 1960, pp. 29–32.

CARROLL, J. B. "Plan for Meeting Individual Differences in Composition and Reading," *English Journal*, November, 1959, pp. 466–472.

CUTTS, NORMA E., and MOSELEY, NICHOLAS. *Providing for Individual Differences in the Elementary School*. Englewood Cliffs: Prentice-Hall, 1960.

FEDORCZYK, V. S. "Providing for Individual Differences in Shorthand from the Beginning," *Business Education Forum*, May, 1961, p. 31.

FLOURNOY, F. "Meeting Individual Differences in Arithmetic," *Arithmetic Teacher*, February, 1960, pp. 80–86.

HALL, NORMAN. "Individualize Your Spelling Instruction," *Elementary English*, May, 1962, pp. 476–477.

JENNINGS, HELEN. "Sociometric Grouping in Relation to Child Development," in *Fostering Mental Health in Our Schools*. Association for Supervision and Curriculum Development 1950 Yearbook. Washington, D.C.: National Education Association, 1950.

MOENCH, L. "Individualized Practice in Arithmetic: a Pilot Study," *Arithmetic Teacher*, October, 1962, pp. 321–329.

VITE, W. L. "Grouping Practices in Individualized Reading," *Elementary English*, February, 1961, pp. 91–98.

WHITAKER, W. L. "Why Not Individualize Arithmetic?" *Arithmetic Teacher*, December, 1960, pp. 400–403.

ZANCO, M. L. "How to Individualize Instruction with a Tape Recorder," *Industrial Arts and Vocational Education*, February, 1963, p. 19.

Meeting Intellectual Differences III: Programed Materials

Perhaps the most publicized innovation for classroom learning in the past decade has been that of programed materials and teaching machines. Although programed approaches might properly belong with the other classroom methods discussed in Chapter 5, we are presenting them separately in Chapter 6 because of their unique characteristics.

Our discussion will center on the nature of programed materials and their apparent contributions to individualizing instruction.

THE NATURE OF LEARNING PROGRAMS AND DEVICES

In the early 1920's, Sidney L. Pressey, an Ohio State University psychologist, invented a simple machine for giving tests to individual students.

It worked this way: A multiple-choice question and four possible answers were shown in an opening on the front of the machine. The student read the question and then chose his answer by pressing one of four answer keys. If his choice was correct, the question flipped out of sight and the next question appeared. But if his choice was incorrect, the original question remained, and the student tried again by selecting a different answer key.

Although this machine was originally designed for testing, Pressey recognized that it could also teach. That is, the machine at once told the student whether his answer was right. And if it was wrong, the student immediately tried again and thus *learned* the correct answer.

Note to Reader: *To check your understanding of the explanation above, read Statements A and B below.*

A. Pressey set out to invent a teaching machine, which incidentally turned out to be useful as a test-scoring device. (If you think this statement is true, turn to page 203.)

B. Pressey invented a machine for administering multiple-choice tests to individuals, then recognized that the device could serve as a teaching machine. (If you think this statement is true, turn to page 201.)

(*From page 204*)
Your answer: "No."

Correct. A pamphlet containing the Constitution in original form is not programed material. Now let us continue with some additional ideas.

Not all self-teaching programs are built according to the same pattern or same philosophy of programing. We shall describe the two most popular types.

The first pattern consists of a single sequence of small subject-matter segments, each accompanied by a question or problem. The student reads the first segment, answers its question, then moves on to the next. If his answer is wrong, he is informed immediately of his error, but no attempt is made to explain or reteach him the information in a different way. He simply tries the question again. This pattern of programing is called "linear" because every student follows the same straight-line program.

The second variety also presents segments of material with accompanying questions. If the student answers correctly, he progresses directly to the next portion of new learning material. But if his answer is wrong, he is sidetracked or rerouted onto a branch line where his error is explained. That is, he is retaught in a different way, then is directed back to the main line. This is called "branching."

QUESTION FOR READER: *Which programing pattern has been used so far in this chapter?*

A. Linear (turn to page 205).

B. Branching (turn to page 202).

(From page 201)

Your answer: "A motion-picture projector used for showing historical films to social-studies classes."

I'm afraid you didn't understand what we meant by "new class of teaching machines."

Although a motion-picture projector is a machine and is often used for teaching, it does not meet the four requirements we described for the "new class of teaching machines." To belong in this class, a machine must provide for:

1. Each student to learn at his own rate.

2. Subject matter to be offered in small, graded portions.

3. Each student to give an answer to a question about each segment.

4. The student to learn immediately whether his answer has been correct.

You may recall that in the typical method of showing motion pictures to a class, the film is run straight through without stopping. Thus the ideas are presented at the pace determined by the people who produced the film. But this pace may not suit the learning rate of each class member. Recall also that subject matter in films is often presented in large, continuous portions, not small ones. And unless the teacher periodically stops the film and asks students to answer questions on the subject matter, the students are not being required to respond actively to each learning segment.

Now turn back to page 201 and select the correct answer.

(*From page 201*)

Your answer:

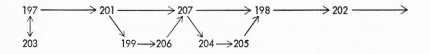

Now let's look over this chapter's organization a bit more carefully. Start with the first page and see where the choices at the bottom of the pages lead you. Note that in each case where the reader makes an incorrect choice and is branched off the main line, he is retaught on another page, then is sent *directly back* to the point where he made the error. The diagram above, however, does not show such a pattern. For example, according to the diagram a student who makes a wrong selection on page 201 is sent to page 199, then directly to pages 206 and 207 without ever having returned to make the correct choice on page 201. But such is not the routing that this chapter really follows.

Return to page 202 and try again.

(*From page 197*)

Your answer: "Pressey invented a machine for administering multiple-choice tests to individuals, then recognized that the device could serve as a teaching machine."

You are correct. This invention was a pioneering contribution to a field that is newly important in education.

Many teaching machines are appearing on the market today. Some are simple mechanical apparatus. Others are complex electronic creations the size of a large television set or, in a few cases, the size of a classroom. But all of this new class of teaching machines provide the following four features.

1. They enable the student to learn at his own pace.

2. They offer subject matter to the student in small, graduated portions.

3. They request or require the student to respond actively by giving an answer to each small portion of learning material before he moves on to the next portion.

4. They provide the student with immediate knowledge of how correct his answer has been.

Question for Reader: *Which of the following devices would properly be included in the new class of teaching machines discussed above?*

A. A motion-picture projector used for showing historical films to social-studies classes. (If you think this is correct, turn to page 199.)

B. A flat box containing a mimeographed sheet of paragraphs, each accompanied by a question. The paragraphs are exposed one by one to the student through a window in the box. For each, the student writes his answer to the question that concerns the material in the paragraph, then turns a crank which exposes the correct answer. (If you think this correct, turn to page 204.)

C. Both devices A and B. (Turn to page 206.)

(*From page 198*)

Your answer: "Branching."

That's right. Not all readers progress through this chapter by the same route. Now let's move ahead.

Today's electronic teaching machines make possible a variety of branching programs—some quite complex—so that students with different backgrounds or abilities can receive material better adjusted to their needs at each step.

An easy way to show different branching possibilities is by picturing the learning sequence in diagram form. The diagram below shows that at Step C in a program there are three possible answers to the Step C question. Students who make the correct choice here go directly to the new material at D. Students who select one of the incorrect choices are retaught at X before returning to C. Students selecting the other incorrect choice are sent to subsequence $M–N$ for reteaching, because their error at C revealed a great lack of understanding.

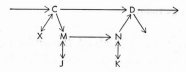

QUESTION FOR READER: *Which of the following diagrams shows the program sequence used so far in this chapter?*

A.

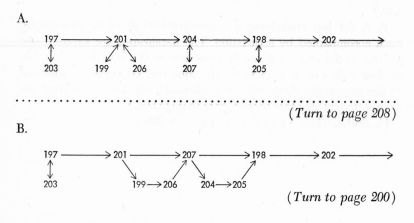

(*Turn to page 208*)

B.

(*Turn to page 200*)

(*From page 197*)

Your answer: "Pressey set out to invent a teaching machine, which incidentally turned out to be useful as a test-scoring device."

Sorry, but you have misunderstood Pressey's purpose. It was just the opposite. He tried to develop a device which would score multiple-choice tests. He hoped that such a test-correcting machine would have two principal advantages: (1) it would relieve teachers of test-marking chores and (2) it would furnish the student immediate information about how well he had understood the subject matter on which he was being tested.

It was more or less incidentally that Pressey recognized that when the machine required the student to find the right answer before continuing, it was doing a teaching job. Or, more precisely, it was doing remedial teaching.

Now turn back to page 197 and select the correct statement at the bottom of the page.

(*From page 201*)

Your answer: "A flat box containing a mimeographed sheet of paragraphs, each accompanied by a question. . . ."

You are right. This device meets the four requirements we described for the "new class of teaching machines." Motion pictures shown in the usual manner do not.

It may have occurred to you by now that this chapter so far also fulfills the four requirements described on page 201. Thus it becomes appropriate for us now to broaden our vocabulary. We need a new term that includes both the "new class of teaching machines" and such reading materials as this chapter's scrambled sequence of pages.

The term we shall use to include both the new-type machines and the scrambled textbook is "programed learning devices." Or we can as well call them "programed teaching devices."

The word "program" here refers to the sequence of short lessons or short subject-matter segments that make up one of these newer self-paced courses of study. A "programer" is a person who creates such lesson sequences. And "programed learning" means that a student follows a pattern of learning material that meets the four requirements, no matter what kind of device is used to present the program to the learner.

QUESTION FOR READER: *Could we properly apply the term "programed learning device" to a pamphlet intended for American-history classes titled* The Constitution of the U.S.: A Copy of Its Original Form?

A. No (turn to page 198).

B. Yes (turn to page 207).

(*From page 198*)

Your answer: "Linear."

I'm afraid not. If this were a linear program, each reader would be moving through this chapter along exactly the same route. But you notice that each time you are asked to answer a question at the bottom of a page, you are sent on to a different page according to whichever answer you have selected. So different readers move through the chapter in different patterns. That is how you have arrived here on page 205. You have been branched off the main line because on page 198 we did not make sufficiently clear to you the difference between linear and branching programs.

So far, this chapter has been built on a branching pattern.

Now return to page 198 and select the correct answer.

(*From page 201*)

Your answer: "Both devices A and B."

You are half right. The flat box containing the mimeographed sheet of questions would properly be included in the "new class of teaching machines" that we described. But the motion-picture projector would not.

It is true that the projector is a machine and is sometimes used for teaching. But if you think of the typical way films are shown to an entire class, you see that the projector would not fulfill the four requirements that we said distinguished the "new class of teaching machines." That is:

1. Each student learns at his own rate.
2. Subject matter is offered in small, graded portions.
3. The student gives an answer to a question about each portion before he moves on to the next.
4. The student learns immediately whether his answer has been correct.

These requirements are, however, met by the box containing mimeographed paragraphs which, along with questions, are exposed to the student one by one. The paragraphs represent the small segments of graded learning material, and the student's written answer represents his active response to the material. When he turns the crank, the correct answer appears, providing him an opportunity to check on the goodness of his own answer.

Now turn back to page 201 and choose the correct statement.

(*From page 204*)

Your answer: "Yes."

Sorry. That's not correct.

Now let's consider again the four criteria we set up for defining programed learning devices. They must:

1. Suit individuals' learning rates.

2. Offer subject matter in small portions.

3. Draw an active response from the learner for each small portion of subject matter he studies.

4. Inform the learner constantly of how well he is understanding the subject matter.

If the American-history pamphlet actually does present the United States Constitution in its original form, it does not fulfill these requirements. Rather, the pamphlet is more the traditional type of text or reading material used in schools. It is not *programed* material.

Turn back to page 204 and select the correct answer.

(*From page 202*)

Your answer:

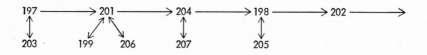

Correct. This is the branching pattern the chapter follows. Now let's turn from branching to linear programing. A linear diagram would obviously look like this:

197 ———→198 ———→199 ———→ 200 ———→ 201 ———→ 202 ———→

Most linear programs today do not offer the student multiple-choice questions. Rather, they ask him to construct an answer or to fill in an incomplete sentence. There is no reason for this difference other than the preferences of the people who have constructed the program.

Although most linear programs, like branching ones, are administered to the student by means of a teaching machine, they can also take the form of a pamphlet or textbook.

So far our chapter has been organized in the branching form used by Norman A. Crowder in his TutorTexts (a series of textbooks on such subjects as algebra, the arithmetic of computers, how to play bridge). Now we shall change our approach. From pages 209 through 212 our material is presented in the linear pattern developed by Robert Glaser. To read this material, you start with Frame 1 on page 209—that is, you begin with the top panel. When you have decided what words best fill the blanks of the incomplete sentence, turn the page to Frame 2 and check your answer. Then read Frame 3 on page 211 fill in the blanks, and check your answers on page 212. Continue until you have completed the entire sequence of panels.

THE TASK OF THE PROGRAMER

Frame 1

When a programer begins to plan a learning sequence in a given subject-matter area, he must ensure that his program starts at the level of simplicity appropriate for the learners. Therefore, as he plans the beginning frames of a program, he must be able to make a good estimate of the students' former _____.

Frame 5

B. F. Skinner, the Harvard psychologist who has led the linear-programing movement, says that each new step in the learning sequence should be rather easy for the learner to take. Thus, when the learner faces a properly written program he can usually expect to make responses that are (1) _____. That is, his answers should seldom be (2) _____.

Frame 9

If the sequence of learning is too steep—that is, if each succeeding step is quite difficult—the student will frequently (1) _____ to answer correctly. This tends to make him feel (2) _____, and he may stop trying to learn.

Frame 13

Norman Crowder, exponent of branching programs, believes that the student's active response is not essential for (1) _____ to take place. But he thinks the response is essential for testing whether or not the student has (2) _____ the segment of material he has just seen.

Frame 2	Answer to Frame 1: "experiences" or "learning" or "education" or "knowledge"

Frame 6	Answers to Frame 5: (1) "right" or "correct" or "successful" (2) "wrong" or "incorrect" or "unsuccessful"

Frame 10	Answers to Frame 9: (1) "fail" (2) "angry" or "discouraged" or "unsuccessful"

Frame 14	Answers to Frame 13: (1) "learning" or "understanding" (2) "learned" or "understood" or "mastered"

Frame 3

The programer must also analyze the body of subject matter. He wants to organize it in a sequence of small learning steps which will progress gradually from very (1) _____ ideas to more (2) _____ ones.

Frame 7

According to Skinner's theory, the student's very act of answering or responding correctly to an item is what brings about the (1) _____. Thus we see the necessity of creating programs that consist of many small segments to ensure that the student gives many correct (2) _____.

Frame 11

Therefore Skinner stresses the desirability of small, graduated learning steps which ensure that the student makes many correct (1) _____ which cause the learning to occur and which motivate the student to (2) _____ working.

Frame 15

Crowder says that the student's response shows whether he is ready for the next new step or whether he should be sent on a different route to be (1) _____ the same material again by a (2) _____ more suitable to his background and abilities.

Frame
4

Answers to Frame 3:

(1) "simple" or "easy"
(2) "complex" or "difficult"

Frame
8

Answers to Frame 9:

(1) "learning"
(2) "answers" or "responses" or "reactions"

Frame
12

Answers to Frame 11:

(1) "responses"
(2) "continue" or "keep on"

Frame
16

Answers to Frame 15:

(1) "taught" or "presented"
(2) "method" or "means" or "technique"

PROGRAMS AND INDIVIDUAL DIFFERENCES

After our brief exposure to the most popular forms of programing —linear and branching—we return to the traditional style of writing to speculate about the contributions these approaches may offer for meeting individual differences.

We need to use the term "speculate," because this field is so new that the appropriate place of programing in the school's repertoire of teaching methods has not yet become clear. Since the mid-1950's, when major interest in programing began, there have been many developments. Throughout the nation at the present time scores of school systems are testing programs and the devices (machines, scrambled books, work sheets, workbooks, punchboards, punch cards) that can be used for presenting them to learners. Programs have been developed in such a variety of subjects as elementary-school spelling and arithmetic, word study, English grammar and usage, reading of foreign languages, algebra and geometry, fundamentals of music, physiology, physics, time telling, shorthand, statistics, basic and advanced electronics, psychology, use of the slide rule, symbolic logic, and how to play bridge. A Center for Programed Instruction has been created to stimulate research and keep educators and psychologists abreast of current developments through its bimonthly bulletin, *Programed Instruction*.[1] Universities are conducting summer workshops in the art of constructing programs. Manufacturing firms and publishers are experimenting with a wide variety of machines and books for use as programed teaching devices.[2]

With so much research being conducted, in the near future we can expect considerably more precise knowledge of the best uses for these techniques in schools. But at present we are safest if we use the results of current studies only as guides to tentative estimates of the ways programing methods will best suit the intellectual dif-

[1] To order the bulletin, write to The Center for Programed Instruction, Inc., 365 West End Avenue, New York, N.Y. 10024.

[2] Two volumes, *Programs '62* and *The Use of Programed Instruction in U.S. Schools*, survey in detail available programs and their experimental uses in schools. Both are available from the Superintendent of Documents, Washington 25, D.C.

ferences of students. The following section, therefore, presents examples of varied uses for programed materials at different grade levels and in different subject-matter areas. The examples illustrate how such materials can serve as (1) the basic text for a class, (2) enrichment for individual students or small groups, (3) remedial teaching, (4) outside assignments to parallel class work, and (5) a course in a specialized subject which the student wishes to pursue on his own.

Basic Text for a Class

In the typical American classroom, the traditional textbook serves as the main source of content as well as the determiner of the sequence in which the materials will be studied. Programed texts, either in the form of books or sequences of lessons on machines, can serve these same purposes and, in addition, enable each student to move ahead at his own rate. When a teacher adopts these programed materials and faithfully follows their plan, his former role of lecturer, discussion leader, and accepter of recitations is altered. He may now function as a supervisor who (1) answers individuals' questions about how to approach their programed material, (2) tests students on units they have completed, and (3) furnishes new units when a student has demonstrated his mastery of the previous one.

The following four examples illustrate programed material serving as a basic text in English usage and grammar, in spelling, in mathematics, and in economics.

A Teaching and Sectioning Device

In the four eighth-grade English classes of a junior high school, the objectives set up for students to reach are (1) to improve their understanding of English usage and grammar and (2) to improve their written composition.

In the fall, each pupil is assigned arbitrarily to one of the four sections. All students begin the year studying English usage and grammar by means of the linear-programed textbook *English 2600* (so named because it consists of more than 2,600 frames; published by Harcourt, Brace and World). The content of this volume is equivalent to more than a year's work in grammar and usage typically taught at this grade level. Each student works at his own pace to complete the units in the text. Because reports from other schools which have used this volume have suggested that brighter students are sometimes bored with the program, the procedure used with these eighth-graders has been altered to counteract boredom by permitting them to take pretests over units. If they score sufficiently high on a pretest, they are permitted to skip that unit.

When a student completes a unit, he informs the teacher, who gives him a test covering the material of the unit. Pupils who score 80 or above move on to the next unit. Those scoring below 80 repeat that portion of the program.

The use of *English 2600* not only suits learning to each pupil's individual pace but also furnishes a guide for sectioning pupils for the remainder of the year's work in composition. That is, the first twenty-five students to complete the programed text form one class; the next twenty-five form another. The 10 per cent of students who find the program too difficult are placed in a special class in which the programed text is supplemented with classroom instruction and more teaching aids.[3]

Spelling with Teaching Machines

A spelling program utilizing simple teaching machines has been used in third-grade classes with such success in one school system that the machine-teaching approach has been expanded for use in the upper grades as well.

The spelling program consists of a series of units, each containing fifteen to twenty different words presented sequentially in fifty to sixty frames. Within a unit, each word is offered from two to seven times, depending on the difficulty of its spelling. Each presentation focuses on a different aspect of the word (such as its prefix or suffix, double letters, or the like). Words selected for use in the program are those most frequently needed by third-graders in their writing.

The machine that presents the program to the pupil is a simple flat

[3] *Programed Instruction,* Vol. 1, No. 4 (February, 1962), p. 3.

box with a slot at one end through which he feeds an 8½ by 11 inch page of teaching material. Each sheet contains five frames of questions and their answers. When a sheet has been inserted in the box, the first frame is exposed through a window in the face of the box. The student writes his answer to this frame on the paper and then turns a knob which pushes the first frame out of reach and simultaneously exposes its correct answer. Thus he checks immediately the correctness of his response. But since the advance knob will not reverse, he cannot turn back to his written answer to alter it if he has been wrong. Therefore the machine, unlike a programed textbook, is "cheat-proof." All errors which the student has committed while studying the program are thus available for the teacher's inspection.

Here is the way the classroom spelling system operates.

At the beginning of the year, the teacher holds training sessions with the children to teach the use of the machine and program sheets.

The pupils are placed in three groups, according to their reading abilities. While the teacher instructs one group in reading, a second group of eight children work independently with the spelling machines at a separate table. At the same time, the third group of children work at their desks on individual assignments: reading, arithmetic, art, and the like. After twenty minutes, the groups rotate. Hence, within about an hour every pupil has spent twenty minutes on each of the three activities: reading, spelling, and individual assignments.

When working at the spelling table, each student follows this procedure.

1. He completes fifteen to twenty-five frames of a unit.

2. Then he takes a test on the words that were presented in the unit. If he spells all the words correctly, he moves directly to Step 4. But if he misses more than one word on the test, he goes to Step 3.

3. Step 3 is to finish the remaining thirty-five or so frames of the unit so as to have enough practice to ensure reasonable success on the final test (Step 4), which few pupils fail.

4. Now he dons earphones connected to a tape recorder which slowly dictates sentences for him to write. The sentences contain the unit's spelling words.

During the first year's trial of the program, the classes using the machines made greater gains in spelling skill than those using traditional methods. The teachers reported that children were quick to learn to handle the materials, machines, word tests, and the charts for recording scores. "They were greatly disturbed whenever anything prevented their having a spelling lesson." [4]

Because so much paper was originally consumed when children wrote their answers on the question sheets, the machines have been altered so that answers are written on a roll of adding-machine paper, and the question sheets can be used over and over.

Individualizing Instruction in Oversize Classes

A high-school staff believed that if students were to receive adequate individual instruction from the teacher in such subjects as English composition, class size would have to be reduced. To accomplish this goal and still maintain the school's present over-all teacher-pupil ratio, the administration decided to increase the size of classes in such subjects as mathematics, where individualization might be accomplished through programed materials.

Consequently TEMAC mathematics programs (available from Teaching Materials Corporation as textbooks or for use in Min/Max machines) were adopted, and mathematics classes were increased to sixty students each. The large classroom was altered by the construction of sixty individual study carrels or semienclosed booths. In addition there were a teacher's consultation and small-group discussion area and a testing area. A secretarial assistant aided each teacher with the added clerical duties that resulted from working with three hundred mathematics students a day.

After their first semester, school officials concluded that the programed approach provided sufficient motivation to keep students working fifty minutes a day, allowed some students to progress as much as eight times faster than others, and made it possible for some to complete a full year of mathematics in one semester. They also concluded:

Teachers who move from textbook teaching to programed learning instruction in mathematics should be given a preschool orientation experi-

[4] Alice K. Egerton and Ruth W. Twombly, "A Programmed Course in Spelling," *Elementary School Journal,* Vol. 62, No. 7 (April, 1962), p. 384.

ence where the theories of automated instruction and the contents, scope, and sequence of the subject matter can be mastered. Teachers with a positive attitude and teachers who enjoy close and intimate contact with students on an individual basis should be selected for programed learning work. Teachers who must lecture and who are inclined to dominate the center of learning activity in the classroom will find frustration in the role played by the teacher who utilizes teaching machines.[5]

A Variation for Slow Learners

A class of slow learners in a high-school economics course did not progress satisfactorily with the traditional teaching methods and textbooks because these pupils (1) rarely met success and thus showed little interest in learning, (2) had great difficulty trying to read typical textbooks, yet did not want to be given a course whose content varied much from that studied by their more apt agemates, (3) had trouble following extended class discussions, (4) were frequently bored and therefore daydreamed, and (5) did not succeed well on essay tests because they did not write well, though they often understood quite a bit of the content.

To teach these students more effectively, the instructor recast the school system's basic economics syllabus into thirty-one lessons that covered 90 per cent of the usual course material. His new programed version eliminated concepts that seemed too abstract for slow learners. A typical lesson in the sequence took two or three days for the class to complete. Each lesson progressed according to these steps: economic terms were defined, problems were solved, progress with the lesson was tested. At the end of a unit, the class held a review and took a unit test. The following illustrates more specifically the conduct of a lesson.

1. *Define terms.* Pupils read aloud definitions of economic terms that form the basis of the lesson. Illustrations to clarify the terms are suggested by students and teacher and are discussed. Pupils' questions are answered.

Sample definitions: "*Stock exchange* is a place where stocks and bonds are bought and sold according to organized rules. Brokers buy

[5] Terrel Howard Bell, "Teaching Machines and Programmed Learning in Weber County," *Journal of Secondary Education,* Vol. 37, No. 2 (February, 1962), p. 111.

and sell for customers. *Capital gain:* The profit made by selling stock at a higher price than the purchase price." [6]

2. *Solve practice problems.* Students read and answer objective-type questions based on the definitions. Answers are reviewed by teacher and pupil.

Sample problems.

(*a*) If you buy a stock at $50 a share and sell at $55 a share, you have earned
 ( ) a profit of $55
 ( ) a dividend of $5
 ( ) a capital gain of $5 per share
 ( ) a capital gain of $55
(*b*) You bought 100 shares of stock at $10 per share and sold these shares at $12 a share. You have made a capital gain of $_____.
(*c*) Although there are about fifteen million Americans who own stock, most people prefer to keep their savings in a bank because of the following reasons. (Check all the correct answers.)
 ( ) You cannot lose money in a savings bank.
 ( ) Little knowledge is required in order to save in a bank.
 ( ) Most people are not interested in getting rich.
 ( ) When you save in a bank, you do not have to pay a broker's fee.
 ( ) Buying stocks and bonds is a greater risk than saving in a bank. [7]

3. *Take test on lesson.* The printed test of five to ten multiple-choice questions is taken, and papers are exchanged, to be marked by classmates. When students receive their marked tests back, they discuss the answers, so that the testing serves also as a reinforcement of the learning. Test items are similar in form and content to the problems shown above.

Although in the strict sense of programing, as defined earlier in the chapter, this economics course is not individualized, it still does provide learning material in small portions. It also furnishes fairly immediate knowledge of results. The objective-type tests enable the

---

[6] Samuel Sierles, "The Slow Learner Can Learn!" *Clearing House,* February, 1962, p. 362.
[7] *Ibid.,* pp. 362–363.

student to display his knowledge without requiring writing talents of him. All these factors, which are also common to certain work-book approaches to learning, were found to be conducive to success with slower learners.

Enrichment

As noted earlier, the students who complete assignments before their classmates are a continual challenge for the teacher. Programed materials can aid such pupils by furnishing activities that enrich their learning without taking the teacher away from the majority of the pupils who usually need more personalized instruction. The follow-ing examples of enrichment are from a sixth-grade and a high-school English class.

Programs in Varied Subject-Matter Areas

To expand learning opportunities for the most apt students, a sixth-grade teacher collected or developed brief programs in the areas of word study, science, and social studies. The programs served as supplementary learning rather than opportunities for ac-celeration. That is, none of the programs taught exactly the subject matter being studied by the entire class.

Topics treated in the science programs included photosynthesis,[8] magnetism, astronauts, conductors and insulators, and weather pre-diction. At the end of each program, several simple experiments were suggested for the student to try at home.

The word-study program was a more extensive commercial one on which students worked over a longer period. (*Words,* Science Re-search Associates, 1962.)

Programs in social studies concerned Hawaii and Alaska, func-tions of the United Nations, map reading, map making, the Bill of Rights, and the geography of the local county.

All were linear programs. With the exception of the commer-cial one on word study, all were reproduced on ditto sheets. As a student completed the sheets, he had to be trusted to cover the an-

[8] Marta Zaborska, "Photosynthesis," *Grade Teacher,* Vol. 80, No. 5 (January, 1963), p. 36.

swer below each frame as he responded to the question in that frame.

Administering the enrichment lessons was a simple matter. If a student completed his regular classwork early, he could choose one of the programs from a cardboard file near the teacher's desk. When he finished it, the teacher gave him a test to measure his learning of the material.

The following excerpt from the beginning of one of the programs, which the teacher adopted from the *Grade Teacher* periodical, illustrates their form.[9]

OUR TWO NEWEST STATES

This is not a test, but a new way to learn. It is called a program. Cover the page with a piece of paper so that you can see only the first sentence. On the paper write the complete word that goes in the blank in the first sentence. Then slide the paper down and read the next sentence. Write the word that goes in that blank, and then check your answer by sliding the paper down again. Continue this way. Look at the program answer promptly, but not until you have written your own answer first.

1. When Alaska and Hawaii were admitted to the United States, the number of states increased from 48 to _ _.

50

2. Alaska and Hawaii are the two newest states. Alaska was the 49th state to be added. The 50th state was H w i i.

Hawaii

3. Look at the map to find this answer. Both Alaska and Hawaii are farther _ _ _ _ than our other states.

(east or west)

west

4. Neither Alaska nor Hawaii touches another state. Alaska borders on Canada. Hawaii is completely surrounded by the _ _ _ _ _ _ _ Ocean. Look at the map to get the answer if necessary.

Pacific.

Speech and Dramatics Enrichment

The faster workers in a high-school English class who completed compositions, reading assignments, and term papers ahead of their

[9] Darlene Haring, "Our Two Newest States," *Grade Teacher*, Vol. 80, No. 2 (October, 1962), pp. 22–23.

classmates were furnished with two kinds of supplementary activities: (1) additional suggestions for expanding their reading interests and (2) opportunities to complete programed units on such topics as stagecraft, dramatics, and phonetic analysis. Some of the programs, such as those on stagecraft, were in scrambled-book, branching form. However, the one on phonetic analysis was dittoed onto letter-size sheets which were used as a linear program in a special manila folder that served as the "teaching machine."

The purpose of the phonetics program was to teach standard symbols used by speech analysts in transcribing the spoken word. The manila folder was converted into a "machine" when three small windows were cut in the front of it to expose each frame to the student in sequence. When the sheet of paper containing the program was placed in the folder, the word or letters which the student was to transcribe were shown in the left window. He wrote his phonetic transcription in the center window. Then, to check his answer, he pulled the paper up about three-eighths of an inch and saw the correct transcription printed below his own answer. If he was wrong, he wrote the correct answer in the right window. But if his first response was correct, he simply slid the paper up to the next word without writing in the right-hand window.

After students had mastered the symbols in written form through study of this program, they were permitted to listen on earphones to tapes on which words were spoken at paced intervals. Again the student used the manila folder as his response "machine." But the sheets for use with the taped words contained no words in the left-hand (stimulus) column. Only the center and right-hand windows were used.

An example of the initial frames of the written phonetics program is given on page 223.[10]

(Size and placement of windows cut one inch below the top of the manila folder are indicated by the dotted lines above the program.)

---

[10] Adapted from Charles John Tolch, "Methods of Programming Teaching Machines for Speech," *The Speech Teacher*, Vol. 11, No. 3 (September, 1962), pp. 233–238.

⅜″   1¼″   ⅝″   1¼″   ⅜″   1¼″

me		
me	i	_____
feet		
feet	i	_____
meat		
meat	i	_____
toot		
toot	u	_____
sue		
sue	u	_____
seed		
seed	sid	_____
brief		
brief	brif	_____

Remedial Teaching

In almost any class where the subject matter is taught in the same manner to everyone at once, some of the students fail to grasp the material adequately. Hence they need to be taught in a different manner or at a slower pace if they are to succeed with their second try. Programed materials can be used for accomplishing this remedial-teaching task, at least in some subject-matter areas and with certain types of students. The two examples below concern teaching algebra to a class of ninth-graders and teaching spelling to a few individuals in a regular fifth grade.

Algebra in Summer School

Thirteen of the class of nineteen ninth-graders in the six-week summer session had enrolled because they had already completed the algebra course during the regular school year with unsatisfactory marks. The other six were students who had taken less than one semester of algebra in a general mathematics class and now wished to complete the course.

The students followed the TEMAC first-year high-school algebra course (Encyclopaedia Britannica Films, Inc.). It consisted of 8,229 linear frames in 1,292 notebook pages. The notebook included a plastic slide which permitted students to answer a frame, then reveal the correct response.

Most of the pupils felt that the two-hour class sessions were not too tiring. Some worked as much as three hours at a time by arriving at class an hour early and beginning work on their own.

The range of individual differences in rate of working was suggested by the fact that at the end of the first week one student had completed 300 pages, whereas another working the same length of time had finished only 150. Each week every student, in conference with the teacher, established his own individual goal of pages to finish. "Faster students remarked that they were relieved by the fact that they did not have to listen to explanations of material they already knew. Slower students appreciated the opportunity to spend as much time on a particular topic as they needed." [11]

At first the instructor found it odd not to be lecturing. But as the course continued, he gained great satisfaction working with individual students. Immediately after a student completed one of the twenty unit tests, it was graded. A ten- to twenty-minute conference was held to analyze the student's strengths and weaknesses before he proceeded with the next unit in the program.

"No student's time was wasted by time spent on explanations of another's mistakes, nor were any of the more timid students' deficiencies ignored. It was this teacher's conviction that he came to

[11] Paul McGarvey, "Programmed Instruction in Ninth-Grade Algebra," *The Mathematics Teacher*. Vol. 55, No. 7 (November, 1962), p. 578.

know the students . . . better as individuals than in any summer school class he had taught before." [12]

Compared to thirteen students who were repeating algebra in a parallel class taught in a more customary manner with a traditional textbook, the thirteen repeaters in the programed class made larger gains in the final test. One student, however, did very poorly in the programed class, just as he had in the previous semester's traditional class. The other twelve met varied degrees of success and completed different amounts of the total program during the six weeks.

Remedial Spelling

In a fifth-grade class, three students who had particular trouble with spelling were given special programed instruction in fourth-grade work in addition to the regular fifth-grade spelling lessons which they completed along with their classmates.

For the remedial students, a commercial spelling program (TMI-Grolier Fundamentals of Spelling) was used in a single Min/Max teaching machine. At specified times during the day when class members were doing seatwork, one of the three students worked for fifteen or twenty minutes at the machine at the rear of the classroom.

By this method, each of the three improved his mastery of fourth-grade spelling without requiring extra teacher time for individualized remedial instruction.

Outside Assignments

There are two basic ways that programed materials may serve as assignments to be pursued outside of class. First, the student may work on the program in class, as in the case of the remedial algebra course discussed earlier, and then take the workbooks home to continue with them as an outside assignment.

In other cases, however, classroom activities may not involve any programing, but each student is assigned programed materials as homework which he can complete at his own rate. For instance, in a high-school biology class the students were taught through lecture, discussion, textbook reading, and laboratory experiences. However, during the unit on human physiology and anatomy, each pupil during

[12] *Ibid.*, p. 578.

his study-hall period spent some time working on Fundamentals of Human Physiology, a TMI-Grolier program used in a Min/Max teaching machine.

A second example is found in a high-school music class whose students entered the course with varied understandings of music fundamentals. The teacher wished to ensure they all gained a similar background in fundamentals but did not wish to spend class time reteaching material which some had already mastered. Hence he tested their understanding of basic musical terms and notation procedures. Pupils who scored below 85 per cent were assigned to work through a Fundamentals of Music program (TMI-Grolier) in workbook form, with the understanding that they were to write their answers on separate paper and not to mark the texts, which might be used again. Class periods were then used for choral work and for discussing recordings to which the class listened.

In other subject-matter areas at all grade levels, teachers can develop short programs treating specific topics (experiments in science, prefixes and suffixes in English, structure of city government) that occasionally can serve as homework assignments.

Specialized Courses

One of the main disadvantages of attending a small high school is that the variety of courses offered is usually much more limited than that in larger schools. As a result, the students in smaller districts miss the opportunity to take work in areas that would be of great interest and profit.

Programed materials promise a solution to this problem by enabling a diligent pupil to pursue on his own, with minimum teacher help, such courses as plane geometry, introductory statistics, trigonometry, stenospeed (an ABC shorthand), measurement-meteorology-astronomy, basic German reading, basic Spanish reading, basic Russian reading, modern Hebrew reading, fundamentals of electricity, the arithmetic of computers, and others.

SUMMARY

Recent years have witnessed the rapid development of new learning materials which have four characteristics in common. They all:

1. Enable the student to learn at his own pace.

2. Offer subject matter to the student in small, graduated portions.

3. Request or require him to respond actively by giving an answer to each small portion of learning material before he moves on to the next portion.

4. Provide the student with immediate knowledge of how correct his answer has been.

Most programed materials are still in experimental stages of development, so we cannot state with confidence the roles they will fill best in education. Research findings to date indicate that in certain subject-matter areas (mathematics, spelling, some sciences) certain kinds of pupils learn more in a shorter time than they would in a traditional class. In other cases, programed and traditional teaching approaches have proved equally effective. It is not yet clear whether the best contribution of programed materials will be limited to factual subjects (spelling, mathematics, language usage, science fundamentals) or whether they can also be adapted effectively for teaching literary judgment,[13] creative writing, appraisal skills in social sciences, and the like. More research is needed.

The preliminary studies that have been made, however, suggest that programing can contribute significantly to better individualized instruction in several ways: (1) as texts for an entire class, (2) as enrichment materials for fast learners, (3) as remedial materials, (4) as outside assignments, and (5) as specialized courses not offered by the school in the form of a class.

SUGGESTED LEARNING ACTIVITIES

1. Secure a program from the library or from one of the sources in the Suggested Readings for this chapter and work enough of the program to answer the following questions: (a) For what grade level do you think this might be appropriate? (b) How might this program be used to care for individual differences? (c) What shortcomings do you think the program exhibits, and how might these be remedied?

2. Invite the local representative of a company that distributes programed materials to demonstrate their use for your class.

---

[13] For an interesting scrambled book in the sphere of literary criticism, see John Clark Pratt, *The Meaning of Modern Poetry* (Garden City: Doubleday, 1962).

3. For a topic in your own teaching area, write a fifteen- to twenty-page program and submit it to a colleague to try out and evaluate. Tell how you might use such a program profitably with a class or with individuals whom you might be teaching. (For guides to program writing, see references in Suggested Readings.)

4. Inquire at nearby schools to learn whether they are using any programed materials. If so, interview the teachers who have adopted programing to learn (a) the success they have met, (b) the problems they have encountered, and (c) suggestions they have for improving the materials or their use.

5. Search through the *Education Index* in the library to locate articles about the use of programed materials in your own teaching field. On the basis of these articles and your own thought about the matter, describe the ways in which you believe programed materials can and cannot be effective for meeting the goals of your field.

SUGGESTED READINGS

Center for Programed Instruction. *Programs '62: A Guide to Programed Instructional Materials.* Washington, D.C.: U.S. Office of Education, 1962. Annotated listing of programs available for school use through 1962. Obtain from Superintendent of Documents, Washington 25, D.C.

————. *The Use of Programed Instruction in U.S. Schools.* Washington, D.C.: U.S. Office of Education, 1962. Survey of programed instructional materials in thousands of the nation's schools. Obtain from Superintendent of Documents, Washington 25, D.C.

DETERLINE, WILLIAM A. *An Introduction to Programed Instruction.* Englewood Cliffs: Prentice-Hall, 1962.

LUMSDAINE, A. A., and GLASER, R. (eds.). *Teaching Machines and Programmed Learning.* Washington, D.C.: Department of Audio-Visual Instruction, NEA, 1960.

LYSAUGHT, JEROME P., and WILLIAMS, CLARENCE M. *A Guide to Programmed Instruction.* New York: John Wiley and Sons, 1962.

MAGER, R. F. *Preparing Objectives for Programed Instruction.* San Francisco: Fearon Publishers, 1961.

MARGULIES, STUART, and EIGEN, LEWIS D. (eds.). *Applied Programed Instruction.* New York: John Wiley and Sons, 1962. Descriptions of programs used by schools, colleges, industry, and the military.

MARKLE, SUSAN M.; EIGEN, LEWIS D.; and KOMOSKI, P. K. *A Programed Primer on Programing.* 2 vols. New York: Center for Programed Instruction, 1962. Guidebook for writing programs.

CHAPTER 7

Working with the Gifted

If you teach an ordinary mixed class, it is likely that you will face each year one or two very bright children plus several others who are somewhat faster learners than the bulk of the class. If you teach a group of students that have been skimmed from the intellectual top of the grade in a large school, you will probably have a quantity of these talented, very apt learners to deal with.

You are best prepared to succeed with them if you (1) recognize characteristics they usually possess, (2) recognize problems they typically face in school, and (3) know effective ways to care for their needs either in a mixed class or in a homogeneous group of pupils with above-average ability. Chapter 7 focuses on these aspects of teaching the intellectually superior.

WHAT ARE THE GIFTED LIKE?

Very bright children certainly are not all alike. Each has his own pattern of strengths and weaknesses, attitudes and interests. Despite these differences, studies show that the gifted as a group *tend* to have certain characteristics in common. As a result, we can construct a portrait of the typical gifted student. And with this portrait in mind, we are better prepared to know what we may expect from the very bright individuals in our classes. This, then, is the typical gifted child or youth.

Intellectually he is very curious and often asks "Why?" or "How do you know?" He learns readily how to search for causes and to draw sound conclusions. He tends to have a wide range of interests and knowledge in many different fields. He knows things which other children are unaware of. His memory is good, and he retains what he learns without much rote repetition. He often desires to do things differently, is creative, is inventive, and shows initiative. He may well be a clever planner and organizer. He is apt at applying his knowledge to new situations. He has well-developed powers of self-criticism.

Educationally he is accelerated in grade placement about 14 per cent above his age, but in mastery of school learning he is perhaps 40 or 45 per cent ahead. Thus his placement is two or three grades below his actual mastery of the curriculum offerings. He learned to read and talk earlier than his average classmates. He is superior to his agemates in all school subjects. This superiority is greatest in reading, language usage, arithmetical reasoning, science, literature, and the arts. His superiority is somewhat less marked in spelling, arithmetical computation, and facts of history and civics. (Terman *in* Witty, 1951.)

Physically he tends to be slightly taller, heavier, healthier, and stronger than the average child his own age.

Socially he tends to seek older companions. If his IQ is between 130 and 140, he will tend to be a better leader and have better social adjustment than if his IQ is above 140 or 150. If his IQ is above 150, he tends to engage in more solitary activities. He prefers more complicated games than the average child, and his knowledge of play and games is more like that of children two or three years older.

Emotionally he tends to be more stable than the average child.

Ethically he tends to be more trustworthy when under the temptation to cheat.

He may come from any race, creed, or socioeconomic level. (CESAA, 1958:76; Magnifico, 1958:5.)

As we cautioned earlier, not every gifted child will fit this composite sketch. But this picture of tendencies does give a general expectation that the teacher can start with when working with a very bright child. And the teacher's own observation of each particular bright child can tell in what ways he differs from the average. There are gifted children who have been born crippled. There are those who are very capable in some areas and quite average, or occasionally below, in others. There are those who are emotionally disturbed and others who are socially unbearable. Yet in general, the tendency is for the intellectually gifted to be blessed with advantageous social, emotional, physical, and ethical characteristics.

THE GIFTED STUDENT'S SCHOOL PROBLEMS

In general, very bright children must face the same variety of problems as their more average agemates. But certain kinds of difficulties are more likely to arise for the intellectually apt because they work in school systems geared chiefly to pupils of lesser abilities. Four of the more prominent of these problem areas involve (1) discrepancies between ability and achievement, (2) social and emotional rejection, (3) a dedication to exclusively intellectual activities, and (4) conflicts with adults.

Discrepancy between Ability and Achievement

If we can assume that it is desirable for each of us to succeed as well as we can, then the most serious problem of the gifted student is that too often he falls far short of his potential. When he is young he may have a curiosity and drive which enable him to speed ahead of his classmates intellectually. His ideas and questions can leap far ahead and dig deep, but the steady pace of the class is too slow for him. If no provision is made for him to exercise his potential and if he is not stimulated to do his best, he may well relax and get by as well as the average pupil by expending almost no effort. Later in life, when he needs good study patterns and the habit of searching diligently for solutions, he does not have them. He may have goals he wishes to reach, but he has lost the early training he needed in ways to use his abilities.

Case studies have revealed instances of gifted students who have never liked school. Their dislike is rooted in a distaste for routine drill over work they have already mastered. They rebel against problems that are too unrealistic or too simple for their intellectual talents. Their rebellion may take the form of neglect of routine work, a course of action resulting in low achievement, and perhaps failing marks. Or they may become aggressive, disturbing the class and embarrassing the teacher. This, in turn, may result in humiliating punishment before the class. So they dislike school. Ironically, it sometimes happens that neither they themselves nor their teachers recognize that these young misfits are really very bright and would have succeeded well under better learning conditions.

In other instances, if the gifted child's talents are not recognized through teachers' careful observations and tests, he may come to think of himself as perhaps a bit different from others, but he may not really recognize that he is potentially quite above average. Consequently, he may well set his sights too low for his ability and thereafter achieve at a modest level because he has never been encouraged to aspire to more suitable, higher goals.

Research on the gifted suggests that "if they are in an unstimulating environment or under emotional stress, they may exhibit a tendency to do well in non-verbal areas and poorly in verbal areas, since verbal ability seems to suffer first from these limiting conditions." (CESAA, 1958:3.)

The solution to these students' problems lies in early recognition of their potential through techniques described in Chapter 3 and suiting schoolwork to their ability level through administrative adjustments and through the kinds of classroom practices suggested later in this chapter.

Social and Emotional Rejection

Studies of bright children have shown that in general the gifted make above-average social adjustment. Perhaps this is partly because they are quick to recognize the way other people react to them, and thus they can learn more easily how to act in order to be liked.

However, good social adjustment seems more typical of bright children *up to IQ 140 or so* than it does of those considerably higher. Apparently a child can be too bright for easy social adjustment. His interests, fund of information, and insight may be so much more mature than his agemates' that he is bored with them, and they in turn cannot understand him. He may be impatient with their inability to catch on quickly to new ideas, jokes, and explanations, and he may express his impatience with a sneer that alienates them. Too, his more average classmates may be jealous of his obvious intellectual talents and may try to punish him through social rejection.

What help is there for the gifted child who is becoming neglected or rejected socially? Although a teacher is not a psychiatrist and cannot endeavor to remake a child's personality, sometimes measures can be taken that may improve the child's social acceptability. One possibility is to transfer a gifted child to a special class for fast learners where he can more readily find companions with interests and abilities similar to his own.

Another possibility is to introduce group projects in class so that a bright child can be placed on a committee with another one or two with above-average ability. This informal cooperation on a project gives children more opportunities to get acquainted with each other than is true in a class where each child sits and works alone at his own desk all day.

Some teachers have had success with pairing students up as partners for drill sessions (as on spelling tests or for mastering number facts). This provides more chances for interaction.

Class discussions sometimes help. That is, as more teachers are better trained in psychology, they can lead discussions of human relations. Young people frequently gain better insight into their own attitudes, as well as the social needs and social plight of others, if in class they discuss how we get along with others, what other people's needs are, what people's feelings are, and the like.

The discussion above has been based on the assumption that the gifted child should have friends, should have amicable social relations. It is assumed that the teacher is responsible for trying to bring friendships about. Although this belief is apparently sound in most cases, psychologists point out that there are instances of children who do not seem to want or need many friends among their agemates. These children immerse themselves in hobbies, in music and art activities, and above all in reading. Through reading they find a great variety of seemingly satisfactory companions. We do not know very surely how much personal friendship some children need for their satisfactory development. As in other areas of human behavior, there seem to be wide individual differences in this need. And we do not know to what extent books and individual hobbies really serve as adequate substitutes for social contacts or how often books are just escapes and second-rate compensation.

In the light of these considerations, it is well for the teacher to study the pupil's behavior carefully before pushing him into friendships. In this way the teacher estimates whether the pupil actually does need more companions. In some cases we should take measures directed at increased social contacts. In other cases perhaps we should not interfere.

Exclusively Intellectual Activities

All lists of goals of American education reflect our belief that everyone needs a "well-rounded" education. The well-rounded young man or woman is usually considered to be one who not only succeeds well academically but also has interest and skill in some physical activities, art, and music and is socially desirable.

In American schoolboy society, skill at sports is important. For the normal boy, physical prowess is one aspect of establishing feelings of masculinity and developing a satisfying image of himself. For girls, success in physical activities is less important.

Usually the bright child is well endowed for engaging in sports. But sometimes he rejects them, participates only when forced to, and may increasingly become a recluse. There can be several reasons for these cases of rejection of physical activities. One is that the gifted child is accustomed to learning with ease in the schoolroom, but on the ball field his learning may be slower, though as satisfactory as his agemates'. This slowness may exasperate him. Instead of persisting to overcome his difficulties, he retires from sports. Or, some gifted children have so many other interesting activities (reading, hobbies) that they have little time to play outdoors. Without practice, they fail to develop the skills needed for success and recognition on the playfield.

Again, as in the social-adjustment situation, we cannot always be sure about when we should leave the nonparticipating child alone and when we should take measures that cause him to join in games so he can gain the skill that brings satisfaction. In general, though, it appears soundest to assume that most young people will be happier if they succeed in physical activities, so we should make attempts to have them participate. If it becomes obvious that his continued unsatisfactory participation is so painful psychologically that

it is worse than never gaining physical skills, the pupil should probably be left alone to compensate for his lack of physical skills
through his intellectual successes. The older the boy gets, the more
difficult it is to begin developing his skill in sports.

Conflicts with Adults

As teachers, we are accustomed to the role of noting students'
shortcomings and pointing out ways for them to improve. But most
of us do not take kindly to the reversal of the role. The gifted student is particularly apt at remembering facts and at seeing inconsistencies in his teachers' arguments. Therefore he may often feel it
is desirable to correct teachers when they err. Since he is often better informed and quicker at solving problems than some of his instructors—especially in the upper grades—he may find himself correcting them rather frequently. This may well result in personality
conflicts between the chagrined, insecure teacher and the bright, aggressive pupil. Other adults, likewise, seldom appreciate being
corrected by children and adolescents. So the gifted child risks the
disapproval of adults unless he develops a sensitivity to their feelings and learns either to hold his tongue on certain occasions or else
present his suggestions in a manner that enables his elders to save
face.

Because of these characteristics of some brighter pupils, it has
been suggested (*Educational Policies Commission, 1950*) that the
teacher who will be most successful and happiest working with
gifted students is one who is not only a well-trained instructor in the
usual sense but has such added qualities as (1) superior intelligence,
(2) a rich fund of information, (3) versatility of interests, (4) an
inquiring mind, (5) unusual ability to inspire and stimulate, and (6)
freedom from excessive sensitivity to criticism. This rather special
person is the ideal one for the school to seek when choosing a
teacher for a special class of superior learners. But any teacher,
though he may not possess all these qualities in large measure, can
still serve the several gifted students he meets each year by adopting what might be considered a "desirable" attitude. That is, he can
strive to:

1. Admit that his gifted pupils have greater aptitudes and needs

for different and more challenging activities than those activities suited to their more average or slower agemates.

2. Control jealousy which he might feel toward the brightest pupils because they have extra talents.

3. Accept, without expressing resentment, the gifted child's occasional criticism of class procedures or his looks of disgust, but at the same time in personal contacts try to aid the bright child in recognizing the social desirability of being sensitive to others' feelings. Basically, it is the home's responsibility to help the superior learner develop social sensitivity and to accept the shortcomings of others. But sometimes a teacher who has gained the bright student's respect can talk with him privately about his abilities, his responsibilities for not injuring other people's feelings, and the wisdom of knowing when to speak up and when to keep quiet. The chances of his being happier in the future are probably greater if he learns not to offend too often by his greater knowledge and his ability to catch on to new ideas quickly.

ACTIVITIES FOR THE GIFTED

When specific activities are proposed for enriching the school program for the most apt learners, the complaint is often voiced by educators, "Those activities are desirable for all students. You shouldn't restrict them to the gifted only. Every pupil can profit from them."

Although this observation is true, it should be recognized that because the superior student learns faster and can handle more complex material at an earlier age, he has more time for a broader, deeper program. At the time when the more average student is still pursuing such necessary learnings as developing basic skills in arithmetic and reading, the gifted student who has already mastered these learnings is ready to move into broader fields. Even though these broader fields would also be desirable for the more average or slower student, they are not as necessary nor, often, as appropriate for his maturity level as are the more basic skills he is working on. Therefore, for the average student the enrichment learnings would be luxuries that would be taking up time he would more profitably spend on necessities. But for the gifted, the enrichment learnings provide him with an expanded education for which he is ready. Without the chance for the enrichment activities, he would simply waste his time in school.

Criteria for Selecting Activities

When seeking experiences to enrich the learning of apt pupils, the teacher needs criteria for determining which activities are appropriate and which are not. The writers suggest the following as basic guides.

Enrichment experiences for the gifted should:

1. *Carry the student toward important goals he has not yet reached.* That is, he should not be merely repeating more of the same kinds of mathematics problems he has already mastered. He should not be coloring outline animals in the workbook day after day. Nor should he be helping the teacher with routines (cleaning the blackboard erasers or correcting objective-test papers) from which he learns nothing that is worth while. He should not be assigned to teach slower classmates unless he is learning something desirable from this experience.

One of the most legitimate complaints about teachers' treatment of the apt students is that they too often exploit his skills or assign him to busywork which makes him either lazy or resentful. This does not mean that he should never be helping the teacher or classmates, but it means that when the pupil is asked to give such aid he should, in the process, be pursuing goals that are worth while for his own development.

2. *When possible, develop skills which make the student increasingly independent and able to work on his own.* It is clear that the teacher's goal, when working with children of all ability levels, is to make them as independent of the teacher as possible. But with the gifted this ambition needs even more stress, for the superior students are the ones most capable of learning to work on their own. By increasing their skills of investigating the world and reacting to it, the teacher helps them expand their learning faster and into more fields. For instance, at all grade levels the superior students can be directed to investigate a question or field of interest on their own and report their findings to the teacher or class. The teacher demon-

strates to these pupils efficient ways to find books and magazines, use source books like encyclopedias and atlases, outline their findings, and report them in a clear manner. In doing so, he expands their abilities to study other topics through use of the same research techniques.

When the teacher illustrates steps in scientific ways of observing and reasoning, he helps the gifted develop skills that serve them well in making science collections, doing experiments, and recording their observations of phenomena in a wide variety of fields. Also, if the elementary-school teacher provides guidance for the superior pupils to learn touch typing, the pupils have at hand another tool to use in producing neater reports, articles, scripts, and stories at a faster rate (and if necessary with carbon copies) than they could by handwriting.

Therefore, as the instructor offers enrichment experiences, it is well for him to stress skills of investigating and reporting that hasten students toward independent learning in a wider variety of areas.

3. *Not treat subject matter that is identical with what the student will be required to study a year or two later.* As mentioned in Chapter 5, many teachers do not know very clearly what is covered in social studies, science, literature and languages, and health education in the grades above them. As a result, when they choose enrichment activities they run the risk of furnishing the more apt students with work that they will meet in the regular course of study a year or two ahead. To avoid this waste of student time, it is desirable for the teacher to acquaint himself with the typical offerings in the content areas in future grades. With an understanding of what the pupils will meet later, the teacher can search out different topics for the gifted pupils in his class.

Examples of Activities

The remainder of this chapter consists of specific learning activities organized under the following subheadings: reading, creative writing, history and geography, other social studies, science and health education, arithmetic and mathematics, languages, home economics, industrial arts, business education, school activities and service, and activities and service outside of school.

In each of these subsections, no attempt is made to differentiate elementary from secondary, because gifted students by their very nature can succeed with tasks that spread over a broad range of years and grade levels. An activity that is suited to a bright ninth-grader may also be appropriate for an exceptionally brilliant fifth-grader. It is left to the individual teacher to inspect the suggested activities and to judge which ones might be best adapted to the needs of a particular gifted pupil or to a group of bright students in his own class.

Reading

Perhaps the simplest, yet one of the most profitable, ways to aid the rapid learner is to provide him with a continual supply of books and magazines. This may be done in several ways. The student may be given the opportunity to visit the school library when he has completed his regular work sooner than his classmates. Or the entire class may have a period when they all visit the library. It is also desirable to have a classroom library, which consists of a series of shelves or a reading table in the corner containing books borrowed in quantity each month from the central school or city library.

The teacher can use several different techniques for interesting students in these free-reading opportunities. One device is to make displays of book jackets on the bulletin board. Another is to provide an individual student with two or three books which the teacher thinks will interest him and which will challenge his level of understanding; the teacher suggests he look them over and select the one he likes. A third technique is the book comment. That is, when a student finishes reading a book he is asked to write a brief opinion of it on a card that is kept either in the library pocket of the book or in a special file. As a result, each potential reader has a series of his classmates' evaluations to inspect as he decides whether to try the book or not. A fourth technique is for the teacher to read aloud a passage from the book to the class or to a small group, to provide a taste of the volume's style and content.

Although the gifted tend to be avid, rapid readers, they do not always voluntarily read in a variety of fields. Therefore it is usually desirable for the teacher to urge them to expand their reading in new directions, providing a truly enriched education. One technique is to divide reading interests into a variety of areas, such as science, biography, adventure, sports, travel, history, recreation, and light verse. Another reading pattern might consist of animal stories, folk tales, tall tales, stories of boys and girls in other lands, and adventures from American history. The gifted student is to read books from each of these fields so as to develop a balance among them. To report his progress, he can construct a chart, perhaps illustrated, recording how he is filling out the pattern.

Reading breadth can also be stimulated through periodicals like *The Reader's Digest, Time, Newsweek, Coronet,* and *The Saturday Evening Post.* These magazines, along with such school publications as *Read Magazine* and the *Scholastic* publications, furnish the student a sample of a variety of subjects. The pupil can report to the teacher which of the articles interested him most, and the teacher or librarian can then suggest further sources of reading on these same topics.

During group or individual discussions of television programs and motion pictures which the students have enjoyed, the teacher can suggest to the gifted pupil books or magazines that treat these same topics. If the teacher himself does not know specific reading sources, he can request that the school librarian aid the pupil.

Often the teacher will find it appropriate merely to stimulate the pupil to read these books without having him report on them in detail. But in other cases it is desirable to help him expand his understanding and skills of expression by suggesting he react to his reading in a specific manner. This may be in the form of a written or oral book report or, perhaps, a conference with the teacher.

When book reports are called for, it is often best to furnish the student some suggested direction his reaction should take. The gifted child will probably profit most if he is not asked simply to relate the plot of the tale but instead to focus his attention on some aspect of literary works that apparently has not commanded his conscious attention heretofore.

For instance, to help the student understand matters of characterization more thoroughly, the teacher may ask him, before he reads the book, to use his reading to answer such questions as: "Which characters did you like best, and why? Which did you like least, and why? What techniques did the author use to tell you what each character was like; that is, did he do it through a direct description of the person, through the person's own conversation, through what others said about him, or through his actions toward others? Did any of the characters change during the course of the story, or were they the same kinds of people at the end as they were at the beginning? If they did change, describe in what ways, and describe the events which brought about these changes."

In other cases, the teacher may ask the student to compare two or three books on the basis of such questions as: Did the authors seem to have a lesson to teach in these books? If so, what was it? Which book had the most humor in it? What were the authors' ways of making the reader feel happy—sad—anxious? Which book do you think had the best ending, and why?

Sometimes pupils are interested in expressing their reaction to literature in a form other than a traditional book report. The student may wish to draw pictures to illustrate the most exciting events or the most interesting characters in the tale, and these can be posted on the bulletin board. He may wish to create several puppets that represent characters in the story and use them for playing out a series of scenes from the tale. Or he may wish to write a radio script portraying events in the book, and with a cast selected from the grade he can—after school or during the noon hour—tape-record the radio play for his classmates.

Enrichment activities in the field of literature may also be shared by a group of rapid learners. Several pupils may read a series of plays together, each speaking a given role in a manner that expresses as fully as possible the way the character would really act. Group reading activities may also be carried out with selections of poetry or with stories that involve dialogue. Some of these readings can also be presented as verse-choir selections, with the teacher demonstrating verse-choir technique and then turning over the direction to a student leader.

Creative Writing

Gifted children typically have active imaginations and enjoy the challenge of creative writing. With stimulation and encouragement from the teacher, they will eagerly reproduce their imaginings in a variety of forms. In the process they also improve their command of the mechanics of writing: spelling, paragraph structure, usage, punctuation.

There are many ways to stimulate creative writing. One is to read students the successful efforts of members of former classes or to suggest they read published stories, verse, and plays of other young people. (Applegate, 1949; Burrows, 1952; *Literary Cavalcade;* Mearns, 1929.)

For the student who feels he has nothing to write about, the teacher may use one of the following as a springboard. Offer three or four pictures from magazines and ask the student to write a story about what was occurring in one of the scenes. Provide the student with the first paragraph or two of a short story he has not yet read and suggest he finish the story; then compare his version with the original author's or with his classmates' versions. Read a short story up to the climax and have the students write the end of it. Suggest that the pupil think of two of his favorite television stars who appear on different programs and write a story which contains both of them in some adventure. Furnish a series of first lines and suggest that the pupil use one of them to begin his story. Sample first lines might be:

1. The two young men buckled themselves into their seats in the nose capsule of the rocket and listened for the count-down signal that came through the earphones.

2. Jane had looked forward to this Saturday evening for weeks. Now that it was here, she was a bit frightened.

3. Doris knew that her birthday tomorrow would bring a surprise, for her mother had warned her, "Don't dare go into the hall closet today."

4. The tall, blond boy stood on the crest of the hill and gazed down on the settlement in the valley below. The smoke from the last embers of the fire that had leveled the houses drifted slowly into the blue sky.

Another stimulus to broaden their writing interests can be provided by a list of character descriptions or by a list of descriptions of settings. Here are some sample characters:

1. Two boys, Bob and Larry, whose summer is spent on a ranch.

2. Mr. Dalrimple, a kindly-looking man with thick glasses, who owns a muscular boxer dog that accompanies him wherever he

goes. Mr. Dalrimple looks like a meek clerk from an office, but he is really a brilliant detective and a judo wrestling champion.

3. A family of rabbits: Father-Jack, Mother-Hop, and two children, Nimble and Stumble. As their names suggest, Nimble is very quick and Stumble is rather clumsy, but nice.

Descriptions of settings may include:

1. A large mansion in the country. Tall pine trees surround it. A tunnel leads from a nearby hidden dry well to a secret door in the cellar of the mansion.

2. A vacant lot in the city. Boys have cleared its center for a playfield and in one corner have built a clubhouse of scrap lumber.

3. An Indian tepee village in the hills. Nearby are woods where deer, bears, badgers, and beavers live. A river with swift rapids and a waterfall curves close to the village.

The gifted students themselves are probably the most fertile source of first lines and descriptions of characters and settings. Once shown how, they will eagerly create a variety of these writing stimulators for their classmates.

A person's motivation to write is usually strengthened by the knowledge that the product he is creating will be shared with others and, he hopes, admired. Therefore the teacher who provides outlets for writing efforts, and thus recognition for the authors, can expect more success with the creative writing program. A common pair of media are the school newspaper and the school literary magazine. But because one newspaper per school provides writing opportunities for only a limited number of authors, it is well for individual classes to start their own newspapers, literary magazines, or booklets. These can be in mimeographed form or can simply be typewritten and stapled to the bulletin board. The town or city newspaper also frequently welcomes pupil literary efforts. The gifted child can also compete in district and national literary contests, such as the *Scholastic Magazine* writing competitions that have stimulated high-quality creative work in many secondary schools in recent years. (See copies of *Literary Cavalcade*—address listed in suggested readings at the end of the chapter.)

Creative writing frequently serves for enriching subject-matter areas other than the language arts. The fast learner in a high-school mathematics class may be assigned the task of reading about the concept of the *personal equation* in science, thus learning of the 1796 incident at the observatory in Greenwich, England, where Maskelyne dismissed Kinnebrook, his assistant, for consistently observing the times of stellar transits almost a second later than he himself did. On the basis of this incident and others related to it, the student might create a series of dramatic scenes that would form an interesting tape-recorded radio program for his classmates. The field of history provides a never-ending source of such dramatic events that may be best developed by the gifted. Or the student may be asked to create a dialogue that might occur between two historical or literary characters who lived in different eras but who, in our imaginations, could meet and exchange views. The characters might be selected from any field: scientific, artistic, military, religious, or political.

History and Geography

Reading activities form the most important enrichment experiences in the area of history. While the bulk of the class is studying a particular era, the gifted student can supplement his learning in at least two ways.

1. By studying three or four other historical accounts of the same period and comparing them from the standpoints of agreement in regard to factual material, the kinds of facts included, the interpretation given to the facts by the writer, the interest engendered by each writer's style, and the books' illustrations. It is particularly useful if the student can read accounts of the same era of history which were written during different decades (such as one history written in the 1920's and another in the 1960's) or in more than one country (the British versus the American view of the American Revolution). Such comparisons help the student understand the important influence of the author's national, racial, religious, social, political and economic views in determining what enters into his historical accounts.

2. By reading novels, biographies, and short stories that depict a historical era. While studying the French Revolution, high-school students can read and compare *Les Misérables, The Scarlet Pimpernel,* and *A Tale of Two Cities.* While studying the American Revolution they can read *The Autobiography of Benjamin Franklin* or biographies of Washington, Jefferson, and the Adamses. An understanding of World War I and the attitudes toward war of the

1920's is deepened by a reading of *All Quiet on the Western Front* and the poems of Rupert Brooke and Siegfried Sassoon.

When historical events of the twentieth century are under consideration, gifted pupils can develop a series of questions to ask elder citizens in the community about their recollection of these events. For example, the student may ask parents and grandparents what roles they played during the depression of the 1930's and during World War II. What was their attitude toward the Japanese in 1942 and 1943? How did these war years affect the local community?

Such accounts help make history live and show pupils how apparently remote events changed the lives of their ancestors or their older friends and, therefore, have also influenced their own lives. These vignettes of local history can be collected in a notebook and placed in the school library as reference material for future classes.

Through research in the community library and interviews with older people and members of historical societies, students can also write accounts of other aspects of local history: the growth of fire protection, the development of principal buildings and landmarks, the sources of community leadership, the origins of street names.

Events of the past can be brought to life further through stories, dramas, radio scripts, and debates that pupils create. For example, a student can write a tale of how a great day in history might have been experienced by a schoolboy or girl who lived at that time. For special holidays, such as Columbus Day or Thanksgiving, gifted pupils can write skits to be acted out by their classmates. Two or three pupils can imagine they are citizens living at a given time in the past, with each of them holding a different point of view toward a current issue. Then they can prepare a debate or discussion that might have been carried on at that time, such as a conversation between a pro-British and an anti-British colonist in 1775.

For events of more recent history, students can make collections of *realia* to be exhibited in the school: old coins, firearms, clothing, kitchen utensils, drawings and photographs, schoolbooks, novels, and newspapers.

The gifted pupil is often well equipped to trace the development of a particular object, institution, or process from its earliest days to the present, because once his interest is captured he has the talent to immerse himself for long periods in a topic. He is also frequently clever in developing ways to present his research to others. Topic possibilities seem unlimited: costumes throughout history, military uniforms, means of transportation and communication, systems of law and forms of justice, sources of food, methods of warfare, exploration, developments in medical and health practices, the development of language and printing, changing economic systems, the growth of musical instruments and art media, and so forth. The report may be written or it may appear as a scroll or in the form of a pictorial time line that is drawn on a roll of shelf paper and pinned above the blackboard in the classroom.

History's inseparable mate, geography, also offers many enrichment possibilities. As the class studies the growth of the United States, a gifted pupil can accept the task of hunting up information about the composition of the country at different periods and constructing a series of maps that describe these changes visually. He can construct pictorial maps showing the products of various nations or of various parts of the United States.

Current events, such as the development of new nations in Asia and Africa, can also be better understood if time-sequence maps are drawn. The changes in the transportation systems or the growth of population in the local community can likewise be described through map sequences.

Small-group activities for the rapid learners of the class include the construction of large papier-mâché relief maps, the building of globes or planets with papier-mâché pasted onto balloons, or the collection of photographs describing different parts of the state, nation, or world.

An understanding of life in other countries can be broadened as the pupil creates illustrated scrapbooks, corresponds with foreign pupils (addresses available from the Junior Red Cross), writes to foreign embassies and travel agencies for free literature, interviews foreigners who live in the community or local residents who have traveled broadly, reads travel and adventure stories, collects stamps or postmarks or post cards or coins, visits homes or restaurants that specialize in foreign foods, and views television programs picturing other lands.

As a supplementary activity, the gifted can locate people who have lived in other countries and are willing to come to the school as resource persons. The students who make these contacts would be expected to prepare ahead of time questions that the class would like the visitor to answer, to ask the visitor to bring along objects that would interest the class, and to aid in exhibiting the pictures or *realia* that are made available.

Other Social Studies

Among the other social-studies areas that provide good opportunities for enrichment are intergroup relations, politics and government, economics and business, anthropology, sociology, and psychology. Although these areas frequently may not be met under these specific titles in the school curriculum, they are all commonly dealt with in some form at both elementary and secondary levels. The following examples suggest some of the possibilities related to them.

To better understand *intergroup relations,* gifted students can be asked to collect from newspapers and news magazines accounts of current examples of relationships between groups—accounts of cooperation as well as descriptions of conflicts. For a given incident of group relations, such as a labor strike or a pact between countries, the students can search out historical roots and can follow the development of the relationships over a period of weeks. The teacher can provide guide questions to promote understanding of the social psychology involved, including such questions as: What human needs are fulfilled by membership in these groups? What are the reasons given for the conflict or the cooperation between the groups? Do you think these stated reasons are the real ones? Who are the leaders of the groups? What role do they play for their groups? What techniques are the leaders using to pursue their goals? If a conflict is involved, what outcome would you predict?

While studying *government and politics,* gifted students can be assigned to visit city-council meetings, attend political rallies, and interview public officials about current political issues or about problems faced in their jobs. The results of these interviews can be cast in the form of written or oral reports. Election time provides a particularly good opportunity for students to collect information about candidates' backgrounds, voting records, and expressed attitudes toward election issues. This information can be compiled by a small committee in the form of charts comparing one candidate with another. A classroom or all-school mock election furnishes opportunities for small-group work centered on organizing support for a given candidate and publicizing his record through posters, debates, and descriptions of his stand on controversial issues. Gifted students can also play key roles in organizing elections for class and student-government offices.

A long-term individualized activity in the area of *business and economics* involves the superior student's assuming he has an amount of money to invest, perhaps $500 or $1,000. With the aid of textbooks and booklets on investment, he studies the possibility of returns on his money should he invest it in bonds, savings accounts, or stocks. He then pretends that he buys certain bonds or stocks, and he keeps a record of the weekly changes that occur in his investment. If several students carry on this financial stock-market game, they can compare the returns on their investments.

A group of students can further their understanding of economics by assuming they create a company, sell stock, and manufacture a certain product. They can then assume that their company succeeds in about the same way other corporations in the same field do, as reported on the stock market. They can pretend to carry out the same types of financial actions as corporations: investing in new plants, paying dividends, declaring stock splits, raising wages, and experiencing strikes.

The fast learners can also interview businessmen in their community to learn how they entered the particular business they are now in, to arrange excursions for the class, to learn what current problems the businessmen face, and in some cases to work for a short time in the business on an apprenticeship basis to gain personal experience with that type of organization.

Books probably provide the best enrichment sources in the area of *anthropology*. The gifted student can be asked to use encyclopedias and anthropology books to write a comparison of various authors' theories about such questions as: Where did human life begin? Did it begin through an evolutionary process, and if so what steps were involved? Why has one group of peoples advanced more rapidly than another in developing an industrialized civilization? Which of our characteristics in our society seem to be universal "human" nature and which seem to be learned characteristics that are not found in the same form in other societies?

In addition to pursuing *sociology* in greater depth through books, the advanced learner can apply what he has learned in his reading by making an analysis of his own community. For example, he can observe and write a report on the apparent social-class structure of the community and the symbols of class that are most obvious, the problems of youth, the marriage-divorce rate, the growth or control of crime and delinquency, and the changes in the citizens' sources of income in recent decades.

Novels showing the influence of social-class factors on individuals' lives make the study of social psychology more interesting. Typical writers in this area are John P. Marquand and Sinclair Lewis.

While studying such *psychological* adjustment mechanisms as repression, rationalization, projection, and fantasy, students can be asked to find examples of these devices in their own lives, in the actions of their acquaintances, and in television shows, motion pictures, short stories, and novels. Instances of neurotic behavior such as conversion hysteria, obsessions and compulsions, and phobias can be found in these same sources.

Science and Health Education

At all school levels, it is desirable for teachers to develop files of supplementary experiences in science for advanced learners. These activities can be organized according to the typical units or topics studied during the semester (such as electricity, volcanoes, atomic energy, sources and uses of minerals), so that when each new topic is met, the extra activities can be easily provided. Frequently it is convenient to maintain these suggestions on cards, each containing (1) the title of the activity or experiment, (2) the scientific principles it illustrates, (3) the equipment used, including helpful diagrams of the equipment, (4) the procedure for carrying through the activity, and (5) questions that the student should answer about the results or about what he has observed. (For many specific suggestions of activities to challenge the gifted student at the elementary and early secondary levels, see the suggested readings at the end of the chapter titled Science Activities for Superior Students.)

The possibilities for supplementary individual and group experiences in science are almost limitless. They include making collections, as of leaves and leaf prints, rocks and minerals, sea shells and other sea life, seeds, butterflies and moths, other insects, pictures of prehistoric animals, model airplanes, biographies of famous scientists, manufactured items at different stages in the manufacturing process (such as plastics), magazine articles on space travel, various types of fabrics, paint and dye samples, and models of different types of machines.

Individuals can develop their own herbariums, terrariums, and aquariums. They can experiment with growing plants under different conditions of moisture, light, heat, and fertilization.

The student can be encouraged to take and develop his own photographs, build his own radio and electric motors, and construct his own weather station and keep weather records.

Those who have a literary bent can be invited to write science-fiction short stories, or they can report on the science aspects of television shows they have viewed.

Scientists in the community may be willing to aid the gifted student by talking with him about their work, inviting him to observe them at work, recommending and lending appropriate books or magazines, or suggesting or directing individual experiments.

A group of gifted students can make a health survey of their homes, their school, or the community to note health hazards and to recommend measures that will improve conditions. Such studies may include analyses of the water supply and inspections of filter plants and sewage-disposal systems. An analysis of the food content of the typical student lunch eaten in the school cafeteria can also be carried out.

Small groups can search out the historical steps in the development of a given invention or a certain area of science and as a report can create an illustrated scrapbook or time line for the classroom. A group can also develop demonstrations or exhibits for the rest of the class.

In many communities, educational television courses in science are broadcast, often with college credit awarded to those who follow the course assignments and take the tests. Gifted high-school students can be urged to enter such classes, either unofficially or for advanced credit that can be applied later to their university records.

Arithmetic and Mathematics

The most apt students can be urged to find different methods or short cuts for carrying out arithmetic processes which they have already mastered in one form. For example, in adding a long column of numbers they can try hunting for groups of tens in the column and thus add by tens at a glance. Or the student can practice adding two or three columns at the same time.

Further insights into number relationships are provided by a comparison of various methods of computation, such as a comparison of these methods of subtraction: the take-away-borrow or decomposition method, the take-away-carry or equal addition method, the addition-borrowing method, the addition-carry or Austrian method, and the complementary method. (Otto, 1957:74.)

Each individual in a group of better students can create problems which he assigns to the other members of the group to solve. In the elementary grades, pupils can also develop number games and puzzles or can locate puzzles in reading sources from the library. Here are examples of two such puzzles or number tricks.

1. The student tells a companion: "Write in a column three nine-digit numbers. Now I will write two more nine-digit numbers under them and will add them very quickly."

The trick involves the following: In writing the fourth nine-digit number, write in the ones column (the furthest right-hand column) a number that when added to the corresponding digit in the first nine-digit number will make a sum of 9. Continue this same pattern until the fourth nine-digit number is complete. Then write the fifth nine-digit number by relating it to the second nine-digit number in this same manner (that is, the second and fifth digit in each column should equal 9). The answer is immediately obvious. It is the same as the third nine-digit number, but with 2 subtracted from the ones (the first digit on the right) and a 2 placed before the number on the left, making it a ten-digit number, as shown below. (Otto, 1957:88.)

$$
\begin{array}{r}
271,286,493 \\
427,865,492 \\
869,742,304 \\
728,713,506 \\
572,134,507 \\
\hline
2,869,742,302
\end{array}
$$

2. The student can gain practice in addition by solving the following "missing number" exercise.

"Supply the missing number in the blank squares so that each up-and-down column will add to 20."

9	6		5
9	8	7	6
5		4	3
	1	6	

At all grade levels, gifted pupils can search through supplementary arithmetic and mathematics books for real-life applications of the functions they are studying in class. They can also interview people in different vocations to learn the practical uses of arithmetic and mathematics in various walks of life. The reports of these interviews can be collected in a booklet for the classroom or school library.

Enrichment can also be provided by individual or small-group study of a topic related to the general field they are studying, such as searching out the history of numbers and different number systems, learning about and developing code systems, making maps of the school area or some portion of the community, organizing a school store which sells items needed by students, laying out a softball diamond or a football field, studying foreign money systems and reducing them to United States values, handling the planning for amounts of food and the transportation costs for class excursions, graphing the school enrollment for a period of years or graphing the records of sports teams, calculating the comparative costs of cash payment versus credit buying, keeping a record of the family budget for a month, figuring the annual per pupil cost of attending the local school, and interviewing utilities officials to learn how they compute costs to customers.

If calculating machines are available in the school office the gifted child can study their uses in adding, subtracting, multiplying, dividing, and deriving square roots.

Lloyd has suggested a variety of popular topics for the more advanced students in high school. These topics may be pursued either in a small classroom group of similarly gifted agemates or in a mathematics club.

The tower of Hanoi, illustrating geometric series, powers of two, and the binary system.

The Chinese Rings, a somewhat more intricate application of the same topics.

Linkages, of many types, illustrating numerous principles in classical and modern geometry.

Construction of conic sections, in a variety of ways, ranging from mechanical devices and paper-folding to projective geometry, and their important uses.

Applications to art, using mean and extreme ratio, the divine proportion and dynamic symmetry.

Applications to science, engineering, and industry.

Mathematics in music, including the harmonic mean, the equitempered scale based on $\sqrt[12]{2}$ and periodic functions representing simple and composite tones.

Proofs of Pythagorean theorem, using cut-outs and other devices.

Pi, developed historically, geometrically, analytically, by probability theory, infinite series, and most accurately by electronic computers.

e, the basis of natural growth, illustrated by continuous compounding of interest; its derivation by either algebra or calculus.

Crystallography and the study of regular solids.

Trisection of angle, its history and influence on discovery of conics and higher curves.

Elements of non-Euclidean geometry.

Measuring instruments and devices of all kinds, both primitive and modern.

Computing instruments and devices of all kinds, both primitive and modern.

Magic squares of different orders and kinds.

Mathematical games such as Nim, Chinese chess, and so forth, using the principle of powers of two.

Logic, or "thought" problems, involving deductive, or indirect, reasoning.

Mathematical recreations and fascinating problems such as Diophantine cases.[1]

Languages

Foreign-language study is usually related to enrichment for the gifted in one of two ways: (1) the apt student in the language class receives out-of-the-ordinary experiences with that language; (2) the gifted student is provided experiences in another foreign language that is not being studied by the rest of his regular class.

1. *Enriched experiences with the language class.* In the regular beginning language class, the teacher may provide additional experiences by assigning the fast learner to read passages or short stories in other beginning language texts whose basic vocabulary is similar to that of the text. In more advanced classes, simple articles from foreign magazines (or the foreign-language *Reader's Digest* versions) and newspapers may be offered the student from the teacher's file, simple short stories may be read, and travel brochures may be obtained from travel agencies and embassies for additional reading experiences.

To enhance listening skills, the teacher may furnish foreign-language recordings which the student can listen to alone through earphones. In cities which show foreign motion pictures, advanced students can be encouraged to attend. They can also be urged to listen to foreign radio stations.

Frequently someone in the community who speaks another tongue is willing to hold periodic conversation sessions with an interested, apt student, thus providing practice in both listening and speaking. Further experience with these skills is gained by a pair or trio of rapid learners who work up dialogues or brief playlets outside of school to present before their classmates. Either the students may

---

[1] Daniel B. Lloyd, "Ultra-Curricular Stimulation for the Superior Student," *The Mathematics Teacher*, November, 1953, pp. 487–489.

act out lines created by some other playwright or they may create their own dialogues. These dialogues may also be tape-recorded and serve as bases for self-evaluation of pronunciation and accent.

Reading and writing skills can be promoted by writing to pen pals in other countries. This may be conducted on an individual or group basis. That is, individual students can write to the nearest embassy or consulate of the nation concerned requesting names of pupils in their country who would enjoy corresponding. Or, through the same channel, the names of schools in the country can be obtained. The individual correspondence usually consists simply of the exchange of friendly letters. The group effort may involve the creation of an illustrated scrapbook which describes, in the foreign tongue, the local community, school, student activities, and student interests.

2. *A further foreign language.* Frequently, at both elementary and secondary levels, school officials wish to broaden the rapid learner's experiences by furnishing foreign-language work as an addition to his regular course. That is, in the elementary grades he may be placed in a small special class with gifted children from other sections of his grade or from a grade above or below him. In the secondary school, he may be assigned to study more than one foreign language.

When this decision is to be made, it is well for school officials to recognize that the relationship between the usual academic intelligence tests and language ability is not perfect. As Carroll has written:

It has commonly been supposed that foreign language aptitude is related to general intelligence. It may indeed be true that certain *kinds* of foreign language instruction place a premium on general intelligence, but my own research findings suggest this is not the case for courses taught with proper emphasis on speaking and hearing the foreign language. . . . Although gifted children *on the average* may do better in foreign languages, it is probably a mistake to select children for foreign language instruction on the basis of intelligence test scores. . . .

If children are to be selected at all, a short preliminary trial of language learning success would probably be the best presently available method. Children who can imitate foreign language sentences quickly and accurately are most likely to succeed. It would seem that foreign language learning ability is almost a special talent like musical or artistic ability (but independent of these, of course).[2]

If a student does show language aptitude, but no extra language is available in the school to care for this need, he may be able to carry out independent study either through the guidance of someone in the community who is willing to teach him individually or through following one of the language-learning programs available on phonograph records. Esperanto is proving a fine base for study of national tongues and also provides worldwide correspondence with students. (EANA, 1837 NE 49 Ave., Portland 13, Oregon.)

Home Economics

It is not difficult in home economics to suggest more complex, more challenging activities in the same areas as those in which the regular class is working. The gifted girl can be assigned to create more complex clothing designs or a more varied wardrobe, to prepare more complete meals, to plan a series of menus for a longer period of time, and to develop interior decorating designs for a larger variety of homes.

In addition, the faster learner may be given major responsibilities for planning fashion shows, dinners, and home-decorating exhibitions in which class members take part. She can make bulletin-board displays of new products which she has obtained through interviews with personnel of local department stores or supermarkets, and she can read the most recent magazine articles on such topics as child care and first aid and report these to the class. She can read the latest books on household budgeting, home finance, automation in the home, grooming, costumes, food preparation, and the history of women's styles.

Finally, she may profit from working part time in such places as a hospital diet kitchen, a dress shop, the dress-design department of a clothing-manufacturing company, the women's-page depart-

[2] John B. Carroll, "Foreign Languages for Children: What Research Says," *The National Elementary Principal* (May, 1960), pp. 13–14.

ment of a newspaper, or a testing laboratory of a food-processing plant.

Industrial Arts

The possibilities for enrichment in industrial arts are similar to those in homemaking. The most apt students can move into more complex woodworking and metalworking activities sooner than their classmates. They may be expected to repair more complex machines with the aid of manuals and factory diagrams under a minimum of instructor supervision.

They can develop a personal library of information on topics that interest them by writing to manufacturers for literature and by subscribing to trade magazines.

The gifted student can either plan excursions for the entire class or make visits by himself to manufacturing plants, craft and hobby shows, do-it-yourself exhibitions, automobile shows, and demonstrations of new industrial products. He may also work for brief periods in different industries to obtain an inside view of their operation and the work their personnel do.

Business Education

Likewise the rapidly advancing student in business-education courses can be challenged by part-time apprenticeship opportunities in business organizations of the community. But when the opportunities are requested, it is important that the cooperating employer be aware that the experience should be a valuable learning activity for the student, not simply a routine of running errands, keeping the office staff's coffee cups filled, or typing letters and running the mimeograph machine day after day.

Sales representatives for business machines are often willing to demonstrate the use of their products to a group of students who visit their offices. The gifted student can take the responsibility for planning such excursions.

The superior learner may also be encouraged to begin a small business himself to gain realistic experience. He may be in charge of the school store, become a dealer in paperback books for fellow students, or take orders for corsages for school dances.

School Activities and Service

Outside of the regular classroom study there are many opportunities for enrichment related to all-school activities or to services
the gifted student can perform for the class or school.

Publications such as the school newspaper, literary magazine, and
yearbook provide enrichment possibilities. The gifted pupil can
be encouraged to join organizations which can broaden his social
contacts and at the same time furnish him training in organizing
activities and in creating program ideas. Such groups include assembly committees, school-dance committees, Red Cross and cloth-
ing-for-other-nations drives, and those in charge of anniversary
celebrations, broadcasts over local radio and television stations, and
corridor displays.

School clubs of many types can be used to enrich the regular
program. The club has the advantage of drawing students who
have a concentrated interest and often special talent in a given
area. Typical kinds of clubs are those focusing on photography,
radio and television communication, mathematics, creative writing,
fashion design, wood carving, music composition, painting, weaving, crafts, leatherwork, ceramics, dramatics, verse-choir work,
modern dance, Spanish language, French language, German language, automobiles, stamp-collecting, international relations, travel,
motion-picture classics, new books, politics, chemistry, physics,
biology, botany, geology, astronomy, letter writing to foreign lands,
and public speaking.

As suggested earlier, the gifted student can often function as a
teacher aide. But when he does there is always the danger that he
will be exploited rather than provided with opportunities to develop himself. If the teacher is always careful to ensure that the
tasks the gifted pupil is asked to perform are truly worth while for
him, the pupil can profit from such experiences as the following:

1. Setting up and operating motion-picture, overhead, and slide
projectors.

2. Collecting a bibliography of suitable book and magazine materials in the library for a particular topic the class will be studying.

3. Selecting free-reading books on a variety of topics and on

different levels of difficulty to be borrowed from the main school library for use in the classroom library for a period of time.

4. Assisting in the school library.

5. Assisting in the school office.

6. Serving as host or hostess for visitors by greeting them at the entrance of the school, guiding them through the school, arranging for their lunch in the school cafeteria, and introducing them to teachers. This helps the student develop poise and courtesy.

7. Preparing scripts for all-school programs as well as arranging for publicity, ticket sales, rehearsals of the cast, and the smooth direction of the final production.

8. Taking responsibilities in organizing programs for parents, exhibits for Education Week or United Nations Week, and the collection of contributions for worthy causes.

9. Representing his class on the student council, where he gains experience in defining problems, proposing solutions, evaluating others' proposals, reaching agreement on action, and carrying out the action.

10. Acting as recorder for the school nurse during health examinations for younger children.

11. Serving as a chairman of a museum committee to collect, label, and organize objects donated to the school or lent for temporary use.

Activities and Service Outside of School

The gifted student is often well equipped to represent his school in the community. He may write articles for the local newspapers or radio stations about school events, serve as a member of discussion or debate teams, speak to luncheon clubs or women's groups about matters important to youth, or serve as a representative on interscholastic committees.

He can head up school groups that initiate worthy projects in the community. He can develop publicity for welfare drives, organize ticket sales for plays and concerts, help tabulate data from surveys conducted by adult organizations, and take a leadership role in such youth movements as the Scouts, Campfire Girls, 4-H Club, or Future Farmers of America.

The superior student can also be encouraged to visit or join clubs or cultural groups that include both younger adults and capable youths, such as model-airplane or railroad clubs, orchestras, choirs, drum corps, stamp or camera clubs, chess clubs, and public-speaking groups.

Adult education classes often furnish desirable enrichment opportunities. The apt learner should be informed of the courses offered in the evening by the public schools' adult program and by such organizations as the YMCA, YWCA, public library, educational radio and television stations, natural-history museum, and the community art gallery.

Correspondence courses, obtained either from colleges or from private schools, furnish additional possibilities for the rapid learner whose talents are not sufficiently challenged by the regular work of the school.

SUMMARY

To meet the needs of the few very bright or gifted students he will find in his class, the teacher should (1) recognize the characteristics that the gifted usually possess, (2) know what problems these students often face in school, and (3) know effective ways to suit schoolwork to their talents.

It is well for the teacher to develop a file of enrichment activities so there is always at hand a ready source of useful experiences which can be suggested to the gifted student. If such a fund of worthwhile activities is not available, there is the danger that the busy teacher will either ignore the rapid learner's special aptitudes or exploit him by assigning classroom chores that contribute nothing to his development.

SUGGESTED LEARNING ACTIVITIES

1. For the grade level or subject you teach or plan to teach, start a card file of specific enrichment experiences that would challenge the most apt learners in your class.

2. Interview a teacher to discover (a) what methods he uses to identify which students in his class have the greatest learning potential, (b) the problems he meets in working with these students, and (c) in what ways he adjusts classwork to their needs. Give your own estimate of the probable adequacy of this program.

3. Visit a nearby school that administers achievement-test batteries to students. Request the opportunity to inspect the achievement-test results of three superior pupils. After seeing where these pupils stood in each subject-matter area in comparison to percentile or age or grade norms, write a brief description of the patterning of each of the student's apparent abilities as reflected by his achievement. If aptitude- or intelligence-test scores are also available, write a comparison of the aptitude-test scores and the achievement-test scores to estimate whether each student's achievement is apparently keeping up with his apparent potential.

4. Survey your own community to determine what kinds of out-of-school enrichment opportunities are available to gifted students at the grade level you teach or hope to teach.

SUGGESTED READINGS

General References

Abraham, Willard. *Common Sense about Gifted Children.* New York: Harper and Brothers, 1958. Popular book for parents.

CESAA. *The Gifted Child: Another Look.* San Francisco: The California Elementary School Administrators Association, 1958.

DeHaan, Robert Frank. *Educating Gifted Children.* Chicago: University of Chicago Press, 1961.

Everett, Samuel. *Programs for the Gifted.* New York: Harper and Brothers, 1961. A case book in secondary education.

Fine, Benjamin. *Stretching Their Minds.* New York: E. P. Dutton, 1964. An approach to education of gifted children pioneered by the Sands Point Country Day School.

Fliegler, Louis A. *Curriculum Planning for the Gifted.* Englewood Cliffs: Prentice-Hall, 1961.

Freehill, Maurice F. *Gifted Children, Their Psychology and Education.* New York: Macmillan, 1961.

Gallagher, James John. *Teaching the Gifted Child.* Boston: Allyn and Bacon, 1964.

Getzels, Jacob W., and Jackson, Philip W. *Creativity and Intelligence.* New York: John Wiley and Sons, 1962. Explorations with gifted students.

Hildreth, Gertrude H. *Educating Gifted Children.* New York: Harper and Brothers. 1952.

Magnifico, L. X. *Education for the Exceptional Child.* New York: David McKay Co., 1958.

OTTO, HENRY J. *Curriculum Adjustment for Gifted Elementary School Children in Regular Classes.* (Bureau of Laboratory Schools, Publication No. 6.) Austin: University of Texas, 1957.

WITTY, PAUL. *The Gifted Child.* Boston: D. C. Heath, 1951.

Sources of Science Activities for Superior Students

BARKER, WILL. *Winter-Sleeping Wildlife.* New York: Harper and Brothers, 1958.

BARR, GEORGE. *More Research Ideas for Young Scientists.* New York: McGraw-Hill, 1961.

BEELER, NELSON, and BRAMLEY, FRANKLYN M. *Experiments in Science.* New York: Thomas Y. Crowell, 1955.

BILLINGS, HENRY. *Man under Water.* New York: The Viking Press, 1955.

FENTON, CARROLL LANE, and PALLAS, DOROTHY CONSTANCE. *Reptiles and Their World.* New York: John Day, 1961.

FREEMAN, MAE, and FREEMAN, IRA. *Fun with Scientific Experiments.* New York: Random House, 1960.

HAMILTON, RUSSELL. *Science, Science, Science.* New York: Franklin Watts, 1960.

HERBERT, DON. *Mr. Wizard's Experiments for Young Scientists.* Garden City: Doubleday, 1959.

LONGSTRETH, T. MORRIS. *Understanding the Weather.* New York: Macmillan, 1959.

MORGAN, ALFRED. *The Boy's Second Book of Radio and Electronics.* New York: Charles Scribner's Sons, 1957.

PARKER, BERTHA MORRIS. *Science Experiences—Elementary School.* Evanston: Row, Peterson, 1952.

PEARL, RICHARD M. *How to Know the Minerals and Rocks.* New York: McGraw-Hill, 1955.

SCHWARTZ, JULIUS. *Through the Magnifying Glass.* New York: McGraw-Hill, 1954.

SPERRY, ARMSTRONG. *All About the Jungle.* New York: Random House, 1959.

SWEZEY, KENNETH M. *Chemistry Magic.* New York: McGraw-Hill, 1956.

ZIM, HERBERT S., and SHAFFER, PAUL R. *Rocks and Minerals.* New York: Golden Press, 1957.

Stimuli for Creative Writers

ANDERSON, DONALD G. "Writers Are Made." *Elementary English Journal,* January, 1951, pp. 24–27.

APPLEGATE, MAUREE. *Helping Children Write*. Scranton: International Textbook Co., 1949.

BURROWS, ALVINA TRUET, *et al*. *They All Want to Write*. New York: Prentice-Hall, 1952.

Literary Cavalcade. A periodical for secondary-school creative writing published monthly by Scholastic Magazines, 33 West 42nd St., New York 36, N.Y.

MEARNS, HUGHES. *Creative Youth*. Garden City: Doubleday, Page, 1929.

CHAPTER 8

Working with the Retarded

America's faith in education and belief in human rights cause us to expect today that a suitable form of secondary as well as elementary education will be provided for all children and youth, except those few with the most marked mental and social deficiencies. Therefore it is not only the primary-grade teacher who can look forward each year to having a few retarded or slower learners in the regular class. Most junior and senior high-school teachers will also have some. And if a particular grade level of students is divided into several homogeneous sections, the teacher who is assigned the lowest section can expect to meet quite a number of the retarded.

As a result, most regular classroom teachers can profit from a better understanding of (1) the characteristics retarded learners often possess, (2) problems they typically face in school, and (3) specific teaching procedures that will help them learn most successfully.

WHAT ARE THE RETARDED LIKE?

The trouble with trying to discuss retarded learners as a group —and trying to give a clear picture that fits them all—is that they exhibit many individual differences among themselves. What we find to be true of some slow learners may not prove true of others.

It is sometimes even difficult to determine who belongs in such categories as retarded, mentally deficient, dull, feeble-minded, or slow learner, because persons relegated to one of these categories on the basis of one criterion may not belong in it on the basis of another. Therefore, it is important at the outset to inspect the matters of definition and measurement in more detail than we did in Chapter 3.

During recent years, the two most common criteria for determining levels of retardation have been the psychometric and the sociological.

The *psychometric* depends on intelligence tests for placing a person in a particular category. This was the criterion that formed the levels of intelligence discussed in Chapter 3 where we noted typical IQ groupings: 0 to 25 signifying the idiot, 25 to 50 the imbecile, 50 to 70 the moron or mentally handicapped, and 70 to 90 the borderline or slow learner or dull.

The *sociological* criterion focuses on the person's ability to manage his own affairs with ordinary prudence. The extent to which a person can fulfill this is typically judged through the use of personal observation, the compiling of a case study, and the use of social-maturity scales and projective techniques. The most famous of the scales in this area was constructed by Doll (1953) and titled the Vineland Social Maturity Scale. In general structure it is similar to the Binet-type intelligence tests, but it measures *social age* rather than *mental age*. For each age level, several common acts that signify social maturity are identified. For instance, the seven-year-old is expected to use a table knife, comb his hair, and participate in preadolescent play. At age fifteen, the scale lists such behaviors as communicating by letter, following current events, going out unsupervised, using spending money, and the like.

For the educator, both of these criteria are important. He can combine both psychometric and sociological data, along with evidence of success in school tasks, to form an *educational* criterion. This educational criterion focuses on the kind of school placement that will probably bring the best success to the child or youth.

It will be found that there is considerable correlation between where a child stands on one of these criteria scales and where he stands on the others, but the relationship is far from perfect. Some children with measured IQ's in the 60's will succeed better in schoolwork and in conducting their daily affairs than others with IQ's in the 80's. Some with IQ's in the low 70's will succeed socially very well, whereas classmates with the same measured school ability will be more successful in schoolwork but badly adjusted socially. Thus we again emphasize the importance of considering each pupil as an individual and of seeking information about him from as many sources as possible. In this way we learn his unique patterning of abilities, knowledge, ambitions, fears, and social background.

With these cautions in mind, we can still recognize that there are certain characteristics which retarded or slow-learning or mentally handicapped pupils often tend to possess in common. As we did with the gifted, we can construct from these characteristics a portrait of a mythical retarded student.

Intellectually the retarded pupil has more difficulty than the average one in seeing relationships between ideas and in reasoning logically. He is less likely to be curious or persistent in asking questions about things and people in his environment. He has more difficulty in memorizing. His language development is retarded, so that by the middle teens, when the average youth has 15,000 or more words in his vocabulary, the retarded youth may have no more than 7,000 words, and the dull or borderline teen-ager may have only 9,000 or so. (Ingram, 1953:25.) He is not skilled at self-criticism. Often he does not plan his work well, and he is much more likely to depend on the teacher for initiating an activity or for suggesting a next step in working than is the average pupil. He misunderstands directions more often. He has trouble predicting consequences and applying to one situation what he has learned in another. He is easily confused and easily distracted.

Educationally he continually faces difficulties and defeats. If he is now beyond the primary grades, we can expect that he may have failed at least one grade and so has been held back. He will have suffered his greatest difficulties with such tasks as reading, arithmetic, and reasoning in the social and physical sciences. He has probably gained considerably more satisfaction in music, art work, and physical education, where his performance is more like that of his classmates.

Physically he approximates the normal child. His height and weight are almost as great as his agemates'. The retarded learner has good general motor control, except in some extreme cases of physical disability. He can walk, run, and jump well. Control of the fine muscles for the hands and fingers is slower to develop.

Childhood speech defects tend to persist longer than in average children, especially with boys. Some investigators have noted that the slow learner is more likely to suffer from a variety of minor physical defects than is the average child. (Orr, 1955:107–108.)

Socially the retarded child prefers children of similar mental ability. He is sensitive and experiences feelings of inadequacy with more normal groups, and he senses his rejection by them. He is less likely to belong to clubs than is the average pupil. In adolescence he—and she—shows the same kinds of interests in the opposite sex as his agemates. He has more difficulty getting along with his classmates and his teachers.

The high-grade mentally defective children and borderline slow learners who are found in school more frequently come from families of low socioeconomic, intellectual, and educational levels. It is not clear whether the low mental functioning of these children is caused by inheritance or a depressed cultural environment. Probably both factors are operative. In contrast, idiots and imbeciles are found as frequently in families of high intellectual ability as in families of low ability. (Kirk, 1952:694.)

Emotionally the slow learner experiences fears, hopes, pleasures, sorrows, and an active fantasy life. He craves the acceptance of other people. Often he is not as stable emotionally as his better-endowed agemates.

Ethically he has more difficulties than do other children. There are probably several causes underlying this. His efforts to succeed in school and outside are more frequently frustrated than are those of other pupils, so he has more reason to copy from others' papers, to cheat, lie, and steal than does the average or superior student. He cannot predict the outcomes of his behavior very accurately, so often he does not realize the consequences of his acts. He may not understand regulations and laws or the reasons behind them, so he breaks them unintentionally. Since the retarded child is more likely to have come from a family that is lower than average on the economic, social, and intellectual scales, he may not have been taught to behave in a way that is acceptable to middle-class and upper-class teachers and pupils. And because he is not as bright as others, he may get caught more often at unethical behavior than will other children who are cleverer at sinning without detection.

Although subnormals in their teens and in adult life have several times as many court records as do normals, the large majority of the retarded who have had special training during school years will later have no trouble with the courts. Tyler (1956:373) concludes, "The results of a number of follow-up studies now make it abundantly clear that in spite of the handicap of low intelligence, as measured by our customary tests, the great majority of morons who have been given special training in school make good after they get out."

These, then, are characteristics which are common among retarded learners.

Before turning to the types of school problems that arise for such pupils, it is desirable to recognize that not all students who display some of these characteristics should be automatically relegated to mentally handicapped or dull or borderline ability categories. Sometimes the pupil is potentially capable enough, but some other factor is causing him to appear mentally retarded. For example, he may suffer from a psychophysical disorder like cerebral palsy which places limitations on his muscular control, so that he has great difficulty expressing what he thinks and understands (though it is true that many children with cerebral palsy are also mentally deficient). In other cases, a mentally capable child who is very emotionally disturbed will perform in school at a low level, misleading the observer into concluding that he is mentally retarded. Undiscovered physical disorders, like subnormal hearing or faulty eyesight, may result in similar false diagnoses of low academic potential. The ability of the child who has faulty speech or a gaping mouth caused by adenoids is also sometimes misjudged by the more casual observer.

Therefore, once again we see the importance of making a careful individualized evaluation of the pupil's abilities and liabilities through the use of various sources of information.

THE RETARDED STUDENT'S SCHOOL PROBLEMS

The retarded learner's most perplexing problems in school involve (1) a discrepancy between his ability and the expectations of the typical school program, (2) his feelings of worthlessness as a result of constant defeat, and (3) his need for more guidance and different activities than his classmates require.

Discrepancy between Ability and the Typical Program

Unless academic schoolwork is adjusted to the ability level of the retarded learner, he finds much of what the class studies to be very confusing. Even when the class meets something that the slow learner might grasp if he were given more time or a simpler explanation, he finds that the others have moved ahead to new matters before he has caught on to this one. So he tends to fall farther and farther behind.

The unhappy consequences of this discrepancy between student ability and the typical school program are many. The pupil's school life is strewn with defeats. He wastes days and days sitting through study sessions that are beyond his comprehension. He receives low marks and so fails to pass, with resultant embarrassment for himself and his disappointed parents. He does not have enough chances to learn the things he will really need in life, for he spends too much time vainly pursuing things that will only be understood by, and of use to, his more able classmates.

The obvious solution to this problem is for the school to suit the *goals* and *teaching methods* more to the student.

The goals usually stressed for the mentally handicapped are (1) occupational competence, (2) social adequacy, and (3) personal adequacy.

Kirk and Johnson (1951:118–119) have clearly specified the objective of occupational competence.

A mentally handicapped child should be trained in such a way that he will be able to support himself partially or totally in some productive activity. Occupational training, therefore, should begin when the child enters school and end when the child has been successfully placed on a job. . . .

Occupational training should not be thought of as specific vocational training. The positions in which the mentally handicapped will be successful later in life are in the unskilled and semiskilled activities. Success on the job is going to depend on getting to the job on time, personal appearance, manners, getting along with other employees and the employer, personal health, ability to handle money wisely, safety on the job, responsibility in following directions and carrying the task through to completion, and many other personal characteristics which are developed from early childhood. . . . Even reading, writing, and arithmetic are parts of occupational education since a child will require a minimum of the academic skills in order to read signs, simple directions, and possibly to communicate by means of writing even at a simple level.

The goal of social adequacy involves preparing the student to learn the personal habits which enable him to get along in a home, raise children, coexist with neighbors, and be an acceptable member of the community. Therefore school activities should stress working well with others and having a degree of respect for their rights and desires.

The matter of attaining personal adequacy will be considered under the second of the major problems the student faces in school: feelings of worthlessness.

As we inspect these objectives for the mentally retarded, it becomes clear that much of the academic learning expected of the normal pupil does not contribute to these goals. So if the retarded learner cannot be placed in a special class, the regular classroom teacher who has him in the group will be expected to adjust both goals and teaching methods (which are discussed in the final section of the chapter) to the pupil's needs.

Feelings of Worthlessness

One of the most serious results of the slow learner's being defeated by the regular academic program is his developing feelings of worthlessness and a lack of self-respect and confidence.

Smith (1954:14–15), as a teacher of slow learners, has written:

When a child comes to my class, if he has had any schooling at all, I know certain things about that child:

He has been the despair of his mother.
He has been the shame of his father.
He has attended too many schools.
He has been shunted from class to class.

He has been thumbed down by too many teachers, whom I cannot blame too much, since most teachers have little actual time, however deep their dedication, to devote to individuals. . . . They kick the dull normal child around, because they have no time to do otherwise.

Kanner's discussions of the child's feelings about himself focus primarily on parent attitudes and how they affect the student.

There is no getting away from the fact that the knowledge of an off-spring's scholastic and social incompetence is a source of perpetual heart-ache. One cannot possibly expect unmitigated Pollyannish acquiescence. But different people react differently to the irreversibility of unpleasant realities. . . .

There is, fortunately, a group of persons who, although they cannot be expected to rejoice over their child's shortcomings, have a healthy capacity for maintaining a warm relationship with him. They neither reject nor overprotect him, but try to assess the extent of his abilities and limitations, and make realistic provisions for his education and his future. They can be helped to follow a program best suited for the needs of the individual child, whether in an ungraded class or in a residential school. They keep their plans in reasonable balance with their economic resources, with their standards of living, with the needs and feelings of their healthy children. . . . An exceptional child reared in such an atmosphere has a good opportunity to accept himself without shame and guilt.

But there are parents who insist on playing ostrich and bury their heads in the sand in order to convince themselves that what they do not see does not exist. This attitude is observed most frequently in fathers and grandparents who do not have the constant care of the child. They go around assuring themselves and others: "There is absolutely nothing the matter with the child. . . ."

Even greater inroads on the child's peace of mind are made by those who, though aware of his limitations, try to change the decree of Nature, not infrequently with the connivance of ignorant pseudo-Joshuas. . . . Tongues are clipped, tonsils are evicted, endocrine extracts are administered, vitamins are prescribed, glutamic acid is given—all to "make the child over." Tutors are engaged to "brighten him up," and he is generally made the victim of numerous scientific, fruitless, and useless procedures. Thus the search for some miracle takes the family on an extended shopping tour among physicians, psychologists, chiropractors, and others, distrusting the truth when it is offered and grasping at any straw, however fragile and hollow. And meanwhile, the parents are making the child miserable through their constant corrective efforts to mend the unmendable. The child . . . cannot help being crushed, defeated, unappreciated, and either pathetically unhappy over his inability to please, or clumsily rebellious against his tormentors.

There are, lastly, those parents who cannot forgive their child that he is not as they want him to be. The child is met with hostility, open and unvarnished.[1]

Although a single teacher cannot hope to remake the personality of a pupil who has developed deep-seated feelings of worthlessness —or to make over his parents—there are several measures that can be taken to improve the situation to some degree.

The first is to adjust the program more to the pupil's ability so that he can succeed at learning and thus have a feeling of accomplishment.

The second is to use types of rewards attainable by the slower learners as well as the faster ones. As suggested in Chapter 5, too often the kinds of rewards that have been furnished in school can be achieved only by the best students—such as high marks, gold stars, listing on the honor roll, membership in the honor society, scholarships, and prizes. Therefore the positive motivation for working hard toward school goals is realistic for only the best students. But if each student is to have satisfaction and a feeling of accomplishment, a type of reward that can be adjusted to each pupil's level of success is needed. The most useful is verbal praise. For instance, the teacher can say to a sixth-grade girl who has finished copying a personal letter she created, "Jane, I want to show you this other copy of a letter you wrote at the first of the school year. Just see how much better this one you are now finishing is compared with this earlier one. The ideas are clearer, the sentences are better, and it's much neater. That's good progress."

Or the teacher of an arithmetic class can say, "You've mastered the way to solve these percentage problems. That's good. There were only two careless errors on the paper. Now we'll go to work on this other kind of problem you've had trouble with, where you figure out how much interest you pay when you buy things on installment plans. I have some problems on this mimeographed sheet that you can practice with, so you'll be able to do this kind accurately, too."

Such techniques of verbal evaluation serve as good motivation

[1] Leo Kanner, *Helping Parents Understand the Exceptional Child* (Langhorne, Pa.: Child Research Clinic of the Woods Schools, 1952), pp. 21–28.

for more than one reason. (1) They help define for the students the kinds of behavior that are expected and approved in the school. (2) They fulfill the pupil's needs for approval in a manner that encourages him to develop additional worthy skills and knowledge. (3) Unlike grades, personal approval is not limited to the mention of success in academic subjects alone but is used to commend behavior in all areas of living. (4) Most important for the slow learner, not only the students with great talent receive praise, but those of little talent receive mention for their minor successes.

A third related measure that can be taken to improve the child's image of himself is for the teacher to accept him emotionally. A smile from the teacher, a pat on the back, and a friendly word often add to the student's realization that he is an acceptable person in the teacher's eyes. This realization helps make him more acceptable in his own eyes.

A fourth way to aid the pupil is to enlist his parents in a coordinated effort of home and school to suit work to the pupil's abilities and to accept his abilities realistically. As the description of some typical kinds of parents cited earlier suggests, this task of establishing a good cooperative relationship with the home will be more difficult in some cases than in others. Occasionally, deep-rooted negative parental attitudes will make a satisfactory relationship impossible. But most fathers and mothers will profit from periodic conferences which the teacher arranges. The conference functions in several ways for the teacher. First, it enables him to make an estimate of the parents' attitudes toward their child's retardation. Second, it enables the teacher to report to the parents concerning the pupil's school progress and any problems he may be facing which they should know about. In discussing the child's tested abilities and progress, it is usually best not to quote IQ scores or percentiles which typically the parent cannot interpret accurately. Rather it is usually more meaningful to give a rough approximation of the grade level at which the pupil is working or the typical age level which his ability or school progress represents. Exactly how far to go in explaining the child's progress, and in what terms this report should be couched, depends somewhat on whether the parents have a receptive or belligerent attitude toward their child's retardation. The teacher must make this judgment as he talks with them. A third function of the parent-teacher conference is that of providing an opportunity to make a cooperative plan of action for the future which is designed to ensure more consistent treatment of the slow learner both at school and at home.

Need for Teacher Time and Different Methods

No one in the classroom needs more personal guidance from the teacher than the retarded pupil and the mentally handicapped one. Whereas the gifted student can often progress well on his own after a brief explanation of an enrichment activity by the teacher, the slow learner needs more frequent and simpler explanations. He learns by more gradual steps, and each of these steps may require a careful explanation by the instructor.

The typical teacher is usually busy enough trying to help the more average bulk of the class. This leaves too little time to give the slower learners all the help they need. In addition, the regular classroom teacher often does not know what types of activities best suit retarded learners. Hence many of the retarded simply sit through much talk that is over their heads or do busywork that is designed mainly to keep them out of mischief. One solution for this is the establishment of a special class for the retarded, containing a limited number of pupils. But this is not a complete solution. Most regular classroom teachers still find themselves dealing with some students with below-average ability. The suggestions for teaching the retarded learner contained in the rest of this chapter are intended to aid the regular classroom teacher in meeting the needs of the retarded.

TEACHING THE RETARDED

In discussing the teaching of retarded learners, we shall consider first some general principles, then specific procedures for use in different subject-matter areas.

General Guidelines

Success in teaching slower learners will usually be greater for the teacher who bases his procedures on the following generalizations.

The goals the student is to pursue should be concrete and specific. Exactly what objective he is to reach, and why it is a good idea to work toward this, should be made very clear to him. Abstract values and general, long-term aims have much less meaning and appeal. He needs to see how the intended learning will pay off for him in his daily living.

He has trouble understanding abstractions and words whose meanings he has not personally seen or experienced. So it is important for the teacher to relate the retarded student's learning activities to his immediate environment. Constant use of audiovisual materials other than reading matter will better ensure his understanding. Models, real-life objects, films, pictures, and field trips suit him well. He usually profits more from experiences which involve his doing something concrete, such as using materials or building something or operating tools, than from having something described.

Learning Activities

The remainder of this chapter consists of specific learning activities or recommendations organized around the following topics: reading, arithmetic, social living and social studies, science and health, speaking, writing and spelling, art and industrial arts, and music.

Reading

The slow learner develops reading ability in much the same way as do other children but at a slower pace. Teaching procedures are basically the same but differ somewhat in emphasis.

Of the different indicators of pupils' ability (such as the IQ, MA, and special tests), the mental age is the most useful guide to what reading level and reading materials are most suitable for a given pupil. Kirk and Johnson (1951:254) have furnished the following guide to aid teachers in judging the ability level of retarded learners.

(1) Children with chronological ages seven to nine and with mental ages of four to six:

  (a) Have not begun to read.

    (b) Should be showing interest in reading, in books, and in pictures, in the interpretation of pictures, labels, their own names, and so forth.

    (c) Should be engaging in an intensive reading readiness program.

(2) Children of chronological ages nine to eleven and with mental ages of five and one-half years to seven years:

    (a) Should be having an intensive reading readiness program with incidental reading of charts, signs, labels, etc., if readiness is not adequate.

    (b) Should begin reading stories of their own experiences from the board and from charts if readiness is established.

    (c) Should be interested in drawing pictures, interpreting pictures, and reading and writing stories about these pictures.

    (d) Should be able to make booklets of their own stories that they have told and which they have read from charts.

    (e) Should begin to read pre-primers, primers, and simple books.

(3) Children of chronological ages eleven to thirteen and with mental ages of seven to eight and one-half years:

    (a) Should be reading first- to third-grade material with adequate understanding.

    (b) Should be grouping words and phrases into thought units, but are slow in reading.

    (c) Should be developing a method of word recognition and should be capable of recognizing new words from context clues, phonic analysis, and so forth.

    (d) Should be interested in reading simple books for information and pleasure, and engaging in out-of-school reading such as newspapers, directions for games, and projects.

(4) Children of chronological ages thirteen to sixteen with mental ages of eight and one-half to eleven years:

    (a) Should be utilizing reading for many activities and using books from third- through fifth-grade level.

    (b) Should be using dictionary, telephone directory, library, and reading newspapers and maps.

    (c) Should have increased vocabulary and fair comprehension with independent methods of word recognition.

    (d) Should be spontaneously reading for information and pleasure.

Reading Readiness. The first stage of reading, as suggested above, involves developing reading readiness. One basic requirement for readiness is sufficient mental maturation. Although in general this is produced only through the internal growth of the child and so must be waited for, there are school activities that can bring this maturation to focus earlier than if we simply wait and do nothing.

If a pupil is to get meaning from reading, he must first recognize that the words he sees refer to something he knows in his own life. Therefore, by furnishing the child with many concrete objects and personal experiences, the teacher or parent is building a background of meanings which help make reading possible. These experiences can be provided through excursions or field trips, objects or animals brought to class, television programs or films, picture booklets and scrapbooks, and the development of projects (such as making a school garden or classroom store, building model villages, building papier-mâché relief maps, and carrying out plays in the classroom).

Another essential of reading readiness is the recognition by the child that certain scribbles or marks—that is, written and printed words—symbolize meanings and spoken words. This recognition can be hastened by labels on items in the classroom, such as a one-word title under a picture or labels on the free-reading table, on the drawing-paper shelf, or on the rack that holds painting smocks.

A desire to read can be stimulated in several ways. One is for the teacher to read aloud to the class. Another is by providing books and magazines containing both interesting pictures and interesting reading text for children to browse through. Still another is by furnishing games that involve some simple recognition of words as one element of play (such as bingo-type games based on simple words rather than numbers). Of course, for the retarded child in the regular classroom a considerable stimulus to read has already been furnished by his classmates' more advanced success in reading.

Any progress the student makes in other language areas, as in speaking and understanding spoken language, also prepares him for reading. Therefore opportunities to express himself in conversations with the teacher, in social activities like school parties or games on the playground, and in simple classroom dramatics are desirable.

Prolonged Beginning Reading. When it becomes apparent that the pupil is ready to begin simple reading, the teacher can follow the basic patterns for teaching beginning reading that are described in manuals accompanying any of the good developmental reading series. But in using a basic pattern of activities, some adjustments must be made to suit the work to the retarded learner. From his standpoint, the reading materials prepared for average children have two major shortcomings.

1. The pace at which new words and more complex sentences are presented is too rapid for the retarded. The slow learner cannot remember the vocabulary presented at a rate suitable for his more normal agemates. Therefore he will need more review of basic words, will profit from the use and reuse of workbook material, and can grasp vocabulary more securely if a selection is read more than once. However, simply reading the same stories over and over is not enough. The teacher needs additional new material that is at the same level of difficulty so the slow learner has much practice but does not become bored in the process. Therefore, it is well to have in the classroom the primers and beginning readers from several different publishers' reading series. When the pupil has finished one first reader or several units in it, he can be given another first reader from a different series that contains substantially the same vocabulary load. Supplementary books in social studies and science with the same basic vocabularies are also available.

2. When the reading difficulty of a book is suited to the reading ability of the slow learner, too often the characters and subject matter of the stories are inappropriate to his interests and chronological age. The activities of Dick and Jane and their little friends in first or second grade are not particularly appealing to a ten-year-old or thirteen-year-old. Thus the teacher is often hard pressed to find reading matter of low difficulty level and high interest level for the retarded reader. In recent years, an increasing amount of such materials has been produced. Some, like the Rochester Vocational Series (Syracuse University Press), have been designed specifically for the needs and interests of teen-agers whose reading skill is still at the primary level or slightly above. Others are stories written in a simple vocabulary but with an appeal for a wide range of interest levels. When a pupil is past the first stages of beginning reading and has some sight vocabulary at his command, easy comic books can capture his interest in a variety of reading matter that most of his agemates eagerly consume.

Whenever possible, the slow-learning pupil in the regular classroom should be given material treating the same kinds of topics being read by his classmates but at a simpler level. For instance, in the area of science the unit-text pamphlets published by Row, Peterson (Evanston, Illinois) each focuses on a particular science topic, but different pamphlets are of different levels of difficulty. The slow learner constantly faces the realization that he cannot do so well as his classmates. Whatever can be done to have him successfully study the same topics as the others will help develop his confidence and his feeling of belonging to the group.

Advancing Reading Skill. As pupils advance beyond the stage of beginning reading, they need continual work on methods of word recognition (phonics, structural analysis, judging meaning from context) and careful guidance in understanding more complex reading materials. The teacher will find his efforts more successful if he recognizes that the retarded reader:

1. Needs more simplified and detailed explanations of what he is to do. Some of the directions in workbooks and in teacher-made exercises will be hard for him to understand. He should try the first one or two items under teacher guidance before he is set to work on his own. This better ensures that he knows what he is doing.

2. Profits from more oral reading. Many slower readers need to vocalize what they are reading in order to comprehend it well.

3. Tolerates repetitive or drill work more readily than his more able classmates and profits from such repetition.

4. Lacks initiative and therefore must have his purpose for reading carefully explained.

5. Is easily discouraged in reading activities, so the material should be easy enough to ensure success. Otherwise his defeats in trying to read will often result in an emotional rejection of reading.

6. Often profits from carrying out some physical motor activity in relation to what he has read, such as acting out a portion of the story, constructing a model of the African village, or drawing a sketch of the Indian camp.

7. Profits in the secondary school by reading materials that will be directly useful to him in his life after school, such as reading advertisements, newspaper stories, directions in shop manuals and cookbooks, directions for mixing paint or for sewing a simple garment, application forms for jobs or a driver's license, and easy magazine articles.

Seatwork. The regular classroom teacher will not have much time to dedicate to the one or two most retarded readers in the class. They must be expected to work at their seats a good part of the time while the teacher is engaged with other groups. Useful types of seatwork that direct the pupil to read for understanding include:

1. Workbooks that accompany reading series, with the understanding that the child cannot simply be turned loose on an exercise but needs a clear explanation of what to do before he begins.

2. Drawings the child can create to illustrate a story he reads.

3. Reading books which are of a difficulty level below that which is currently considered his work level in reading. The teacher should not shame the pupil by saying, "Oh, that's too easy for you" or "That's a little child's book" if the pupil willingly tries to read it. The pupil should be encouraged to read as much easy material as possible.

4. Sentence-completion exercises which consist of mimeographed portions of stories already read but with certain words omitted. The child's task is to insert the proper words.

5. Games that are useful in building word recognition and phrase reading, such as the Dolch series of games and flash cards (Garrard Press, Champaign, Illinois).

6. Matching pictures from magazines with a series of words or appropriate titles typed by the teacher or copied from the chalkboard by the student.

Sometimes children of similar ability can work in pairs to drill each other with flash cards on word recognition and phrase reading.

Such a program as this can carry the child toward the goal of being able to read basic materials that will be important to him in his daily life. The program does not pretend to focus on complex concepts, remote times, or remote places and peoples.

Arithmetic

As with reading, the retarded child will be ready to learn arithmetic later than his agemates, and he will progress more slowly. The fact that retarded children have trouble understanding general principles and applying them to new situations becomes important in planning their learning activities in arithmetic. The slow learner needs more time working with concrete objects (such as blocks, beads, abacuses, measuring cups, rulers) and semiconcrete items (such as pictures of groups of cars, horses, pints of liquid) before he can handle these quantities adequately on the symbolic number level. He will need to spend more time counting on his fingers than will his more apt classmates. Therefore, the teacher needs to provide more concrete situations for a longer time in teaching the meaning of number as well as in teaching fundamental number processes (adding, subtracting, dividing, multiplying).

In planning the kinds of goals the slow learner should pursue, we should keep clearly in mind what he is going to be doing with quantities in his life. Arithmetic programs for average and superior learners usually endeavor to provide the pupil with computational skills needed in everyday living and also to furnish a basis for the more abstract thinking needed in the algebra and geometry they will meet in high school and beyond. The typical arithmetic program also tries to show the student various ways to arrive at solutions so that a sophisticated understanding of number and quantities is developed. The goals for the slow learner's program need to be more modest. All his work should focus on number concepts, computation, and measurements he will need as a family member and as a worker in a nonskilled or service occupation. Studies of the problems typically met by adults in daily life have indicated that the average citizen's needs are well cared for if he has understanding and skill with:

1. Time concepts: minutes, hours, weeks, months, years.

2. The nominal use of numbers, such as house numbers, room numbers, telephone numbers.

3. Ordinal use of numbers, such as first, second, third.

4. Whole numbers and a few common fractions representing quantities, along with the ability to count, add, subtract, multiply, and divide them.

5. Money values, because the greatest number of adult daily problems deal with the buying and selling of goods.[2]

6. Linear measures (inches, feet, yards, miles), liquid measures (pints, quarts, gallons), and weights (pounds, tons).

[2] G. M. Wilson, *A Survey of the Social and Business Usage of Arithmetic,* Teachers College Contributions to Education, No. 100 (New York: Teachers College, Columbia University, 1919).

7. Simple ratios.

8. Some arithmetical and mathematical terms.

The program for the slow learner should aid toward developing these kinds of understandings and skills with their use in specific everyday problems that the pupil has already met or can readily understand in his environment.

As with reading, the mental age of the child is perhaps the best single guide to what types of arithmetic learning he is able to handle. Kirk and Johnson (1951:292) have furnished the following estimates of arithmetic readiness:

With a mental age of seven to eight years, a child should be able to recognize, write, and relate symbols to 100, tell time, have a concept of the ordinal numbers, know all the addition and subtraction combinations not requiring carrying or borrowing, use inches, yards, feet, cents, and the calendar for names of the months, names of the days of the week, and the date, form groups of objects (as a basis for division and multiplication), and use the fraction ½ correctly.

At mental ages of eight to nine years the children should learn to understand money values through one dollar (including ability to make change), and identify larger quantities, use the fractions ½ and ¼, carry in addition, borrow in subtraction, and do simple multiplication and division.

The sequence of teaching arithmetic concepts and skills to the retarded is the same as to the normal child. Therefore the upper elementary-grade teacher can find a teaching plan and a quantity of practice materials by securing the primary-grade textbooks and workbooks from several of the leading textbook publishers. The junior-high teacher can likewise turn to upper elementary-grade arithmetic texts and the accompanying teacher's manuals for aid.

In addition to the regular systematic teaching of arithmetic by itself, it is well for the teacher to take advantage of quantitative problems that arise during the school day and have the students solve these. In science projects, arithmetic problems are common. Distances and amounts of people, houses, and products are dealt with in the social studies. Art and craft activities involve measurements. Planning class parties, making school posters, or collecting contributions furnish further opportunities. Simple problems in these areas can be given to the retarded learner to figure out as part of his arithmetic study. Such problems have the advantage of being practical, immediate ones, the kind that are best understood by the child of lower mental ability.

Social Studies and Social Living

A *social studies* program is often said to aim at helping the student understand his social world: his community, his nation, the people of other lands, and conditions in the past that have led to the varied forms of social development found today.

A *social living* program is often said to focus on changes in the pupil's personal conduct with the people he meets daily. It concerns his adjustment to his immediate social environment.

Both these areas are accepted today by most schools as being their concern. But in the case of the retarded learner, the greater focus is on the second.

Cause and effect in history, struggles between nations for power, ideological differences between governments, and other matters remote in time and place from the pupil's daily experience tend to have little meaning for the retarded student. He is more concerned with how to find his way around his own community, how to understand people and be understood by them, how to find a job and keep it, how to get to nearby places, how to be liked and how to make friends, how to find good recreation, where to buy things, and how to get the most out of money.

For the very retarded student, the social-living program can well become the sole program. For the borderline or higher mentality, more social studies focusing on things farther from his immediate life are reasonable, though the stress is still more on the immediate social relationships in his own life.

Keeping in mind this concept of a social-living emphasis, we shall illustrate suggestions for teaching under three different classroom conditions: (1) a homogeneous class of slow or retarded learners, (2) a heterogeneous class in which all students are being taught as one group, and (3) a heterogeneous class which is divided into subgroups.

A Homogeneous Class of Slower Learners

In classes composed entirely of rather slow learners, the two most typical ways to adapt social studies to their level are (A) accepting the school's general course of study which was designed for the average pupils and altering the methods of teaching so the material better suits the less apt ones and (B) replacing the usual course of study with objectives and material suited specifically to the needs and abilities of the less apt.

A. *Same Goals, Different Methods.* We can illustrate one pattern of adapting the regular course of study as we view a junior-high class of slower learners who are expected to pursue the same general goals of American history and citizenship as those outlined for the average and superior students of the grade. By the end of the year, the pupils are all expected to know the main characteristics of the American Constitution and Bill of Rights, the causes and progress of the American Revolution, outstanding political developments and personalities of the nineteenth century, and something of current national and international events.

To adapt work to his students, the instructor of the slow learners has made two major adjustments in the plan suggested for the grade. He has selected a relatively few events and people of these periods on which to concentrate, and he has substituted other methods of communication for the textbook reading which the higher-ability classes are doing.

His procedure can be illustrated by the way he approaches the Bill of Rights. First, he has eliminated several of the early documents that the more apt classes study and has chosen the Bill of Rights as the one early document to stress. For each item in the Bill he has collected many illustrative anecdotes, both from history and from current everyday life. In some cases he has created problem situations or adapted them from newspaper stories, such as problems of people carrying weapons or of houses and citizens being searched. To begin each day of this unit of study, he describes the item from the Bill that will be considered, writes it on the blackboard, and tells an anecdote, such as one about a policeman who has searched a man whom he suspected of selling narcotics to high-school students. In this instance, the man subsequently sues the police department. After relating this incident, the teacher asks whether the students think the policeman was violating the Bill of Rights item or not. A class discussion takes place, and the teacher tells what the court's decision was in this case. Similar examples are given over a period of days to show by many specific cases the meaning of this basic historical document as it applies to things the pupils know in their lives. The students are asked also to bring up similar problems for discussion.

Throughout the year the teacher also emphasizes a few concrete major acts of Washington, Jefferson, and Lincoln, usually in anecdote or story form. The instructor does not expect the class to remember dates or other names or the types of struggles that Whigs and Tories, Democrats and Republicans, engaged in.

Although several copies of a junior-high textbook are in the classroom for the few better readers in the group, the instructor does not depend on textbook study as the source of most of the information. The anecdotes or historical tales that he relates, some comic books on American history topics, motion pictures and film strips on the selected subjects, and collections of pictures for the bulletin board serve as the basic resources.

For the weekly current-event day, the instructor emphasizes use of television news programs and picture news sources like *Life* and Sunday supplements of newspapers. The better readers are also asked to bring in whatever articles they can from daily newspapers, but no great stress is placed on this source.

With these approaches the instructor directs the class toward the usual goals set for the grade level, but at the same time he adjusts his expectations and teaching methods to the slower learner's talents.

B. *Different Goals, Different Methods.* Many schools provide a program especially suited to the slower learner's social and vocational needs rather than trying to adapt the usual academic offerings to his ability level.

For example, in a junior high school a combined social-studies and English class for slow learners focuses on the following kinds of activities:

1. Reading labels on bottles and boxes, street and building signs, advertisements in newspapers, recipes, directions for assembling simple objects, directions for getting from one place to another, street maps, fire-prevention rules, traffic rules, business letters, and stories with simple vocabulary but plots appropriate to junior-high pupils' interests.

2. Writing friendly letters, notices and signs, letters of applica-

tion, requests for items from a catalogue or from an advertisement, directions for how to perform different kinds of jobs, and notes from information given over the telephone.

3. Hearing stories read by the teacher and discussing the behavior of characters in the stories.

4. Conducting meetings of the class to determine ways for pupils to work together in carrying out some activity, such as planning a trip to the airport or to the electric power plant or planning bulletin-board displays on different vocations. In this way they practice methods of arriving at group decisions, of dividing up the jobs among the class members, and of taking individual responsibility for the success of a group project.

Such topics as history, complex political relationships, international problems, grammar, and the literature from other places and other eras are not pursued in this slow-learner section.

A Heterogeneous Class as a Single Group

In a class containing pupils of varied levels of ability, it is obviously more difficult to suit the work to those at every level. Perhaps the most practical way to meet this problem is to give somewhat different assignments to different pupils within the class. The following examples illustrate three ways to accomplish this.

In a high-school class studying American history, the teacher asked all class members to study two kinds of reading materials: the basic text and supplementary sources. The supplementary sources in most cases were books borrowed by the teacher from the school library on long-term loan. In addition, there were comic books and magazine articles on historical topics which the teacher had collected. There were also scrapbooks which students of past years had put together for different events in American history. The teacher assigned these readings to pupils according to their abilities. He did it by typing each student's assignment on a slip of paper along with a couple of questions to guide his study of the reading material. In a general class discussion about a given topic, the students were asked to contribute what they had learned from both the text and their individual readings. These discussions helped the less apt readers learn some of the things the more able ones had covered.

The key to the success of this approach lies in the teacher's ability to maintain a card catalogue related to each topic studied during the semester. Each card under such a topic as the Civil War contains (1) the title of the book or magazine article or comic book, (2) the pages related to this topic, (3) a code letter indicating the difficulty level of the material (such as A for *advanced*, GL for *at grade level*, E for *easier*, and VS for *very simple*). With this system, several students who have similar reading abilities may be assigned the same reading materials. Since collecting these varied resources and preparing the card file involves teacher time and work, the instructor will find it most practical to develop the card file and supplementary materials gradually over a period of years.

A second way of differentiating assignments involves taking the students to the school library to browse through a variety of reading sources on a topic, such as looking through books and magazines on Africa for an elementary-school class which is studying that continent. Each pupil, in order to answer a series of questions which the class has outlined during a discussion, is expected to collect material from two of the library sources. The teacher sometimes suggests certain books to individuals, but the final choice is up to the student himself. With this approach, students usually choose materials appropriate to their level of understanding.

A third pattern does not require that pupils use reading materials as the lone source of information. Rather, when a topic such as Climate and People's Ways of Living is studied, the class can suggest many sources of information about the subject, such as television travel programs, interviews with people who have lived in other countries or states, calendar and magazine pictures, motion pictures and film strips, as well as books, pamphlets, and periodicals. Then the teacher can either assign a source to each student according to his apparent ability or allow each student to select the medium he will use.

Each of the foregoing techniques aims at permitting pupils of varied talents to pursue the same topics together without having assignments which overwhelm the slower ones or bore the gifted.

A Heterogeneous Class with Subgroups

In the illustrations above, the teacher has kept the class in one group physically while in his own mind he has subgrouped them by differentiating their assignments. The subgrouping process is also sometimes done in an open manner so that it is obvious to everyone. There are two popular ways of grouping. (A) One involves placing the pupils of similar ability together on a committee. (B) The other entails dividing the students so that each group contains some members of high ability, some of moderate ability, and some of low ability. We shall illustrate these two varieties so their purposes and operation are clear.

A. *Ability Grouping within the Class.* There are two principal ways in which the class can be divided so students are working in subgroups with classmates of similar talents.

One pattern involves all pupils in studying the same topic, but each subgroup within the class is responsible for a different type of activity. For instance, in a fifth grade all members of the class are studying transportation. The unit of work has begun with the teacher's posing several questions which the pupils talk over during a general class discussion: What does transportation mean? What are some examples of transportation? How was transportation different when our parents were children? And how was it different when our grandparents were children? How do new advances in transportation change people's lives? What are the safest kinds of transportation? What new methods will we be using ten or fifteen years from now?

During this initial discussion, it becomes evident that the pupils do not agree on the proper answers to several questions, and other questions which need answering have also arisen. Obviously the class needs more information. The teacher recommends that they list their questions on the chalkboard as a guide to their study for the next four or five weeks. He and the class members together suggest ways they may work in five committees to locate information and present it to the class.

That evening, the teacher lists the names of children who will be assigned to the five committees. One group is composed of pupils whose reading skill and mental age are high; another, of those with low academic talents. The remaining three groups contain members of moderate ability.

The instructor assigns the most complex questions to the group containing the most apt pupils. The questions include ones like:

How long did it take Magellan's ships to sail round the world? How long does it take a jet plane to circle the globe? How long does it take a manned space capsule? When you consider both cost and speed, what is the best way to send animals from Africa to America? To send a Christmas package from our city to New York? To send automobiles from Detroit to San Francisco?

The teacher assigns the group of slowest learners some tasks which require the least academic ability. For example, the committee is to produce three scrapbooks. One is to contain pictures of devices for land travel, the second for sea travel, and the third for air travel. The pupils are to cut pictures from magazines and newspapers or draw them with crayons. A caption or title is to be lettered beneath each picture, and the students are to be able to tell something about each of these modes of travel.

The three groups of pupils who have moderate abilities are also assigned questions and tasks that the teacher believes suit their talents.

Each committee has a chairman who sees that everyone in his group understands his job and does it on time. The teacher serves as general supervisor. He spends his time visiting the groups and aiding them in their work of finding materials, taking notes, and organizing their information.

During the final week of the study, each group sets up a bulletin-board display and reports its findings to the entire class so that their learning is shared.

In the foregoing example, some cohesion was maintained among the different ability-level groups because all were studying the same general topic. But it is also possible for the groups to work on different topics. When this is done, the instructor is actually teaching more than one social-studies class within the same room. This is like the one-room country school, except that in our present example the pupils are all at the same grade level.

An illustration of this style of teaching in a small high school is seen in a tenth-grade class which is divided into two groups. The majority of the students are studying The Place of the United States in International Affairs. A minority of six, who are the least academically apt, are studying vocations.

The majority use a textbook and do supplementary reading in

weekly news magazines and the daily papers. Their activities include reading, class discussion, map making, and giving oral and written reports on international relations.

The minority study vocations for which they might qualify in the community. They learn about safety factors in different kinds of work, the advantages and disadvantages of union membership, social security and health insurance, and the like. Their study techniques include reading fairly simple pamphlet material, interviewing employers and workers, and visiting factories and business houses to view working conditions.

Two of the most vexing problems a teacher faces in such a dual-purpose class are those of (1) trying to conduct discussions with one portion of the class without disturbing the other portion and (2) preparing assignments that the slower students willingly pursue on their own during the times the teacher works with the larger portion of the class.

B. *Forming Heterogeneous Groups within the Class.* Teachers who organize students into committees to study different aspects of a problem sometimes wish to have a range of talent represented in every subgroup rather than have all the best students on one committee and all the slowest on another. When this is done, it is necessary to have a division of labor within each committee to suit tasks to the individual aptitudes of the members.

An example of this pattern is found in a high-school class that is studying American problems. During a three-week period, the focus of attention is labor-management relations. The class is divided into six groups, each composed of five or six members. In determining committee membership, the instructor uses the following criteria.

1. Each group should have at least one student who is very apt in social studies and at least one who is capable of organizing the members, dividing the work fairly among them, and encouraging them to work hard. (In some cases, one student will have both the desired social-studies aptitude and the organizational qualities.)

2. The pupils of average talents should be spread evenly among the committees.

3. The slowest learners should be distributed among the groups.

4. Students who apparently dislike each other and probably

would not work well together should, if possible, not be placed on the same committee.

On the first day of the labor-management study, the teacher reads excerpts from newspaper and magazine articles which point up a variety of labor-management incidents that have been newsworthy in past months. The purpose of this is to furnish an introduction to the types of issues that would concern the class during the three-week unit. During the ensuing discussion, a variety of questions arise about labor and management in the local community. The teacher suggests that these questions might best be answered if the class were divided into several groups, each group to be responsible for studying the relations in a local business or industrial field. As homework, students are to think of industries they might select.

The following day during class discussion, they settle on the areas of communication, food processing, farm-equipment manu-facturing, barbering, home construction, and police and fire pro-tection.

The teacher divides the class into six committees. Each group is to find answers to questions about labor-management relations in the field assigned to it. He appoints a chairman for each com-mittee. Most of the class members are asked to browse through their textbook and past issues of *Time, Newsweek,* and *U.S. News and World Report* to gain an overview of labor-management problems.

At this same time, the teacher meets with the chairmen to define their tasks. Since they have worked in groups before, their general responsibilities are not new to them. One thing the teacher stresses is the need for chairmen to see that each committee member be assigned a task with which he can succeed. This means that every committee will have to meet and determine what kinds of informa-tion it should collect, how to collect it, and how to report it later to the class. Then every chairman will divide this work into jobs of different degrees of complexity and ask each member to work on certain of the tasks. The teacher will aid the chairmen in deciding which assignment would perhaps best fit the different members.

Here are some of the kinds of tasks that are deemed most suitable for the slower learners.

Interviewing. Every student will be responsible for interviewing someone concerned with labor-management relations. Each of the slower learners, armed with a series of specific questions to ask, will interview either a barber, a factory worker, a truck driver, a carpenter, a construction worker, or the like. In doing this, not only will the student learn something of value to his committee, but he will become acquainted with some of the types of jobs which he may later fill as an adult. The results of these interviews will be reported orally to the committees.

Map Making. Although the more academically inclined students will plan community maps on which to locate the businesses being studied, the less apt ones can aid in drawing and painting the maps.

Searching for Materials. A slower learner can be paired up with a more capable classmate, who is appointed director of the pair. Their task is to search through magazines and the indexes of library books for information on topics specified by their committee. The director can suggest which books it would be best to inspect and show his partner which words to hunt for in the indexes. When the slower learner locates pages or sections he thinks are worth while, he can check his judgment with the director's to see whether the book should be checked out for committee use. (This plan assumes that the director of the pair has been briefed by the teacher about his responsibilities to work in an understanding way with his partner.)

When a teacher uses the foregoing pattern of teaching, he is trying to ensure that (1) each group contains rather capable leadership and therefore will probably succeed at its tasks, (2) the slower learners are not clustered together so that they will flounder when trying to work on academic tasks by themselves, (3) the slower learners do not feel segregated from their more capable classmates, (4) everyone is assigned tasks which challenge but do not overwhelm him, and (5) the chairmen gain experience in designing jobs of varied levels of complexity and in assigning members to these jobs in a manner that encourages them to participate wholeheartedly.

Summary of Social-Studies Procedures

Of the variety of teaching patterns we have discussed in this social-studies section, which is the easiest for the teacher to use and the best for meeting individual students' needs?

As suggested earlier, the answer to this question depends on such factors as the range of talent in the class, the size of the school, the teacher's background, and the availability of supplementary learning materials. In a large school where several different sections of a course are possible, the slower learners will probably be easiest to teach if they are in one class and if that class contains not more than twenty or twenty-two pupils. In classes of mixed ability levels, the problem of planning to meet individual needs is more complex. But for many smaller schools, heterogeneous grouping is the most feasible pattern. In these cases the teacher can make the adjustment to individual differences within the class by some of the approaches suggested above.

Science and Health

In teaching science and health practices, we can organize the class in the same variety of patterns as described for teaching social studies. We shall not describe these patterns again. Rather, we shall suggest some types of science and health activities that will aid the slow learner within whatever class organizational pattern he finds himself.

Our discussion focuses on (1) health and safety, (2) biology and botany, and (3) electricity and mechanics.

Health and Safety

The retarded learner's need for training in health and safety practices is often very great. Because of his intellectual limitations, he may not pick up health and safety information outside of class as readily as his more average classmates. Hence he needs to be taught these things directly.

Instruction in first aid is usually valuable. The slow learner will profit most from this instruction if it is not simply on the verbal level but includes direct practice in cleansing wounds, giving artificial respiration, recognizing when to move an injured person and when to leave him alone, fashioning a stretcher, treating burns, and knowing which simple medicines to use for different kinds of injuries. He should also learn to avoid the misuse of common medicines and poisons. For example, he should know the dangers of taking too many aspirin or sleeping pills and of using tablets or syrup from unmarked bottles. He should recognize that the skull and crossbones symbolizes poison and that the antidote for the poison is often printed on the label of the bottle.

A knowledge of basic physiology can help the student understand safety and health practices. Today there are excellent charts, build-up models, and films to illustrate the location and function of the principal organs of the body. These visual teaching materials should be used liberally with slow learners. The gifted pupil may understand the heart's relation to the lungs and to the stomach and blood vessels when he hears a lecture or reads about these topics. But the student of below-average verbal ability will often be confused by such verbal explanations. A lecture illustrated with a diagram or model of the human torso will be much more effective in teaching him why cigarette smoking reduces an athlete's stamina or why a tourniquet should be placed on the wrist when a vein in the forearm is cut.

In studying proper dietary practices, the slow learner will gain more from demonstrations of ways to prepare food to retain vitamins than he will from trying to read about them. Pupils can illustrate the desirable components of meals by cutting pictures of foods from magazines and placing them on posters.

Classroom demonstrations, films, and pictures of food-handling techniques are useful for teaching sanitation. After students have viewed such demonstrations, they can show their understanding by creating scrapbooks and charts. They may also imagine they are experts who give advice to a radio or newspaper audience that inquires about health problems. The teacher can play the role of the audience, and the students are to answer his questions about how to deal with such problems as unsafe drinking water, nonrefrigerated meat, moldy bread, and a restaurant cook who has a very bad cough for several weeks.

In studying safety, the pupils can take inspection tours of the school and their homes to identify hazards. Upon returning, they can draw posters showing ways to correct the hazards. Posters and demonstrations can also focus on safety practices for pedestrians, bicyclists, and motorists.

Throughout this instruction, stress is laid on topics of practical use in the pupil's daily life. Teaching methods emphasize demonstrations, charts, posters, pictures, and films. Whenever possible, the student should take part in the safety and health activities directly, not merely hear or read about them.

Biology and Botany

The slow learner does not gain much from studying cell structures, theories of evolution and matter, and the schemes scientists use for dividing living things into kingdoms and phyla. He gains more from the practical experience of caring for plants and animals.

Therefore it is desirable to conduct classroom experiments with plants, such as growing one flower box of beans in the light and another in the dark, or growing one in sandy soil and another in loam. Pupils may visit a neighbor's garden to learn which plants are considered weeds and which are flowers. They can be encouraged to plant a garden at home and keep a record of how often they water it, what plant foods they add, and what kinds of plants grow most rapidly.

The study of animals can follow a similar pattern. Field trips to farms and zoos show clearly the animals' appearance and habits. When the slow learner has pets of his own, frequently he is strongly motivated to learn how to feed and exercise them properly and how to care for their injuries. He may wish to collect and mount butterflies or beetles. He may build and stock an aquarium or terrarium or an ant farm in a bottle.

Such activities as these not only teach him biological facts but furnish visible proof of accomplishment. This can bring self-satisfaction and recognition from classmates.

Electricity and Mechanics

Since he lives in a world of machines, it is useful for the retarded pupil to learn to use them safely and efficiently. In some cases he will develop considerable mechanical or manual skill. As shown in a later chapter, academic ability and mechanical aptitudes do not seem to be closely related.

A practical understanding of electricity can be taught through a variety of direct experiences. For instance, the pupil can learn to repair frayed electric wires and to replace an electric plug which has pulled loose from its cord. He can learn the dangers of poking metal objects into electric sockets and of touching electrical appliances when he is standing in water, such as in the bathroom. As the teacher gives demonstrations and explains diagrams, the student can see that wire which resists the passage of electricity will heat up and thus serves a useful purpose in hot plates, toasters, irons, and electric heaters.

With a length of bell wire, a dry-cell battery, and a large nail, the pupil can create an electromagnet. Adding a wooden frame and metal strip to this gadget changes the magnet into a telegraph set.

Pupils learn principles of levers by using and discussing wrenches, screw drivers, and crowbars. The properties of gasoline and kerosene and the proper handling of these fuels can be illustrated with posters, diagrams, and demonstrations. A discarded lawn-mower engine can be disassembled to show its components. A model-airplane engine can be operated in class.

These kinds of experiences, as well as others related to earth science and weather, are especially well suited to the slower learner because they involve specific objects that he meets in everyday life; and they may be explained in a simple enough way so that he can use the objects more effectively.

A wide selection of such activities is found in elementary-school science books and in the kinds of references listed under Simple Science Experiences at the end of this chapter.

Speaking

The retarded learner needs the same kinds of speech opportunities as average pupils. He should have chances to engage in conversations and group discussions and to give reports to the teacher and the class.

Since the slow learner is not very skilled in verbal reasoning, he needs more help than his classmates in giving oral reports. In the lower grades, the teacher can help him organize his ideas by asking leading questions during the report. The oral report thus becomes a type of interview, with the teacher asking the questions and the student offering answers. When the retarded student is older and more capable, he may be able to organize his ideas ahead of time as a list of topics he will talk about. Often he is not able to develop a well-ordered outline on his own. It is usually best if the teacher helps him plan the sequence of topics beforehand so he will be more successful in his appearance before the class.

Some slow learners have been laughed at for saying things which have sounded silly to others or they have been teased about enunciation defects. Such treatment has made them reticent. They have come to realize that a person who keeps his mouth shut is unlikely to be teased for what he says. In these cases, the teacher faces a dual problem: building the child's confidence so he will try to talk, and helping correct errors that appear in his speech. This is not an easy task, because it usually takes a quantity of individual or small-group conversations between the teacher and the retarded child before he will emerge from his shell of reticence. And when he has become brave enough to emerge, the content of his speech will still often reflect the shortcomings of his mentality. The teacher cannot guarantee that he will never be laughed at again, but it can be emphasized throughout all classwork that every student should respect others' opinions and should not embarrass them by snide remarks and teasing.

Retarded pupils have a higher percentage of speech defects than do normals. In most instances, these defects are not particularly complex. They tend to be cases of poor enunciation or the carry-over of articulation patterns learned in early childhood. However, correcting these disorders demands more time and patience than is usually needed with similar difficulties in normal pupils. The techniques described in Chapter 16 can be used for helping pupils improve faulty speech habits.

Writing and Spelling

The procedures for teaching handwriting to mentally retarded pupils are basically the same as those used with normal ones. However, the retarded child will be taught writing when he is chronologically older, usually at about the time he can learn to read and spell. This may be at age nine or eleven rather than six or seven. Since the subnormal pupil's retardation is usually more pronounced in mental than in motor abilities, by the time he is intellectually ready for writing his skill in manipulating a pencil is already quite adequate. The nine-year-old retarded pupil has better manual skill than a normal six- or seven-year-old. Thus the slow learner needs less emphasis on motor coordination during writing instruction than do younger children of his same mental age.

Most schools teach manuscript writing (lettering or printing) in the first grade and then change to cursive writing (connected script letters)in about the third grade. This is because the unconnected manuscript letters seem easier to form, are more legible, and resemble the printing in the books the child reads. This same pattern of teaching is suitable for subnormal pupils. However, if the child has a very marked intellectual deficiency, it is probably wise not to try to make the transition to cursive writing at all but to have him continue through school with manuscript letters. (Special techniques have been recommended for teaching handwriting to the brain-injured handicapped child. Strauss, 1947:184–190.) Throughout the grades, the emphasis should be on legibility rather than speed.

The slow learner's major writing problem is not that of forming legible letters but of deciding what to write about and how to say it. Therefore the same techniques suggested for aiding him with oral reports can be used to help him with the content of his writing. The teacher can ask him questions whose answers he can write out. Thus he organizes his ideas in a sensible sequence. The instructor can help the older student list a succession of topics which guide the organization of ideas he plans to write down.

All the pupil's writing assignments should focus on his practical needs in school and outside so that he continually sees the value of learning to write. In the lower grades, he can letter labels for pictures in a scrapbook he has made, write a short thank-you note to the proprietor of a dairy the class has visited, and keep a record of what he has spent money for during the week. In the upper grades, he can write for an item he wishes to buy from a mail-order house, write a letter of inquiry about a job, and fill out an application form. The retarded learner's abilities are not so well suited to creative assignments, such as writing original short stories and poems.

Spelling is often difficult for the slow learner because he tends to have trouble in both perceiving and memorizing words. For spelling lessons, he should be given considerably fewer words than his normal classmates, and he can be expected to require more practice with a word before he masters it. Often the act of tracing a word with his finger or writing it out several times will help him remember its spelling.

Art and Industrial Arts

In the areas of art and industrial arts, the retarded child often finds his greatest satisfactions. Typically he has become painfully aware of his shortcomings in the academic studies which form the greater portion of schoolwork. But in manual activities he is usually a better match for his normal classmates, so it is in these art areas that he is more likely to experience some success.

Because an entire chapter in the next section of the book is dedicated to graphic arts, at this point we shall suggest only a few of the ways arts and crafts can correlate with the academic studies of the slow learner.

At all grade levels, retarded pupils can draw illustrations for stories and poems they have read or heard. They can construct model villages representing other cultures and draw maps containing pictures of products of industries in their own community. They can create safety and health posters, mold clay or papier-mâché animals and fruits, and make cardboard models of stores and homes. These activities enable slow learners to visualize more clearly the ideas derived from their reading. And since retarded pupils usually cannot concentrate as long on academic tasks as normal students, art work which relates to their academic studies serves as a desirable diversion from constant verbal activities. In addition, art work furnishes tangible evidence of their efforts.

Music

Like manual and artistic abilities, musical talent does not necessarily go with academic ability. Therefore slower learners are often able to participate successfully with their normal agemates in singing and in playing instruments. In classes designed especially for mentally handicapped pupils, music typically plays an important role because the pupils respond to it emotionally and derive satisfaction from both listening and performing.

In Chapter 11 we shall discuss individual differences in musical ability. Therefore in this present chapter we shall merely mention a few of the ways that music can be used in conjunction with other subject-matter areas to aid the retarded pupil.

In the social studies, many folk songs are available which relate to historical topics and to life in various nations. In some instances, pupils understand an era better if they listen to or learn to sing songs about elections, war, love, or heroes of the times. Catalogues of the major recording companies list songs of these types.

Health and safety songs, though sometimes considered trite by more sophisticated students, often appeal to the retarded and handicapped.

Singing activities can further help the slow learner improve his enunciation, articulation, and voice quality, especially if direct instruction is given in proper voice placement.

Among the lowest mentalities, the process of learning a new song may be somewhat different from that used by normal or borderline pupils. For instance, the least apt pupils cannot be expected to read either the words or music. Songs chosen specially for them are best if they have a melody that is not longer than twelve or sixteen measures. Tunes containing repetitious phrases and a very limited range of notes are especially suitable. Learning a song is easiest for them when the vocabulary and sentence structure are familiar and reflect natural conversation.

SUMMARY

The pupil whose academic aptitude is well below average can succeed best in school if the goals he is to reach are concrete rather than abstract. He can understand the here and now better than distant places and times. He learns most readily those things which he can see will profit him in daily living.

He cannot read as well as other students, so he will learn more adequately when pictures, films, excursions, models, and work projects supplement or supplant the textbook assignments that his agemates are expected to pursue. He cannot plan ahead very well, so he should be given definite short-term tasks rather than be expected to make long-term plans on his own. He requires simpler explanations and more teacher time than do his normal classmates.

The slow learner will have his greatest difficulties with the verbal activities that form the typical school's academic program. In art, music, and manual work he can participate on a more nearly equal footing with his agemates.

SUGGESTED LEARNING ACTIVITIES

1. In the *Education Index* to periodical literature, look under such categories as *backward children, individual differences,* and *mentally handicapped* to locate two articles about teaching the mentally retarded or mentally handicapped. After reading the articles, list the suggestions, if any, which they contain to aid the regular classroom teacher in working with slow learners whom he would meet in his class.

2. Interview a local teacher who works regularly with slow learners. Ask about (1) how teaching methods and materials have been adapted in his or her class to suit the pupils' abilities, (2) specific reading materials that have proved most useful for them, and (3) provisions which have been made to improve their relationships with normal agemates.

3. Interview a teacher whose class contains a wide range of academic ability. Ask about (1) the kinds of problems encountered in working with the less apt pupils of the class, and (2) the measures the teacher takes to adjust the goals and teaching methods to the slowest learners.

4. Visit a public or school library. Select a topic which you might be teaching. Search among the books and pamphlets on this topic to locate reading materials that would be understandable to the slow learners you might find in the class you would teach. Make a list of these materials and indicate why you think each one would be appropriate for below-average students.

SUGGESTED READINGS

References on Teaching the Retarded

CRUICKSHANK, WILLIAM M., and JOHNSON, G. ORVILLE (eds.). *Education of Exceptional Children and Youth.* Englewood Cliffs: Prentice-Hall, 1958.

DOLL, EDGAR ARNOLD. *Measurement of Social Competence* (manual for the Vineland Social Maturity Scale). Minneapolis: Educational Test Bureau, 1953.

INGRAM, CHRISTINE PORTER. *Education of the Slow-Learning Child.* New York: The Ronald Press Co., 1953.

KIRK, SAMUEL A. "Experiments in the Early Training of the Mentally Retarded," *American Journal of Mental Deficiency,* April, 1952, pp. 692–700.

———, and JOHNSON, G. ORVILLE. *Educating the Retarded Child.* Boston: Houghton Mifflin, 1951.

ORR, KENNETH N. "Helping the Slow Learner," *Social Education,* March, 1955, pp. 107–108.

PERRY, NATALIE. *Teaching the Mentally Retarded Child.* New York: Columbia University Press, 1960.

SMITH, MARION FUNK, and BURKS, A. J. *Teaching the Slow Learning Child.* New York: Harper and Brothers, 1954.

STRAUSS, ALFRED A., and LEHTINEN, LAURA E. *Psychopathology and Education of the Brain-Injured Child.* New York: Grune and Stratton, 1947.

WALLIN, J. E. WALLACE. *Education of Mentally Handicapped Children.* New York: Harper and Brothers, 1955.

Descriptions of Retardation

MASLAND, RICHARD L.; SARASON, SEYMOUR B.; and GLADWIN, THOMAS. *Mental Subnormality* (Biological, Psychological, and Cultural Factors). New York: Basic Books, 1958.

TYLER, LEONA E. *The Psychology of Human Differences.* New York: Appleton-Century-Crofts, 1956.

Mental Retardation Explained to Parents

HEISER, KARL F. *Our Backward Children.* New York: W. W. Norton, 1955.

KANNER, LEO. "The Emotional Quandaries of Exceptional Children," *Helping Parents Understand the Exceptional Child.* Langhorne, Pa.: Child Research Clinic of the Woods Schools, 1952. Pp. 21–28.

LEVINSON, ABRAHAM. *The Mentally Retarded Child.* New York: John Day, 1952.

Simple Science Experiences

BAER, MARIAN E. *Sound: An Experiment Book.* New York: Holiday House, 1952.

GREENBERG, SYLVIA S., and RASKIN, EDITH L. *Home-Made Zoo*. New York: David McKay, 1952. Inexpensive ways to care for a variety of small pets.

LYNDE, CARLETON J. *Science Experiences with Home Equipment*. New York: D. Van Nostrand, 1955.

————. *Science Experiences with Inexpensive Equipment*. New York: D. Van Nostrand, 1955.

ROGERS, MATILDA. *A First Book of Tree Identification*. New York: Random House, 1951.

SCHNEIDER, HERMAN, and SCHNEIDER, NINA. *Science Fun with Milk Cartons*. New York: Whittlesey House, 1953.

SELSAM, MILLICENT E. *Play with Plants*. New York: William Morrow, 1949.

CHAPTER 9

Teaching Reading Skills

Because skill in reading so strongly affects students' chances for success in almost all subject-matter areas, we are dedicating a chapter to ways of caring for reading-skill differences at all grade levels. The chapter focuses on (1) the range of reading ability to be found in typical classrooms, (2) ways of appraising students' reading abilities, (3) administrative provisions for reading, (4) methods for teaching basic reading, and (5) methods for meeting differences in ability to read in various subject-matter areas.

THE RANGE OF READING DIFFERENCES

The dispersion of reading talent found in typical fifth- and ninth-grade classes was suggested in Chapter 1. To broaden our scope, we shall now inspect reading-test scores at three other grade levels: third, eighth, and eleventh.

Figure 9-1 shows the reading ability of boys and girls in the third grade of two schools in a West Coast city at the beginning of the school year. The graph shows not only that the third-graders' reading abilities spread over a range of five grades but that the distribution of these abilities will differ somewhat from one school to another. The superiority, on the average, of the Hill School pupils might be expected when we recognize that Hill draws its clientele primarily from middle-class socioeconomic-level homes. Central draws a greater percentage from lower-class families, including those who are bilingual and migrant. At least part of the Hill students' higher reading level is due to the greater opportunities their homes offer for reading.

But even though Hill pupils on the average score higher than Central pupils, a heterogeneously grouped classroom in either

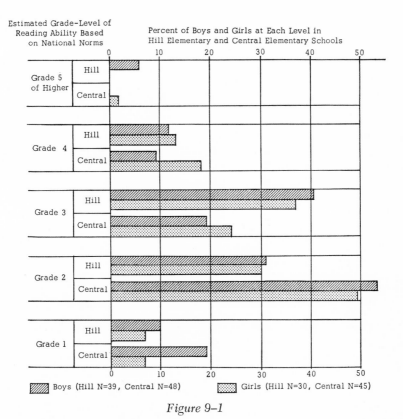

Figure 9–1

Range of Reading Ability of Third-Graders in Two Schools

school will contain a range of at least five grade levels in September. By the following May the range should be even greater, because the slower readers continue at their slower pace and the most apt speed ahead.

In addition, it is noted that although a larger percentage of boys than girls are found among the poorest readers (which is a typical condition in all schools), neither excellence nor inadequacy in reading skill is the exclusive fate of either sex. Both boys and girls are found at each level.

By the beginning of eighth grade, the range of reading ability is much greater than that found in third grade (Figure 9–2). It can span more than ten grades. (The fact that so many pupils are bunched in the Grade 12 or Higher category in Figure 9–2 suggests that the test norms were not well suited to the most apt. If norms for college had been available, some of these eighth-graders would apparently have shown up as well as the average college freshmen and sophomores.)

As with the third-graders, the socioeconomic level of the junior high groups is reflected somewhat by their reading scores. There are two junior high schools in this city in the Southwest. Jefferson is located in the older part of town and draws pupils both from the industrial area and from a middle- and upper-class residential district on the Upper South Side. Lincoln School is in a new, rapidly growing section to the east where people such as young businessmen, skilled craftsmen, faculty members at the technical college, and executives for the plastic industry have settled.

It is clear that the junior high schools that were used throughout the nation for establishing grade norms did not have as capable readers, on the average, as do either Jefferson or Lincoln. More than 50 per cent of Jefferson and Lincoln pupils scored above the national average for eighth-graders. Thus, in some other communities eighth-grade teachers must expect to work with a greater percentage of less adequate readers than are shown here.

By eleventh grade, the problem of coping with a wide range of reading ability is even more serious (Figure 9–3). The graph shows a spread of reading talent encompassing twelve grade levels. But it is clear, on the basis of other studies of reading differences, that if norms had been available for college seniors and graduate students, we would find that the best of the eleventh-graders can read as well as the average senior or master's degree candidate. So in a heterogeneously grouped class, this spread of fourteen or more grades is what the high-school teacher may meet.

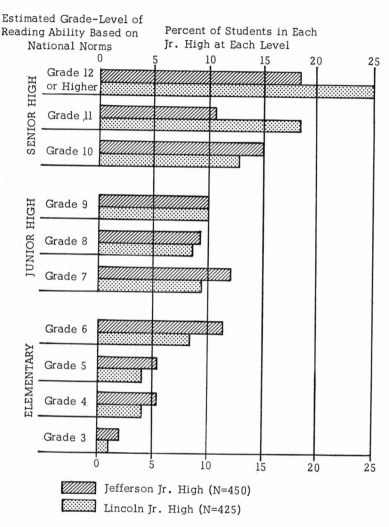

Figure 9–2

Range of Reading Ability of Eighth-Graders in Two Junior High Schools

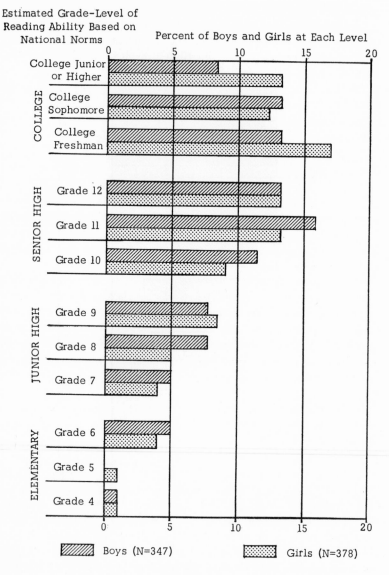

Figure 9–3

Range of Reading Abilities of One School's Eleventh-Graders

Actually the problem of teaching reading at any of the foregoing grade levels is even more complicated than the graphs suggest, because the figures reflect only general, over-all reading scores. Each score is actually an average of several subabilities whose individual natures are beclouded by the averaging process. For instance, a student's vocabulary knowledge may not be at the same level as his ability to gain meaning from a paragraph or to draw inferences or to read rapidly. This is why we can expect the task of teaching reading to be more complex than the graphs imply.

EVALUATING READING DIFFERENCES

Whether you are a third-grade teacher who is responsible for reading skills or a high-school instructor whose job is to teach history or science, you will profit from discovering each pupil's reading ability early in the year. This discovery enables you to set realistic expectations for him.

The desired information may be obtained in several ways. Students' records that are passed to you from last year's teacher will serve as an initial guide to their reading talents. But because pupils often lose, or sometimes gain, skill over the summer, you may wish to obtain your own more accurate estimate of their September status. The simplest way to make this estimate in all grades above the lowest primary levels is through use of a standardized reading test.

In the primary grades, the teacher may prefer to have each child read aloud a few passages from books of a graded series rather than use a formal test. This informal reading examination is usually an interesting task for the child, and it enables the teacher to observe such things as the pupil's understanding of punctuation and his method of discovering the meanings of unfamiliar words.

Instructors at all grade levels can make less formal evaluations during regular classwork by (1) assigning students to answer questions—either orally or in written form—about the content of what they have read, (2) giving teacher-made tests that measure comprehension and ability to draw inferences, and (3) having students read aloud to reveal whether they can sound out unknown words or whether they skip some words and guess blindly at others.

ADMINISTRATIVE PROVISIONS FOR READING

In Chapter 4 we inspected in detail the administrative techniques that schools use to meet individual differences. So at this point it is not necessary to review these at length but only to note which ones are most commonly used in meeting reading differences.

One approach is through ability grouping. That is, in some cases reading skill is one of the criteria the school authorities use in deciding whether to assign a pupil to a fast, average, or slow-moving section. In other cases, reading skill is not singled out as a criterion, but because it is so often highly correlated with academic success, ability groups formed on the basis of academic marks may incidentally be somewhat homogeneous in reading skill.

One particular variety of ability grouping has become known as the Joplin plan because of the publicity given to its use in Joplin, Missouri. The plan consists of taking all children from two or three grade levels—such as fourth, fifth, and sixth—and reshuffling them for one period a day to compose a number of reading classes. Each reading class consists of pupils of similar reading ability, regardless of their official grade level. A teacher who normally teaches fourth-graders in other subject-matter areas will, during reading period, perhaps have a medium-progress reading group composed of pupils from fourth, fifth, and sixth grades.

Remedial-reading classes are often provided to aid students whose skill is two or more years below the average for their grade level. In the elementary school, the remedial pupil is usually removed from his regular class for a portion of each day, or perhaps three times a week, to receive tutoring or attend a special class. In the high school, the student is usually not removed part time from another class; rather, the remedial-reading course is a regularly scheduled class which he attends daily.

Some secondary schools offer special reading classes that are not designed solely for retarded readers. Instead, they are organized for small-group and individual work adjusted to the needs of any student who wishes to improve his reading. An academically apt youth who wants to gain speed or to improve his scanning skills or vocabulary is as welcome as the one who is markedly retarded in reading.

METHODS FOR TEACHING BASIC READING

By "basic reading" we mean the initial skills of gaining meaning from the printed page and of developing methods to figure out the meaning of strange words. The pupil also learns to draw inferences, understand figurative meanings, and recognize implied meanings. The basic reading program is principally a responsibility of the elementary school, but it continues into the secondary grades for pupils who have not developed sufficient mastery at the elementary level.

In formulating a basic-reading program, the teacher needs to answer two questions: (1) What kinds of materials, such as books or pamphlets, best suit the pupils' needs? (2) How can the class be organized so as to meet individual needs and at the same time efficiently utilize the teacher's time?

Although these questions can be answered in numerous ways, the most prominent solutions and their chief variations can be described through the use of three illustrative classroom programs. The first involves permanent reading groups that use a single basic-reading series. The second is an individualized program in which each student reads a separate book. The third is a multiple-approach scheme that utilizes various classroom organizations and various reading materials different days.

Reading Groups Using One Basal Series

The reading program in most elementary schools is built around the use of *basal* or *basic* readers. These texts typically are published in a series, beginning with wordless picture books that furnish reading-readiness activities for the kindergarten or first-grade child. The readiness books are followed by preprimers and primers which are typically used in the first grade. One or two volumes are provided for each of the succeeding elementary grades. Every book in the series is more difficult than the previous one. Each introduces new vocabulary in a controlled pattern and regularly repeats words that were introduced in earlier volumes. Workbooks that accompany the readers furnish practice in comprehension, phonetic analysis, using prefixes and suffixes, drawing inferences, and the like.

The basal series itself does nothing to care for individual differences. It only tries to ensure a graduated sequence of reading experiences through the grades. But the teacher can attempt to accommodate for pupils' varied skills with the use of a basal series by grouping the class for reading activities. The most advanced pupils read through the volumes at a faster pace than the less apt. So all cover the same material, but some groups do it faster than others.

The most common method of grouping in primary grades consists of dividing the class into three parts. There is no compelling reason for three groups rather than four or five, except that three seems to be about as many as the typical teacher can manage with comfort. The teacher tends to think of these as the fast, average, and slow groups but usually avoids mentioning these labels to the class. Rather, the groups are given names which do not impugn the aptitudes of the slower readers, such as the Jets, Rockets, and Astronauts or Jack's group, Helen's group, and Nancy's group. It should be recognized, however, that this euphemistic titling serves chiefly as a courtesy. It does not successfully hide from the children the reading skill represented in each group. Primary graders quickly recognize the true hierarchical nature of the groups, no matter what they are named.

In handling the class, the teacher proceeds in the general pattern described for the second grade in Chapter 5. She spends about twenty minutes with each group during the morning and perhaps an equal period in the afternoon. While she gathers one group in a semicircle around her at the front of the room to read, the others work on individual assignments at their desks.

Two of the most difficult problems faced in administering this program are (1) providing worth-while assignments for the children who are not meeting in their reading group and (2) ensuring that each student knows how to do his individual assignment.

Activities for Those not in Reading Group

Some teachers give too little thought to the activities they assign to the children who remain at their seats while the teacher handles a reading group at the front of the room. As a result, the pupils are too often assigned busywork like coloring outline designs or pictures, completing workbook exercises involving skills they have already mastered, and copying poems into composition books. But with thoughtful planning beforehand, the teacher can provide activities which do not just keep children occupied and quiet but stimulate worth-while learning. Such activities include the following.

1. *Student-Led Group Work.* While the teacher aids one reading section, the other groups, under the direction of pupil-leaders, can work on projects or skills related to other phases of classwork like:

Murals, perhaps of storybook characters, scenes in folk songs, vocations in the community, or chief characteristics of a country being studied, a history of air or land transportation, or uses of lumber or rubber products.

Maps, such as salt-and-flour relief maps of a country, product maps featuring drawings of the principal crops and industries of a state, or maps of the travel routes of explorers.

Simple dramatics with the teacher giving initial aid, then putting one of the more apt pupils in charge so the group can rehearse on its own.

Construction projects, such as table-top villages, a display of types of dwellings or modes of transportation of various lands, a clothing display, or a model fortress.

Drill activities, such as flash-card practice on sight vocabulary or spelling or arithmetic facts (only after understanding of the arithmetic process has been ensured), the development of quiz-program questions on social-studies or science topics to ask the rest of the class later, or use of reference books to answer questions assigned to the group for a social-studies unit.

2. *Individual Activities.* Frequently pupils work on individual interests or assignments while the teacher is with one reading group. Such assignments include:

Workbook exercises or teacher-made work sheets designed to aid children in specific reading, language, or arithmetic skills. Sometimes all children can profit from the same kind of exercise, so all will be assigned the same pages in the workbook. But on other occasions, not all need practice on the same skill, so some may be assigned one exercise, some another. A common fault of many workbooks is that the children cannot do them successfully on their own. Thus they may require that the teacher work with them as they begin a new page. After they understand what tasks the page involves, they can move ahead alone. Often the less apt readers should not be expected to work unaided in the workbook that accompanies their reader, but they need work sheets that are less difficult, perhaps derived from a lower-level book of some other publisher's reading series.

Creative art work, not mere coloring in or pattern cutting. Pupils may draw illustrations of stories they have read, heard, or created. They may draw their versions of such topics as "My Happiest Day" or "Busy Day at the Supermarket" or "Workers Building the New Road."

Recreational reading or research in books to find material for social studies or science.

Writing reports, stories, poems, thank-you letters, or letters to friends in other lands, or completing arithmetic assignments.

Ensuring that Individuals Can Do Assignments

The principal techniques for making sure that individuals working at their seats understand their assignments seem rather obvious. But the fact that some teachers fail to use these techniques suggests that we may not be amiss in reviewing them briefly.

Perhaps the most common approach is for the teacher to write on the board ahead of time each group's assignment. At the beginning of the reading period, before pupils move into their groups, she goes through the first step of each group's seatwork with them (when workbook or work-sheet problems are involved) or instructs them in the steps of the day's activity (when group projects like murals or dramatics are in order). Sometimes the teacher can assume that students already understand the day's activity because they have had similar experiences before. But to check this assumption, she may wish to ask them, rather than tell them, what they intend to do.

In all grades above the second or third, student-leaders can help ensure that seatwork or group activities proceed efficiently. Ahead of time, the teacher meets with the leaders to explain the tasks of the day. The leaders are then responsible for explaining the tasks to their members and for checking members' progress and giving them help during the period.

The instructor can often take a few minutes away from her reading group to cruise around the class and inspect the work of people at their seats. For instance, in a first-grade reading group when the pupils have been assigned to read a page or two silently, the teacher can move to the pupils working at their seats to see how well they are progressing.

Variations of the Reading-Group, Basal-Series Plan

The foregoing description illustrates only one of several popular variations of the grouping and basal-reader plan. Some instructors prefer not to have the average and slower groups simply following along later in the same books that the faster group uses. Thus, instead of buying thirty-five copies of a single reading series, they purchase eight or ten copies from each of three different publishers' series. The advanced group may then read in the Ginn series, the average group in the Scott-Foresman series, and the slowest group in the Row-Peterson series. The advantages of this scheme are that (1) the slower readers do not meet stories each day which they may have overheard twice when the medium-speed and fast groups read them earlier in the year, (2) the slower readers feel they have their own books about which they can talk to the others without a sense of simply dragging along far behind them, (3) the teacher is not so bored from doing the same story three times a year (a boredom which may communicate itself to the pupils), and (4) a greater variety of books is available in the classroom from which the more apt pupils may choose to read when they have completed other tasks ahead of time.

Another variation of the grouping plan enables the teacher to spend more time with the average and slower readers. It consists of training the most capable pupils to handle their own reading sessions. This system can work effectively at the third grade and above, so long as there are some capable readers in the class. But it does not succeed unless the teacher carefully instructs the members of the fast group in proper teaching methods. The teacher introduces pupils to the plan gradually by perhaps saying, "I want you to pay close attention today to each step we take during our reading period. The reason is that each of you will have a chance to be the teacher of this group during the coming months. So you have to be well prepared. On this sheet of paper you see my lesson outline. Now watch what we do first in the lesson and see why we do it."

In such a manner, she clarifies for them the anatomy of a reading lesson. Then, during the coming week as she continues to work each day with the group, she assigns one student to try teaching one segment of the lesson and another student to try a different segment. Eventually each member has experience with every step. Thereafter the teacher can assign one student each week to serve as the group's instructor while she is working with the middle and low reading groups. To make sure the pupil-leader of the high reading group understands his task, each day the teacher discusses the lesson outline with him ahead of time. Some of the most capable students can occasionally develop lesson outlines themselves, aided by the teacher's guidebook that accompanies the reading series.

Obviously this pupil-leader approach demands careful supervision, but it can work very successfully, and as an added advantage it can provide the most apt pupils with leadership experience. Even though a pupil-leader system appears to be succeeding well in class, it is usually wise for the teacher not to let the group operate constantly on its own. It is well for her to take over the group once or twice a week to check their progress and to furnish special instruction of which a pupil-leader is not capable.

Individualized Reading Program

Some educators believe that three or four permanent reading groups using the same basic text do not adequately meet individual differences. Rather, they believe each child should be on his own and use a book or magazine best suited to his unique needs and interests. Thus they recommend an individualized reading program. We may illustrate how such a program operates by considering the sources of reading matter, the pupil's role, and the teacher's role.

Sources of Reading Matter

For an individualized program to succeed, there need to be reading materials treating many areas of interest at various levels of difficulty. For instance, in a fifth-grade class an appropriate selection would usually include books on animals, sports, adventure, mystery, biography, folk stories, life in foreign lands, grooming for girls, automobiles, airplanes, science fiction, explorers, science experiments and activities, hobbies, history, and humor. Because in a typical fifth grade the reading abilities may range from first grade through ninth or tenth, the books should represent a similar range of difficulty, with a larger number suited for Grade 3 through Grade 7 where the greatest concentration of abilities will lie.

When a teacher first launches into such a program, one of his knottiest problems is that of securing all these books. If the school administration is enthusiastic for the plan, some special money may be provided. Then the teacher, with lists of appropriate books and the assistance of the librarian, can purchase a basic classroom library. But often the administration will not or cannot furnish sufficient funds. In this case, other resources need be used to provide the three books per child which some writers feel is the minimum required to operate the program properly. (Veatch, 1959:41.) Teachers can:

1. Trade some copies of presently owned basic and supplementary readers to other teachers who have a quantity of different ones on hand.

2. Request books from room parents or the PTA.

3. Borrow twenty or thirty books from the local city or county library on a month-long loan.

4. Ask pupils to bring books which classmates might borrow.

5. Ask all libraries in the community for a gift of books which they were planning to discard.

6. Have the students conduct a book drive in their neighborhood to obtain copies that neighbors will donate.

7. Ask the principal or supervisors for the sample books they often receive.

8. Request friends and neighbors to contribute discarded magazines (*Boy's Life, Child Life, Reader's Digest, National Geographic, Seventeen, Life, Popular Mechanics*).

9. Take the class to the local library to browse, and have each pupil obtain a library card. Throughout the year encourage pupils to use the card.

10. Take the class periodically to the school library to browse and check out books.

The Pupil's Role

The student's first responsibility is to look over the books which the teacher has displayed and choose one which he thinks he would like to read. If he starts one and decides it does not suit him (too difficult, uninteresting, or confusing), he is free to return it and try others until he finds one that is appropriate.

While he is reading his book silently at his desk, he is also supposed to be planning how he will report his reading to his classmates and teacher. Upon completing his book, he is given an opportunity to present the report, the nature of which he has already determined in conference with the teacher. For instance, he may wish to read an exciting passage aloud to the teacher or the class, or he may draw a picture illustrating one scene and explain the incident as he displays the picture. He could describe the most interesting character, the most frightening scenes, or the funniest and saddest incidents.

Often each pupil keeps a reading diary. Every day at the end of the reading period he writes a sentence or two about the day's reading activity. The diary serves as a record of progress. Typical entries are:

"October 6: I finished *Little House on the Prairie* and I read some of it to Mr. Sorenson. I like it. He said *Farm Boy* was a book about the same family. I'll try it tomorrow.

"October 7: I read to page 18 in *Farm Boy*. It's a good story. Not many hard words either."

In some classrooms the library-card pocket inside the cover of every book contains a folded sheet of paper on which each student who completes the book writes a one-sentence evaluation for the guidance of classmates.

Pupils are permitted to help each other select books and, during reading session, to aid each other with difficult words.

The Teacher's Role

After securing a supply of books of varying levels of difficulty, the teacher places them in three or four areas of the classroom to reduce the crowding and confusion that might occur if all students hunted for new reading matter at the same moment at a single bookshelf.

In some classrooms, all books at one location are adventure stories, at another location biography and history, and so forth.

When a new batch of books is obtained from the library or purchased by the school, the instructor takes time to introduce each one briefly to the class by perhaps reading a synopsis from the dust jacket or telling about its main characters or reading the first page or two.

During reading period each day, the teacher typically locates himself in one corner of the room with an empty chair alongside. The pupils are either at their desks reading or at the bookshelves hunting for a book. One child at a time comes to sit with the teacher for a personal conference, which lasts about five minutes. Some teachers establish a conference schedule at the beginning of the period by asking who wishes to read aloud today and talk about his book. Other teachers make out a regular schedule that ensures each child a conference every three or four days.

The purposes of the conference are (1) to enable the teacher to evaluate the child's comprehension, his word-attack skills, and his ability to read aloud and (2) to enable the child to share what he has learned with an interested adult and to receive help with his unique reading problems without fear of making a spectacle of himself in front of his classmates.

To record his appraisal of the pupil's strengths and weaknesses, the teacher keeps a notebook with a page for every pupil or a card file with a card for each one. Perhaps a child's mispronunciation of phonetic words during the conference reading shows that his understanding of phonics needs improving. Thus the teacher may work with him on phonics rules and their application or give him a couple of dittoed work sheets on phonics to complete. If several pupils display the same shortcoming at about the same time, the teacher may collect them into a group the following day and work with them for part of a period or two. Then the group is disbanded, and the students continue reading individually.

The characteristics of the individualized reading program as compared to ability-grouped reading have been summarized by Veatch [1] (1959:12–13) as follows:

[1] Jeannette Veatch, *Individualizing Your Reading Program* (New York: G. P. Putnam's Sons, 1959), pp. 12–13.

| *INDIVIDUALIZED READING* | *ABILITY–GROUPED READING* |

I. Reading Material

A. Large number and variety of trade and textbooks used in instruction.	A. Single basic or supplemental readers used in instruction.

II. Classroom Organization and Procedure

A. Children choose what they read.	A. Teacher chooses what children read.
B. Motivation arises from child's interests.	B. Motivation comes from teacher using the manual.
C. Instruction on individual one-to-one basis.	C. Instruction on group basis.
D. Grouping is short term and for specific, immediate purpose.	D. Grouping is semipermanent and for indeterminate purpose.
E. Reading lesson prepared independently and seatwork has element of self-determination.	E. Reading lesson prepared in a group and seatwork determined by teacher.
F. Remedial work integrated with other activities.	F. Remedial work entails separate operation.
G. Planned sharing period (with teacher).	G. No special sharing period.
H. Individual peak reading level checked and evaluated.	H. Various and indeterminate reading levels checked and evaluated.

III. Effects on the Child and His Reading

A. Gifted child progresses at his own pace.	A. Gifted child must gear progress to group's.
B. Slow reader not publicly stigmatized.	B. Slow reader publicly stigmatized by group and book assignment.
C. Close personal interaction with teacher serves child's psychological needs.	C. Child loses advantage of close personal interaction with teacher.

D. Reading at own interest and ability level fosters development of skills.

E. Acquiring skills only as needed assures their normal development.

F. Oral reading promoted by genuine audience situation.

G. Reading becomes its own reward.

D. Working at group interest and ability level may hinder development of skills.

E. Acquiring skills when not needed may hinder reading competence.

F. Oral reading suffers through absence of genuine audience situation.

G. Extrinsic rewards may debase intrinsic value of reading.

Upon reading this summary, which casts the individualized program in such a better light than the grouping plan, advocates of grouping and basal readers would hasten to point out that this comparison has come from the hand of a strongly biased supporter of the individualized approach. They would state that Miss Veatch has compared the best possible individualized class with the worst possible grouping scheme. They would indicate that some of the virtues she claims for her approach are questionable, and numbers of the disadvantages she claims for grouping are not characteristic of grouping when it is conducted properly. For example, they would note that checking only a child's *peak* reading level (which results when the child rather than the teacher decides which passage he will read aloud) may conceal important weaknesses in the child's skills which would have been evident if the teacher had selected the passage. Furthermore, the defenders of grouping would reject the claims that "working at group interest and ability level may hinder development of skills" because research on the two methods does not support such a contention.

Then where does the truth lie? Is grouping superior to individualizing? There is no sure answer. Children are learning to read well under either plan. For example, in an experiment comparing the two approaches at the sixth-grade level, Wilson and Harrison [2] found both methods equally good for developing vocabulary and reading comprehension. It is probable that for most teachers the

[2] Richard C. Wilson and R. Harrison, "Skill Growth with Individualized Reading," *Elementary English*, Vol. 40, No. 4 (April, 1963), pp. 433–435.

grouping plan works better in the primary grades where the pupils are taking their first steps toward reading skill. In the middle and upper grades, however, they may profit more from the individualized approach, for they can now read effectively by themselves for extended periods of time without teacher aid, thus allowing the teacher opportunities for individual conferences. Sheldon (Robinson, 1959:140) has suggested that a teacher may wish to begin with a grouping plan and then move to the individualized program.

The advantage in teaching children in three groups using basal readers lies in the fact that plans have been provided for each lesson. There is also a provision of continuity and sequence in vocabulary, word analysis, and comprehension development. The two- or three-group basal reader approach has proved to be of great help to the inexperienced teacher. As the teacher gains experience he can depart from comparative rigidity to a more flexible approach to meet the needs of those above and below each group.

Combination Reading Programs

It should be apparent by now that the grouping and individualized plans are not two completely separate entities. Rather, they are two ends of a continuum, and a teacher may follow a program of his own that lies somewhere between the poles. That is, he can take advantage of the elements of each that best suit his own teaching skills and the reading abilities of his pupils.

Examples of the reading program in two classes, one at the sixth-grade level and one at the high-school level, will illustrate two varieties of combination plans.

A Sixth-Grade Class

The instructor has divided his class of thirty-one pupils into three basic groups. The first consists of the fourteen best readers whose abilities range from Grade 7 into senior high school. The second consists of the fifteen pupils whose reading skills are similar to those of the average fourth- to sixth-grader. The two remaining pupils, who read at about the first-grade level, form the third group. On a typical day the reading period in the middle of the morning follows this pattern.

The teacher meets with Group 2 (the fourth- to sixth-grade readers) and introduces the story of Amelia Earhart's last flight which the fifteen group members find in their copies of the basic reader. During his introduction, the teacher tries to stimulate their interest and to orient them to the historical significance of the story. He also asks different students to try to tell the meaning of several words found in the story which he thinks some of the group may not understand. Then, before they begin silent reading, the teacher indicates six questions on the blackboard which they are to answer in written form after completing the tale.

During this time, when the teacher is working with Group 2, the two pupils in Group 3 are being taught by one of the most advanced readers in the class, a girl from Group 1. Of the two retarded readers, one is a boy who has never been able to get much meaning from books. He is now making some progress in first-grade books. Although he does not resist reading the stories in the regular first-grade primers which the teacher has borrowed from a primary class, he is obviously not elated by reading material that is of more interest to six-year-olds than twelve-year-olds. He is happier about the present day's lesson, which is in the easiest book of the Cowboy Sam series, for the content is not aimed so directly at the interests of primary pupils. The other member of Group 3 is a boy from Germany who recently entered the class with almost no knowledge of English. Although he seems to be profiting from the first-grade reading material at the present time, it is apparent that he will soon need more advanced work as he becomes better acquainted with the language.

The Group 1 girl who works with the pair of boys follows a lesson plan which the teacher has provided. He has trained her, along with four other Group 1 students, to follow the lesson plan and to give appropriate help to the two retarded readers. These five pupil-teachers take turns with the regular teacher on different days in working with the Group 3 boys. Today, after the pupil-teacher has listened to her pupils read aloud and answer oral questions on the contents of the story, she gives them a work sheet on word analysis to do silently at their seats. She then returns to her desk to pursue her own reading assignment until the end of the period.

While the teacher has worked with Group 2 and the girl has

helped Group 3, the fourteen best readers who compose Group 1 have been reading silently in books of their own selection. This is because Group 1 students actually do not work as a unit on most occasions. Rather, they follow an individualized program, each pupil reading his own book.

It is after the teacher has set Group 2 students reading the Amelia Earhart story that he begins holding individual conferences with the best readers. The first boy he signals brings his book to the teacher's desk and reads aloud a portion to demonstrate his oral fluency. Then the teacher asks him several questions about such matters as the plot, the characters, the writer's style, and the local color of the story. On the basis of the oral reading and the pupil's responses to the questions, the teacher writes a comment in a reading-record notebook that contains a cumulative report of each one's progress. Then another student from Group 1 is invited for a conference. These interviews continue until the end of the period. At this rate, the instructor finds that he can talk to each pupil in Group 1 about once every three days.

Although this is a typical reading period for this sixth grade, the program is altered occasionally so that the instructor can work with the entire class on some topic that he believes will benefit all. For instance, if he wishes to focus everyone's attention on a verse form, like the limerick, or on the techniques which different authors use to begin stories, he either reads illustrative passages aloud or has the students pair up to read together silently from the sixteen available copies of one of the two basic-reading series in the classroom.

The program is sufficiently flexible so the teacher can form other kinds of temporary groups that best suit pupils' needs and make efficient use of his own time. If several students in Group 1 and several in Group 2 show common weaknesses in phonics skills, he withdraws them from their usual assignments for several days to form a temporary group who practice phonics with him while their classmates read in books of their own choice.

When the teacher is questioned about the wisdom of having Group 1 pupils serve as pupil-teachers for the two retarded readers, he says, "It would be better if I had the time to spend twenty or thirty minutes a day with the two boys, but if I do that I sacrifice the rest of the class. Our slowest boy in Group 3 is practically a nonreader. He gets remedial-reading work outside of class three days a week. So I work with him one day a week, and the pupil-teachers teach him and the German boy the other four days. I think it helps the pupil-teachers by giving them practice in teaching someone who requires their patience and clear explanations. I don't think it harms the pupil-teachers' reading by taking this time for aiding the slower readers. The pupil-teachers are in an individualized program, so they aren't missing group instruction, and they read omnivorously at home. This is the best I can do in the circumstances."

A Tenth-Grade English Class

The English teacher intends to help his students pursue the following goals:

1. Increase reading speed and comprehension.
2. Understand and enjoy several types of poetry.
3. Read a variety of kinds of literature.
4. Analyze the way such elements as plot, character development, local color, suspense, mood, character delineation, and dialogue contribute to the success of different stories.
5. Increase vocabulary and word-attack skills.
6. Improve understanding of figures of speech, distinctions between facts and opinions, and ways to check the validity of factual material.

To achieve these goals, the teacher carries on a program that includes the following activities, requiring several types of reading materials.

Speed and Comprehension Practice

During the first half of the class period three times a week, the students all work on speed reading and comprehension by using the Science Research Associates Reading Laboratory IVa, College Prep Edition.[3] The laboratory is actually a box containing two- or four-page folders of reading material plus a series of objective-type

[3] SRA reading laboratories for all elementary and secondary levels are available from Science Research Associates, Inc., 259 East Erie Street, Chicago 11, Illinois.

test items about the reading. Each folder is a complete reading selection, different from each other one. Some are trimmed in orange, some in red, some in other colors. Each color represents a particular grade level of reading difficulty, ranging from Grade 8 through Grade 14. Half of the folders or large cards are called "power builders" because the articles or stories printed on them are intended to extend the student's ability to understand increasingly complex material and to apply this knowledge in making decisions. The decisions are in the form of questions which the student is to answer after he reads the passage. The other half of the cards are called "rate builders" because they require the student to increase his reading speed and subsequently answer multiple-choice questions on what he has read in a three-minute interval.

The instructor follows the carefully described directions in the teacher's handbook that accompanies the SRA Lab. That is, one student in each row of desks in the classroom is designated as the lab leader. It is his task at the beginning of class to inspect each pupil's record book to see which cards the student has completed and to select another card of the same color for that student. The leader delivers appropriate cards to each pupil in his row, and everyone sets to work on a power card. When a student has finished answering the questions accompanying his card, he goes to the lab box and selects an answer key with which to check the accuracy of his responses. After marking his answers and checking to see what he had misunderstood in those he missed, he records his score on his individual score sheet that has also accompanied the lab. Therefore the routine of the reading plan is operated chiefly by the students themselves, leaving the teacher free to converse with individuals and determine which ones are ready to move up to a new color level (that is, to a new grade level in reading difficulty).

Both the students and teacher are highly pleased with the power and speed reading sessions. Each student works at his own speed, readily sees his own progress on his record form, and typically enjoys the selections, which were chosen for their appeal to maturing adolescents.

Because these SRA materials have some vocabulary and word-attack practice built into them, they serve as materials for pursuing

Goals 1 and 5 for the class, and they contribute somewhat to Goals 3 and 6.

Analysis of Literature

Since the SRA program consumes only part of the week and is completed well before the end of the semester, there is sufficient time for several other kinds of activities that focus on the other goals of the class.

Each student has a copy of the anthology that serves as a text in which the class as a group read stories and verse. The instructor has a special purpose for studying each of the selections that they analyze together. One day they will take turns reading aloud to investigate the effect of different oral interpretations of verse, drama, and prose. Another day the teacher poses questions which students are to answer after reading a selection silently. Typical questions are: What words and situations did the author use to give the tone of fear to the story? Which character changed most during the story, and how could you tell he changed? How do you decide whether the author's picture of life is realistic or true? What figures of speech did the author use; were they clichés or original creations?

To provide students opportunities to apply some of the skills of analysis which they have met in the study of the anthology, the teacher assigns each one to make a collection of twenty poems he likes and to read at least six books outside of class.

When a student hands in his collection of best-liked poems, each verse must be introduced by a brief written explanation of why it has been included. The teacher wants the class members to feel free to include verses they really enjoy rather than simply collect those they believe the teacher would like. To better ensure that this is done, he informs them ahead of time that the anthologies will be graded only on completeness (twenty verses, twenty introductions) and neatness, not on whether the teacher also likes these particular selections.

So that students will delve into various types of literature, they are required to include at least four of the following areas when they choose their minimum of six books to read outside of class: biography, drama, mystery, science or science fiction, history, travel, and contemporary life. Reports on four of the books are made in written form. Reports on the other two are given orally on the occasional days that the class divides itself into five groups and students take turns giving one another ten-minute analyses of a book read outside.

For at least one book read during the semester, each student must try to answer several of the questions that arose during discussions of the anthology selections read in class.

In summary, we note that the teacher provides common learnings for the class through the anthology-reading sessions. But individual interests and abilities are served as the students attempt to apply these learnings to their own selections of verse and outside books. The SRA materials automatically suit themselves to the speed and comprehension levels of the individuals in the class.

Other Variations of Combination Plans

As noted earlier, the sixth- and tenth-grade classes illustrate only two of many ways group and individualized instruction can be combined. The teacher's skills and experience, the students' range of abilities, the number of students in the class, and the variety of reading materials available are all variables which affect the decision about which combination will serve best in a given classroom. There is no single correct solution.

Perhaps the greatest hope for additionally valuable approaches to meeting individuals' reading needs lies in the development of new kinds of reading materials. Some years ago the Lyons and Carnahan company produced a double series of basal readers for the intermediate grades of the elementary school. It was double in that the regular text for fifth grade had a parallel "classmate" edition containing exactly the same stories written in simpler sentences and vocabulary so that the less apt pupils could read the identical material as their classmates but at an easier level. Though these parallel series have been a step in a desirable direction, they have not sufficiently cared for the wide range of talent met in the grade. The more recent SRA materials are proving to be better suited to the true range of skills in typical classrooms. Publishers other than Science Research Associates are preparing similar sets of materials, patterned after the SRA laboratories, that propose to improve literary tastes as well as increase reading speed and comprehension.

Research with these materials is now needed to determine just how effectively they do teach the variety of skills of which over-all reading ability is composed.

READING PROBLEMS IN OTHER SUBJECT–MATTER AREAS

Pupils' differences in reading skill form some of the most irksome problems faced by teachers of social studies, mathematics, science, home economics, and industrial arts. Although it is the poor reader who causes the greatest difficulties, the best reader also poses problems when he becomes bored by materials beneath his level of sophistication.

The attitudes that teachers in such subject-matter fields take toward poor readers might be placed on a scale. At one extreme are those who feel that reading problems are not their concern. They often say, "My field is history, not English. I wasn't hired to teach the skills of reading which students should have mastered years ago. If they can't read their history assignments, they'll have to accept the consequences." At the other extreme are instructors who observe, "If pupils haven't learned to read well enough to understand the science assignments, they aren't going to learn much in my class. So I feel I have to take the time to teach them science reading or to reach science goals through means other than books." Many other teachers adopt a position somewhere between these two extremes.

This final section of the chapter should interest only those teachers who place themselves on one end of this scale, that is, the ones who feel responsible for aiding the inadequate readers through (1) giving help with the types of reading usually met in the subject-matter field, (2) providing reading materials of varied levels of difficulty, and (3) utilizing teaching methods that circumvent sole dependence on reading for attaining the subject-matter goals.

Special Reading Instruction

Two of the main questions faced by the subject-matter instructor who wishes to improve students' reading are: What reading skills should be stressed? How should reading instruction be worked into the class schedule?

To answer the first of these questions, the instructor needs to carry out at least a cursory diagnosis of the pupils' shortcomings. Often they need practice in such basic skills as sounding out new words, recognizing prefixes and suffixes, and paying attention to punctuation. For techniques in teaching these skills, the instructor without special training in the teaching of reading will profit from consulting the following books listed at the end of this chapter: Anderson, 1952; Austin, 1961; DeBoer, 1960; Durkin, 1962; Gray, 1963; Gray, 1960; Harris, 1963; Heilman, 1961; and Russell, 1961.

But if the subject-matter teacher feels he lacks the time and training to teach basic skills, he may still improve his students' reading by clarifying some of the reading problems unique to his subject-matter area. That is, some students' greatest difficulties lie in their lack of understanding of the vocabulary peculiar to the course: quotient and multiplicand, empire and eighteenth century, iambic and participle, factor and integer, piston and cam, blanch and iodized, transistor and fulcrum. Therefore, at the time he gives a reading assignment, it is well for the instructor to list the specialized or new words the class will meet and explain them before the reading is done. Subsequent vocabulary tests should reveal which pupils still have not understood, and some small-group explanations or aid from a classmate may help clarify the vague terms.

In addition to learning specialized vocabulary, pupils often profit by explanations of specialized kinds of reading problems that are prominent in the subject-matter field. For instance, in arithmetic and mathematics classes the prime reading task is that of discovering which mathematical operations a verbal problem is requiring the student to perform. In home economics and industrial arts, the student's reading problem is often that of following directions and diagrams, such as for cutting out a dress or installing brake drums. In history class, a series of somewhat specialized reading tasks may be posed by the textbook: mentally arranging in chronological order a series of historical events, recognizing which statements are facts and which opinions, keeping in mind a map of a continent so that the relationship between places mentioned in the reading is clear, and others. In science there are such specialized reading tasks as understanding which variables in an experiment have been controlled and which have not, recognizing the difference between a tentative hypothesis and an assumption, and understanding classification systems of animals and plants.

The best readers in the class will often learn the specialized vocabulary and the unique organization of materials in a field simply by reading the assignments. These are the same students who, in the early elementary grades, unconsciously construct adequate phonics rules for themselves when no phonics instruction has been given. But the average and poorer readers will profit from direct instruction and from practice exercises focused on the reading tasks peculiar to the subject-matter field.

The problem of when and how to carry out such instruction is often a difficult one, but there are several ways to attack it. If the entire class lacks the skill, such as map reading in a social-studies class, all the students may obviously be instructed as one group. But more often it is a segment of the class that needs special aid. In such cases the teacher may:

1. Meet with the small group while the rest of the students are completing individual assignments at their desks.

2. Work with the less adequate readers during study-hall period, before school, or during lunch hours.

3. Ask each of the less adequate readers to choose a classmate who can aid him with some specific reading problem. When the pupil himself rather than the teacher selects the helper, he often works more willingly. If this approach is used, it is appropriate for the teacher to provide the helper with a description of the specific ways he can best assist his classmate. For instance, in an arithmetic class the teacher can furnish a page of verbal problems in a workbook along with several questions which the helper should use while guiding the inadequate reader to think through the steps he should follow in reading the problems.

4. Invite a parent to school, and explain how his child can be helped with special reading assignments or practice exercises at home.

5. Request the school principal to schedule the inadequate reader for remedial sessions with a specialist. Subsequently the subject-matter teacher can ask that the reading specialist spend some sessions focusing on the reading assignments for the class.

Varied Levels of Reading Materials

Even teachers who cannot take time to offer specific instruction in reading can still provide for the range of their students' reading talents by furnishing materials for different levels of ability. For instance, the social-studies or science instructor who uses a problems approach may first outline the problems to be investigated, then assign different students to seek answers in the kinds of reading sources commensurate with their talents. Some of the materials may be made available in the classroom; others may be sought in libraries or the students' homes. Or if an arithmetic class is subgrouped according to ability, each of the ability groups will probably be assigned a different textbook or workbook. Furthermore a few supplementary copies of additional books may be kept on the classroom shelf for use in assignments that enrich the learning of the most apt pupils.

The types and sources of this broad selection of reading materials that suit individual differences may be summarized as follows.

Textbooks. Because the textbook has been for some decades the basic source for learning in most classrooms, millions of copies are sold annually. This makes textbook publishing a big business. In a typical subject-matter field, like American history or chemistry or arithmetic, several publishers will vie for the schools' business. To compete successfully for school sales, each publisher tries to make his product more attractive and a more successful guide to learning than those of his competitors. In the case of one publisher, the attraction may be in the form of easier vocabulary, though the text covers substantially the same material as the others. In the case of another, the attraction may be more complex material to challenge the better learners. In science, one volume will include more experiments for students to try than will another. In foreign languages, one text will stress simple phrases for everyday conversation, whereas another will emphasize a more formal study of grammar.

Because this variety of texts is available in each subject, a teacher may often find similar topics treated in different volumes at varied levels of reading difficulty. Thus it becomes feasible to buy simpler books for the less adequate readers or perhaps to purchase one or two copies of several texts which will not be used as textbooks but as supplementary reading for pupils of varied abilities.

In the past, many publishers printed on the book cover the number of the grade level for which the book was intended. However, this practice places the teacher in an awkward position when he wishes to assign a ninth-grade boy to a fifth-grade book that suits his reading ability. The boy will usually reject what is obviously material intended for elementary pupils. Today there is a trend for publishers not to label texts by grade level, especially in the secondary schools. Thus teachers can safely assign easier materials as individualized reading sources to the less apt students without insulting them.

To secure copies of various publishers' textbooks for purposes of examination, teachers may obtain lists of publishers from school or city librarians or by consulting Appendix A of the Thomas and Swartout (1963) volume at the end of this chapter.

Supplementary Books. As educators have recognized the need of pupils for a variety of materials to suit individual talents, publishers have responded with hundreds of books and pamphlets that supplement pupils' basic learning sources. An especially wide selection of supplementary materials is available in the areas of literature, science, and social studies. Because these books wear no grade label, they can be assigned to students at a variety of school levels. When the school library purchases one or two copies of such volumes, a class may secure them for use during the study of a topic pertinent to them, or individual students can check the books out of the library.

Teachers who wish to locate lists of new supplementary books for purchase by the school may secure annotated titles from a librarian or may find descriptions of new books in educational journals.

Free Materials. Hundreds of free pamphlets and brochures are issued by government agencies, medical and dental societies, foreign governments, manufacturers and business groups, trade-unions, chambers of commerce, and similar organizations. A few sample titles and the organizations offering them suggest the variety of topics treated: *The Story of Oil* (American Petroleum Institute), *Talking Plastics* (Society of the Plastics Industry), *The Story of Aluminum* (Kaiser Aluminum and Chemical Corp.), *Brazil at a Glance* (Brazilian Government Trade Bureau), *Student's Kit on*

Canada (Canadian Embassy), *For What Purpose—Which Glasses* (Better Vision Institute), *How to Sharpen Tools* (Behr-Manning Co.), *Frank Visits the Dentist* (American Dental Association), *Song Birds and Wild Flowers* (National Wildlife Federation).

The problem of locating such free materials has been simplified by the publication of the following lists, which are available in many city, school, and college libraries or may be purchased at low cost from their publishers:

1. *Elementary Teachers Guide to Free Curriculum Materials.* Educators Progress Service, Randolph, Wisconsin.

2. *Sources of Free and Inexpensive Teaching Materials.* Field Enterprises, Inc., Educational Division, Merchandise Mart Plaza, Chicago 54, Illinois.

3. *Free and Inexpensive Learning Materials.* Division of Surveys and Field Service, George Peabody College for Teachers, Nashville, Tennessee.

4. *Sources of Free and Inexpensive Teaching Aids,* edited by Bruce Miller. Box 369, Riverside, California.

5. *Educational Aids for High Schools.* National Association of Manufacturers, Education Department, 2 East 48th Street, New York, New York 10017.

Reference Books. Encyclopedias are perhaps the most useful reference books. An encyclopedia permanently located in the classroom can be a constant aid in social-studies, science, and English courses. School librarians who have only one set of a single publisher's encyclopedia should be urged to purchase another one or two sets that are suited to varied levels of reading difficulty.

When a teacher assigns students to consult encyclopedias, he should realize that some sets are considerably more difficult to understand than others. For example, those appropriate for pupils with the reading skills of an average fifth- to eighth-grader include: *Book of Knowledge, Britannica Junior, Compton's, New Wonder World, Our Wonderful World, World Book, Lincoln Library of Essential Information,* and *Volume Library.* Most of these are also well suited for high-school students, because the articles are mature in approach in most cases even though relatively easy to read. Encyclopedias which demand greater skill and are thus best suited to average or better high-school readers are the *Americana,* the *Britannica,* and *Collier's.*

Since dictionaries and atlases are also published for different reading levels, students in upper elementary and secondary grades should have more than one level of these resource books available.

Periodicals. Three kinds of periodicals are probably of most value for expanding the reading resources of the class: educational newspapers, daily newspapers, and magazines.

Periodicals like *The Weekly Reader, The American Observer,* and *Scholastic* are written specially for school use and at varied reading levels. That is, there are different versions of each of these publications designed for average reading abilities at several grade levels. A teacher can clip articles pertinent to his class's studies from past issues discarded by grades below and above his own. The articles easiest to read can be pasted into a small scrapbook for later use with less adequate readers. The ones of moderate difficulty can be pasted into another, and the most difficult in a third. In this manner scrapbooks can be developed on such topics as world population growth, new technology, ethnic and race relations, invention, space travel, studies of the sea and stars and earth, safety, life in other lands, and so forth. Students who are later assigned these scrapbook readings are usually unaware of the grade levels for which they were originally intended, so the less adequate readers are less likely to feel insulted.

Daily newspapers and Sunday supplements are obvious sources of material on a great variety of topics. To expand the classroom's reading materials, pupils can develop the kinds of scrapbooks described above with materials from newspapers and magazines on science, history, current events, sports, medical advances, business and economics, religion, art, music, weather, and the like.

Perhaps the greatest expansion of classroom reading resources is made by general monthly periodicals like *Reader's Digest,* general news weeklies like *Life* and *Newsweek,* and magazines directed at specialized fields like *Business Week, Design, Plays,* and *Science Digest.* As with encyclopedias, these periodicals are written at varied levels of reading difficulty. Although most high-school students can read articles in *Reader's Digest* with understanding and interest, only a limited group of the better readers will profit from *The Reporter, The Atlantic Monthly,* and *The Saturday Review.*

Comics. To a limited degree, comic books expand reading offerings in the areas of social studies, literature, and science. The reluctant or inept reader in the upper elementary and secondary grades will sometimes willingly learn from the Classics Illustrated versions of *The Red Badge of Courage* or *The Story of America* when he would not learn from the regular American history texts used by the class.

When a teacher has located a variety of the foregoing kinds of materials, he needs to determine for what reading level each is best suited. Although there are several reading-difficulty formulas that may be used (Dale, 1948; Flesch, 1951; Lorge, 1939), their efficacy for the classroom teacher is questionable. Experienced teachers can often judge the level of material simply by inspecting it. When in doubt, they try out the reading on some of their students whose comprehension level they already know. For instance, the teacher may enlist a pupil's willing aid by asking him to help judge how well a given article or book is suited for the class. The student is then asked to read a portion aloud and subsequently to answer several questions about the contents of the selection. He is also asked whether the material is interesting. If he has made several errors in the oral reading (words miscalled or puzzled over) and does not recall the contents accurately, the material is considered too difficult for readers of his ability. If the teacher wishes to have the difficulty level of several magazine articles or books judged at the same time, he may omit the oral reading and simply ask several students to read the passages silently and write answers to several written questions he has provided about the contents of the material.

Students can further aid in rating the difficulty and interest levels of books by annotating the bibliographies of term papers and written reports. The annotations indicate which of the resources were most readily understood and most valuable. This same kind of information can be requested on written book reports.

All the foregoing guides to reading level, as well as judgments printed in publishers' and librarians' descriptions of new books, aid the teacher in making appropriate assignments of materials.

Circumventing Reading Problems

When students' reading disabilities prevent them from learning adequately from texts and periodicals, instructors sometimes circumvent dependence on reading by utilizing other teaching media: lectures, discussions, demonstrations, debates, student oral reports, interviews of authorities in the field, experiments, films, photographic slides, charts, graphs, mounted pictures, blackboard cartoons and diagrams, television or radio programs, models and specimens, tape recordings, and classroom dramatics.

These nonreading approaches for poor readers may be fitted together with reading approaches in a variety of ways. For example, the instructor who assigns his class to read in the textbook in order to learn the main points and details of a topic may later in class emphasize once again the main points by means of illustrated lectures and discussions. By this means he hopes that pupils who did not master the assigned reading will comprehend at least the main points during the lectures and discussions.

Another teacher may occasionally assign the most apt members of the class different topics on which to give oral reports. Each speaker is asked to introduce his illustrated talk by writing on the chalkboard the questions his classmates should be able to answer by the end of his report. If at the end of the report the answers have not all been made clear for the listeners, the speaker is required to explain the vague points.

When the most apt learners have completed their work early for a social-studies or home-economics or business-education assignment, they may then create a tape-recorded radio drama or debate based on the reading topic. The rest of the class, or at least the segment of it containing the least adequate readers, then listen to the tape to understand the topic better.

A student who has understood the reading assignment is sometimes willing to explain its high points to a classmate who has not. This approach, when used occasionally, can profit both the good reader, who reinforces his understanding by having to teach someone else, and the poor reader, who learns the main points of the topic. It should be evident that this procedure is unsuitable if either of the pupils in the pair resents the arrangement.

A poor reader can also profit from small-group projects. If he is part of a trio conducting an experiment in general-science class, the better readers on his team can read aloud the procedures they are to follow, and together they can carry out the experiment and observe the results. Small-group discussions in social-studies and English classes enable the inept reader to learn the subject matter from the comments his fellow group members make about their reading. It is also true, however, that the inept reader in small groups is often embarrassed by not being able to contribute enlightened comments himself.

Through such teaching methods as the foregoing and those described in Chapter 8, worth-while subject matter can be learned by pupils whose reading disabilities would usually prevent them from succeeding at all in academic work.

SUMMARY

Variations in reading skill in the typical classroom are so marked that teachers at any grade level cannot hope to serve pupil needs adequately if they do not differentiate their methods and materials to suit these variations.

The most popular methods for meeting individual differences in teaching basic reading are the grouping and the individualized approaches or some combination of the two. Research studies suggest that neither of these approaches is generally superior to the other in all teaching situations.

Instructors in academic subject-matter areas can help pupils learn these subjects despite reading disabilities if the instructors (1) furnish aid with the specific kinds of reading that is faced in that field, (2) provide reading materials of varied levels of difficulty, and (3) utilize teaching methods that circumvent sole dependence on reading for attaining the subject-matter goals.

SUGGESTED LEARNING ACTIVITIES

1. Secure several textbooks in a subject matter you will teach, and rank them according to their apparent levels of reading difficulty.

2. Ask four pupils individually to read two pages aloud from a textbook which you believe is suitable for their grade level. On the basis of their performance (three errors per page means the book may be unduly difficult) and ability to answer three comprehension questions per page, you should be able to tell which of the children you think should be assigned such a text. If the book is unreasonably difficult for any of these children, tell how you might provide for his learning needs if he were in your class.

3. Interview a teacher who has classes in the subject area you wish to teach. Ask what kinds of reading problems he has found among his students and what he does about them. How adequately do you think he understands the variety of reading skills represented in his class—that is, do you believe he really knows the range of reading talents of his students? How adequately do you think he is meeting this variety of skills?

4. Select a topic or problem which could serve as the theme of a month's study for a class you might be teaching. Estimate the range of reading levels you would find among your students. Locate textbooks, supplementary books, and periodicals treating this topic and appropriate for the varied reading skills of the pupils. How would you propose to assign these materials to the students? How would you determine, during the progress of the month's study, whether your estimates of reading levels have been accurate?

SUGGESTED READINGS

ANDERSON, IRVING H., and DEARBORN, WALTER F. *The Psychology of Teaching Reading.* New York: The Ronald Press Co., 1952.

AUSTIN, MARY C.; BUSH, CLIFFORD L.; and HUEBNER, M. *Reading Evaluation, Appraisal Techniques for School and Classroom.* New York: The Ronald Press Co., 1961.

DALE, EDGAR, and CHALL, JEANNE S. "A Formula for Predicting Readability," *Educational Research Bulletin,* Vol. 27 (1948), pp. 11–20, 37–54.

DEBOER, JOHN J., and DALLMAN, MARTHA. *The Teaching of Reading.* New York: Henry Holt, 1960.

DURKIN, DOLORES. *Phonics and the Teaching of Reading.* New York: Bureau of Publications, Teachers College, Columbia University, 1962. Descriptions of ways to teach phonics and a summary of research on phonics issues.

FLESCH, RUDOLPH FRANZ. *How to Test Readability.* New York: Harper and Brothers, 1951.

GRAY, LILLIAN. *Teaching Children to Read.* New York: The Ronald Press Co., 1963. Clear explanation for a novice in the area of reading instruction.

GRAY, WILLIAM. *On Their Own in Reading.* Chicago: Scott, Foresman, 1960.

HARRIS, ALBERT J. *Readings on Reading Instruction.* New York: David McKay, 1963. Useful sections on grouping, individualized reading, content areas, and gifted and retarded readers.

HEILMAN, ARTHUR W. *Principles and Practices of Teaching Reading.* Columbus: Charles E. Merrill, 1961.

LORGE, IRVING. "Predicting Reading Difficulty of Selections for Children," *Elementary English Review,* Vol. 16 (October, 1939), pp. 229–233.

ROBINSON, HELEN M. (ed.). *Reading Instruction in Various Patterns of Grouping.* Chicago: Supplementary Educational Monographs 89, University of Chicago Press, December, 1959.

RUSSELL, DAVID. *Children Learn to Read.* Boston: Ginn, 1961. Excellent description of process of teaching basic reading.

————, and FEA, HENRY R. "Validity of Six Readability Formulas as Measures of Juvenile Fiction," *Elementary School Journal,* Vol. 52 (November, 1951), pp. 136–144.

THOMAS, R. MURRAY, and SWARTOUT, SHERWIN. *Integrated Teaching Materials.* New York: David McKay, 1963.

VEATCH, JEANNETTE. *Individualizing Your Reading Program.* New York: G. P. Putnam's Sons, 1959.

PART III

Artistic and Motor Differences

In Part III we consider the aptitudes which appear to require talents that have little, if any, relation to those required in traditional academic pursuits. Individual differences in graphic-arts abilities are discussed in Chapter 10, those related to music in Chapter 11, and those involving other types of gross and fine muscle coordination in Chapter 12.

CHAPTER 10

Graphic Arts Abilities

People seem to agree rather closely on "What is arithmetic?" and "What is a good arithmetic student?" Similar consensus is found in such areas as handwriting, reading, and health education. But the graphic arts are another matter. People can differ radically in their definitions of "What is art?" or "What is good art?" or "What is artistic ability and how do you measure it?"

Because a teacher's viewpoint toward art affects his treatment of students in this area, we shall begin by examining various views of art to which teachers may subscribe. After this introduction we shall consider the two major issues of the chapter: How are individual differences in art ability identified? How can teachers care for these differences within the school program?

DEFINITIONS OF ART AND CREATIVITY

Whether you are a painter, sculptor, teacher, or art critic, usually you do not judge works of art from only one viewpoint. Rather, you see them as having several facets, or you judge them according to several scales or dimensions. For example, you may enjoy the subject matter of a portrait painting but dislike the slick surface which a liberal use of linseed oil has given to the canvas. In this case, you have seen the painting from two vantage points: that of subject matter and that of technical handling of the paint. Or you may believe a figure drawing is quite imaginative and like its clean pen strokes, but you may not understand the symbolic message the artist tried to convey. In this instance, you have judged the work according to three scales: creativity, technique of handling the medium, and efficiency in communicating a meaning.

We believe that a person will understand his own reactions to art more clearly if he recognizes the facets or dimensions he uses in judging art works. To illustrate the nature of such facets, we shall describe eight of them as dimensions or scales and suggest what variety of positions a person can adopt along each of these scales. We shall label the eight facets as follows.

1. A *realistic-nonobjective* dimension. This one focuses on how literally the art work reflects the appearance of things as they are seen in nature.

2. A *design-principles* dimension. This means the degree to which the art work adheres to a series of tenets that relate to the organization of line, space, mass, and color.

3. An *expression* dimension. This deals with the extent to which the art work expresses what the artist wanted to state.

4. A *communication* dimension. This means how well other people understand what the artist tried to say.

5. A *technical-skill* dimension. This deals with the artist's mastery of his media, such as his skill in mixing paints or his control of chisel strokes.

6. A *growth-process* dimension. This means how much the artist's personality or view of life changes during the time he is painting a picture or carving a wood block.

7. A viewpoint toward the *appropriateness of subject matter*. This deals with the question: "Is the artist's subject matter suitable for an art work?" (This facet is called only a viewpoint rather than a dimension, because it is not readily turned into a linear scale.)

8. A *creative* dimension. This focuses on the amount of originality the artist has displayed.

Throughout the ensuing discussion, it will become obvious that these eight are not mutually exclusive. At various points their inter-relationships are evident.

Realistic-Nonobjective Dimension

Copying Nature

Some painters view a scene in nature, then paint a picture which reflects the scene with photographic identity. All objects are located on the canvas in exactly the same size and position as they appear in nature. Colors and shadow patterns are reproduced with great exactness. Many people are entranced by such a painting. To them the best work of art is that which reflects most literally the appearance of nature.

Reorganizing Nature

Some artists criticize the exact copying of nature. They say such products are not art. They believe a camera can do the job faster and better. They define art as an interpretation of a natural scene by the artist. Thus the finished painting is not a copy but a skillful reorganization of a view from nature.

Those who subscribe to this belief say that a work of art gains its worth from the kind of interpretation of life that it provides. When the painter creates his picture, his interpretation may deviate only slightly from photographic realism or it may deviate greatly. A slight deviation might consist of eliminating the details of leaves on the trees so that the entire tree becomes a flat green area. Or the painter may deviate more by drawing a portrait in which he uses no curved lines, only straight lines and angles. In a profile view of an old woman, the artist may emphasize the model's prominent nose by making it much larger than it is in real life. Or the painter may show three different views of an object on the single flat plane of the canvas. Such terms as "caricature," "stylization," "cubism," "pointillism" have been used to label some of the different styles of interpreting and reorganizing natural scenes.

When the artist takes so much freedom with the natural forms that the original scene or model may be hardly recognizable on the finished canvas, the painting may be labeled "abstract." That is, the artist has caught some impression or emotion when viewing a scene or having an experience like falling in love, and he has tried to abstract the essence of this in his painting. The result may be an obvious deviation from the appearance of the original stimulus in real life.

Disregarding Nature: Nonobjective Art

Some painters ignore natural scenes entirely. They concern themselves solely with the placement of colors, lines, and shapes in interesting patterns. They believe that the best art does not attempt to reflect the appearance of nature at all.

Therefore we see that one way of viewing an art work is according to how realistically it reproduces the appearance of natural objects. Some people believe the closer the painting is to photographic realism, the better its art quality. Others prefer different types and amounts of departure from the literal appearance of nature. Still others will happily accept any degree of adherence or deivation from realism. For them, the matter of realism is not the issue in art, but some other facet, such as communication or creativity, is the crucial element.

Design-Principles Dimension

A two-year-old is capable of holding a camera and clicking the shutter. But it is doubtful that many of the pictures he takes will be considered artistic by a jury of art critics. The jury would probably reject the child's casual chopping of scenes from nature on the ground that the photographs are poor compositions. The pictures show a lack of attention to design principles.

People who consider design principles important believe that a work of art should be a complete, satisfactory unit within itself. It should not give the impression of being an incomplete segment from nature transposed to a canvas in a manner that leaves something wanting. Nor should the picture simply be disorganized paint dashed onto a board. Rather, the area within the picture frame should arrest the viewer's attention and impress him as being comprehensible, interesting, balanced, and complete. When it does all these things, it is a good composition.

For centuries, artists have tried to extract from the most famous art works the characteristics of organization that have made them last. The characteristics have been stated as design principles. Many people use such principles, either consciously or unconsciously, to distinguish good from poor art.

The principles have been labeled by such terms as "dominance," "subdominance," "variety," "balance," "rhythm," "repetition," and "center of interest." For our present purposes, it will suffice to illustrate three of them briefly rather than discuss all in detail.

The principle of dominance states that a painting is most pleasing and best organized if it has a dominating color rather than containing equal amounts of several quite different colors. That is, the picture should give the impression of being basically a blue painting or a cool-color painting (consisting mostly of greens and blues and grays) or a tan and brown painting. This idea of dominance also applies to the kinds of shapes and line directions the work contains. For instance, the picture should not consist of equal amounts of vertical, diagonal, horizontal, and circular lines. Instead, it should contain more of one of these types if it is to be most readily comprehended as an artistic unit.

But dominance is not the only characteristic. The art work also needs variety. A picture containing only one tone of green and only straight vertical lines certainly has a dominant color and a dominant line direction. But for many people it is boring. They would be happier with some variety in color and line direction to maintain their interest. Thus a few small areas of the opposite color, red, or of an adjacent color like yellow, plus some circular shapes, could relieve the monotony of the work but still not destroy it as a comprehensible, complete unit.

In addition to dominance and variety, the painting needs a center of interest. All parts of the picture should not be equally demanding of the viewer's attention. At some place on the canvas, not too near the edge, there should be a limited area that draws his attention more insistently. The other areas of the canvas should be organized around this center of interest in a manner that prevents the viewer's eye from wandering out of the picture.

So it is that such design principles can be used as criteria for judging the goodness of an art work. They can apply to any variety of subject matter from realistic to nonobjective.

Expression Dimension

Drawing, painting, modeling, and carving are commonly considered to be expressive arts. They are channels the artist uses to state what he feels or thinks.

At one end of our expression dimension, we can place art works which have enabled the painter or sculptor to state his ideas and emotions completely. After he has finished the painting or carving he experiences great relief and satisfaction because the art work states precisely what he intended. At the other end of the scale, we find drawings and carvings which have failed abysmally to express what the artist has felt. Between these extremes are many gradations of success in expression.

On this theoretical level we shall find few, if any, people who will quarrel with the belief that art is expression. But when we come to the practical task of judging the worth of different art products on the basis of their expressive quality, troubles arise. The teacher who considers art to be the expression of an individual's ideas and emotions is hard pressed to defend any grade or mark given the student for his work. Until scientific advances someday enable us to partake directly of other people's minds and feelings, the artist himself remains the sole judge of whether he has expressed what he intended. He must be asked to report how closely his painting has reached the the goal of self-expression.

Sometimes a change in the painter's general behavior from *before* to *after* he has completed the art work is used as a measure of how successfully he has expressed himself. That is, in the treatment of psychological disorders, psychiatrists have found that painting, modeling, and weaving activities sometimes have helped relieve symptoms of disturbance in patients. However, from the art standpoint it would appear unwise to assume that such a diminution of symptoms of maladjustment is an adequate measure of artistic expression.

We conclude that art may be considered expression, but the critic or teacher cannot very adequately evaluate the artist's products on this dimension. A teacher might ask the student to tell how successfully he has expressed what he intended, but this source of information may often be of questionable validity.

Communication Dimension

Some people consider art to be communication. The purpose of the painting or carving is to convey the artist's ideas and emotions to the viewer.

This aspect of an art work, like those already considered, can be placed on a scale. At one end is perfect communication between artist and viewer. At the other end is extreme misunderstanding between the producer of the work and its consumer. Between these two opposite poles are various shades of adequate communication.

The task of judging a painting's communicative efficiency is sometimes rather simple, but more often it is very elusive. The task is simple when the teacher assigns the class to paint a scene of six Holstein cows browsing in a field beside a red barn. If the pupils' final paintings contain easily recognizable cows and barn, communication has succeeded. The teacher can even grade each student on how nearly his painting resembles the assigned scene.

But what about communication in cases where the artist has set his own goal, that is, where he has given himself his own assignment? In these cases, how is the teacher or art critic to know whether he understands adequately what the artist wished to convey? What about Salvador Dali's painting of the limp watches? What is the message there? Did Dali intend a symbolic meaning, or did he merely wish to show visual images in unusual relationships? What mark should Dali receive for efficiency of communication?

One way people have tried to answer such questions has been to ask the artist what he meant. These inquiries have been met with various replies. Some artists try to explain in detail the ideas they had hoped to convey. This explanation may clarify their intentions or, as is sometimes the case when painters turn to words, the explanation may simply compound the confusion. Other artists say that if the viewer failed to get the idea upon seeing the picture, there is no use trying to explain it.

In any case, we should recognize that judging the communicative efficiency of an art work is frequently an elusive, difficult task and sometimes impossible.

In connection with art as communication, it should be recognized that occasionally the viewer misleads himself into believing he has understood the creator's purpose. But what has really occurred is that the viewer has brought his own meanings to the colors and shapes on the canvas. This phenomenon is demonstrated daily in the psychological clinic where patients interpret the meaning of Rorschach ink blots in a great variety of ways, each way representing one person's individual style of interpreting life. Likewise it is possible that a given painting may be enjoyed by a viewer and contain important meaning for him. Yet this meaning or emotional response may be only his own projection and not the one intended by the artist who created the work. This fact of misinterpretation should not lessen the value the art product has for the viewer personally. But simply because the viewer feels that he himself finds meaning in the work, he cannot properly conclude that the artist has communicated efficiently.

Technical-Skill Dimension

Much of the artist's training and practice usually focuses on gaining command of the tools of his art. He learns to mix paints so the exact colors he desires are achieved. He learns how much oil to add to give the desired surface appearance on the canvas. He learns which kinds of brushes or palette knives to use for producing the right variety of effects. He practices sketching the human form so he can draw a hand or leg or head in any position he desires. Thus he tries to achieve complete mastery of art media so he is able to fashion every impression that arises in his imagination.

This technical-skill aspect of art is complex. However, we could think of it as being composed of a variety of dimensions, each ranging from excellent skill to poor. Every dimension focuses on one aspect of technical skill—one on skill in mixing paints, another on draftsmanship, another on wood carving, and so on.

Some people judge the quality of art works from this viewpoint. A major reason they like a certain painting is the artist's craftsmanship in representing the splashing of surf, the shining silk of a blue party gown, or the twinkling of a maiden's eyes. They dislike another painting because of its dull, muddy colors and the awkward shapes of the figures in it.

If a teacher wishes to use this dimension in judging students' art products, how difficult will his task of evaluating be? It will not be especially troublesome if he establishes clearly in his own mind what standard each variety of skill is expected to reach. That is, he needs to decide what constitutes good figure drawing, what comprises good color combinations, and so forth. Then, if he explains these standards to the students and they accept his expectations as being proper, no particular confusion occurs. The students strive to reach the same goals of technical skill that the teacher holds.

But difficulties do arise when a teacher's or an art critic's standards differ from those of the artist. For example, an artist squeezes quantities of thick oil paints from their tubes onto the canvas, without first mixing any of them to reduce their brightness or alter their tones. He uses a palette knife to smear the paints like thick butter, thus creating the figure of a chunky, heavy-featured dock worker. When a critic inspects this picture, several questions about the painter's technical skill may come to mind: Did the artist use the unblended paint directly from the tubes simply because he lacked the talent to mix them and achieve more lifelike tones? Did he apply the paint in coarse strokes of the knife because he lacked skill with a brush? Did he form the figure in a rough fashion only because he lacked the draftsmanship needed to cast figures in truer proportions and detail? Or was the artist really a master of color, brush, and draftsmanship but consciously chose to render the dock worker in raw colors, heavy strokes, and bulky form because he believed such technical treatment best reflected the worker's rough life?

The question of what constitutes technical skill is a knotty problem in contemporary art. This is because so many different approaches are being used to painting and sculpturing. Certain painters are being accused of adopting nonobjective or primitive styles because they lack the drawing ability to succeed with more traditional approaches. It is quite probable that in some cases such accusations have validity. But it is difficult to know. Some artists have turned to abstract or primitive styles only after having first proved themselves skilled craftsmen in more traditional forms of painting.

We may conclude that a technical-skill dimension can be set up for judging works of art. But when a teacher or art critic establishes his standards for technical skill, he should recognize that his standards will not necessarily be accepted by other teachers and critics. An inspection of art history shows that standards of technical skill change in certain respects with the passing of centuries.

Growth-Process Dimension

Some art educators believe the process of creating a picture is more important than the picture itself. Although they enjoy viewing a child's paintings, they believe the real significance of his art work is the growth process that occurs during the time he is creating it. By "growth process" they do not mean that the pupil is simply improving his ability to handle a pencil or brush more adeptly. Rather, they believe that when the child creates a picture called "I Help Daddy in the Garden," he is defining for himself who he is in relationship to his father and is explaining to himself the meaning of such work as gardening. The art process is thus believed to make important contributions to the child's establishing his self-image and to his defining his physical and social world.

For this facet of artistic endeavor we can suggest a dimension. It ranges from much significant psychological growth at one end to no growth at all at the other.

Teachers who believe in this growth dimension are usually not so interested in collecting finished pictures as they are in (1) providing many opportunities for art activities and (2) judging the amount of growth pupils achieve during their art experiences. The task of providing activities is much easier than that of judging the students' growth. There seem to be three principal ways teachers attempt to make such judgments.

1. The instructor questions the child about his completed drawings or carvings. He asks the child what the drawings mean, what he thought about as he made them, and how he felt about them.

2. The teacher collects drawings the child has produced over a period of time, then compares the earlier products with the later ones to determine what changes in the child's life seem to be reflected in his paintings.

3. The teacher observes the child's behavior as he paints or during a period of time when he is producing quantities of art work. The purpose is to find signs of the child's gaining confidence, becoming better accepted socially, or making more mature remarks about his world and his place in it.

Each of these three channels to evaluation has serious shortcomings. In regard to the first method, the child frequently cannot say what the painting means to him, because his self-understanding and his vocabulary are both too limited.

The second method is also very questionable. Frequently psychologists and teachers have tried to understand a child's inner life by interpreting his art work. But when the research studies on psychological interpretations of children's art are summarized, it seems that you first need to understand the child's inner life before you can understand his art products, not vice versa. (Hartley, 1952:248, 254–269.)

When observations of the child's general behavior are used for evaluating the effectiveness of the art process, we are again on slippery ground. Let us imagine that the child actually does reveal in his behavior that he is gaining a more mature understanding of human relationships and that he is more self-confident. Are we now warranted in attributing this growth to his art activities? What about the other influences in his life at this time, such as books he has read, television programs he has viewed, the way his family has treated him, his Cub Scout experiences, a recent success on the soft-ball field? How can we filter out the contribution, if any, that art experiences have made to his personality development?

In summary, we conclude that the art process may very well be significant in carrying the child toward mental and emotional ma-turity. But at our present stage of skill in evaluating personality growth, we lack the techniques for judging the way this process may operate in pupils' lives, at least in most cases.

Appropriateness of Subject Matter

A few decades ago, a group of American painters jolted the tradi-tional art world by painting scenes of back alleys and slums. They were dubbed the "ash-can school" of art and were condemned by art critics who believed that the broken fences and dissolute souls of big-city life were not fit subjects for serious artists. The criticism was not aimed at design or color or draftsmanship but at subject matter.

Likewise many people admire pictures and carvings because of the subject matter portrayed rather than because of design qualities or creativity. Cases in point are Whistler's painting of his mother, Norman Rockwell's covers for *The Saturday Evening Post,* and the statues of Civil War officers who sit astride bronze horses in village squares throughout America.

All of us, after a little pondering, could list what we think are appropriate subjects for art work, those that we consider less desirable, and some that we regard as not appropriate at all. Teachers' preferences for certain subjects will affect what they tell their pupils is good art. Many a teacher will give a warmer reception to an awkward sketch of a pony trotting at a fair than to a well-designed, graphic painting of the insides of a dead horse.

Creativity Dimension

Visitors to museums like the Louvre in Paris may see a painter sitting at his easel in front of an old masterpiece making a copy of it. In some cases the copyist produces such an exact likeness that it takes an expert to distinguish the original from the reproduction. Two questions may be asked about this: Should the copy be considered a work of art? Can the painter of it be considered a significant artist?

Similar questions may arise when you visit an American classroom and see a display of twenty-five almost identical drawings, each one the product of a different child. The teacher has exhibited these sketches because they are such faithful reproductions of the sample sketch she drew on the blackboard at the beginning of the art period. Is this copying activity to be regarded as good art instruction? Are the children's pictures to be considered good child art?

If we limit our conception of good art to technical skill in painting and drawing, we shall perhaps commend the copyists at the museum and in the classroom and label them real artists. However, many people are not willing to award the title "artist" simply for technical skill with brush and crayon. They require that the artist also display creativity. By this they mean that his work should include something different, original, unique, or individualistic.

This component of originality can be achieved in a variety of ways. One is to deviate from the manner in which artists of the past have painted scenes from nature. Van Gogh, Cézanne, and Picasso gained some of their distinction from giving a new treatment to nature's appearance. Or the artist can digress from accepted treatment of design and color. He may wish to produce a feeling of confusion by breaking with the tradition of providing a dominant color tone in his picture, so he uses equal amounts of many different hues. He may veer from familiar forms of balance or rhythm. Or he may be original in the subject matter he selects. Among the nineteenth-century French painters who used subject matter that was uncommon in their day were Degas, who chose ballerinas, Gauguin, who favored South Sea islanders, and Toulouse-Lautrec, who selected Parisians in cafés. Today we find a great variety of unusual items brought together on a single canvas by some of the artists who are striving for originality.

This dimension of creativity or differentness is one which ranges from literal copying, on one end, to extreme deviation from former works of art, on the other. Probably few, if any, people would accept the extreme-deviation end of the scale as a desirable position to adopt. A work which was drastically different in every way from all others probably would not make sense to viewers. Most of us seem happier with art works which have some familiar controls (such as traditional design elements or customary subject matter) but depart enough from past works to furnish the spice of a new interpretation of life.

When the modern-day painter strives to be original, the path for him is more difficult than for those who have gone before him. This is because he is operating with a long tradition of many varieties of originality behind him. As he tries to escape from the past, his deviations must become more extreme if they are indeed to be unique and not reflections of innovations by previous artists. Thus, today we find many works of art not understood by the general public because the artist's striving for uniqueness has carried him far beyond the experiences and tastes of laymen.

When the teacher tries to judge the degree of creativity in a student's art work, he must answer for himself this important question: Is a student to be considered creative if what he produces is unique in his own experience, even though it is rather common in the experience of the teacher? It should be recognized that the child has had limited contact with life and with the art products of other people. He does not know all the varieties of interpretations used by artists of the past and present. Hence, in his attempts to express his own ideas in graphic form, he may hit upon a design or treatment of nature that is quite original from his own standpoint. However, the teacher may recognize his picture as being rather typical of what other children of similar age have produced in the past. In this case, it would seem unwise to scorn the pupil's efforts and to recommend that he do something "more original." Rather, if indeed he has not copied someone else but has offered his own interpretation of life or nature, he would seem to deserve commendation for creativity. He will probably profit from encouragement to continue such attempts.

A Point of View

The foregoing discussion has been furnished to encourage teachers to analyze their own views of what art is. So far, we have described only the attitudes a person might hold on each single dimension. Now we wish to consider the over-all point of view a person may adopt when his position on one dimension is combined with all others into a general attitude toward the nature of graphic arts.

Perhaps the simplest way to illustrate some of the many possible over-all viewpoints is to describe three teachers and show how they vary in their definitions of art and their treatment of students because they have different attitudes toward the individual dimensions.

Teacher A's Viewpoint

Teacher A works with children in the primary grades. She believes the real worth of art for the child is found not in the product but in the process. She stresses the expressive and psychological-growth aspects of art. The final picture or product is regarded as a reflection of what is happening to the child in his growing up psychologically.

Teacher A guides children toward drawing subject matter related to their own immediate lives and activities. Pupils choose their subject matter during open discussion at the beginning of periods dedicated to art work. The teacher controls the choice by suggesting what they will talk about during the discussion. For instance, she suggests they look out the window at the winter landscape and asks what kinds of things they can do in the snow. When they mention making snow men, throwing snowballs, and sledding, she asks them to imagine how it feels to make a snowball.

"Show me with your hands how you pick up the snow and pack it into a ball," she suggests. In a similar manner she asks them to act out or to imagine building a snow man, falling in the snow, or sliding, sledding, and shoveling. She wants them to become conscious of the feelings and the body movements involved in these activities before they begin to draw.

Next the class is asked to propose a variety of titles for pictures they might create about these subjects, such as "I Make a Snow Bear" or "We Roll Down the Hill" or "We Play King of the Snow Mountain." Then each pupil begins a picture of his choice to express some winter experience.

In the pupils' pictures, a variety of deviations from visual reality is acceptable. That is, on the realistic-nonobjective dimension the teacher accepts very realistic sketches as well as deviations from the real appearance of natural scenes. Although for this assignment she does not consider a nonobjective design proper, on other occasions she suggests, "Let's draw interesting lines and colors and spaces on the paper." Thus she holds a very broad view of what is acceptable on this dimension.

From the standpoint of communication, she believes that she should try to understand something of the child's view of life through the art products he creates. She uses his paintings and carvings to estimate whether he is more clearly defining his world and his place in it. She also tries to determine whether he is ridding himself of disturbing emotions which would upset him if he did not have art as a form of psychological catharsis.

Teacher B's Viewpoint

Our next instructor teaches art classes in a secondary school. She presents illustrated lectures to her class on such topics as principles of art and of perspective. She teaches the students about the color wheel and how to mix hues in complementary and adjacent combinations. She assigns them to draw and paint portraits, clothed human figures, landscapes, and still-life compositions. Pupils whose pictures closely resemble the literal appearance of objects and conform to principles of composition receive the greatest commendation and best marks. Sometimes the pupils draw nonobjective designs which they believe would be suitable for wallpaper, linoleum, and holiday wrapping paper. However, they are not to use abstract or nonobjective designs for their other painting assignments.

This instructor strongly believes that art should communicate. She contends that the artist best expresses himself when he conveys a scene accurately to others. She considers drawings which distort the human form or natural perspective to be only bad draftsmanship, not art. She states that art should be creative, but it should not deviate pointedly from the appearance of things in nature.

Teacher C's Viewpoint

The third instructor also teaches at the secondary level. She says she wants her students to show "enlightened creativity" in their work. By this she means they will express a uniqueness which is founded on craftsmanship and an understanding of tradition.

During the year in her drawing and painting class, the students learn traditional art principles and practice drawing objects as accurately as possible. They inspect and discuss prints and photographic slides of art works of the past and present in order to understand the kinds of subject matter, compositions, colors, and media used by some of the world's outstanding painters. (They do not study the history of painting formally nor do they memorize dates and names.) In making practice sketches, they try to simulate some of the styles of the masters. They discuss originality and try to identify evidences of it in the works of nineteenth- and twentieth-century artists.

Finally, each student tries to develop his own drawing and painting style, one which he feels suits his tastes and talents best. Based on the drawing and composition skills he has studied, he tries to express his own variety of uniqueness in his works.

This instructor accepts from students any variety of adherence to, or deviation from, the realistic appearance of objects in nature. She thinks art is principally a medium of expression and that if the artist himself is satisfied with the work, it is successful. If other people like it also and seem to gain meaning from it, that is an extra bonus of worth.

Needless to say, with this philosophy she finds the matter of grading students' work rather awkward. She solves the marking problem by basing grades primarily on how diligently each student has completed the numerous demanding assignments rather than on how closely a student's final painting resembles what she herself would paint.

In the foregoing examples, we have seen three different attitudes toward art which can result from teachers' adopting different combinations of beliefs regarding the dimensions described earlier. Obviously a variety of other over-all viewpoints will result from other combinations. If a teacher is to be honest and efficient in teaching art, he seems obligated to identify his own over-all viewpoint.

Creating and Appreciating

Our discussion of dimensions so far has focused on only one of the school's goals: that of teaching students to produce art. Another goal is to teach them to appreciate art from the standpoint of a viewer or consumer.

The skills involved in appreciating seem related to those of producing art works, but they are not identical. For instance, there are art critics who themselves are not at all adept at creating paintings, but they enjoy art and can describe in detail the compositional characteristics that have made a given work successful.

This matter of art appreciation is often confusing because the term "appreciation" frequently means different things to different people. Some use it as a synonym for "liking." When they say they appreciate a work of art, it means they enjoy looking at it. Others use appreciation to mean *understanding the design principles* employed by the artist to achieve a successful composition. They also know the way he has applied colors to achieve various shading effects. In short, they understand the artist's techniques. Still others use appreciation to mean *respect* or high regard for the artist's talents and his perseverance, though they would not desire to look at his paintings daily, and they do not understand his symbolic message or his painting techniques. Another meaning of appreciation is *a knowledge of the historical place* of the artist's work, its effect during his own time and its role in the subsequent development of art. Still another related meaning is *an ability to identify many artists' works and style* by sight and to tell the date and occasion of each painting or sculptured figure.

When we use the term "appreciation" in this chapter, we shall specify which meaning we intend at the moment so that communication will be clear.

As a final note, we should explain that the observations made in the foregoing discussion about drawing and painting apply also to other varieties of visual arts: sculpturing and carving, weaving, paper cutting, metalwork, and print making.

EVALUATING INDIVIDUAL DIFFERENCES IN ART ABILITY

Just as students within a typical class vary distinctly in academic abilities, so they will also vary greatly in the ways they perform on the dimensions described in the early portion of this chapter. There are three main reasons why teachers may wish to evaluate these individual differences.

1. To *predict* how well a pupil can probably succeed with art in the future. This is sometimes called "aptitude testing." On the basis of such appraisal, the school may determine what types of future art experiences, if any, will be appropriate for the student.

2. To determine specific *strengths and weaknesses* he has at the present time. This is called "diagnosis." It enables us to describe the next specific steps he needs in his training, though it does not necessarily commit us to predicting his future success.

3. To judge how much the student has *learned from his art training*. This is achievement testing. On the basis of this evaluation, we can summarize his progress and, if we wish, assign him a mark which describes how well he has succeeded, compared to what we expected of him.

So far in this chapter we have touched on evaluation techniques only incidentally. Now we shall focus directly on the ways these tasks of predicting, diagnosing, and judging achievement can be carried out. Our discussion treats art tests and methods of observing art work.

Art Tests

Art tests can either be bought from publishing companies or created by the teacher. As will be shown, each of these sources has its own advantages and limitations.

Standardized Art Tests

Most published art tests in use today were first developed at the end of the 1920's or during the 1930's. Several have since been revised. Most of them are designed for secondary-school students and adults rather than elementary-school pupils.

Some tests require the student to do some drawing, thus focusing on the production aspect of art. Others require him to judge which of several drawings is the best; thus they are treating aspects of art appreciation. (The degree of relationship that exists between creative skills and appreciation abilities has not been established.)

In the following summary of six published art tests, each one is described by name, date of publication, grade levels for which it is intended, types of items included, and the uses for which it is probably valid. The Meier, Graves, and McAdory instruments focus on appreciation or judgment. The Lewerenz, Horn, and Knauber tests emphasize drawing ability.

Meier Art Tests: I, Art Judgment (1929, revised 1942: Bureau of Educational Research and Service, State University of Iowa), Grade 7 to adult. The test consists of one hundred pairs of pictures in black and white. Most of the drawings are of scenes or figures, but some are abstract designs. In each pair, the two pictures are alike except that a small portion of one has been altered to change the composition. The subject selects the better of the two. Since the correctness of choices was originally established by agreement among art experts who took the test in its try-out form, the examinee is actually matching his judgment against that of professionals. The test is supposed to measure general aesthetic judgment, but a more cautious interpretation would be that it measures judgment of linear and pattern qualities in black and white compositions. It is not known whether a person's score on the test would also serve as an index to his judgment of pictures containing color and of sculpture, architecture, furniture, or industrial design. It has not been determined whether a student's high score on the test is a result of some innate art sense or of his past art experiences, nor is it known whether the test accurately predicts a student's future art success.

We seem safe in concluding that the Meier test best measures how closely the student agrees with experts in judging matters of composition. There is no evidence that the test appraises creativity, ability to control art media, or talent for communicating or expressing ideas.

Graves Design Judgment Test (1948: Psychological Corporation), Grade 7 to adult. The test consists of ninety items; each item includes two or more abstract or nonobjective drawings, from which the subject is to select the best composition. Because all designs are abstract, the subject's judgment of composition is freed of the influence that such content as landscapes, people, and the like might exert on him. The test is intended to measure the examinee's reaction to the design principles of unity, dominance, variety, balance, continuity, symmetry, proportion, and rhythm. The items included in the test were selected on the basis of:

(*a*) agreement among teachers of art . . . as to which of the two or three designs in each item was best, (*b*) greater preference for the design by art students than by non-art students, (*c*) greater preference for the design by those who achieved high scores on the entire test than by those receiving low scores (internal consistency). (Michael in Buros, 1953:335.)

The Graves test seems to measure about the same thing as the Meier: judgment of traditional design principles.

McAdory Art Tests (1929: Bureau of Publications, Teachers College, Columbia University), all grades and college. The test consists of seventy-two items, each involving four variations of one picture. Each variation is to be ranked in order of merit. The pictures are of six groups of materials: furniture and utensils, texture and clothing, architecture, shape and line arrangements, dark and light masses, and color arrangements. The McAdory instrument is intended to measure aesthetic judgment and appropriateness of materials to their design. Like the other tests of this general nature, it does not have an established predictive value. Because the McAdory test includes such things as furniture and architecture, many of the items are out of date and inappropriate today, thus making the instrument of more historical than practical interest.

Lewerenz Tests in Fundamental Abilities of Visual Arts (1927), Grades 3–12. Nine subtests intended to measure recognition of proportion, originality of line drawing, observation of light and shade, knowledge of art vocabulary, visual memory of proportion, analysis of problems in cylindrical perspective, problems in parallel perspective, problems in angular perspective, and color matching. As the description of items suggests, the tests measure some elements of draftsmanship and visual perception rather than the over-all aesthetic judgment of compositions. The Lewerenz battery has been criticized for (1) measuring unconnected skills rather than ability to produce a finished, integrated work of art, (2) including too little scope for aesthetic judgment and originality, and (3) providing no data on the predictive value of the test scores. It is probable that a student's score on these tests will be strongly influenced by his former art training, so they should not be considered necessarily a measure of innate artistic potential.

Horn Art Aptitude Inventory (1939, 1953: C. H. Stoelting Company), Grade 12 through adult. The inventory contains two parts, each a test of drawing skill. Part I requires the examinee quickly to sketch twenty familiar objects (such as a house, six circles, a book, a corkscrew) in small scale. Part II consists of twelve rectangles, each containing a few lines. The examinee is to use the lines as stimuli for creating a picture within each rectangle. To some degree, both parts of the test evaluate imagination, neatness, compositional sense, and general sketching skill. Although it should be useful in furnishing evidence about the presence or absence of several desirable elements of creative aptitude, its value as an over-all predictor of ability has not yet been demonstrated. It does not test color sense or aptitude for work in specific media like oil paints, water colors, wood, and such.

Knauber Art Ability Test (1932, 1935: Alma Jordon Knauber), Grades 7–16. The test asks the student to reproduce a design from memory, draw a figure of Santa Claus, adapt given designs to other conditions, draw objects in perspective, create pictorial compositions making use of designated elements or themes, check drawings for accuracy in perspective and shadow, and work out light and dark arrangements. From the nature of the items, the test apparently measures certain sketching abilities, an understanding of perspective and shadow patterns in nature, and some design principles. It is entirely probable that a student's score results as much from specific training as from a more basic art ability.

To summarize, we can say that published art tests measure some aspects of design principles, particularly as they are found in two-dimensional black and white drawings. Some of the tests approach art from the viewpoint of the critic or appreciator (Meier, Graves, McAdory), others from the viewpoint of the producer or creator (Lewerenz, Horn, Knauber). Although most artists and critics would probably agree that the skills measured by these tests are important or even essential in art, few, if any, would hold that they are inclusive enough to be valid indicators of real creative talent.

In the scarce validity studies available, art tests have correlated only to a moderate or low degree with marks in art classes or with teachers' estimates of students' ability. (Freeman, 1950:288.) The currently available art tests are thus of quite limited value for estimating a student's potential, analyzing his current strengths and weaknesses, or determining his achievement.

Teacher-Made Tests

Tests developed by individual classroom teachers usually serve to measure achievement at the end of a unit or semester. In some cases, a test may be given at the beginning of the semester to determine the present stage of the pupil's knowledge or skill so the teacher can better judge what kinds of instruction he needs.

The main advantage of teacher-made tests over published ones is that they can be designed to measure more precisely the kinds of skills the individual instructor considers important. We may illustrate this with the kinds of tests constructed by the three instructors described earlier: Teachers A, B, and C.

Teacher A gives no tests at all. Her stress is on the psychological-growth aspects of art, not on the compositional elements of the final product nor on the appreciation of other people's work. She judges growth by observing the changes in the completeness and complexity of the pupils' drawings, their comments about their work, their enthusiasm for art activities, and changes in their general behavior in class.

It will be recalled that Teacher B instructs students on principles of design, perspective, the realistic drawing of objects, and the use of color. Periodically throughout the semester she gives tests. Since she is interested in students' gaining both art-production and art-appreciation skills, her tests contain items that are similar to those in the published tests we have discussed. For instance, to measure skills of criticism she provides pairs of drawings and asks which is the better and why. To measure drawing skills, she (1) furnishes sketches whose perspective is distorted and asks students to correct them, (2) has students make quick sketches of objects displayed at the front of the room, and (3) asks them to color geometric designs and then write a defense of their color scheme, basing the defense on theories of color which have been presented in class.

Teacher B has two immediate uses for the test results. One is to diagnose students' weaknesses and thus to know how she might adapt her instruction to strengthen specific skills that individuals seem to lack. The second is to give the students their periodic report-card marks and written evaluations. She also uses the test results as partial evidence for predicting students' probable future success in art. She assumes that those who have succeeded best on tests and on drawing and painting assignments will have the greatest aptitude for art in the future.

Teacher C, as described earlier, believes that students should express their own individuality in their art, but their individual styles should be founded on craftsmanship and an understanding of the art of the past and present. Periodically she evaluates pupils' progress in understanding design principles and color theory by displaying three pictures and asking the students to write a comparison of them, stressing whatever design factors or drawing and painting techniques they have been studying recently. For instance, on various occasions they may be asked to analyze color organization, light-dark patterning, placement of forms, flow of line and form throughout the picture, the detailing of foreground compared to background, methods of suggesting a third dimension, the amount of adherence to realism, or the methods of applying the paint to the canvas.

The instructor uses these test results primarily for diagnosing students' strengths and weaknesses in understanding composition principles. The results are used to some extent in deciding a student's final mark, but most of his grade is determined by his diligence in fulfilling the drawing and painting assignments.

So it is that teacher-made art tests may take many forms. Some tests that are intended to measure skills of appreciation may require the student to identify the titles of historically important works, their creators' names and nationalities and eras. Others ask the student to identify the art media used in several original works which are displayed.

Evaluating by Inspecting Art Products

Some estimate of a student's appreciation of art can be made from what he writes or says about it. But the ultimate evaluation of his ability to create must come from analyzing the picture or the carving he has produced. Thus the teacher needs some ability to appraise students' art products (unless, of course, the instructor believes art is only expression and therefore the creator himself is the only judge of its adequacy).

To appraise efficiently, an instructor needs to answer three questions for himself:

1. What is my philosophy of art, or what do I conceive good art to be?

One way to answer this is for him to analyze where he stands in relation to the dimensions described earlier. For instance, does he think art should be realistic and should adhere to traditional art principles but may involve any variety of subject matter? Or is art a very original expression of an individual's deepest emotions in the form of designs that do not reflect the usual appearance of objects in nature? Or is art something still different?

2. Can this concept or philosophy of art be analyzed into components, and if so, what are they?

This is the problem of whether an aesthetic visual experience can be or should be transformed into words. It is also the problem of whether a picture or carving should be perceived only as a unit or *Gestalt* or whether we can legitimately analyze it into meaningful different aspects.

A few people apparently believe an aesthetic experience is exclusively a direct one: the eye sees the picture; the brain is impressed with its image. They believe we cannot properly translate such a visual experience into another medium, such as words or music. A visual experience must remain exclusively a visual one.

We cannot accurately communiate about it with talk. If we thoroughly accept such a belief as this, we seem obligated not to analyze a picture into its color combinations, compositional qualities, and the like. Rather, we simply look at the painting and accept the impression emotionally. We may express an "I like it" or "It leaves me cold" reaction. But we should not discuss what elements we think might have contributed to its success or lack of success. A teacher who might adopt such a philosophy would not analyze a picture into components and evaluate these but would simply give an over-all expression of liking, feeling indifferent, or disliking. Perhaps such an evaluation would please the student whose work is liked, but it is not very useful to the student whose work is not. When he asks, "What specifically don't you like about it?" or "How can I improve?" he receives no help.

But most people probably believe that a picture can be analyzed into elements, both graphically and verbally. That is, even though it is true that a picture does produce a direct visual experience that cannot be completely transposed into words, still it is possible to identify characteristics of dominance, variety, and rhythm of line and color. On the basis of this analysis, the teacher can instruct the student in how to change the composition to bring it into better harmony with the teacher's idea of satisfactory art or the student's idea of what he wanted to show.

As noted earlier, there are individual differences among people's ideas of art. So the elements that one teacher believes make up a proper work of art can differ from those accepted by another. Though we have no right to demand that teachers all hold identical philosophies of art, we do have a right to ask that each one define clearly the components he believes make up an art work so he can more adequately evaluate students' art products and make useful suggestions for improvements.

3. After a teacher identifies the various components in his conception of good art, he faces a third question: How can the analyses of an art work be best recorded and communicated to the student?

The most common way for a teacher to record his observations is simply by remembering. He tries to keep in mind what strengths and shortcomings a given pupil's drawings or block prints have shown in the past. In other cases, he may write a brief note or give the student a mark in the roll book or may record the observations on a rating scale or check list.

The most common way teachers communicate their analyses to students is orally. They say:

"I like the color scheme. The dominance of dark blues and greens nicely suits the idea of a cold night in a forest. But there's no center of interest, no highlight to arrest my attention. My eye wanders all over aimlessly, searching for a place to land."

"Your idea of flowers blowing through the sky is good. It's quite original. But I think your paints are becoming mixed together too much on the palette. Some of the colors are muddy and indefinite. They lack life. This yellow flower is bright and has a hint of vitality, but did you really want the others to look like that?"

In addition to giving such verbal appraisals, a teacher can develop a check list or rating scale focusing attention on the components of art which he considers most important. Let us illustrate one such instrument which might be used by one of the instructors in our earlier examples, Teacher C.

RATING SHEET FOR PAINTINGS

Student's name ____Hal Johnson____ Date __March 17__

Subject matter of painting being judged __Air view of a landscape — almost abstract__

COMPOSITIONAL QUALITIES

1. UNITY OR HARMONY. Colors, forms, lines, and painting style appear to belong together to form a complete picture that does not have parts missing and is not cluttered with undesirable or confusing elements.

    A. *Hues unified?* ___Yes _X_Partially ___No

    Comments: Dominance of color is split among brown, black, and white.

    B. *Dark-light pattern unified?* ___Yes ___Partially _X_No

    Comments: Too large a mass of white at lower left. Picture appears to split into two segments — a white one and a brown-black one.

C. *Forms, lines harmonize?* ___Yes _X_Partially ___No
   Comments: Changing the dark-light pattern would bring better harmony to patterns of form and line.

D. *Drawing and painting style unified?* _X_Yes ___Partially ___No
   Comments: All done with bold strokes of palette knife.

E. *Is there an area of emphasis or a center of interest which makes the picture easily comprehended?* _X_Yes ___Partially ___No
   Comments: But it covers the entire lower left corner of the picture. Altering the dark-light placement would add stability to the composition.

2. VARIETY OR INTEREST. Within the dominant color, dark-light, form, and line patterns there is enough variety to maintain the viewer's interest and attention. The viewer does not find the picture boring.
   A. *Sufficient hue variety?* _X_Yes ___Partially ___No
      Comments:

   B. *Dark-light pattern varied enough?* _X_Yes ___Partially ___No
      Comments:

   C. *Form and line varied enough?* _X_Yes ___Partially ___No
      Comments:

CONTROL OF MEDIUM

1. Mixing Paint. Paints are mixed to achieve color qualities that are:
   __Dull, lifeless _X_Lively __Unpleasantly raw, blatant
   Comments:

2. Applying Paint. Paints are applied in fashion that is:
   _X_Precise, confident __Worked over too much __Inconsistent
   Comments:

CREATIVITY. Does the picture evidence an individualistic interpretation or expression rather than a copy of someone else's work?
_X_Yes __Partially __No
What seem to be the most creative aspects? *Color combinations, bold patterning of color and dark-light areas. But I feel that this originality has taken the composition beyond the limits of pleasing, stable design. The picture is striking but not satisfying for me to view.*

In devising the foregoing rating device, the teacher does not assume that the qualities of paintings or sculpture can be completely reflected in a set of scales. He does not assume that a visual experience can be completely transposed into words. Nor does he imagine that this scale is a highly objective device, free from personal opinion.

Rather, he only assumes that certain qualities of art can be approximated by verbal descriptions. These verbal descriptions, as defined in class by pictorial examples previously shown to the students, are useful in focusing teacher and student attention on the qualities. A rating scale containing the descriptions helps the teacher communicate his reactions to the student.

It should be noted that none of the individual ratings on the scale was converted into a numerical score. Nor was an over-all score derived from totaling individual ratings. This is because, as the *Gestalt* psychologists have implied, the whole effect of an art work is something more than a simple summing up of its individual, segmented parts.

Whether a rating device like the one above would be given to the student or only kept among the teacher's records depends on why the teacher is making the evaluation (prediction, diagnosis, achievement) and how the student would probably react. If the student is mature and confident so that he could profit from knowing the uncomplimentary portions of the appraisal, it would be proper to give him the appraisal sheet. But if the scale shows the painting to be quite inadequate in many respects, and if the instructor thinks the student would be discouraged by seeing such an evaluation, the scale would better remain in the teacher's record folder. In this case, the teacher might orally commend any praiseworthy aspects of the work but point out only one shortcoming which he feels the student could accept and profit from at his present stage of progress.

Evaluation Summarized

We conclude that students can differ markedly from each other in the kind and quality of art they produce. Teachers evaluate them to predict future progress, diagnose strengths and limitations, or judge achievement to date. The two commonest approaches to evaluation are through teacher-made tests and teacher observations of student art products. Standardized art tests have been used on a limited scale, especially for predicting art ability, but their actual value as predictors is still unknown.

The greatest obstacle to devising standardized evaluation techniques in art is the fact that art means different things to different people. Universal criteria against which evaluation devices might be validated have not yet been established and possibly never will be. Each teacher, therefore, is obligated to determine the criteria he himself will use. Only then is he prepared to select the evaluation devices which will enable him to judge the qualities of students' work and communicate his judgments to them.

PROVIDING FOR INDIVIDUAL DIFFERENCES

So far, we have identified several viewpoints teachers may hold toward art, and we have discussed methods of appraising students' art work. In this final section we shall identify some of the ways art may be taught to suit individual differences among students.

We shall begin by assuming that the two most basic goals of the typical school art program are (1) to help every pupil create art products that furnish him personal satisfaction as well as desirable recognition from other people and (2) to help him appreciate the art works of others (in whatever senses the particular school interprets the term "appreciation").

Within this framework of goals, there are several ways that individual talents and tastes can be served. We shall consider them under the headings of variety of media, breadth of subject matter, degree of realism, and stage of progress.

Variety of Media

Perhaps the most obvious way for the school to suit art activities to individual differences is to introduce pupils to many art media. One student may find his greatest satisfactions in tempera painting, another in weaving, still another in clay modeling. Since the breadth of possibilities of media may not be obvious to all readers, we shall suggest some of the types that pupils can profit from meeting during their school careers.

Drawing and Painting

The most common drawing tools are crayons, soft pencils, and pens.

Crayons are suitable for any grade level. They can be used for making line drawings. Or, stripped of their paper cover, they can be used with the flat side against the picture to produce varied shading and modeling. When cloth is thumbtacked tightly across a board or cardboard box, pupils can draw on it with crayons to make flags, wall hangings, or classroom curtains. After the cloth drawing has been pressed with a hot iron between sheets of wrapping paper, it is permanent and washable.

Scratch drawings are created by coloring white cardboard with areas of solid crayon hues. Then a layer of black India ink is painted over the crayon. When this is dry, a sharp tool can be used to scratch a drawing into the surface of the ink, allowing the crayon and white cardboard to show through the scratches.

India ink in lettering pens yields sharp black line drawings. Since India ink is waterproof, the dried drawing can have transparent water colors painted over certain portions to provide highlights of color. This line-and-wash technique is usually handled most adeptly by secondary-school students. It is less appropriate in the lower grades because the lettering pens demand a sure hand.

Felt-tip or brush-point marking pens have become popular as drawing instruments because they are available in a variety of widths and produce a stroke that dries immediately and is permanent. They allow the pupil to draw more quickly and with freer sweeps than is possible with other types of pens.

Chalk drawings can be successful at any grade level. Some of the most pleasing ones are done on colored paper, such as white or yellow chalk on black or chocolate-brown construction paper. In the secondary school, the more advanced students can produce highly finished drawings with the fine-grained pastel chalks which are available in a wide variety of hues.

In the primary grades, finger paints are popular because they do not demand skill with drawing instruments. The child simply smears the creamlike paint across dampened paper, deriving more pleasure perhaps from the sensation of gooey fingers than he does from the final product. Finger paints can be purchased ready to use, or they can be produced in class by mixing soap flakes with dry poster paints and water. In the upper grades, finger paints serve to decorate scrapbook covers or produce holiday wrapping paper.

Tempera or poster paints in bright hues are suitable at any level. In kindergarten and primary grades, children dressed in smocks paint at easels. In higher grades, they produce murals of historical events on wide rolls of wrapping paper. In the secondary school, a chalklike binder may be mixed with the paint powders to furnish a medium appropriate for more mature studio paintings.

Transparent water colors, available in the typical tin school box or in tubes, are best suited to older students' talents. The transparent paints can yield precise and delicate paintings of professional quality, but they demand a sureness of hand and mind. Once the brush touches the paper, the stroke cannot be sucessfully covered over or revised if it was not exactly right.

Oil paints are also more appropriate for secondary-school students. They are more costly than water colors and demand more patience than tempera usually does. In addition, dried oil paint does not easily come out of clothes. But for the older student, oils can be a most satisfying medium. They can be handled in a variety of styles, and they produce permanent work. If considerable linseed oil is added to the paints, a smooth-surface painting is produced. More body is given to the paints if wax is added instead of oil.

Modeling and Carving

Clay serves the modeling needs of younger and older students alike. With it they can mold bowls, vases, and ash trays, model human figures and animals, and create three-dimensional abstract designs. After water-base clay objects are dry, they can be painted; but in this form they chip easily. If fired in a kiln, they become waterproof and resist chipping. If dipped in glaze and placed again in the kiln, they achieve a permanent, glassy finish.

Plastic clay, available in several colors, does not dry completely, so after the pupil tires of an object which he has modeled he can use the material to build something different.

One of the least expensive and most useful modeling materials is papier-mâché. To make a mask, you simply tear strips of newspaper, dip them into creamy wallpaper paste, and crisscross layers of the strips over a clay mound that has been modeled into the general features of the mask. When a half-dozen layers have been applied and have dried, the clay can be dug out, leaving a lightweight but durable mask.

If a quantity of newspaper or paper toweling is torn into bits and mixed with paste, a sticky mass is produced and may be used for modeling figures or puppet heads. When sawdust has been added to this mixture, a coarser texture of modeling substance results.

Plaster of Paris makes good carving material. The plaster powder is first mixed into water until it becomes like thick cream. It should be poured immediately into a mold, where it hardens in a short time. Saucers may be used as the molds if the pupils wish to carve small circular wall plaques in bas-relief. When a milk carton has served as the mold, the student obtains a plaster block suitable for sculpturing human figures, model ships, or abstract forms.

Bars of soap and soft wood also serve as carving materials. The more advanced secondary-school students may wish to try sculpturing in soft stone, such as firebrick or sandstone.

Print Making

Print making in the primary grades can be started with vegetables as the stamping tools. The child cuts a potato or turnip in half, carves a simple design into the flat cut surface, presses it on an ink pad and stamps the design onto paper or cloth.

Older pupils may cut designs into linoleum or wood blocks to produce prints of some quality. Or they may cut stencils from paper and apply this design to paper or cloth with tempera paint, printer's ink, crayon, or dyes.

High-school students can master the silk-screen process and produce quantities of posters and prints in varied colors and sizes.

Weaving and Dyeing

In the lower grades, looms can be made by stretching yarn back and forth between notches cut at opposite ends of a sheet of cardboard. Another color of yarn is woven over and under the strands of this grid to produce simulated Indian doll blankets or hot-dish mats. A sturdier loom can be constructed from a wooden box with rows of nails at each end to hold the warp threads. On larger, commercially built looms, the older student may produce scarves, rugs, and table cloths of professional quality.

These weaving activities are particularly well suited to certain types of disturbed students. Weaving is a repetitive activity which produces a visibly pleasing object. As such, it appears to have a therapeutic influence on many disturbed individuals. Pupils of rather low mental age may succeed with simple weaving when they lack the original ideas needed with other art media.

Tie-and-dye techniques furnish another way of making designs on cloth. The pupil may place a marble in the center of a square white scarf, then draw the scarf together tightly around the marble so the marble looks like the small covered head of a puppet and the rest of the scarf hangs below like the body and skirt. A quantity of string is wound tightly round and round the scarf below the marble, covering an area of perhaps one or two inches beneath it. If the cloth is then dipped into dye and allowed to dry, the string and marble can be removed, revealing a newly designed scarf. There is a colored circle in the center, a wide white circle around it (where the layers of string kept the dye from the cloth), and the rest of the scarf is the color of the center. Different designs result when string is wound round other portions of the cloth.

Advanced high-school students might wish to try the batik dyeing technique of Java. In this case hot wax is dripped onto cloth in a pattern from a small spout in a tin cup or tiny pitcher. When the waxed sketch is complete, the cloth is dipped into dye. The dye does not touch the waxed areas of cloth, so when it dries and the wax is washed out with warm water, the waxed portions form a white design against the dyed background.

Summary of Media Possibilities

The foregoing examples do not exhaust the kinds of art media which can serve students' individual tastes. They merely suggest the variety available. Other useful activities involve paper cutting and paper sculpturing, the creation of mobiles and stabiles, wire sculpturing, needlepoint work, leather carving and tooling, woodworking, metal carving, the burning of designs into wood and leather, jewelry making, the creation of collages by attaching objects of various textures to a surface, glass and metal etching, and carving in plastic. Further possibilities, along with specific directions in how to develop them with pupils, are suggested in the readings listed at the end of the chapter.

With such a range of media available, teachers should be able to locate some which will suit the needs of each student, despite the individuality he may exhibit.

Breadth of Subject Matter

Early in the chapter we noted that different teachers may consider different types of subject matter as being proper for art. The question at this point is: Which kind of teacher would best care for students' individual differences in choices of subject matter for art work? It seems evident that the teacher who accepts the greatest variety of subject matter as being proper will be the one who can most adequately care for the broadest diversity of individual tastes. The broader the range of subjects the teacher considers admissible, the more likely it is that pupils will find something to paint or carve that interests them.

Sometimes, however, students are restricted in choice of subject matter simply because they do not understand the breadth of things the teacher will accept, not because the teacher wishes them to limit their choice. Some instructors give too little attention to encouraging a student to explore a great range of possible subjects. They are caught up in a routine of displaying only a limited selection of still lifes, landscapes, animals, and human figures. They would willingly accept students' deviations from these familiar paths, but they simply have not thought about suggesting more possibilities. Therefore, it is desirable to take positive steps to broaden pupils' scope. There are several ways this may be done.

The teacher can exhibit and discuss pictures that illustrate a diversity of subjects. Or he may project colored slides of many kinds of objects and scenes that he has photographed in the community.

Students themselves can be assigned to suggest new subject matter. They may be asked to list possibilities observed around their home and neighborhood. They may describe subjects suggested by television programs, newspaper articles, and fiction. They may be asked to make a dozen sketches of subjects they have never tried to draw before.

Sometimes individual items, such as a rose or a car or a horse or a circus poster, are not new subject matter for the pupil. But new combinations can be made of them. The dew-tipped rose may be pictured atop a stark, dry skull. The horse may be pictured looking at the circus poster plastered on the rear of the battered car. When students are encouraged to imagine new combinations, they often expand subject-matter possibilities in quite original ways.

The discussions that arise during these activities also enable the teacher to clarify for the class the standards he uses in determining what is appropriate subject matter for art work.

Degree of Realism

In our earlier discussion of a realistic-nonobjective dimension, we noted that some teachers will accept a wider variety of deviations from literal realism than others. From the standpoint of individual differences, the teacher who welcomes many kinds of deviations (such as caricature, cubism, nonobjective art) will be providing more opportunities for students than the teacher who accepts fewer variations.

Whatever his position on this dimension, the instructor will help meet individuals' artistic needs more adequately if he makes clear to them the range of styles he considers proper. The situation here is similar to that described for subject matter. Sometimes students do not know the degree of deviation from realism that an instructor will accept because he has not bothered to tell or show them. Often he would welcome more originality than students realize, but he has assumed they know this without being told.

To make his beliefs clear to the class, the instructor can show them a series of pictures illustrating the variations he considers good art and others he considers unartistic or improper for art works. Students can be assigned to sketch in a variety of styles (such as literally realistic, abstract, stylized) and they can discuss why they prefer one of these to another. They can try to develop new departures from realism and can judge them according to the criteria suggested by the instructor.

Through such activities, the class members not only learn the teacher's philosophy of art but can also be stimulated to inspect their own beliefs and to develop personal standards with which they feel comfortable. Thus they are better prepared both to create art work and to understand or appreciate that of others.

Stage of Progress

In addition to providing varieties of media, subject matter, and degrees of realism from which students may choose, the art teacher can adapt classroom procedures to fit the different stages of development found among pupils. For instance, one student may be ahead of his classmates in basic drawing skills, so he is ready sooner for more sophisticated problems. In ceramics class, a few may have finished making their clay bowls and be ready for slip-casting dishes while the others are still trying to master the most basic pottery techniques.

The ways teachers can care for these differences in rate of progress are similar to those described for meeting differences in the more academic studies. If a small group is working on one kind of task, the teacher can meet with it in a corner of the room while the rest of the class pursues different activities. If one or two secondary-school students are ready to learn a new technique or style, the teacher may direct them to read magazine articles or books which illustrate and explain the technique. Several pupils may stop after school or during recess to learn a new approach which they can later develop on their own in class with only occasional help from the instructor.

Compared to most teachers of academic subjects, art instructors are usually more accustomed to conducting class in a way that promotes individualized instruction. Students are freer to move about the room and to ask questions of classmates. The instructor often introduces the problems on which the group is to work, then spends his time visiting each student, offering suggestions and adjusting the general assignment to individual needs and talents.

SUMMARY

From the standpoint of individual differences, the field of graphic arts is at once an opportunity and a puzzlement.

Opportunity exists because art is a field in which originality is usually encouraged. Pupils with varied abilities and interests can probably all gain some degree of success if they have teachers who show them the breadth of possibilities available. Because there is apparently little or no relation between art talent and aptitude for the usual academic subjects, a student who is not adept at academic work may well be able to succeed in art.

The puzzlement in art results from a lack of agreement among artists or art teachers about what constitutes good art. It becomes the teacher's uneasy duty to decide what philosophy of art he himself will adopt and to explain this philosophy clearly to his students, knowing all the time that other people may be telling them something different.

Two principal techniques are used for judging students' differences in art work: tests and analyses of art products. Standardized tests have very limited usefulness because they measure only segments of the entire creative process. They have not proved efficient in appraising present skill or predicting future success in art. Teacher-made tests and analyses of art products, based on the instructors' own criteria, seem to be the most defensible approaches to evaluation (unless, of course, we hold a philosophy which deems the artist himself the only rightful evaluator of whether he succeeded in what he attempted).

Teachers can more adequately meet individual differences when they (1) introduce pupils to many different art media, (2) suggest many possibilities for subject matter, (3) illustrate varieties of ways they may interpret life or deviate from realism in art work, and (4) adjust classroom procedures so students can move ahead at their own rates of development.

SUGGESTED LEARNING ACTIVITIES

1. To learn something of your present concepts of art, inspect pictures in an art book or art gallery. Rank them according to which you like best and which you like least. Then try to determine the criteria you have used to distinguish the best liked from the least liked. Write out this analysis and compare it with your classmates' apparent standards of art judgment.

2. List any types of subject matter which you think are inappropriate for art works. Then describe the standards you believe you have used for distinguishing the acceptable from unacceptable subjects. Write a similar type of analysis for the realistic-nonobjective dimension.

3. Visit a classroom during an art period to hear what the teacher says

to students and to see the kinds of art work they produce. On the basis of this visit, try to estimate where the art teacher stands on two or three of the dimensions described in this chapter.

4. Interview an art instructor to determine what range of individual differences he finds in his class, what problems (if any) these differences cause him, and how he adjusts classwork to meet these differences. Inquire about the criteria he uses for grading pupils.

5. Read the introductory chapter (or chapters) of two art-education books or read two articles. Write a summary of the agreements and disagreements in philosophy of art which you may have found between the two authors. In what ways do you agree or disagree with them? In what ways do you question their viewpoints?

SUGGESTED READINGS

BARKAN, MANUEL. *Through Art to Creativity.* Boston: Allyn and Bacon, 1962. Contains visits to art classrooms to see exactly what teachers say to stimulate creative work and what the children do.

BUROS, OSCAR K. *The Fifth Mental Measurements Yearbook.* Highland Park, N.J.: Gryphon Press, 1959. Evaluations of art tests.

————. *The Fourth Mental Measurements Yearbook.* Highland Park, N.J.: Gryphon Press, 1953. Evaluation of art tests.

CONANT, HOWARD, and RANDALL, ARNE. *Art in Education.* Peoria: Charles A. Bennett, 1959.

D'AMICO, VICTOR. *Creative Teaching in Art.* Scranton: International Textbook Co., 1953.

DeFRANCESCO, ITALO L. *Art Education, Its Means and Ends.* New York: Harper and Brothers, 1958. Chap. 11: Art and the Exceptional Child.

FREEMAN, FRANK S. *Theory and Practice of Psychological Testing.* New York: Henry Holt, 1950.

HARTLEY, RUTH E.; FRANK, LAWRENCE K.; and GOLDENSEN, ROBERT M. *Understanding Children's Play.* New York: Columbia University Press, 1952.

HORNE, JOICEY. *Young Artists.* Toronto: Longmans, Green, 1961.

JEFFERSON, BLANCHE. *Teaching Art to Children.* Boston: Allyn and Bacon, 1959. Illustrates what teachers say in guiding art activities. Chap. X: Importance of the child's individuality and experiences.

LORD, LOIS. *Collage and Construction in Elementary and Junior High Schools.* Worcester: Davis Publications, 1958.

LOWENFELD, VIKTOR. *Creative and Mental Growth.* New York: Macmillan, 1957.

McFEE, JUNE KING. *Preparation for Art*. San Francisco: Wadsworth, 1961. Chap. 4: Individual Differences in Development in Art.

WICKISER, RALPH L. *An Introduction to Art Education*. Yonkers-on-Hudson, N.Y.: World Book Company, 1957.

CHAPTER 11

Musical Abilities

Even a casual observer recognizes distinct differences in musical ability among children and youth. During a kindergarten music session, one child sings in tune and with accurate rhythm after hearing a melody only a few times. Another recalls the general form of the melody but deviates somewhat from the original version. A third drones along in a tiresome rhythm that hardly resembles the song. This same range of talent is observed at all grade levels and with instruments other than the voice.

Differences are also obvious in listening tastes. When left to their own choice, some teen-agers limit their listening to the repetitive chants of the current dance tunes. Others prefer folk songs. Some like semiclassical and classical works. Still others enjoy all these.

If a teacher is to work most effectively with students who exhibit such varieties of taste and talent, he will profit from knowing answers to the following questions: (1) Does musical talent consist of one over-all ability or of specific abilities that are not necessarily related? (2) How are musical taste and talent best measured? (3) Are musical abilities basically inborn, or are they a result of training? (4) What activities can the school provide to enable each student, despite his level of talent, to achieve the most in music? Chapter 11 proposes answers to these questions.

MUSICAL ABILITY OR ABILITIES?

Is musical talent one all-encompassing ability which determines a person's success in all aspects of musical endeavor? Or do different kinds of musical efforts—composing, playing piano, playing cello, listening—depend on somewhat different talents which a person may possess in varied amounts? These questions are important to teachers for two principal reasons.

First, if musical talent is a single quality, then a single test will predict how successful a student will probably be in whatever musical activity he attempts. But if a person's skills for one kind of activity, such as playing the oboe, can be different from his level of skill for success in another, like creating songs, then we need more specific measures of each of these areas to determine his chances of success in each.

Second, if musical talent is a single characteristic, students who have more of it are the only ones who can hope for much success in any musical pursuit. But if a variety of somewhat independent abilities exist, then a more varied music program in the school which takes advantage of different students' areas of strength can be provided. Many students can be expected to have some measure of success in at least certain activities.

We can seek an answer to this problem of single ability versus groups of abilities in two ways. One is the logical analysis of the skills that various musical activities require. The other is a comparison of the ways people succeed on various kinds of musical-ability tests.

Music Activities Analyzed

The rich assortment of skills found when we survey all varieties of musical experiences suggests strongly that many subtalents, rather than a single all-pervading one, make up musical success in its broadest sense. Not everyone would be likely to have all the subtalents in the same pattern or degree. To illustrate this hypothesis, let us look briefly at the three most basic kinds of musical experiences: composing, performing, and listening.

Composing can consist of so simple a behavior as a child's clapping a new rhythm or humming a tune he has created. Or it may consist of the complex skills demanded of the creator of operas. He conceives a structure for his entire musical drama, then develops compositions that combine melodies which fit the mood of the lyrics

and harmonies and countermelodies that challenge the most sophisticated listener's intellect. His orchestrations must suit the vocal
ranges of the singers and the personal characteristics of the orchestra
instruments.

Not only do composers vary in the complexity of skills they
possess, but they vary in the manner of expressing their creations.
A child may sing his new tune. An instrumentalist may improvise
on the piano or trumpet. Some composers conceive harmonies so
clearly that they write directly from imagination with the aid of no
instrument and know exactly how the creation will sound when
played.

The realm of performance also involves unquestioned diversity
in the skills required. Finger dexterity, field of vision, aural acuity,
and vocal-cord structure all help determine whether a person will
be better at singing than at playing the organ or flute. A violinist
who cannot hear any finer tonal distinctions than half tones will
constantly irritate listeners by playing out of tune. But a pianist
who can make only these same gross distinctions may play very
well. A snare drummer needs an accurate sense of rhythm and some
manual agility but requires no tonal sense at all. Yet the tympanist
beside him must discriminate tones accurately enough to retune his
drums each time the music changes key.

Performance is also affected by the musician's creative abilities.
Not only is this true of the calypso singer or jazz musician who spontaneously composes as he performs, but even musicians who play
others' compositions are expected to insert their individual interpretation and style into the rendition.

Listening to music is often called a music-appreciation activity.
Confusion about appreciation often exists among teachers and students because there is no common agreement about its meaning.
For some, it means liking to hear a composition. For others, it means
understanding the music's structure, such as differentiating a rondo
from a sonata or analyzing the counterpoint of a fugue or the chord
progressions in a symphony. For still others, appreciation means
recognizing the historical significance of the music or the role it
played in the composer's development. And some people believe
it means all these.

We thus conclude that music appreciation or taste means many things to many people, and the talent and training that bring success under one definition are quite different from those which bring success under another.

These observations about composing, performing, and listening suggest that the term "musical *ability*" is a misnomer. Because such varied skills are required for different musical pursuits, it appears that several somewhat independent abilities are involved. To offer further evidence on this issue, we now turn to musical-ability tests.

A Comparison of Musical-Ability Tests

We have three purposes in describing the following tests: (1) to acquaint the reader with six of the more prominent musical-ability scales, (2) to illustrate how statistical comparisons of them cast light on the issue of music ability versus abilities, and (3) to suggest what role these kinds of tests may best play in the school program.

All the tests described here are administered in the same general manner. The rhythms and melodies are on phonograph records or tapes to be played to students, who mark printed answer sheets in response to what they hear. But none of the tests is designed to measure exactly the same things as the others.

The oldest, and perhaps still the most popular, was created by C. E. Seashore (1919, 1939) to measure what its author believed were six inborn physiological capacities upon which musical talent was founded: tonal memory and the discrimination of pitch, loudness, time, timbre, and rhythm. Although Seashore admitted his battery did not measure all capacities that might contribute to musical talent, he thought it measured enough of them to be the best predictor of one's probable success in music.

The Seashore items consist of groups of tones or rhythms that do not pretend to represent melodies. Critics of the battery complain that this approach is unmusical and thus furnishes an unrealistic experience to the listener whose potential is supposedly being predicted.

Here arises our question regarding the unity or multiplicity of musical talent. If musical ability were one all-encompassing faculty, we should expect students who score high on one of Seashore's six capacity tests to score equally high on all others. But statistical comparisons have shown this is not true. With the exception of tonal memory, which is the one subtest that correlates appreciably with the others, the relationship among the six is very slight.

A second question of interest to teachers is: How well have the Seashore tests predicted success in music? A variety of studies have been conducted on this question. Some have shown little or no correlation between test scores and later success in music, while others have revealed considerable relationship. In summarizing this research, Farnsworth (1958:239–240) has written:

> Intelligence tests have been found to be of more worth than the Seashore tests in forecasting music grades in academic classes, e.g., history and appreciation of music, while the Seashore are of more value the more the classes are tonally conducted, e.g., classes in harmony. . . . it is apparent that the Seashore tests have at least some validity.

These studies have indicated that the test battery as a whole is a more secure predictor than are any of its parts.

A second musical-ability test of long standing, the Kwalwasser-Dykema battery (1930), measures the same six qualities as does Seashore's instrument. In addition, it tests pitch and rhythm imagery. One might assume that the relationship between the Kwalwasser-Dykema tests and their counterparts in the Seashore battery would be very high. But with the exception of tonal memory, such is not the case. (Farnsworth, 1958:240.)

The most recent revision of the Drake Musical Aptitude Tests (1954) measures musical memory and rhythmic ability with specially composed melodies and a rhythmic portion pitting metronome against voice. The correlation between Drake's and Seashore's rhythm tests is rather low (.17), but the relationship between the tonal-memory portions of the two batteries (.55) suggests that a more nearly common factor is being measured by the tone tests. (Farnsworth, 1958:244.)

Lundin (1949) has attempted to measure somewhat different aspects than previous tests treated. The five sections of his battery focus on abilities to discriminate (1) musical intervals, (2) changes of key as interlinked with changes of melody, (3) musical modes, (4) melodic sequences, and (5) rhythmic sequences. In a study conducted by Lundin, he found the total scores for the battery correlated with six professors' combined ratings of music students between .43 and .70 for such musical tasks as the ability to take melodic and harmonic dictation and skill in performing.

A British psychologist, H. D. Wing (1949, revised 1961), devised seven tests to measure chord analysis, pitch change, memory for tunes, rhythmic accent, intensity, phrasing, and harmony. Most American test constructors apparently believe that rather independent musical subabilities are being plumbed with the individual tests in their batteries, but Wing contends that factor analyses show a strong single common factor running through all of his tests. He concludes, therefore, that there is a general musical ability undergirding a person's performance on all subtests, even though the individual's success on one subtest is not completely identical to his success on the others.

The *Farnum Music Notation Test* (1953) focuses on a different combination of talent and training. The examination requires the student to listen to forty four-measure melodies while visually following a printed musical score that periodically deviates from the recording in either pitch, rhythm, or time. His task is to mark the measures in which deviations occur. The test has been found to correlate substantially with certain of the foregoing musical ability batteries and with ratings of instrumental performance.

From the foregoing survey of six batteries, it is apparent that different authors have focused on somewhat different aspects of musical listening in their attempt to measure musical ability. Although certain British psychologists, notably Wing, have felt that a strong single musical ability permeates all these measurements, the bulk of American studies suggest that many of the subtests (rhythmic memory, interval discrimination, mode discrimination, and the like) correlate so slightly with each other that they may be considered rather independent factors. Of the subabilities, tonal memory is the one which has most consistently appeared to correlate more highly with the others and also with subsequent musical performance.

Before discussing implications that these results hold for classroom teachers, let us inspect a second issue of interest: Are musical abilities inborn or a result of training?

MUSICAL ABILITIES: INHERITED OR ACQUIRED?

Music psychologists have expressed strong opinions on both sides of this question. The following statement by Schoen (1940:161–163) reflects the position that both he and Seashore adopted:

Musical talent is first an inborn capacity . . . bestowed by nature upon different persons very unequally. In the first place, we have the extremes of very marked talent, of the musical genius on the one hand and no talent at all on the other, and all the degrees of talent between the two extremes. Then again, there is the person who is equipped by nature with the sensory, the affective, and the intellectual basis for talent, but is deficient in the motor or technical requisites for effective musical production. . . .

If such a stand is accepted by an educator, and if he also accepts the existing tests as good measures of the inborn capacity, then students who fail to score high on such tests are not worth trying to train. If they can never succeed anyway, why inflict music lessons on them?

However, this hereditarian position has been hotly challenged in recent years. Studies of supposedly basic "capacities" like pitch sensitivity have shown that with proper training students can improve this skill enormously. (Farnsworth, 1958:186.) It has also been demonstrated that judgments of consonance and dissonance are culturally determined. This phenomenon is readily illustrated in the reactions that people from Western cultures typically exhibit toward music of the Orient. (Lundin, 1953:82–92.)

In contrast to Schoen and Seashore, Lundin has adopted a position toward the environmentalist end of the continuum.

There will obviously be individual differences in musical reactions just as there are in other areas of behavior. These will be a function of the biological equipment one has as well as the presence or absence of musical stimuli at various stages in one's development. What we are arguing against is the inheritance of mental powers for musical reception and performance.

That musical talent is the result of previously acquired skills and not inherited genius should be clear by now. No great composer or performer ever achieved his goal without long hours of apprenticeship and struggle.

Musical accomplishment is not the mere result of inherited inspiration but the product of hard work.[1]

Farnsworth (1958:186), after reviewing the evidence on each side of this nature-nurture issue, arrived at a conclusion that seems most reasonable for educators to adopt.

> . . . an ability is always the resultant of the interplay of heredity and environment. The organism limits or facilitates achievement in many ways. The environment likewise aids or inhibits. From these two sets of interacting limitations and facilitations abilities develop. Musical abilities seem in general no more or less inherited than abilities in many other areas.

IMPLICATIONS FOR TEACHERS

If we accept the assumption that one responsibility of the school is to further students' growth in music skills, the discussion so far of musical abilities seems to support the following recommendations for school practice.

1. Because somewhat different talents are needed for different kinds of musical activities, the elementary and junior-high years should introduce pupils to many musical possibilities and should furnish instruction in varied areas so that each child can discover the activities at which he can best succeed.

2. Since musical success is apparently influenced so strongly by environment, rather than being set almost entirely by heredity, teachers should not neglect the instruction of children who do not initially exhibit pronounced musical potential. It has been noted that proper training can improve even the basic physiological "capacities." It is, of course, unrealistic to expect that training will equalize all children's aptitudes. Some students will still be found to progress more rapidly and attain greater proficiency because inherited characteristics put them at an advantage.

3. Available musical-aptitude tests apparently have little value at the elementary-school level and are of questionable usefulness in the secondary school. In the elementary and junior-high grades, all children should have opportunities to study music. Thus tests

---

[1] Robert William Lundin, *An Objective Psychology of Music.* Copyright 1953 The Ronald Press Company, p. 190.

are not needed to determine which ones should receive instruction and which should not. Furthermore, if the school offers all pupils many musical experiences, tests will not be needed because individual differences will be revealed during the normal progress of class activities. Any homogeneous grouping for music classes that seems desirable in the secondary school can best be founded on students' success in previous classes rather than by tests. When prior success in music is used as the basis for predicting future potential, the teacher not only has evidence about such musical-ability components as aural acuity and note-reading ability, which tests could have measured, but also has evidence of such nontestable variables as willingness to practice.

However, if a student entering high school has not had rich opportunities to study music at elementary and junior-high levels, musical-ability tests may be of some aid in estimating the individual's proper placement in a music class.

MEETING MUSICAL DIFFERENCES

The remainder of this chapter consists of specific suggestions of ways to carry out the foregoing implications. The recommendations are presented in three sections: (1) a broad range of activities for the elementary and early junior-high grades, (2) a variety of music-class activities for secondary schools, and (3) ways that secondary teachers of subject matter other than music can enrich students' learning through musical experiences that relate to these other subject-matter areas.

ELEMENTARY SCHOOL MUSIC

As suggested above, we believe the elementary school best cares for individual differences by introducing many music activities and furnishing instruction in them. Thus, pupils can discover which musical pursuits appeal to their talents and tastes. In keeping with this concept of the school's role, the following material consists of an overview of a wide range of specific musical experiences in order to introduce teachers to (or at least remind them of) the variety of possibilities available.

For the sake of convenience, the following suggestions are offered under three headings: composing, performing, and listening. Although no activity is cited as being appropriate for only one grade level, those surveyed below are generally arranged in an order from the simpler to the more complex. Thus, the ones appearing earlier in the discussion are usually more adaptable to the lower grades, and those that appear later are more typical of upper grades.

Experiences with Composing

There are many approaches to stimulating children to create their own songs and rhythms.

One of the simplest consists of the teacher's reciting a two-line verse, then announcing that she plans to make up a tune which suits the words. In front of the class, she tries out different melodies, which she sings or plays on the piano, and then asks pupils which they like best. After settling on a tune to fit the words, she can recite another two-line verse and ask for volunteers to think up tunes which might go with it. In this way pupils see how songs are created and learn that they themselves can do it.

Another composing activity begins with interpretive rhythms. For instance, the teacher says, "I'm going to pat on the table with my hands. Listen to this rhythm. Tell me whether you think it would make people want to march or run or fall asleep." When she taps a regular march cadence, it is assumed that the class will label it a march. Further examples, such as a gallop or Indian war dance, establish for the class the idea that rhythms can represent actions and moods. Then the teacher reverses the task by asking individual pupils to tap rhythms which they think suggest such things as a squirrel scurrying over a branch, an elephant plodding along a jungle path, children running on the playground, and rain falling on a car roof. This activity can be expanded to include the creation of melodies that represent these same actions or moods.

Composing can be profitably combined with listening experiences as pupils hear several songs by noted composers and discuss the way rhythm, cadence, melody, and mode combine to suit the music to its lyrics. Songs that provide contrasts in these characteristics include "Yankee Doodle," Brahms's "Lullaby," "Jump Down and Spin Around," "Oklahoma," "Whistle While You Work," and "Greensleeves." The children are then expected to apply these principles of suitability to their own compositions.

A further introductory experience, focusing only on melodies rather than combining melodies and words, consists of the teacher's playing four bars of a tune and asking different children to sing a tune of four more measures that would go well with the first measures. From this easy beginning, children can more readily move to the stage of creating their own melodies without the aid of an initial musical phrase.

As the teacher encourages upper elementary and junior-high pupils to try creating an entire song, they will often benefit from starting with an analysis of the underlying structure of simple songs. They may begin with a binary song ("Dixie" or Brahms's "Lullaby") which is founded on two principal themes, that is, divided into two distinct or contrasted sections, each the same length (theme A and theme B). Next, they may analyze a ternary or three-part song ("All through the Night") which consists of two principal themes with the first repeated after the second (form A–B–A). Then they can inspect the most common form for popular songs, the A–A–B–A pattern, which is composed of an original melody of perhaps eight measures, followed by a repetition of this tune. A contrasting melody of eight bars forms the third part, and the song concludes with the original melody. By analyzing such patterns, students can determine consciously, rather than only intuitively, satisfying structures for their own compositions.

Setting poetry to melodies is an activity appropriate at every grade level. In the elementary school, this experience is usually most satisfactory when the teacher introduces it by having the children read the poem in unison to get the full meaning and rhythm of the words. A second reading may be accompanied by a tapping or patting of the rhythm to establish this clearly in mind. Next, the teacher may play the tonic chord on the piano to give the class a feeling for the "home tone," or key. Then as many pupils as possible are asked to sing a melody they believe is appropriate for the first phrase. The class choose the one they like best, and they proceed to creating the next phrase. This activity, repeated several times during a semester with different poems, furnishes a pattern for children to follow in creating their own individual songs at home. In the upper grades, the more apt students can create songs to accompany skits or plays they produce.

Performing

Most of the performing experiences of value to children are rather obvious ones. Yet many children are not offered these experiences in school. The reasons for this neglect are apparently several: (1) lack of thought or awareness on the teacher's part, (2) too little time in the school schedule, (3) the teacher's ignorance of how to offer these opportunities, (4) the teacher's conviction that an introduction to performance possibilities other than singing is not the responsibility of the school.

The following illustrations of useful activities are provided for teachers who have been unaware of simple performance possibilities and of ways to carry them on in the classroom.

Using Instruments

The primary-grade rhythm band furnishes the simplest activity. As the teacher plays a march or dance on the piano or record player, pupils accompany the piece on such percussion instruments as drums, triangles, wood blocks, sandpaper blocks scraped together, rattles made of tin cans or small boxes containing pebbles, coconut-shell halves, sleigh bells on a strap, tambourines which can be tapped or shaken, cymbals, and a wood block six inches long with a hollowed-out center to produce a resonant sound. When they hear the melody, the class decide on which beats different instruments will play. In each four-beat measure, the drums may play only on the first beat, the sleigh bells on the first and third, and the sandpaper blocks and tapping sticks on every beat.

Early experiences with melodic instruments are possible with toy xylophones, tonettes, melody flutes, and harmonicas. Not only can pupils pick out tunes on these simple instruments but they have a chance to learn to read music by number, which is an easy step toward transferring to reading by note. When an entire class performs on tonettes, the occasional errors of the less adept are covered over by the group in a way that furnishes all of them the satisfactions that some would not experience if they were required to display their errors in solo.

With rhythm-band and simple melody instruments the mood of different kinds of music can be simulated by various combinations of the instruments. For instance, a recording of a Japanese, Chinese, or Balinese composition can suggest the individualistic quality of the music of these nations. Then children can experiment with various simple instruments to find a combination that reflects these Oriental moods. A wood block, tapping sticks, a gong, and drums may reflect the Oriental quality, accompanied by a five-tone melody on a tonette. A combination of drums may give the impression of Indian or African music. Tunes played on the black keys of the piano simulate the pentatonic scale of the Orient.

In a classroom containing a piano—and a teacher who can tolerate noise—pupils can learn to play simple melodies before and after school or during recess and lunch periods. For many children, this will be the only opportunity they will have to try playing a piano. If the teacher first uses a blackboard diagram or cardboard keyboard models to explain the piano keyboard, she can write out notes or numbers for simple melodies that pupils may learn on their own.

The autoharp, with its push-button simplicity, enables children to add chord accompaniments to their songs. A ukulele in the classroom introduces children to simple ways to make chords on a stringed instrument.

Although it is common for elementary-school teachers to introduce pupils to the sight and sound of orchestra instruments, it is not so common to let children try them out. Pupils' understanding and interest are usually increased when they have a chance to blow the trumpet or bow the violin. It is true that such an activity is not always feasible. Teachers hesitate to pass germs from one lip to another via the trombone mouthpiece, and musicians are understandably hesitant to let children toy with their instruments. Still, it is frequently possible to borrow an inexpensive violin or small guitar or cornet for a week, and rules can be set up for its use. A student monitor can be appointed to ensure that the mouthpiece is washed with soap and water before another child takes his turn and that the violin bow is not used for dueling.

In most schools, some children take private music lessons. If invited to perform at school, they not only gain welcome recognition for an accomplishment but also introduce classmates to new possibilities for musical pursuits.

Singing

The most obvious vocal activity, appropriate at all grade levels, is the singing of rote songs. By "rote," we mean learning a song by hearing it several times rather than by reading it. If the teacher is not confident of her ability to sing or accompany the children on the piano or autoharp, the children can learn from a recording. In this case they may benefit from listening to the recording played the first time, then try humming the tune as it is played again. Later they can learn the words. Those who can read will profit from having the words written on the board or on a sheet of paper so that they do not suffer the occasional aural confusion of believing "The Star-Spangled Banner" begins, "José, can you see?"

To parallel their early singing activities, pupils will benefit from tone-matching sessions. This will improve their abilities to hear accurately and to sing in tune. Tone-matching or ear-training sessions can be conducted at a number of levels of complexity. At a simple level, the teacher sings a tone on a neutral syllable like *loo* or *lah* and points to individuals, who sing the same tone after her. A slightly more advanced variation consists of the teacher's singing two sequential tones representing a common musical interval that is met in songs, such as the *do-so* interval or the *mi-do* or *do-la* combination. These can be sung on neutral syllables or can be related to sounds from life. For example, in practicing octave skips (low *do* to high *do* or vice versa) and smaller interval jumps, the teacher can imitate a train whistle (too-too), imitate the wind (oo-oo), call to a friend (yoo-hoo), imitate a clock (tick-tock), or call good-by. To furnish additional variety to tone-matching sessions, the teacher may call students' names like Kathy or Harry or can sing a question like "What's your name?" to which the child answers, in matched tones, "Jenny."

Part singing can be introduced through such familiar rounds as "Row Your Boat," "Three Blind Mice," "The Pufferbillies," "White Coral Bells."

When teachers introduce music-reading activities, they must realize that there are marked individual differences among pupils in this area. Some students will never succeed well, despite long hours of work, in reading vocal music accurately.

Listening to Music

If each child is to have opportunities to gain the most from music, he deserves to learn that music can be listened to for a variety of purposes. Thus teachers have a responsibility to organize lessons that illustrate these purposes clearly. Some of these purposes are illustrated below.

Pupils can learn that some music is intended to tell a story (program music), whereas other compositions are intended only to furnish an enjoyable experience with sound (absolute music). A recording of *Peter and the Wolf* will illustrate the former, a Bach fugue or Chopin *étude* portion the latter.

To illustrate the ways that music may suggest the mood and characteristics of people, animals, and places, the teacher may play "On the Trail" from Grofe's *Grand Canyon Suite*, Anderson's "Typewriter," Schumann's "Wild Horsemen," "The Flight of the Bumble Bee," "Sleigh Ride," "Songs of the Zoo," and "Carnival of the Animals." The characteristics of toys are simulated by Haydn's *Toy Symphony*, Victor Herbert's *Babes in Toyland*, and Tschaikovsky's "Dance of the Flutes" of the *Nutcracker Suite*.

Pupils learn to recognize the sounds of orchestra instruments and to describe the moods and personalities which the various instruments can reflect. These skills are produced through the pupils' seeing the instruments, hearing them played, and identifying their sounds on records. Some of the recordings that best promote these skills are "Rusty in Orchestraville," "Pee Wee the Piccolo," "Toy Trumpet," "Yankee Doodle," "Instruments of the Orchestra," "Turkey in the Straw," "Fiddle-Faddle."

A series of lessons on different kinds of dances helps students recognize the differences among waltzes, fox trots, minuets, Indian dances, square and country dances (*contredance*), polkas, the schottische, the Sicilian Circle, and music appropriate for ballets.

The roles music has played in occupations, either by aiding workers or reflecting aspects of their lives, are illustrated in such songs as sea chanteys ("Blow the Man Down," "I'll Go No More Aroving"), railroad songs ("Casey Jones," "I've Been Working on the Railroad," "John Henry"), canal-worker songs ("The Erie Canal"), cowboy songs ("The Red River Valley," "Home on the

Range," "The Colorado Trail," "Night-herding Song"), and others like "Water Boy" and the "Volga Boat Song."

Music as a stimulus to fantasy can be emphasized when the teacher instructs pupils, "Listen to the recording I'll play, and let your imagination run along with the music. See what pictures come into your mind or what feelings you have as the music plays. Then be ready to tell the rest of us what the music helped you think about." A variety of individual reactions results from such selections as "Stars and Stripes Forever" march, "Dixie," Debussy's "Hurdy Gurdy Man," Poldini's "Waltzing Doll," Pierné's "March of the Little Lead Soldiers," and Stravinsky's *Firebird Suite.*

A variation of the foregoing free-imagination lesson is the type in which the teacher tells something of the composer's intention, then plays the recording. For example, she may say, "A composer named Smetana had a favorite river. To tell what he felt about it, he composed a piece which we're going to hear. As you listen, pay attention to the way that the first part of the music sounds different from the last part. Why do you think he made this difference? And what instruments did he seem to use to give his idea?"

To combine creative imagination with listening, the instructor can ask the class to tell what kind of music they would make up if they were to write a composition called "The Snow is Dancing." That is, what instruments would be featured? What would be the tempo? What might the tune sound like? After several students express their ideas, invite them to hear the way one composer, Debussy, carried out this theme in his *Children's Corner Suite.* The same type of activity can be used as an introduction to Copland's *Rodeo,* to the storm portion of Rossini's *William Tell Overture,* and to the storm from Grofe's *Grand Canyon Suite.*

Relationships between visual arts and music are established when the teacher asks, "What kind of picture would you paint in order to tell your feelings about the piece we will play?" The students, to demonstrate their answers, can paint or make chalk drawings while listening to such compositions as "The Sea and Sinbad's Ship" from Rimski-Korsakov's *Scheherazade Suite,* Ketelby's "In a Persian Market," "The Blue Danube," "The Drummer Boy and the Cook," and Anderson's "Jazz Legato and Jazz Pizzicato."

From the earliest grades, relationships between music and body movement can be developed. In the primary grades, pupils can begin by moving to rhythms. For instance, they can walk to 4–4 or 2–4 time in imitation of marching soldiers, a parade of toys, animals, and elves. They can run in different ways to 4–4, 2–4, or 6–8 rhythms to represent rain falling, fast-moving trains, or animals of various kinds. Hopping to music can suggest frogs or rabbits. Jumping represents children jumping rope. To simulate horses, they may gallop to 6–8 rhythms. Swinging arms and body to 3–4 time can represent someone in a swing or flowers and trees swayed by the wind.

Free-rhythm play encourages children to create movements that represent a theme. For example, a circus melody inspires them to pretend the band plays, acrobats and clowns perform, elephants waltz, horses do tricks, and the lion tamer directs the big cats. Rhythmic activities can also be created around such themes as the change of the seasons, the work on a farm, kinds of transportation, a sports day, or Olympic Games.

As they listen to music, pupils can engage in mimetic play, that is, imitate movements occurring in everyday life like climbing a ladder, going to the store, pitching and catching a ball, hoeing the garden, hammering and sawing, and riding a bicycle.

Some of the favorite singing games that also involve actions are "London Bridge," "The Farmer in the Dell," "Jim Along Josie," and "Jack Be Nimble."

Ballads also provide opportunities to dramatize the text in pantomime. Some appropriate ones are "The Old Woman and the Peddler," "Oh, No John," "Wraggle Taggle Gypsies," "Good King Wenceslaus," and "Soldier Boy, Soldier Boy."

Musical plays furnish even more challenging acting opportunities. *Peter and the Wolf* is a particularly apt one. Deems Taylor's *Through the Looking Glass* is also appropriate.

Pupils can sometimes adapt a story like *Snow White* by acting out parts to rhythms which the teacher plays on the piano, or the pupils may choose records with appropriate rhythms. For instance, Snow White can run through the woods (6–8 time), clean the dwarfs' cottage (3–4 time), meet the dwarfs upon their return home (3–4 time), see them dig in the mines (4–4 time), and be awakened by the prince who gallops to her rescue (6–8 time).

Along with listening to folk songs, students can learn some folk dances and can create their own Indian dances to match such recorded music as "The Eagle Dance," "Snake Dance," "Sioux Shuffling Feet," and "Cheyenne War Dance."

Suiting Activities to Individuals

Throughout the foregoing discussion, we have recommended that a wide variety of musical experiences be offered elementary-school pupils so that each child may better identify those musical pursuits that best fit his tastes and talents. Many of the same activities suggested for the entire class can also be directed at individuals or smaller groups within the class as enrichment or supplementary work.

For example, a teacher may wish to expand the musical opportunities for a fifth-grader who continually completes her reading assignments before her classmates. The pupil may be furnished a recording and a study-guide sheet with helpful questions such as, "What instrument plays the first melody? What other instrument takes this same melody next? What ideas or pictures does the music suggest to your mind?" If the record player has an earphone attachment, the pupil can listen at the back of the classroom without disturbing classmates. If not, she can perhaps listen in a nearby office or storeroom.

Other listening activities which pupils can carry out independently with the aid of guide questions are: comparing two versions of the same piece and deciding which they like better and why; analyzing songs to determine whether they follow an A–B (binary), A–B–A, or A–A–B–A form; selecting compositions which they wish to organize into a brief program to play for their classmates, along with introductory material explaining the selections; and identifying characteristics of music from different countries.

Likewise, pupils can be asked to listen to radio and television broadcasts at home. Individual assignments to read about composers' lives and the stories behind particular musical compositions can also be prepared on cards and kept in a file which the teacher utilizes to enrich the learning opportunities of more rapid workers or pupils with special music interests. Many stories that are told in music are described by Sid Skolsky in *The Music Box Book* (New York: E. P. Dutton, 1946).

Encouragement from the teacher stimulates some pupils to work hard at home creating songs, poems that can be put to music, and plays that relate to topics studied in class and that can include songs made up by class members. Such projects as these can be pursued by individuals or small groups which meet with the teacher during recess or after school for brief guidance sessions.

In summary, the elementary teacher aids individuals by teaching the entire class the many ways music can be enjoyed and by encouraging individuals and small groups to follow these leads on their own.

Secondary General Music Classes

Many junior and senior high schools provide classes in general music for those students who do not enroll in one of the specialized organizations like band, orchestra, or chorus. It is on these general music classes that we shall focus our attention.

The music curriculum of the secondary schools is basically an extension of the activities we have described for the elementary grades. If the elementary program has been varied and intense, the secondary activities can be a continuation to provide further variety and greater sophistication in composing, performing, and listening. If the elementary program has been weak, the early secondary curriculum consists of many of the more basic activities we have already described. Thus the secondary-school teacher of general music first needs some information about the students' background in music in order to suit the new work to their present level. This information is obtained in several obvious ways: (1) inspection of the music course of study of the elementary schools, if there is one, (2) a discussion with teachers of the elementary schools, and (3) testing early in the semester to discover the pupils' talents and knowledge. The last of these is usually the most satisfactory. Thus, the first week or two of the general music class can well consist of singing by rote and note (for groups as well as individuals), identifying instruments and types of music heard on records, and answering written test questions about music theory (key and time signatures, note and rest values, identification of musical intervals played on the piano). When the students' success with these activities has been analyzed, the teacher is better prepared to offer the work appropriate for them.

Respect for Individual Tastes

One important issue that can cause friction in secondary classes or can alienate some students is that of what music is the proper music. It is our conviction that many teachers are inordinately self-centered and self-righteous in regard to which music or art or literature is good or acceptable. Too often they limit the term "good music" or "the right music" to the compositions they themselves prefer. They press these values on their students. There are also teachers who do not urge their own values on pupils, for they are often uncertain of their own values; but they give lip service to operas, symphonies, and ensembles because they believe "the experts" approve of these forms. Thus these instructors feign such preferences and scorn pupils' interest in popular dance tunes, folk songs, cowboy tunes, and the like. We are convinced that such intolerance of students' choices is both philosophically indefensible and pedagogically unwise.

In regard to the philosophical position concerning a single standard of "good" or "proper" music, we agree with Leopold Stokowski's statement:

Fortunately there is no such norm or standard, because if there were a norm, music could not grow and evolve in new directions but would always be circling around that norm—like an animal in captivity chained to a post. . . . Each one of us feels music differently because of that sacred thing inside us—our individuality. . . . If we compare the opinions of a thousand persons from different countries all over the world, we will find immense variations of opinion as to what is good or bad music. They will sometimes contradict each other completely, with scarcely any two people feeling and thinking exactly alike.[2]

This does not mean that the teacher need hide his own preferences. In fact, it seems appropriate for him to tell what he likes and why he likes it. But it is also desired that he explain that other people

[2] Leopold Stokowski, *Music for All of Us* (New York: Simon and Schuster, 1943), pp. 41–42.

have tastes that differ from his own, and these tastes are to be respected.

The pedagogical wisdom of respecting a variety of musical preferences, though still retaining one's own tastes, is founded on the fact that when students are invited to bring their own songs and records and to explain why they like such music, they often become a more willing audience when the teacher offers other kinds of compositions for their consideration. It is through this give-and-take discussion that two important generalizations about music may be learned: (1) A given composition may serve one purpose well but be very inadequate for another. So a work for a stringed quartet may provide a quiet background for reading or offer the sophisticated listener an opportunity to analyze the subtleties of the sonata form, but it does not produce the rhythm desired at a high-school dance. (2) Individuals' tastes differ according to their moods, their musical training, the frequency with which they have heard a given piece; these varied tastes deserve the respect of others—especially the teacher.

Composing in the Secondary School

In the junior and senior high schools, students can be encouraged to continue setting poems to melodies, creating their own lyrics which are set to tunes, and deciding the piano or guitar chords which may be appropriate to the simpler melodies. The more apt individuals or small groups can attempt such projects as creating songs with parts for two or three voices. This harmonizing activity can well be preceded with class analysis of the basic chord or harmony principles underlying simple songs.

One of the most successful stimuli to song writing is the teacher's suggestion that class members create new school or class songs: pep songs for athletic events, a new alma mater, or a humorous ditty for the school variety show. Other stimuli are nature, tragic events which may elicit ballad attempts, and young love. A more advanced piano student, who is used to creating chords to match melodies, can team up successfully with a student talented in writing stories and verse in order to produce a brief operetta that the class can produce.

A booklet of songs and melodies composed by class members can be compiled and kept from one year to the next as an inspiration for pupils in subsequent years.

Performing in the Secondary School

Most of the performance on instruments in junior and senior high schools is done in individual and class lessons, in the band and orchestra, and in instrumental ensembles. However, the general music class can also serve, as did the elementary school, to introduce students to a variety of instruments. Many general music students are strongly interested in the guitar, banjo, and ukulele and will benefit from a few days of basic instruction in these instruments. Those who show sufficient interest to obtain an instrument can perhaps be organized into a small group that work up several songs on their own. As in the elementary school, pupils can be given a chance to try bowing a violin or cello or playing a flute, clarinet, or snare drum.

The greater part of the performing in general music classes is vocal. In carrying out this part of the program successfully, the teacher faces several problems: coping with changing adolescent voices, selecting appropriate songs, and teaching music reading.

Adolescents are usually quite sensitive to the opinions of their peers. This sensitivity can affect their behavior in music class. If a boy's voice is changing and thus makes unpredictable squeaks when he sings, he is going to be very reluctant to perform before his classmates. A girl who has learned to feel she sings out of tune or has a limited singing range will likewise try to avoid exposing her shortcomings. Thus it is usually wise for the instructor who is testing voices at the beginning of the year to do so in private with students who he suspects might be sensitive performing in front of others. The less apt adolescents gain their greatest pleasure from singing with a group which keeps them in tune and covers their mistakes.

The selections for secondary students can include both unison and part songs. At the junior-high level, they need to be chosen with the range adapted to the voice changes occurring at that age. The teacher can profitably use songbooks developed for school use in finding compositions that will illustrate how songs can appeal by their harmony, melody, rhythm, or text. The students will also probably wish to suggest some currently popular numbers. A simple range of songs suitable for general music class use is indicated by the following list: "Cielito Lindo," "Camptown Races," "Dixie," "Ain't Gonna Grieve My Lord," "Big Corral," "Sourwood Mountain," "Short'nin' Bread," "Funiculi-Funicula," "The British Grenadiers," "Swing Low," "Down in the Valley," "Loch Lomond," and Christmas carols.

What level of skill in music reading should be expected of all students? This question continually vexes teachers of general music, because by whatever method is used (stationary or movable *do*, numbers, or solfeggio), some students readily learn to sing a score, whereas others work for long periods with little success. Individual differences in this skill are very noticeable. The most realistic approach is to offer all students opportunities to learn music reading. That is, class sessions should be dedicated to learning notes and time values and to practicing hearing and singing intervals, but the major portion of class time should not be dedicated to music reading. More time should be spent on listening and on singing songs that can be learned by rote. Those students who show greater aptitude for reading vocal music can be encouraged to work in small trios or quartets at noon or after school, or they can be routed into the school chorus.

Listening Activities

The same varieties of listening experiences suggested for the elementary grades can be profitably extended to the secondary levels. The range of worth-while advanced activities is suggested by the following examples.

A unit of study can be organized around the forms in which music has been cast. It is often best to start with forms already familiar to the class and to compare them from the standpoint of purpose, length, complexity of themes and organization, tempo, orchestration, mode, social setting, and the audience to which they tend to appeal and why. The unit might begin with a comparison of American folk music, jazz, and popular dance tunes. Then other familiar dance forms can be added, such as recordings of Grainger's "Irish Reel," Strauss's waltzes, Chopin's "Mazurka in B-Flat Major," Brahms's

Hungarian dances, "The Russian Sailor's Dance," "Mexican Hat Dance," the cancan from *Orpheus in the Underworld*, and Ravel's "Bolero." Other forms with which students are usually less familiar are:

Art songs: Schubert's "Ave Maria," Schumann's "Two Grenadiers," Tschaikovsky's "None but the Lonely Heart."

Chorales: Bach's and those performed by local church choirs.

Études: Chopin's.

Sonatas: Debussy's No. 2 for flute, viola, and harp; Beethoven's No. 23 for piano.

Suites: Grofe's *Grand Canyon*, Anderson's *Irish*, Carpenter's *Adventures in a Perambulator*.

Symphonic tone poems: Saint-Saëns' *Danse Macabre*, Dukas' *Sorcerer's Apprentice*.

Musical comedies, operettas, and operas: A musical comedy like *Oklahoma, My Fair Lady*, or *South Pacific* can serve as forerunner of operettas (Gilbert and Sullivan, Victor Herbert) and operas (plot outline and recorded excerpts from Gershwin's *Porgy and Bess*, Bizet's *Carmen*, and Menotti's *The Medium*).

In addition to those on musical forms, units can be built around such themes as ancient music, songs of many nations, music that tells a story, Negro spirituals, band music, varieties of American music, Christmas in many lands, modern religions and their music, great Americans that are real or imagined, mountain people's music, ballads of England and America, and new directions in modern music.

Another technique for coping with individual differences is the use of varied classroom activities on different days. For example, a time line drawn on the chalkboard or on a strip of shelf paper above the bulletin board enables pupils to locate the dates of different composers and their compositions. A world map on the bulletin board, with labels indicating the names of composers and compositions pinned to appropriate countries, helps students understand music's geographical settings.

Some pupils who do not find much intrinsic appeal in knowing composers and their styles of writing will sometimes have their interest piqued by "twenty questions" types of games. After a recording is played, the pupils try to identify the composer or name of the piece or the country of its origin by asking a limited number of questions. Students can bring records from home and serve as the teacher for this kind of review activity.

The teacher can show the class the ways classical compositions have been adapted to current popular tastes by playing recordings of dance tunes, popular songs, and television theme songs and background music based on compositions of the past. When the popular adaptation and its original are played, the students can analyze how rhythms, instrumentation, harmonization, melody, and the length of the composition can be changed to suit the music to different purposes, such as the adaptation of a symphonic theme to ballroom dancing.

Some students are interested in the lives of composers, the experiences which apparently influenced them, and the problems they faced. Interest in this direction can perhaps be stimulated better by relating colorful incidents in the composers' lives than by only reciting such facts as birth and death dates and the names of principal compositions. "He wrote this on a menu in a café" is more interesting than "Composed in 1819."

One disturbing problem for the teacher of general music is the presence of some students, usually boys, who disrupt the class. Their disorderly conduct may arise from various causes. A common one is a total rejection of school, which they find to be a place of defeat. Another is embarrassment at the unpredictability of their changing voices. Still another is resentment at being in class with more accomplished musicians. The presence of such students may well cause the teacher to search for activities that may more readily appeal to them than the ones he is currently furnishing. Andrews and Leeder (1953:86–87) have suggested the following variety to meet the needs of students who have a limited musical background and negative attitudes toward music class.

1. Start with music they know and want, such as:
   A. *Hillbilly music.* Learn how it developed from folk music; how to accompany it with simple chords on such instruments as the guitar, autoharp, ukulele, and piano; how to phrase it in different ways; how both nasal and clear tone quality are produced and what they sound like on different hillbilly or country-music recordings.

B. *Ballads.* Learn the history of balladry; the role of minstrels, bards, troubadours, ballad singers; the stories told by various ballads which may be heard on records or sung by class.

C. *Cowboy songs.* Learn stories behind them and colloquial expressions used in them; how to accompany them with simple chords; how to play them on tonettes, harmonicas, or ocarinas.

2. Study other types of folk songs. Utilize:

A. Recordings, including two different singers' versions of the same song to illustrate individuality in arranging and phrasing.

B. Two versions of folk songs that use the same basic tune, such as "Camptown Races" and "Sacramento."

C. Several versions of same basic folk song to illustrate how they change as they are passed around, such as "Shenandoah" and "Cross the Wide Missouri."

D. Live performers, even the nonprofessionals from the student body of the high school and people from the community that play novelty instruments like the musical saw.

E. Folk-song groups from the class, including accompaniments by guitar, washboard, and "jug" blowing.

3. Study the history of jazz, disk jockeys on the radio and how they help popularize songs, dance-band styles, current hit-parade songs, background music from films, hi-fi and record players and how to keep them in good repair.

Individualizing the General Music Class

Three organizational techniques seem most feasible for differentiating work for individuals: offering outside assignments, excusing gifted students from regular classwork, and dividing the class occasionally for group projects.

As suggested in Chapter 5, several approaches can be used in differentiating assignments. Assignments kept in a card file can be distributed to different students or to subgroups within the class according to the teacher's estimate of individual abilities and interests. In a class discussion, students can suggest a variety of kinds of assignments around a particular topic, such as musical forms or composers' lives or collections of favorite songs, and pupils can select the ones they prefer.

It is sometimes true that a gifted student profits little from the classwork that is suitable for most of the others. Thus he may benefit more from being excused from the regular program to pursue individual projects which he outlines in conference with the teacher. In a sense, he makes a contract with the teacher to complete a special task. Projects that are often suitable for the advanced student include composing and harmonizing a march or waltz or sonata, arranging a song for a vocal quartet, rehearsing on the piano or violin a piece to be performed at an assembly, analyzing orchestrations of various compositions and then orchestrating a piece of music himself, making a chord analysis of a chorale or sonata, analyzing art songs and comparing them to contemporary songs, searching out the history of ballads and folk songs, or reading books on musical composition and reporting on them. In some cases the gifted students can work as individuals, in other cases as teams of two or three.

Some large high schools can provide a course or two in advanced musical theory so apt pupils can learn harmonizing, arranging, and composing. When such opportunities are not available in the classroom, the more advanced students can be given individual or small-group lessons, either through the school or by private teaching from musicians in the community.

Sometimes it is desirable to divide the general music class into small groups. Compared to many other subject-matter areas, music poses a special problem, because it often involves making noise. Groups of music students working in one room are more apt to disturb each other than are social-studies discussion groups or groups working on murals in art class. Thus the music teacher must find other rooms for the groups, so one committee may work in the classroom, another in the main seating area of the auditorium, another backstage, and one in a storeroom or the teacher's office. In some instances, all the students will be carrying out the same kind of activity, such as practicing part singing or preparing their own interpretation of a unison song. In other cases, they will be involved in different activities, each task suited to particular skills or interests of the members of the group. Eight pupils may work out square-dance steps that one of them has already mastered, a quartet may be practicing the part singing of a cowboy tune, a student who already knows guitar chords may teach three or four others, several may be in the library looking up the background of cowboy songs and learning the origin of the colloquialisms in them, and the remainder of the class may practice folk songs, with each student taking a turn conducting the group.

It is obvious that such a variety of activities demands that the students take considerable responsibility for their own behavior. Usually this requires that they really be sufficiently interested in the proposed activities to conduct themselves in a businesslike manner while under the leadership of a classmate. It is desirable for the teacher to help them set short-term goals and to require a progress report or a display of the product of their work every day or so. During the class period, the instructor typically moves from one group to another to observe progress, offer suggestions, and ensure that students are working at their tasks, not simply recreating.

Music Related to Other Subjects

Individual and small-group music projects can also serve as enrichment activities in English, social-studies, science, mathematics, art, and physical-education classes. The following examples suggest some of the ways this correlation between music and other subjects may be accomplished.

English and Languages

Several of the most useful projects for relating English and music have already been noted: setting verse to music, writing operettas, and selecting background recordings for verse or short-story reading.

In addition to these activities, which begin with words and move to music, experiences that begin with music and move to words are also useful. For instance, an instrumental selection like Debussy's "Afternoon of a Faun" can be played to a small group as they view a series of words the teacher has furnished: "peace, battle, freezing, dreaming, sharp, humorous, shaded." Each student's task is to select the words which he thinks best express the music. He then compares his choices with those of other group members to learn that even when music carries similar moods for people, different individuals may still interpret it in slightly varying ways, all of which deserve respect. Following several of these experiences, each student can accept the assignment of selecting a recording and preparing a list of words for the group members to try on another occasion.

Music can also be played to set a mood that stimulates pupils to create apt phrases, prose descriptions of what they imagine, and poetry.

When students read such Shakespearean plays as *Twelfth Night* and *As You Like It*, they may listen to recordings of the songs which have been put to music by well-known composers. The original spirit of the numbers is well conveyed by singers who accompany themselves on the lute.

Pooley has described the way music in a literature class can illustrate the artistic point of view of a particular period.

> I have used music of the 17th century, particularly the part-song and madrigal to show the music that Samuel Pepys and the men of his age would have been familiar with. I play some Purcell and follow this up with Handel and Haydn. In a senior high school English literature course I have even introduced some of the operatic music of Buonocini for them to see something of the rococo ornamentation of this style. This in turn would be followed by examples of the early romantic movement and then something of the realistic music of the later 19th century.
>
> For poetry of the 19th century and current times there are quite a few musical settings. I think particularly of such things as Kipling's "Recessional," Tennyson's "I Shot an Arrow into the Air," and some of Browning's lyrics. In America some of Longfellow and Whitman, as well as Edna St. Vincent Millay have been set to music.[3]

Although Pooley has described these as general class activities led by the teacher, they can serve equally well as enrichment experiences for individuals. That is, a student can be assigned to locate recordings appropriate to a particular era or author, select one particularly interesting composition, and prepare a commentary to use when it is introduced to the class.

When the class is studying drama, interested individuals may select plays that have been cast in musical form and compare the musical version with the original. Appropriate selections include *Pygmalion* (which became *My Fair Lady*) and *Green Grow the Lilacs* (*Oklahoma*).

[3] William R. Sur and Charles F. Schuller, *Music Education for Teen-Agers* (New York: Harper and Brothers, 1958), p. 204.

In foreign-language classes, students benefit from learning foreign songs and attempting to translate them. They may enjoy listening to a quantity of music of the foreign land and analyzing the differences between it and ours. These analyses may include descriptions of the subject matter and mood that typify the music, the rhythms (rumba and tango of Latin countries), instrumentation (Latin American marimba bands, German brass bands), and musical form (the *paso doble* Spanish march).

Social Studies

In connection with history, a wide variety of topics for individual reports can be drawn from the area of music. For instance, a student may collect war songs and analyze the way the ideals and feelings during one war and in one nation may result in different kinds of songs than are found in another war or another nation. Another student may collect and analyze national anthems. Election songs from different eras of American history enliven the study of presidential campaigns. Labor-union songs reflect the struggles of workers to achieve fair working conditions. Ballads tell the trials and tragedies of both the nobility and the common people. The role of music in religion enriches students' study of man's spiritual history.

During a unit on foreign lands, one or two students can study the music of a country to learn which types are popular and what roles these varieties of music play in the life of the people in different segments or social levels of the society. If this study of foreign music as a social phenomenon includes not only a description of the country's indigenous music but also that imported from other nations, an estimate can be made concerning which outside societies are exerting the most influence on the nation's changing culture. For example, to what extent are the youth of Japan and Indonesia being affected by American music? By Russian or Chinese music?

In the area of geography, individuals may search out songs relating to such geographical features as rivers, bays, mountains, and cities. An analysis of these compositions may suggest some of the ways these features have affected such people as the composers.

An apt pupil in a high-school psychology class may wish to read and report on such books as Edward Podolsky's *The Doctor Prescribes Music* (New York: Frederick A. Stokes, 1939), Doris Soibelman's *Therapeutic and Industrial Uses of Music* (New York: Columbia University Press, 1948), or Max Graf's *From Beethoven to Shostakovich: The Psychology of the Composing Process* (New York: Philosophical Library, 1947). In a sociology class, a student might wish to read Max Weber's *Rational and Social Foundations of Music* (Carbondale: Southern Illinois University Press, 1958) which describes the evolution of scales in different cultures and explains the rise of part singing in Western culture.

Science and Mathematics

Enrichment activities for physics and mathematics students can center on projects about (1) the nature of sound, harmonics, the physical characteristics of different scales (major, minor, pentatonic), pure tones, overtones, partial tones, (2) harmony and discord, (3) acoustics of a room and how to measure and improve acoustics, (4) logarithmic relationships of tones in scales, (5) comparisons of the tone production of string, brass, percussion, and reed instruments as well as that of electric and pipe organs, (6) hi-fi, stereophonic, and monaural recording and production. In addition to reading about these topics, students may carry out experiments with sound suggested in high-school and college physics texts and in such volumes as Harry F. Olson's *Musical Engineering* (New York: McGraw-Hill, 1952) and Charles A. Culver's *Musical Acoustics* (New York: McGraw-Hill, 1956).

Individuals may wish to construct musical instruments while studying the principles on which their tone production is based. Some of the more obvious are the xylophone (redwood sticks ¾ inch by 1½ inch cut to varied lengths work well), bamboo flute, cigar-box violin or ukulele, soda-straw oboe (pinch together one end of the straw and poke one or two holes farther down the straw for the finger stops), water-glass chimes filled to different heights with liquid to produce various tones, and tin-can and nail-keg drums (stretch leather or inner-tube rubber over the end as a drumhead).

Art

We have already suggested that recordings of various types of music can suggest a mood which pupils may express with paints, colored chalk, or clay. They can also draw illustrations which reflect the story suggested by operas, cowboy songs, folk songs, national anthems, tone poems, and religious compositions. They may design stage settings for operettas and musical comedies.

Physical Education

The most obvious correlation between music and physical activities is in the area of dance. In addition to learning dances in class, the most apt and interested individuals can be taught to read dance-step diagrams and can be provided dance descriptions on mimeographed sheets or in dance instruction books. Social-dancing steps can be practiced at home. Folk-dance and square-dance steps can be practiced by a group of students who meet after school.

Some boys who might otherwise be reluctant dance enthusiasts will enjoy learning some square-dance calls from records or books.

Individual girls who have had some basic instruction in creative dance will welcome the assignment of designing a dance at home to a recording of their own choice. To stimulate their imaginations, the teacher may wish to furnish them with a list of suggestions to try, such as:

1. Improvise appropriate movements to illustrate the feeling you get while listening to one of the following musical numbers: Bernstein's theme music from *West Side Story*, Tschaikovsky's "None but the Lonely Heart," Stravinsky's *Firebird Suite*, Harry Belafonte's recording of "Noah" and "Scarlet Ribbons," or Ravel's "Bolero."

2. Improvise movements that reflect the idea of the central character or object in each of the following: Rogers and Hammerstein's "Oh, What a Beautiful Morning," Rimski-Korsakov's "Flight of the Bumblebee," "The Streets of Laredo," "Sourwood Mountain," "Yankee Doodle," Anderson's "Typewriter," and "Water Boy."

Pianists in the class may wish to create their own music to which other students dance. Individuals may make a drum or borrow a tom-tom from the school to work out rhythms at home to which the class can dance.

Thus, not only are individual differences cared for in the regular class as the teacher encourages originality, but the more interested members of the group have opportunities for enrichment beyond classwork.

SUMMARY

Contrary to popular belief, musical ability is not a single power or factor but consists of subabilities which tend to correlate rather slightly with each other in most cases. Thus we are more accurate in discussing musical *abilities* and in determining which of these abilities are needed for various musical pursuits, such as playing a stringed instrument, singing, enjoying symphonic numbers, composing, and the like. It is apparent that the cluster of abilities possessed by a particular child may equip him better for one type of musical pursuit than for another. It is also apparent that currently available tests of musical aptitude are of such limited validity that in most school situations the teacher will find it more practical to estimate a pupil's potential from his performance in class than from test scores.

We have suggested that the school best cares for individual differences in musical talent and taste by (1) introducing all students to as wide a variety of musical experiences as possible and giving enough instruction to enable the student to select for further study those activities which best suit his own abilities and likes and (2) enriching the more apt and interested pupils' experiences through small-group work, individual assignments, and projects allied to other subject-matter areas.

SUGGESTED LEARNING ACTIVITIES

1. For one of the following subject-matter areas, prepare a lesson plan at a grade level of your choice. The plan should provide for small-group or individualized assignments that would suit the individual abilities and interests of the class and would correlate the study of a topic in the subject-matter area with music. The areas are English, foreign languages, social studies (including history, geography, psychology, sociology, contemporary social problems), science or mathematics, art, and physical education.

2. Assuming that you teach music at either the elementary or secondary level, compile a list of songs appropriate to a grade level of your choice. The list should contain a range of songs suitable to a variety of musical tastes and abilities among your students. Be able to defend your choice of each one.

3. For your own community, prepare a list of the out-of-school musical experiences that you might recommend to individuals to enrich their learning beyond the opportunities the school can provide. Indicate the types of students to whom these recommendations should be made and how you might make the suggestions most successfully.

SUGGESTED READINGS

ANDREWS, FRANCES M., and LEEDER, JOSEPH A. *Guiding Junior-High-School Pupils in Music Experiences.* New York: Prentice-Hall, 1953. Many specific teaching suggestions, sample lessons, recording lists.

DYKEMA, PETER W., and CUNDIFF, HANNAH M. *School Music Handbook.* Evanston: Summy-Birchard, 1955. Strong background material for elementary and junior-high levels.

FARNSWORTH, PAUL R. *The Social Psychology of Music.* New York: The Dryden Press, 1958. Thorough and interesting treatment of the development of scales, intervals, melody, musical taste, and musical abilities.

LEEDER, JOSEPH A., and HAYNIE, WILLIAM S. *Music Education in the High School.* Englewood Cliffs: Prentice-Hall, 1958.

LUNDIN, ROBERT W. *An Objective Psychology of Music.* New York: The Ronald Press Co., 1953.

NYE, ROBERT EVANS, and NYE, BERNICE TROUSDALE. *Music in the Elementary School.* Englewood Cliffs: Prentice-Hall, 1957.

SCHOEN, M. *The Psychology of Music.* New York: The Ronald Press Co., 1940.

SUR, WILLIAM R., and SCHULLER, CHARLES F. *Music Education for Teen-Agers.* New York: Harper and Brothers, 1958.

THOMPSON, CARL O., and NORDHOLM, HARRIET. *Keys to Teaching Elementary School Music.* Minneapolis: Paul A. Schmitt Music Co., 1949. A most practical book for teachers not well versed in methods of teaching music; tells specifically how composing, performing, and listening activities can be taught.

SELECTED MUSIC TESTS

Drake Musical Aptitude Test. Chicago: Science Research Associates, 1954. Age 8 to adult.

Farnum Music Notation Test. New York: Psychological Corporation, 1953. Grades 7–9.

Kwalwasser-Dykema Music Test. New York: Carl Fischer, 1930. Grades 4–12.

Lundin Musical Ability Tests. Described by R. W. Lundin, "The Development and Validation of a Set of Musical Ability Tests," *Psychological Monographs,* Vol. 63, No. 10 (1949). Probably Grade 5 to adult.

Seashore Measures of Musical Talent. New York: Psychological Corporation, 1939. Grade 5 to adult.

Wing Tests of Musical Intelligence. London: National Foundation for Educational Research, 1949, 1961. Probably Grade 7 to adult. Revision procedures described in Herbert D. Wing, "A Revision of the Wing Musical Aptitude Test," *Journal of Research in Music Education,* Vol. 10, No. 1 (Spring, 1962), pp. 39–46.

CHAPTER 12

Motor Abilities

The term "motor abilities" refers to physical skills involving muscular coordination and/or speed and strength. In school, these abilities are displayed during activities in physical education, crafts and industrial arts, handwriting, home economics, business-machine operation, instrumental music, and laboratory science. They include such gross bodily movements as running, jumping, turning, and kicking as well as the finer hand movements required in sewing, weaving, carving, cutting, drawing, lettering, typewriting, hand-writing, playing the guitar or flute, sawing, drilling, planing, and manipulating such equipment as microscopes, telescopes, and test tubes. Individual differences in these abilities are important to teachers for several reasons.

First, instructors should know that motor abilities improve with age and that some types of abilities are sufficiently developed at one age for a given school activity but not mature enough at that time for success at more complex activities. Teachers need to recognize what expectations regarding physical skills are generally reasonable at different age levels. Most third-graders are not sufficiently strong or well coordinated to saw a straight line in a half-inch board, but most ninth-graders are.

Second, teachers should recognize that among a group of children of the same age there will be wide differences in rates of physical maturation and thus in physical skill. Therefore, even at a time when most of the pupils in a class have sufficient arm and finger coordination to write well-spaced and uniform letters on a line, some still may not be well enough developed to accomplish this task. In a sixth grade, one boy may be as strong and as well coordinated in pitching a baseball as the average ninth-grader, whereas another boy may have only the pitching skill of an average third-grader. The teacher who is aware of these differences is better able to set reasonable tasks for individual pupils.

Third, if a teacher knows how motor skills are best measured and how one skill is related to another, he is better equipped to guide students to courses or vocational goals which are suited to their physical talents.

Fourth, teachers should recognize that the preadolescent and teen-age peer cultures usually give considerable importance to certain physical abilities. Especially in the case of boys, status is often strongly affected by skill in playing games and, to a lesser extent, by skill in construction activities like building airplane models or repairing an automobile. Furthermore, teachers should remember that an individual's feelings of confidence and self-esteem are governed to a great extent by the way others react to him. The child who is given status by his peers is more likely to feel confident and at ease than the child who is ignored, laughed at, or rejected. The teacher who realizes these relationships is better able to: (1) help students set realistic aspirations in physical skills, (2) help them improve those abilities that can be increased through practice, and (3) encourage them to use substitute skills to compensate for those motor shortcomings that cannot be fully overcome.

Chapter 12 attempts to aid teachers in accomplishing these goals through answering the following questions: (1) What is the range of variation among students in some typical motor abilities? (2) How are motor abilities measured? (3) What are the interrelationships among different motor abilities? (4) What teaching techniques can be used to suit the motor-skill differences met in physical education, industrial arts and home economics, and handwriting instruction?

TYPICAL MOTOR–ABILITY DIFFERENCES

To illustrate individual differences in motor skills, we shall inspect students' scores in pull-ups, sit-ups, the fifty-yard dash, the standing broad jump, manual reaction time, and typing speed.

TABLE 12–1

PHYSICAL–FITNESS SCORES OF
HIGH–SCHOOL BOYS *

Number of pull-ups	N	Number of sit-ups in 90 seconds	N	50-yd. dash in seconds	N	Standing broad jump	N
22	2	81–82	1	6.4	3	8′4″–8′5″	2
21	0	79–80	0	6.5	3	8′2″–8′3″	3
20	1	77–78	0	6.6	6	8′0″–8′1″	5
19	0	75–76	2	6.7	9	7′10″–7′11″	2
18	1	73–74	2	6.8	9	7′8″–7′9″	10
17	0	71–72	2	6.9	6	7′6″–7′7″	11
16	0	69–70	3	7.0	17	7′4″–7′5″	13
15	3	67–68	3	7.1	13	7′2″–7′3″	12
14	4	65–66	8	7.2	16	7′0″–7′1″	17
13	3	63–64	12	7.3	15	6′10″–6′11″	16
12	4	61–62	13	7.4	17	6′8″–6′9″	11
11	9	59–60	17	7.5	9	6′6″–6′7″	16
10	13	57–58	11	7.6	13	6′4″–6′5″	15
9	7	55–56	13	7.7	8	6′2″–6′3″	10
8	9	53–54	11	7.8	10	6′0″–6′1″	10
7	11	51–52	8	7.9	8	5′10″–5′11″	6
6	15	49–50	15	8.0	5	5′8″–5′9″	1
5	14	47–48	13	8.1	4	5′6″–5′7″	1
4	19	45–46	6	8.2	3	5′4″–5′5″	0
3	20	43–44	5	8.3	1	5′2″–5′3″	2
2	9	41–42	4	8.4	5	5′0″–5′1″	0
1	10	39–40	1	8.5	3	4′10″–4′11″	2
0	29	37–38	0	8.6	0	4′8″–4′9″	2
		35–36	2	8.7	1		
		33–34	1	8.8	3		
		31–32	1	. .			
		. . . .		9.2	1		
		19–20	1	9.3	0		
				9.4	1		
				9.5	1		
	183		155		190		168
Median = 5		Median = 55–56		Median = 7.3		Median = 6′10″–6′11″	

* Distributions of scores for sophomores, juniors, and seniors were so similar that they were combined.

As Table 12–1 suggests, physical-education teachers can expect a very wide range of scores from a typical class of high-school boys who attempt such physical-fitness tasks as pull-ups (chinning up to a horizontal bar), sit-ups (from a supine position), the fifty-yard dash, and the standing broad jump. For instance, 29 boys failed to do even one pull-up, the average boy did five, and the most success-ful one did 22. In sit-ups the most adept did 81, the average did about 55, and the least adept did only 19 within a period of 90 seconds. The fastest boy ran the fifty-yard dash in about two-thirds the time (6.4 seconds) that it took the slowest boy (9.5 seconds). In the standing broad jump, the best jumpers went almost twice as far (8 feet 4 inches) as the poorest ones (4 feet 8 inches). In each of these activities, except for the pull-ups, the bulk of the boys clustered around the average, with a gradually reduced number found at the high and low extremes.

To determine the rapidity of eye-hand coordination among girls, a group of first-grade, seventh-grade, and tenth-grade pupils took part in a reaction-time experiment.[1] The reaction-time task required each pupil to press a telegraph key as soon as she saw a light flash on. The graph in Figure 12–1 not only shows the variability of reac-tion speeds for the three age groups but also indicates that the first-grade girls were on the average slower and more variable within their group than the older girls.

The range of abilities that a high-school instructor of beginning typewriting can expect to meet by the seventh week of the semester is suggested in Figure 12–2. In a three-minute speed test, the least-skilled pupils typed only eight correct words per minute, while the most-skilled typed 53. The average (median) was 20. Interviews with individual students in these beginning classes indicated that the striking differences in performance were not only the result of basic motor agility. The performances were also influenced by the amount of home practice each pupil had conducted since school began and the extent to which he had previously experimented with typing on his own initiative before entering high school.

If we were to extend our survey of motor abilities beyond these examples in physical fitness, reaction time, and typing, we should

[1] Jean Hodgkins, "Influence of Age on the Speed of Reaction and Movement in Females," *Journal of Gerontology*, October, 1962, pp. 385–389.

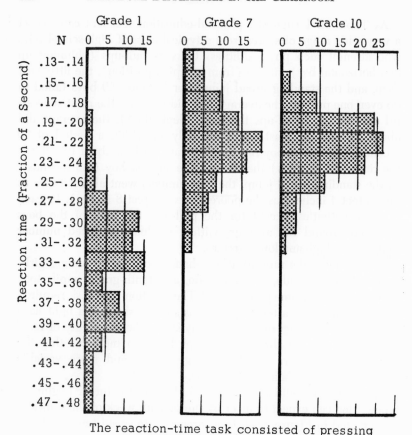

The reaction-time task consisted of pressing
a telegraph key when a light flashed.

Figure 12–1

Reaction Time of Girls

find that similar distributions of skill may be expected in all physical
activities.

MEASURING MOTOR ABILITIES

A great variety of measures of motor skills have been developed.
The best-known ones are designed to measure the large-muscle
movements of physical-education activities. Actually any sport is

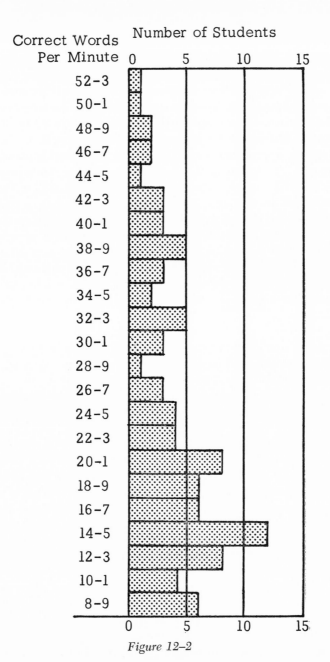

Figure 12–2

Speed of Beginning Typing Students after Six Weeks in Class

a test of the coordination, strength, and endurance of certain groups of muscles. Tests have also been developed to measure certain of the specific acts which are common to several sports. In some cases, these individual tests have been organized into batteries intended to yield an over-all motor-ability score that may be used by physical-education instructors for homogeneously grouping their classes or for setting appropriate expectations for individual students' performance. For instance, the Scott Motor Ability Test (Mathews, 1963:132–135) for high-school girls measures their skill in throwing a basketball for distance, broad jumping, rebounding a basketball off a wall, and racing around obstacles. The Larson Motor Ability Test (Mathews, 1963:140–141) for secondary-school boys is likewise intended to yield a general score to predict over-all athletic aptitude. It consists of running around obstacles, chinning, dipping (pushing up while holding onto parallel bars), jumping vertically (to touch as high as possible on a board), and throwing a baseball for distance.

In addition to the measures of gross bodily movements, a variety of tests for hand and finger dexterity have been developed by vocational counselors who have wished to predict success in vocations requiring manual speed and agility. A typical test in this category is the Minnesota Manual Dexterity Test (also called the Minnesota Rate of Manipulation Test), which consists of a form board containing sixty shallow holes. Sixty identical disks, each somewhat larger than a checker, fit into the holes. This device may be used either as a placing test (examinee takes disks one at a time from the table and places them in holes) or a turning test (disks are already in holes; examinee is to turn each over). Two other widely used measures of manual skills are the O'Connor Finger and Tweezer Dexterity Tests. The device used for measuring finger dexterity is a metal plate containing one hundred holes, each large enough to hold three metal pins one inch long and .07 inches in diameter. The testee is to pick up three pins at a time with his preferred hand (i.e., right hand if he is normally right-handed) and place them in a hole until all holes are filled. The device for measuring dexterity with tweezers consists also of a metal plate containing one hundred holes, but in this instance each hole is only slightly larger than the pins so that only one pin can be placed in a hole. The examinee's task is to see how quickly he can pick the pins one at a time from the table with the tweezers and fill the plate. (For other tests of fine-muscle coordination, see both Buros and Super in the readings at the end of the chapter.)

Besides the foregoing evaluation techniques, there are handwriting scales which have been used by teachers for many years to estimate in a somewhat formal manner the quality of a student's writing. The most prominent of these have been the Ayers, which measures legibility, and the Thorndike, which measures the apparent beauty and character of the writing as well as legibility. The most recent well-standardized handwriting scale by Freeman (1959) provides improvements over the other scales; for example, there are five specimens of handwriting for each grade level against which the teacher judges a pupil's written work.

Despite the existence of these formal tests of motor skill, most teachers base their estimates of pupils' motor abilities on the less formal measures that are a regular part of classwork, such as scores achieved on informal class tests like the number of times a boy can hit a target with a baseball or the number of words a girl can type per minute. Or the estimates of ability are made through observations, as in an over-all impression of a pupil's physical skills in games or a judgment of the general legibility of his handwriting.

INTERRELATIONSHIPS AMONG ABILITIES

By administering a variety of tests and computing correlations among them, researchers have furnished answers to several important questions concerning motor skills.

1. Is motor skill a general ability (a single factor) which determines the quality of a person's performance at all large-muscle activities as well as the fine-muscle movements? Or are there various distinct motor abilities, so that a person's aptitude for gross movements may well be different from his aptitude for fine movements?

Studies have shown the second of these possibilities to be true, especially for older youths and adults. Not only are gross and fine motor skills independent of each other (Tyler, 1956:145), but a given gross motor-skill sport like football or basketball may itself be composed of various factors or subabilities that are somewhat independent of one another. Mathews' (1963:123) review of twenty-eight factor-analysis studies showed that researchers have identified more than a score of factors which combine to determine the level of proficiency in various physical activities. Those most frequently noted were strength, velocity, and muscular coordination. Others were motor educability, body size, height, weight, force, endurance, balance, agility, dynamic energy, ability to change direction, flexibility, peripheral vision, good vision, concentration, understanding of the mechanics of the activities, absence of disturbing or inhibiting emotional complications, timing, rhythm, and coordination.

Even the seemingly related movements of finger, arm, and hand dexterity are not highly interrelated. A measure of one of these skills does not help very much in determining a student's potential in another. (Super, 1962:210.)

2. To what extent is a person's mental ability, as measured by academic-aptitude tests, related to his motor abilities?

The relationship is very slight, particularly at the later adolescent and adult levels. (Tyler, 1956:417–447.) Knowing a person's score on a finger-dexterity test does not aid in predicting his score on an academic-intelligence test.

3. Are specific abilities more independent of one another in late adolescence than in early childhood?

As already implied, yes. The reason for this lies in the fact that children mature at different rates. The more rapidly maturing child usually does not advance in just one ability (such as speech or running or numerical problem solving) but in many areas. At the same time, the late maturer will tend to develop at a slower pace in these areas. But a child's maturation rate is not the only factor affecting his ability level. Obviously, different children are born with different potential. One child's nervous system is built to reach a higher eventual level in understanding abstract verbal material than is another child's, regardless of their maturation rates. The same is true of manual skills. Therefore we need to recognize that two internal influences tend to cause the differences between children in their various skills: (a) basic neuromuscular endowment and (b) maturation rate. (Though learning experiences, motivation, and opportunity to learn also obviously affect skill, we are at this moment confining our considerations to internal or innate factors.)

The maturation-rate factor tends to cause some correlation among abilities. But this correlation is reduced or eliminated by adulthood, and differences in basic endowment and learning opportunities among adults make clearer the fact that motor and intellectual skills are relatively independent of each other.

4. What general implications do these facts hold for the classroom teacher and the high-school counselor?

They suggest that when a teacher tries to predict a pupil's apparent potential for an activity involving motor coordination, he should use a measure that is as much like the activity as possible. In particular, he should not use an academic-intelligence test to predict manual abilities or to group physical-education classes homogeneously. Even at the elementary-school level, where correlations do exist between physical and mental measurements, the correlations rarely reach .30 and thus are unreliable for predicting one skill from a measure of the other.

When a teacher contemplates using a test labeled "manual dexterity" or "general motor abilities," he should not accept the scale at face value but should first inspect the precise acts required by the test items to make sure they closely match the muscle coordinations he is trying to measure or predict. Names of tests are sometimes misleading. Super (1962:198) illustrated the specificity of motor abilities when he summarized studies on the predictive value of the Minnesota Manual Dexterity Test and concluded that ". . . arm-and-hand dexterity as measured by the Minnesota test is important in packing, wrapping and inspection jobs and in gross-manual assembly and machine-operation jobs; however, the predictive value of the test depends somewhat upon the specific factors in the job and the degree to which they are tapped by the test."

Furthermore, studies of the relationships between test scores and the actual performance of a motor task in life indicate that in many instances success in the task is more strongly influenced by factors other than pure muscle coordination or agility. For instance, experience with the O'Connor Finger Dexterity Test suggests:

. . . wrist-and-finger dexterity is likely to be important during the period of initial adjustment to fine manual jobs [like assembling electrical components, repairing watches], and . . . it is likely to be related to success on the job when people with approximately equal amounts of technical understanding or trade knowledge are being compared. When the latter vary considerably, among applicants or employees, differences in them are likely to outweigh the importance of differences in finger dexterity. (Super, 1962:211.)

MATCHING LEARNING ACTIVITIES TO MOTOR–ABILITY DIFFERENCES

The general techniques for adapting learning tasks to differences in motor ability are the same as recommended for intellectual differences. First, the teacher discovers the range of abilities in the class. Second, he determines which of several approaches will be most practical for meeting these differences (ability grouping, individualized assignments, giving the same assignment but expecting different levels of work from different students).

In this section we shall illustrate how these general techniques may be applied to the areas of physical education, industrial arts, home economics, and handwriting.

Physical Education

Especially in secondary schools, the physical-education classes are scheduled according to students' ability levels, or else one large class is subdivided into squads or teams, each composed of members with similar skills. Grouping according to skill and size helps ensure that pupils receive the level of instruction they need and compete with others of similar proficiency, strength, and size.

Sometimes teachers divide a large class into permanent subgroups or assign students to permanent sections for an entire year or semester. In other instances, the subgroups within a class are temporary. They are organized only for the particular activity or unit being followed at the time. For example, a pupil may be in one group for football and another for swimming, depending on his proficiency in each of these activities.

Two of the most popular methods of classifying pupils into permanent groups are those utilizing (1) age, height, and weight and (2) general motor-ability tests.

A typical age-height-weight scheme is McCloy's (1954). At the elementary-school level, only age and weight are used. At the secondary level, height is also considered. McCloy considers age to be more important than weight as an index of physical maturity, so he has given age somewhat more importance at the elementary level. This gives a classification formula of: $(10 \times \text{age}) + \text{weight} =$ classification score. At the secondary level, the score is obtained by: $(20 \times \text{age}) + (6 \times \text{height}) + \text{weight}$. Pupils who receive similar scores are placed in the same subgroups.

The age-height-weight scheme furnishes only a rough measure for homogeneous grouping. When classed in this manner, numbers of students will be misplaced. Therefore, when time for testing is available at the beginning of the school year, it is more efficient to classify pupils on the basis of their scores on a general motor-ability test. (See Mathews, 1963:132–158, for sample tests.) But even these scores will result in the misplacement of some students. Hence, teacher observations of students' success in physical-education class early in the semester may result in transferring some to more appropriate sections.

When temporary groups are being formed for a specific activity, like swimming or tumbling, tryouts in the activity itself may serve best as the basis for classification. That is, one or two days may be used for initial instruction in the activity with the class as a single group. During these instruction periods or during tests of the skill following the instruction, the teacher rates the current skill level and apparent teachability of the pupils. On the basis of these ratings, he divides the class into squads, each squad composed of students of like abilities, needs, or size.

When the size or ability squads have been formed, the instructor decides what kinds of activities will best fit the needs of each one. He usually makes one of three choices.

1. Have all groups follow the same activity and at the same level of sophistication, but the students compete only within their own group. Such a plan is most appropriate for contact sports like football, wrestling, and boxing, in which weight and strength are decisive factors. Because the smaller boys in lightweight squads may be as skilled as some larger boys in heavyweight squads, all the groups may profit from the same type of instruction. Thus the same types of lessons may be provided for all.

2. Have some squads receive advanced instruction while others

work on more fundamental skills. This approach is most feasible when there is a marked discrepancy between the skills of the best and the poorest athletes so that a different kind of instruction is needed for each. For instance, in a swimming class all may be focusing on a crawl stroke, but the more adept may be in one group emphasizing turns at the end of the pool when racing, whereas the less adept group may be practicing the basic stroke and proper breathing.

3. Have different squads follow entirely different activities. This plan is most appropriate when:

(a) Some pupils should restrict their physical activity for health reasons. Several pupils with a heart condition or with reduced stamina due to illness may form a subgroup that pursues very moderate exercise while the rest of the class engages in basketball or track events.

(b) The instructor wants students to choose from several activities the ones that interest them most. The physical-education class may offer badminton, archery, and volleyball, from which class members select one to follow for the ensuing three weeks. In this case, the grouping is according to student interest rather than size or skill.

(c) Each student is trying to develop skill in an activity with which he is only slightly acquainted or in which he is weak. For a portion of the semester in a class offering gymnastics and body-building activities, the teacher may assign students to activities in which their strength or skills are low. The purpose of this plan is to help students develop well-rounded skills and strength.

After the instructor has divided the class into groups, he faces the problem of ensuring that the various squads diligently pursue their assigned activities even when he is not with them. This is usually best accomplished through the appointment or election of student-leaders: team captains, squad leaders, playground supervisors, and referees. These leaders usually work most efficiently if they are given training in their duties by the instructor before they are assigned to their supervision tasks. When a supervisor's or referee's duties remove him from actively taking part in sports and games, it is best for the instructor to rotate the supervisory job among different students so that all have opportunities to participate.

When able student-leaders are in charge of games like speed-ball or events like broad-jumping, the teacher is freed to circulate among the participants and offer them the individual help they need. Since physical-education instructors are so often accustomed to operating classes with the aid of student-leaders and subgroups, they are frequently more successful than teachers of academic subjects in suiting classwork to the individual differences among their pupils.

Industrial Arts and Home Economics

The boy with poor hand and finger coordination and little strength usually faces difficulties in the industrial-arts class where he is expected to be skillful in hammering, sawing wood and metal, fitting bits of wood together and gluing them, inserting small bolts into narrow spaces and screwing nuts onto them, manipulating wrenches and screw drivers, and painting objects with a steady stroke. Likewise, the girl who has poor hand and finger dexterity meets problems in home-economics activities that require her to thread needles, sew with straight and evenly spaced stitches, operate a sewing machine, create flower arrangements, decorate cakes, wrap gifts attractively, and make minor repairs on appliances used in the home.

The three main reasons that industrial-arts and home-economics teachers should be aware of the motor abilities of their pupils are that (1) tasks should be within the range of the pupils' motor ability without causing them constant frustration and disappointment, (2) the teacher's expectation about the quality and speed of a student's work should take into account the pupil's motor skill, and (3) the organization of the classroom should be suited to the differences in students' abilities.

How, then, does an instructor measure manual abilities? The most feasible method in both industrial arts and home economics is to observe pupils systematically early in the year as they perform manual tasks requiring both simple and complex coordinations. On the basis of these observations, the teacher may rate or rank the class members. At this early stage the rating should be tentative, because it is not always clear whether a pupil's lack of agility results from his unfamiliarity with the tools or from a more basic lack of motor skill. As the semester progresses and students' experience with tools increases, the instructor can draw a more adequate conclusion about the level of pupils' underlying motor abilities.

There is some hope that in the future there will be standardized tests directly useful to industrial-arts and home-economics teachers to improve the prediction of motor skills in those fields. One of the most encouraging attempts to develop predictive measures has been that of Fuzak.[2] He used a hand dynamometer to test the strength of grip of 322 junior high-school boys and then compared these strength scores with the skills the boys later demonstrated in industrial-arts activities. Fuzak's study supported his two initial hypotheses that:

1. The level of physical maturity attained by a junior high-school boy determines the level of his ability to perform complex finger coordinative activities.

2. The strength of grip, as measured by a simple hand dynamometer, is an effective indicator of the level of physical maturity of secondary-school boys and of their ability to perform complex finger coordinative activities.

Fuzak was thus able to suggest the dynamometer as a simple testing device for industrial-arts teachers and to indicate several implications that variations in manual abilities hold for teaching, including:

1. The junior-high industrial-arts teacher needs to measure the range of readiness for complex finger coordinations in his class. On the basis of these measurements, he should plan a broad variety of activities that will accommodate the wide range of maturity levels among his students. If all class activities which are feasible for junior-high students were to be ranked according to their degree of complexity, the instructor could assign different activities to class members according to students' abilities to perform the manipulations successfully. This means that not everyone will be doing the same assignments, nor will everyone be expected to reach the same high quality of performance.

2. All teachers whose class activities require finger and hand

---

[2] John A. Fuzak, *The Role of Physical Maturation in Determining the Ability of Junior High School Boys to Perform Finger Coordinative Activities in Industrial Arts* (Chicago: American Technical Society, 1958).

dexterity should recognize that many pupils may be driven away from classes involving complex movements because these pupils lack physical readiness to perform well. Teachers of industrial arts and home economics often lament the fact that the intellectually adept students do not enjoy their classes or take the work seriously. Although there are various reasons why the academically brightest students usually do not enroll in large numbers in nonrequired courses in these fields, one of the contributing causes may be that in junior high their teachers have held such pupils to unreasonable motor-ability standards. Fuzak has noted that manually immature pupils find "much of the time and effort they expend is wasted. This is probably true in particular of the more intelligent pupils. Many of them are somewhat accelerated in school, while duller pupils are somewhat retarded."[3]

Perhaps the most successful classroom procedure for meeting individual differences in industrial arts and home economics is that of assigning pupils individual projects. The following examples illustrate two ways of making such assignments.

During a woodworking unit in a junior-high industrial-arts class, the instructor introduced the boys to the use of common tools by demonstrating each tool's potentialities and proper care. Every student then practiced with the tools by building a simple flat-roofed birdhouse according to a mimeographed plan. During this initial project, the instructor moved about the class, giving aid and rating each pupil's apparent motor skill as shown by his success with the tools. As a boy completed the birdhouse, the instructor made a final rating of his work and apparent dexterity. On the basis of this rating, the pupil was given one of four lists of activities from which to choose a second project. The instructor had created the four lists by placing project possibilities in four sets, each set representing a different level of motor-coordination difficulty. There were at least ten mimeographed projects in each set. Thus the instructor could designate the set that appeared appropriate for a given student and let him decide which of the construction activities in that list interested him most. As the semester progressed, the students were encouraged to conceive projects of their own, draw appropriate plans, and construct the objects.

[3] *Ibid.*, p. 81.

In a high-school auto-mechanics class, the instructor gave lectures and demonstrations early in the semester to acquaint the students with the basic divisions of auto mechanics (ignition systems, fuel systems, bodywork), then instructed the boys in reading auto-repair booklets they would use to guide their work on various automotive jobs. Following these introductory sessions, students worked individually or in pairs on auto-repair projects. The instructor moved from place to place in the auto shop, helping individuals and groups with their tasks. However, frequently he was helping one person with a project at the time other individuals or groups needed his advice. To furnish more immediate assistance to such groups as the semester progressed, the instructor created a job-experience chart. Each boy's name was listed in the left margin and each popular type of repair or maintenance job (such as grinding valves, refinishing fenders, packing wheels) was listed across the top of the chart. When a student had successfully completed one of these jobs, an X was written beside his name in the column assigned to that project. Thereafter, when the teacher was busy helping one person, another individual or group that needed help could consult the chart to find the name of a classmate who had already gained the experience the group needed. This classmate was then asked to help. Similar student-aid plans are also adaptable in woodworking, metalworking, and drafting classes as well as in sewing and cooking courses.

By creating subgroupings within the class, the instructor can also help meet individual differences. For example, one group in a home-economics class may work on a cooking assignment at the stoves while another completes home-decorating plans. Or the more advanced students in a sewing class may work on dresses while less apt subgroups are completing simpler hemming assignments. The techniques, described in Chapter 5, that teachers may use to succeed with several groups in a class are generally sound methods in home economics and industrial arts.

Handwriting

For the typical classroom teacher, the motor abilities of most interest are those related to handwriting. The individual nature of handwriting is obvious. Banks cash checks on the distinctiveness of a person's signature, and courts accept the individuality of a person's handwriting as proper legal evidence.

The three handwriting questions that concern us here are: How is hand-coordination maturity related to the type of writing that should be taught at different ages? How much individuality in handwriting style should be allowed or encouraged? Should the pupil who seems naturally to favor his left hand be encouraged to change to his right for writing?

Elementary-school educators usually distinguish between two general styles of handwriting: manuscript and cursive. Manuscript writing is known also as printing or lettering. Each letter is written with short, simple strokes. One letter in the word is not connected to another letter. Cursive writing, on the other hand, is the traditional form of handwriting. The letters within a word are connected to each other, and the writing is typically slanted. Most American schools today teach children manuscript in the first grade, then change to cursive writing in the second or third grade. This pattern is followed because of teachers' convictions that the younger child's manual abilities are better suited to the simpler separate strokes required by manuscript writing than they are to the continuous sweeps and reversing movements required by a cursive style. Experience with the two styles suggests that this is probably true, so that the prevailing practice of teaching manuscript first and transferring to cursive in the upper elementary grades appears to be sound. However, because of individual differences in motor abilities, there are first-graders who succeed with cursive and there are third-graders who still do not produce clear manuscript writing with any marked ease. By observing pupils during writing practice, the teacher can learn which children can be expected to meet higher standards of attractive handwriting and which ones, even when they try hard, cannot coordinate eye and hand well enough to produce even, well-spaced writing. Research conducted on the speed and legibility of cursive and manuscript has produced no conclusive evidence that one style is superior to the other in the upper grade levels.

The matter of how much individuality should be allowed in handwriting has always posed a problem for teachers. Some people make their handwriting so distinctive, either purposely or unwittingly, that it is almost unreadable, so it is apparent that writing should be sufficiently standardized to communicate. On the other hand, requiring everyone to produce an identical style in letter form, slant, and spacing is unnecessary for communication purposes, and from what we know of differences in motor ability, it is asking for the impossible. In past decades, teachers generally were strict about insisting that children adhere to a specified way to form, slant, and space letters. For instance, in schools following the Palmer method of handwriting, the children were urged to duplicate Palmer's style as precisely as possible. Certificates were awarded to those who accomplished this most faithfully. Today, however, the trend is for teachers to stress legibility and allow for individual variations in slant, size, and form of letters so long as the writing is easily read. Such an expectation is in keeping with individual differences in both eye-hand coordination and personal taste.

Studies of the teaching of legible handwriting suggest that children's practice in forming proper letters should also be individualized. After the teacher has introduced the letter forms to the entire class and everyone has gained some practice, further practice sessions should focus on each child's improving on the writing faults that are peculiar to him. Not everyone should be practicing the same things. This individualization can be accomplished if the teacher uses samples of each child's handwriting to diagnose his shortcomings. Studies by Pressey and Pressey and by Newland[4] have shown that a relatively few letters—a, e, n, t, r, o, s—account for the major portion of handwriting illegibilities. Thus it is likely that several children in the class will exhibit faulty formation of these letters and therefore can be gathered as a subgroup for practice. On the other hand, some children's faults will be more personal. They will require specialized individual practice to correct their errors.

In almost every classroom there are two or three left-handed

[4] Sidney L. Pressey and Luella C. Pressey, "Analysis of 3,000 Illegibilities in the Handwriting of Children and Adults," *Educational Research Bulletin*, Vol. 6 (1927), pp. 270–273.

Ernest T. Newland, "An Analytical Study of the Development of Illegibilities in Handwriting from the Lower Grades to Adulthood," *Journal of Educational Research*, Vol. 26 (1932), pp. 249–258.

pupils. They pose special problems for the teaching of handwriting because school facilities (like desks) and teaching procedures (like handwriting instruction) usually favor the needs of the right-handed majority and neglect the left-handed ones. There are two principal questions about handedness that concern the typical teacher. (1) Should the young child who tends to favor his left hand be encouraged to write with his right hand for his own comfort in a predominantly right-handed world? (2) If the child is so definitely left-handed that he should not be changed, what special teaching procedures should be used for him?

There is no easy answer to the first question. To begin with, it is impossible to divide the population clearly into right-handed and left-handed persons, because different people exhibit varied degrees of handedness. Some show a strong preference at an early age for one hand and continue to exhibit that preference in a host of activities throughout their lives. Other people develop a distinct preference only in the primary grades, or perhaps later. There are also people who prefer the right hand for one act, like writing, but bat left-handed in baseball. A few people show skill with either hand.

The question of whether to try to change a left-handed child's preference would also be easier to answer if we knew whether handedness is a matter of inborn cerebral dominance or learned from experience or a result of both heredity and environment. If handedness is not inborn, we may feel confident about trying to alter it.

A third problem regarding efforts to change the left-handed child's writing hand is the belief which has prevailed among educators and psychologists in the past that efforts to alter handedness often precipitate reading disabilities, emotional confusion, and such speech defects as stuttering. The research on this issue is not conclusive. In recent years, some specialists in this area have come to believe that the change of handedness itself has not brought about the reading and speech defects. Rather it has been the harsh method or the undersirable emotional climate used in forcing the change that has caused the psychological problems.[5] On the basis of present evidence, the soundest policy seems to be to allow the child with

[5] Lawrence T. Dayhaw, "Guiding Handedness in the Development of the Child," *Education*, Vol. 74 (1953), pp. 196–199.

a very definite, well-established preference for the left hand to continue using it in writing. But the primary-grade child whose preference does not seem particularly well established should be encouraged, without force or embarrassment, to try using his right hand. If he does make the change readily, he will probably find it easier to live in a world that is built chiefly for the right-handed.

In teaching handwriting to the left-handed pupil, several rather obvious procedures should be followed. When pupils are shown how to place their paper on the desk, how to sit while they write, and how to hold their pencil, the teacher should not confine her demonstrations to right-handed positions. There should also be a demonstration for the left-handed pupils. When teachers fail to illustrate appropriate posture for the left-handed, pupils frequently adopt awkward writing positions that stay with them the rest of their lives. For instance, cursive writing is most convenient for the right-handed student when the paper is slanted with the top of it pointed toward the upper left area of the desk. But if the left-handed student tries to write on a sheet in this position, he usually finds himself hooking his arm and wrist across the top of the paper to avoid smearing his work as he writes. If, however, he is taught to aim the top of his paper toward the upper right corner of the desk, he can place his hand on the sheet in a posture comparable to the position of his right-handed classmates. Even so, he still faces the problem of obscuring what he has just written by the fingers of his left hand. One way to alleviate this is to hold the pencil with the fingers at least an inch from the point.

Finally, the teacher can aid the left-handed pupil's adjustment by ensuring that the school equipment is suitable for his handedness. In case the desks typically supplied for the class have adequate armrest space only on the right side, obviously other desks or tables that allow the left-handed students to work comfortably should be requested.

SUMMARY

Wide variations exist among students in the motor abilities used in physical education, industrial arts, home economics, handwriting, typewriting, and the like. Teachers should recognize not only that motor abilities are rather independent of intellectual talents but that one type of motor skill may be quite independent of another. Therefore a student who is not very apt in one motor activity, like kicking a football, may be skilled in some other, like manipulating mechanical-drawing instruments. Instructors should not use the results of one type of motor-skill test as an indication of a student's probable skill in an unrelated motor task.

In physical-education, industrial-arts, and home-economics classes, individual differences in motor skill can often be met most adequately through subdividing the class into more homogeneous groups and by giving individualized assignments to class members.

In teaching handwriting, the instructor of elementary-school children can best meet their individual needs by introducing the simpler manuscript writing a year or two before the more complex cursive style, by permitting individual writing styles so long as the material is easy to read, and by knowing the writing positions most appropriate for both right-handed and left-handed pupils.

SUGGESTED LEARNING ACTIVITIES

1. Select six children of the same chronological age and administer the tests listed below, keeping a record of each child's score on each activity. From an inspection of your results, try to answer the following questions: Which child generally showed the greatest motor skill? Which showed the least? If you were teaching them physical education, what individualization of instruction, if any, do you think would be desirable? Did the same child achieve the highest scores on all activities? Did the same child achieve the lowest scores on all activities? Do the results of your testing the six children tend to confirm or refute the discussion of the interrelationships of motor abilities given earlier in this chapter?

The test activities: (*a*) A soccer ball or beach ball is placed on the ground, and the child kicks it as far as possible, first with his right foot, then with his left. Pupils are ranked according to how far they kicked the ball. Each receives a ranking for his right foot and for his left. (*b*) Pupils race together a distance you feel is appropriate to test their running speed. For their scores, they are ranked in the order of crossing the finish line. (*c*) Each pupil is asked to take a turn threading first a large-eyed needle, then a small-eyed needle. For their scores, they are ranked according to how quickly they succeeded in each task, the fastest child receiving the rank of 1, the next child 2, and so on. (d) A fifty-cent piece is placed on the table about two feet in front of the child, who is asked to draw on a sheet of paper a circle that is the same size as the coin. Each child's rank is determined by how accurately his circle matches the fifty-cent piece in size and shape, in the opinion of the tester.

2. Interview a teacher of industrial arts, home economics, physical education, or typing to discover (a) what problems of motor-ability differences have arisen in this instructor's classes; (b) what techniques the teacher uses, if any, to suit class work more adequately to the motor-skill differences among pupils.

SUGGESTED READINGS

Buros, Oscar K. (ed.). *The Fifth Mental Measurements Yearbook.* Highland Park, N.J.: Gryphon Press, 1959.

————. (ed.). *The Fourth Mental Measurements Yearbook.* Highland Park, N.J.: Gryphon Press, 1953.

————. (ed.). *The Third Mental Measurements Yearbook.* New Brunswick: Rutgers University Press, 1949.

Freeman, Frank N. "A New Handwriting Scale," *Elementary School Journal,* January, 1959, pp. 218–221.

McCloy, C. H., and Young, Norma Dorothy. *Tests and Measurements in Health and Physical Education.* New York: Appleton-Century-Crofts, 1954.

Mathews, Donald K. *Measurement in Physical Education.* Philadelphia: W. B. Saunders, 1963.

Super, Donald E., and Crites, John O. *Appraising Vocational Fitness.* New York: Harper and Row, 1962.

Tyler, Leona E. *The Psychology of Human Differences.* New York: Appleton-Century-Crofts, 1956.

PART IV

Psychophysical Differences

In the discussion of intellectual abilities in Part II, we gave as much attention to pupils deviating in a positive direction as to those deviating in a negative direction. That is, the intellectually gifted child received as much consideration as the retarded. In Part III, the student blessed with greater artistic or musical aptitude than the average received the most notice.

But in Part IV we shall focus almost completely on psychophysical deviations in a negative direction. We shall be concerned with individual differences that are usually considered to be disorders, handicaps, or defects. Vision problems are discussed in Chapter 14, hearing defects in Chapter 15, and speech disorders in Chapter 16. A variety of less common difficulties that regular classroom teachers occasionally face are presented in Chapter 17: crippling conditions, cerebral palsy, epilepsy, heart conditions, disfigurements, malnutrition, allergies and asthma, and diabetes.

Some writers have called these conditions only "physical" handicaps. However, we shall use the term "psychophysical" because in each case both physical and psychological causes and symptoms may be involved. Oftentimes the psychological aspects are the more important.

Although these different handicaps are of quite varied types and arise from diverse causes, they are often much alike in the types of special social-psychological problems they precipitate for pupils. Therefore in Chapter 13 we discuss these problems which are common to many handicaps, rather than presenting them repeatedly in the subsequent chapters.

Part IV

Psychological Differences

Social-Psychological Difficulties
of the Handicapped

The social-psychological problems faced by handicapped students frequently center on one or more of the following: (1) relationships with parents, (2) relationships with agemates, (3) self-acceptance and self-esteem, and (4) the role of the handicap in determining what the pupil expects of other people. These topics form the focus of this chapter.

RELATIONSHIPS WITH PARENTS

We cannot expect parents to be glad that a handicapped child has been born into the family. Nor can we expect them to be pleased when a normal son or daughter becomes handicapped through accident or illness.

Probably the parents' displeasure arises mainly from their strong identification with their children. By "identification" we mean that the child is felt by the parent to be an extension of the parent's own personality. So the child's successes are experienced by the parents as their own, bringing them esteem and contentment. But less happily, the child's failures and defects are also felt by the parents to be their own, at least in many cases. Thus, we are not surprised when fathers and mothers are upset by the advent of a handicapped child in the family. We can understand that they might feel embarrassed or disgraced and that they might wish to alter or deny this offending extension of their own egos.

Parent Reactions

The actual way parents' disturbed feelings will manifest themselves in everyday behavior differs from one person to another. It depends on the particular parent's personality structure and the nature of the child's handicap. But in general, research in this field suggests that there are four dominant kinds of reactions that mothers and fathers commonly exhibit. (Kanner, 1952:26; Lowenfeld *in* Cruickshank, 1955:255–259.) It is true that in a given parent these reactions may not always appear in a pure form. Instead, they may be seen as a mixture of two or more varieties. However, it is also true that one of these reactions or attitudes often dominates a given parent's reaction to his defective issue. Teachers who are aware of the nature of the following four types are better prepared to understand the kinds of influences that have molded the personalities of handicapped children in their classes.

1. *Acceptance of the Child and His Handicap.* This is the attitude we would hope for, because it typically leads to the healthiest personality development for the child. The parents have accepted the handicap in an objective way. They neither reject nor overprotect the child. They say, "He's our child; he has this defect; and together we'll make the best of it." They plan realistically for his education and his future. They do not express guilt or anger at the handicap.

Somewhere in their lives, these parents have developed a philosophy to care for this situation. In a study of parents of blind children, it was concluded that "in most cases religion gives [the parents] mental and spiritual support." (Cruickshank, 1955:256.)

2. *Overprotection of the Child.* Mothers, more often than fathers, exhibit this reaction. They are overcome with feelings of pity for the child or guilt for having produced an offspring so poorly equipped to face the world. Thus they protect the child too carefully, do too much for him, and prevent him from making decisions or carrying responsibility for himself. In response to such treatment, he may remain infantile and overdependent. He avoids trying many tasks of which he is quite capable. In some cases the child becomes domineering. His parents (usually his mother) become his slaves.

Mothers who adopt this role may actually be assuaging their own guilt feelings through their penitent dedication; or perhaps they fulfill their need for a person in whom to invest their love.

Sometimes the parents' oversolicitous attitude is really a disguised rejection of the child. They consider the handicap a disgrace. But because society takes a pitying attitude toward such children and because the parents have punitive consciences, they cannot outwardly reject their child. So they play the overprotective role. In doing so, they may harm the child's personality as much as if they expressed undisguised dislike for him. For instance, some parents of this type make it obvious to the child that they are denying themselves a normal life by their dedication to him. This causes the child to heap destructive guilt and shame on himself for being faulty.

3. *Overt Rejection of the Child.* This type of parent openly resents his handicapped child. The parent is aware of his own resentment and dislike but assuages his own guilt feelings by projecting the blame onto the environment: onto society for its negative attitude toward the handicap, onto the doctors who have not seriously tried to help the child, onto the teachers who are prejudiced toward him, and onto the child himself for his resisting normality—"He does not half try to succeed as other children do."

4. *Denial of the Handicap.* Some parents will not accept the fact that the youngster is handicapped and that different aims and different treatment are needed for him than for other children. Typically they set overambitious goals for the child, insist on high achievement, and fail to accept guidance in planning a realistic future for him. Therefore the pupil suffers because too much is expected of him and he is not given the special aid that could often improve his adjustment. But at least when parents have this attitude the child is permitted to try participating in the activities of normal children. He is not overprotected.

The Teacher's Techniques

As the teacher tries to determine which of these attitudes or combination of them is held by the parents of a given pupil, he can profitably turn to the following sources of information: observations of the child's behavior at school, interviews with the parents, cumulative records, and remarks of other people who have worked with the child.

Observations of Child Behavior

During his first five years of life, the child is developing the basic structure of the personality he will have the rest of his days. He is developing fundamental attitudes toward other people. He is learning which methods of adjustment (such as whether to be aggressive, retiring, apologetic, complaining, guileful) will best fulfill his needs. In this process of personality development, the most important influences on the child are usually his parents. They play the greatest role because they are the prime people with whom he must interact in learning to fulfill his needs. Typically the techniques the child has learned in adjusting to his family are the ones he uses with people outside.

As a result, some idea of the parents' relationship to their handicapped child is often gained from observing the ways the child reacts to the teacher and schoolmates. Kanner (1952:25) has observed:

Those who have become acquainted with and dealt with a large number of exceptional children are able to tell how an individual child feels about himself and his place in the scheme of things. Even the very seriously retarded child will give ample evidence of this in the manner in which he responds to the approach of the examiner or any other adult. The youngster who has been treated fondly, and who has good cause to feel accepted at home, will usually have confidence in people, accept kindness, and conform readily within the limits set by his handicap. The child who has been pushed beyond his capacity, criticized, coerced, and punished will shrink from adults, anticipate rough handling, and may even prepare himself for physical injury by putting up his arm in a defensive posture.

The teacher, in addition to observing the general reaction a pupil displays toward others, can make some estimates of parent-child relationships through discussions arising from classwork and from the use of simple projective devices.

For instance, if the student has read a book like *Tom Sawyer* or *Huckleberry Finn* or *The Yearling*, where parent-child interaction plays a significant role, the teacher may ask the student his opinion of different aspects of the story. Included in the questions may be one or two focusing on the parent-child relationship, such as: "Do you think Aunt Polly treated Tom well? Why? What do you think the best kind of parent would have been for Tom? And why?" Or "Do you think there are really parents like Huck's father? In what way do you think most parents should understand their children better?"

It is true that questions of this kind will not inevitably elicit accurate information about the handicapped child's reaction to his own father and mother. Caution should be used in drawing any firm conclusions from these roundabout explorations. But in some cases this book-report type of interview provides an opportunity which the child will welcome to voice his opinion of the parent role.

Projective techniques have proved useful in furnishing information about the parent-child relationship as seen from the child's viewpoint. By "projective techniques" we mean those devices which stimulate the pupil to express his attitudes toward his world and toward himself. The most famous of these are the Rorschach ink blots and such picture-story devices as the Thematic Apperception Test and Symonds Picture Story Test. These are most appropriately used by professional psychologists highly trained in their interpretation. But the classroom teacher, with his more modest psychological training, can often gain useful hints about pupil attitudes from stories they write and from sentence-completion tests they fill out.

For instance, occasionally in English composition the class may be assigned a topic like "If I Had a Million Dollars," "If I Were a Parent," or "If I Had Six Wishes." Sometimes the handicapped pupil's paper on such a topic will contain information disclosing the kind of relationship he has with his parents.

In other cases, the class may be asked to write a short story. The nature of the story can be an open choice for the pupils, or it can be developed around a theme the teacher suggests; for example, a teen-ager wants to do something of which his parents do not approve, a family goes on a trip together, or a child brings home a new puppy given to him by a neighbor.

As the instructor reads these efforts, he should be cautious in drawing conclusions because the story may function differently in different children's lives. One child may place his own parents literally in the story and thus show the fictional parents acting just like his own. Another will use the story as an opportunity for creating the kind of parents he would like, so the characters in the story may be idealized and quite different from his true-life father and mother. Therefore the teacher should consider these creative efforts only as hints or possibilities that must be checked with data from other sources.

Incomplete sentences have been found profitable for investigating handicapped students' attitudes toward their culture and toward themselves. This device consists of a list of phrases which the student is to complete as sentences. The phrases are designed to touch upon psychologically important aspects of the person's life. The following typical items from such a test indicate that certain phrases focus on parent-child relationships and some focus on other facets of the pupil's environment. (Cruickshank, 1955:301–302.)

1. Most of all, I want to . . .
2. I'm afraid of . . .
3. I would do anything to forget the time I . . .
4. My father hardly ever . . .
5. Boys think I . . .
6. If people would only . . .
7. I know I could succeed if . . .
8. Girls think I . . .
9. My mother and I . . .
10. If my father would only . . .

It should be clear that the purpose for giving such a series of incomplete sentences is not simply to gain information about the attitudes of a single handicapped child. A better understanding of many other pupils in the class may also result.

The teacher can introduce this activity to the group in some such manner as the following.

I am passing you each a dittoed sheet with incomplete sentences on it. Your task is to complete the sentences. You won't find this difficult, because this is not a test. There isn't any correct answer to any sentence. This is just a chance for you to write down freely your own ideas, and it will give some practice in sentence writing. The reason we are doing this is because I, as a teacher, am interested in what you young people think.

If I know more about your ideas, perhaps I can arrange our class activities to take up more things that interest you. I'm the only one who will be reading your paper. Just put down whatever comes to your mind first. I think you'll find this interesting to do.

Parent Interviews

The parent interview can serve several functions. It can inform the teacher of the attitudes which parents hold toward their handicapped child. It can inform them of his progress in school. It may, in some instances, help the parents develop a better attitude toward their child. And it can enable the teacher and parents to work out a cooperative, consistent program for aiding the pupil.

In preparing for an interview, it is well for the teacher to get clearly in mind which of these purposes he hopes the discussion will fulfill. Thus he can prepare appropriate questions and answers ahead of time and be able to face the interview with more assurance.

There is no single proper way to conduct such an interview. We cannot state specifically what the teacher should say, because any counseling situation is governed by the two personalities involved and by their sensitivity to each other's feelings and thoughts. However, we can describe two basic generalizations about counseling parents of the handicapped which have been found useful. With these generalizations in mind, the classroom teacher may experience better success with parent interviews.

Generalization 1: Parents deserve a sympathetic listener. It is difficult to be the parent of a crippled child or of one who stutters or has a harelip. These disorders produce out-of-the-ordinary embarrassment and bother. So we can expect parents to harbor some resentment and disappointment. A teacher can frequently develop a closer relationship with parents by being sympathetic toward their feelings. In a noncondemning spirit, he can listen to their expressions of negativism and understand them. To open the way for the mother or father to voice such opinions when they exist, the teacher may use some such indirect inquiry as "What kinds of problems do you feel that a hearing difficulty like John's causes for you as his parents?" Or "How does Frances get along at home as compared to her brothers and sisters?" Or "Is Harvey an easy child to handle at home?"

Mothers and fathers may build up hate and guilt which they have no direct opportunities to express. After they have been able to tell these things to an understanding listener, they are sometimes more ready to face the realities of their plight and to plan a sensible program for the child. So this opportunity to release negative feelings can have a therapeutic effect in the first stages of the interview.

But it must be remembered that this does not always work. Some parents feel resentment but never express it. They separate themselves from the teacher by a hard shell. Others welcome the chance to voice their complaints and resentment, but this never seems to help them adopt a kindlier attitude toward their offspring.

Generalization 2: The teacher needs to analyze the pupil's true status and to explain this status to the parents at an appropriate time. It is important for the interviewer to recognize the difference between (1) accepting a parent's feelings and (2) agreeing with a parent's inaccurate picture of the pupil's status. The educator has a responsibility to give his estimate of the child's prospects as accurately as possible, whether this estimate fits the parent's hopes or not. Therefore, prior to the interview it is well for the teacher to gather as much factual data as is available and to have in mind as true a description as possible of the child's assets and liabilities.

How these two generalizations or principles can operate in the interview situation is illustrated by the following example of a teacher talking with the father of a ninth-grade boy who stutters badly. The boy's parents have come to the school's annual evening open house held in the fall. Although the mother is much interested in her son's school, the father is apparently a reluctant guest at the open house. The English teacher is seated next to the father during the refreshment period in the cafeteria. Since no one else is sitting near enough to overhear their conversation, the teacher has decided to broach the problem of the boy's speech difficulty.

TEACHER: One thing I'd like to do this year is help Dan with his speech problem.
FATHER: I wish you luck.
TEACHER: I assume he's had this trouble for some time.
FATHER: Yeah. Since he was little.
TEACHER: Has he had much help with it?
FATHER: We did everything we could. I don't think it's any use.

Teacher: What kinds of help did he receive?

Father: Oh, I've told him for years to think before he talks. And I've told him to slow down. He tries to talk too fast. That's the trouble.

Teacher: I imagine it's been quite a worry for you.

Father: Yeah. You don't like to see a big kid like that stuttering. I don't want people laughing at him.

Teacher: No, that's understandable, all right.

Father: I thought he'd grow out of it, but he isn't getting any better, as far as I can see.

Teacher: Are there some times he stutters worse than others?

Father: He can sing without stuttering at all. That's funny, you know. That's why I figure he could stop stuttering when he talks if he'd just think about what he's saying.

Teacher: Well, it's quite common for stutterers to sing without any trouble. They can often read aloud with no difficulty. But apparently it isn't a matter of not concentrating or talking too fast. Partly it's because they're afraid they might stutter. Because they're afraid of certain words, they hesitate. Actually they're usually concentrating too hard on these words. By trying too hard, they get tense. Does Dan stutter more when he's excited or under special pressure to speak well?

Father: I . . . I guess he probably does.

Teacher: One thing we try to do to help stutterers in school is to take some of the pressure off. We try not to make them embarrassed about stuttering. In fact, we've found that when a student accepts his own stuttering and can admit his difficulty to other people, he rather automatically doesn't stutter so much. It's because he isn't trying so hard. He's more relaxed.

Father: Then you don't teach him to slow up when he talks?

Teacher: No. We don't talk about slowing up. And even when he's trying very hard to say a word which he can't get out, we never say the word for him. We wait for him to say it in his own good time. That's usually the best help we can give. Try to take the pressure and embarrassment off. When he's not so nervous about doing well he usually won't stutter so badly.

Father: You think this really works?

Teacher: People who work with stutterers all the time find that it does in many cases. We have a new speech clinic in the county. I think they could help Dan, if you'd like him to go there.

Father: They can cure him?

Teacher: I don't know. Stuttering is sometimes very hard to cure completely. But I'm quite sure they can help him, and maybe a great deal. Besides that, they could suggest ways for me to help him in school and for you and your wife to help him at home.

FATHER: We can't spend a lot of money on this thing when we've already tried to help him ourselves for so long and it hasn't done any good.

TEACHER: There's no charge. It's paid for by the county schools. You might try and see.

FATHER: Well, I guess we could try it.

Cumulative Records and Others' Opinions

Sometimes cumulative records include notes made by the pupil's earlier teachers concerning conferences they have had with parents. Or sometimes the school nurse or guidance worker will insert such information in the report. Therefore it is desirable for the teacher to consult the pupil's record folder when trying to understand parent-child relationships.

Although there may be no written information in the record folder regarding parents' attitudes, the teacher who had the child last year can be asked for impressions about his family conditions. The principal, art teacher, or physical-education instructor may also furnish useful opinions.

Through these channels the teacher may gain an insight into the handicapped student's home life and may help in adjusting school treatment to his needs.

Relationships with Agemates

The handicapped child is more likely to be rejected by his agemates than the nonhandicapped. In general he can expect more curious stares, more questions about his condition, more teasing, and fewer invitations to join in games or go out on dates. This is because child society, like its adult counterpart, puts emphasis on conformity. As children enter adolescence, this pressure to be like their peers increases, so the teen-ager is often in even greater need of aid with social adjustment than the younger child.

Smock and Cruickshank compared handicapped with nonhandicapped children's responses to the Rosenzweig Picture Frustration Test and concluded that the handicapped evidenced anxiety and fear especially in the area of social relationships. "There seems to be no question but that the handicapped child is basically insecure in his relationships with others and that he feels quite inadequate in dealing realistically with external appraisal or criticism by others." (Smock, 1952:163.)

The study also suggested that the two most significant barriers or threats to the satisfaction of need were the internal threat resulting from the handicap itself and the external threat of social disapproval which the child feels. Whereas the normal children concentrated more attention on resolving problems, the handicapped were more likely to project blame and hostility on the agent of their frustration.

Teachers may aid these pupils toward better adjustment in school by (1) emphasizing similarities between the handicapped and their peers, (2) helping them develop or display skills that gain peer respect, (3) providing opportunities to practice social skills, and (4) enlisting the aid of classmates to include the handicapped students in activities.

Emphasizing Similarities

Some years ago, when the needs of the handicapped first began to receive attention, their unique problems were given great emphasis. As a result, special schools were designed for their needs. But in more recent years it has become clear that special schools separate the exceptional child too much from his normal agemates. He has too few chances to learn to live with people other than those who also have his disorder. This often compounds his original social-psychological handicap, for when he later attempts to enter the larger world, he lacks sufficient social skill.

Consequently, experts in special education today usually recommend that teachers and parents place more emphasis on what the handicapped child has in common with agemates. Most children who have a hearing or speech disorder are similar to their classmates in more respects than they are different. Keeping this in mind, the regular classroom teacher can emphasize these similarities in many ways and thus help both the handicapped student and his classmates regard him more as one of them.

For example, the teacher should not give the handicapped child an all-encompassing excuse from participation but should excuse him from only those activities in which he obviously should not or cannot take part. Some teachers pity the child too much or lack knowledge of what limitations the handicap actually places on him. Therefore they excuse him from too many events in which he could well participate. The student himself often takes undue advantage of this pity in order to escape from hard work or from embarrassment that might result from his trying an activity and failing in front of others. So, when a task is a reasonable one for the handicapped child, it is desirable for the teacher to be firm in requiring him to participate as a regular member of the class.

Comments which the teacher makes during the school day can reflect his own regard for the exceptional student's abilities. It is hoped that the other students will come to regard the handicapped as more of an equal when they hear such teacher remarks as:

(To a boy who wears a hearing aid) "Fred, you read at about the same speed as Herb, so why don't you two share a book while we read together."

(To a girl who wears a brace on her leg) "Marilyn, you and Jane and Ellen will look good standing together for the photograph, since you're all about the same height."

(To a boy with a large, disfiguring birthmark on his face) "Mike, you're having the same difficulty with dividing fractions as Bill and Eddie, so I'll work with the three of you together."

(To a girl who is a noticeably slow learner) "Kathleen, you and Helen are the strongest sopranos, so why don't you stand in the back row while we sing the national anthem. That will help the girls in front."

Displaying a Skill

The handicapped pupil's chance of being accepted by his classmates may be improved if he displays some talent which they will respect. Therefore it is desirable for the teacher to discover skills or hobbies the pupil already has or to help him develop some which can be displayed.

For instance, at the beginning of the school term the teacher can ask students to list their hobbies or interests on a sheet of paper so he can become better acquainted with them. Or in conversation with the handicapped pupil, the teacher may learn whether he collects stamps or sea shells, plays a musical instrument, builds model ships or cars, draws or paints, assembles radios, or writes letters to students in foreign lands. He can be invited to show the results of his hobby to the class.

If he has traveled, won awards in contests, or met people of note, the handicapped pupil can be asked to describe these experiences.

If he is not already pursuing a hobby or developing skills, the teacher may wish to help him do so. This help may be in the form of books or magazines, an invitation to join Saturday classes at the local art or natural-history museum, or an opportunity to work with some adult in the community who follows an intriguing pastime.

Practicing Social Skills

Frequently the handicapped student is so afraid of other people's opinion of him that he avoids social contacts. In other instances, his reaction is not simply avoidance but active antagonism; when age-mates try to include him in their group, he becomes so obnoxious that they shy away from future relationships with him.

Teachers sometimes can help promote his social skills by:

1. Giving him opportunities to greet guests that come to the class-room or to show visitors round the school. When the teacher gives such an assignment to the handicapped child, it is well if he first reviews with him the way he might talk with the visitors. The student can be more sure of himself if he has some preparation for what the visitors might ask and what he himself might say.

2. Furnishing pamphlets on teen-age etiquette and methods of getting along well with peers.

3. Carrying out classroom sociodramas in which the teacher de-scribes a hypothetical social situation and then places students in various roles to play out spontaneously the way they believe this situation would develop in real life. The sociodrama is not conducted solely for the benefit of the handicapped pupil. All of the class can profitably learn from it, but the handicapped is the one who can perhaps gain the most.

For those teachers who have had little experience with socio-drama, the following incident may clarify the use of the technique.

In a fifth-grade class, the teacher wishes to focus attention on different reactions pupils can exhibit toward losing and winning a game, and he wants the pupils to judge which of these reactions is the most acceptable to agemates. Therefore, he describes the following situation:

> Four boys have been tossing darts at a target. They've decided to divide up into two teams for a competition, with two boys on each team. Each one throws eight darts at the target. When they add up the final scores, they learn that the team of Hal and Tommy has won. Jim and Jack have lost.
>
> Now, I'm not going to tell you any more about this incident. Instead, we'll let four of you boys show us what you think might happen. That is, I'll choose four of you to come to the front of the room and act as if you were the boys. We'll imagine the game has just finished. You talk among yourselves the way you think they might really talk.

At this point the teacher selects four boys who he believes will do a good job of acting out this initial incident. He warns the class:

> This isn't just a joke. So don't try to be funny. This can be quite interesting if you give the boys a chance. Don't be silly about it. Let's see if they act the way you think real boys would. And when they're through, we'll decide which ways of behaving after the game are the ones you think are best in real life.
>
> All right, I'll tell each of you boys the kind of person you are in this play. Jack is the kind who is very angry about losing. Jim doesn't like to lose, but he doesn't seem to get angry about it. Hal is very happy to win; he teases the losers. Tommy is happy to win also, but he realizes that if they played again the other team might beat his. So let's begin. They have just finished adding up the scores. Perhaps Hal can speak first, showing how glad he is that his team won.

As the pupils act out the social situation, the teacher and class watch. In some cases, the teacher has to prompt the actors a bit, especially if sociodrama is new to the group. After they have played their parts awhile, the teacher stops the drama, thanks the actors for their performance, and asks the audience:

> "What do you think about Hal? Is he the kind of person you like to be around? And what about Jim? Is that a good way to behave when you lose?"

From the discussion that follows, pupils often gain a clearer idea of appropriate ways to act toward others. The handicapped child, if he is shy, perhaps should not take part in the first role-playing demonstration. But after he has seen some of his classmates participate, he can profitably become one of the actors as well.

The technique of sociodrama has several advantages over lecturing or reading stories. First, it places students in situations important to them; yet because it is a drama in which they are assigned roles, they can feel psychologically protected and are able to reveal feelings and attitudes which they would not otherwise admit in public. Thus, the role-playing situation provides them with psychological distance or protection from sensitive emotions. In addition, sociodrama not only provides the content of social relationships but conveys the emotional tone to the class better than a lecture or class discussion would. Sociodrama illustrates the ways a variety of kinds of personalities interact in real life, giving the class a concrete situation in which to view such factors as shyness, rudeness, one person dominating another, compromise, indecision, humor, and fear, as they operate in human relations. The technique can be used at any grade level. When well done, it can hold pupil interest better than many other teaching methods.

Social situations around which the teacher may create hypothetical incidents include: greeting a person whom you have newly met, asking directions in a strange town, developing a conversation with a seatmate on a bus trip, congratulating a person who has won an award or has performed well in class, asking a girl for a date, inviting a friend to a party, disagreeing with someone who holds a point of view different from your own, thanking someone for a gift, and chatting with an acquaintance who has an interesting hobby.

Enlisting Other Students' Aid

Some children and youth seem insensitive to the handicapped person's feelings. They bluntly tell him, "Your arm sure looks awful twisted like that," or they dub him "Four-eyed Toad" or "Hop-Along Chester."

But many other children are sensitive to his plight and are willing to stick up for his right to join in their activities. Such sympathetic agemates often can do more than the teacher to see that the exceptional child is welcomed by his peers.

Sometimes the teacher can initiate this process of assimilation by talking privately with one of the pupils who is considered by the others to be a leader. During this conversation, the teacher can explain that handicapped pupils often feel odd and rejected. This act of asking the leader's aid frequently flatters him sufficiently to elicit his willing cooperation.

Occasionally it is desirable for the teacher to talk with the entire class about a handicapped pupil's problems. When students understand the nature of their classmate's disorder and when they are sensitized to the psychological pain he suffers, they tend to treat him with greater friendliness. Here is the way a teacher talked to a seventh-grade class about a student who suffered from crossed eyes.

Since Barry is out of the room on an errand, this is a good time to discuss something concerning him. I noticed last week that some students in the hall made faces and crossed their eyes as he passed. Then they laughed about it. Well, I can see why they might think this was funny. People laugh at Ben Turpin's crossed eyes in the old silent movies you see on television. But before we make fun of Barry, we should think about how he must feel.

First, you should understand a little about crossed eyes. The problem is caused by the muscles in one eye pulling too hard, so the eyes don't look straight forward together. When a small child has this trouble, the doctors can often correct it, perhaps with an operation. But if it isn't corrected early, the weaker one of the two eyes soon doesn't work at all. The person becomes blind in one eye. It's that way with Barry. He can see only with his right eye. If you hold your hand over your own left eye and try to walk around that way for a day or so, you'll see what kinds of problems it causes. You can't judge distances properly, it's hard to read, and you can't see things toward your left side.

But there's something often more serious. When you have crossed eyes, people stare at you. They may mimic you and laugh. Sometimes they consider you very ugly, so they don't want to look at you at all. This makes you feel terrible. You may really be a fine, talented, kindly, interesting person. But because of this muscle problem, which isn't your fault, people consider you a freak. They never give you a chance to show your real worth. And all the time you realize that you must bear this problem all your life. That's a tough burden to carry.

We all like fun. We like to make jokes. But there are plenty of other ways to make jokes which don't hurt a classmate. After all, an accident might occur to any of us and we might end up with some kind of handicap. Think how you would want to be treated by your classmates if that happened.

SELF–ACCEPTANCE AND SELF–ESTEEM

Each person carries within his mind an idea of what he is like. It is his own answer to the question, "Who am I?" This ideal can be called his "self-image" or "self-concept." He thinks of himself as being tall or medium or short, handsome or plain, aggressive or retiring, lighthearted or depressed, talkative or quiet, hesitant or confident, healthy or sickly, wealthy or poor, and so forth.

Besides this self-image, he also has an idea of what he should be like or what he wishes he were like. This goal or aspiration can be called his "ego-ideal" or his "ideal-image."

Your self-image and ideal-image are usually not identical. That is, most people, at least part of the time, do not think that they are quite the kind of person they aspire to be. Some philosophers believe that happiness results from a person's making these two match as closely as possible. So the closer your self-image comes to the ideal-image you have set up, the more content you are. Likewise, the greater the gap between what you think you are and what you would like to be, the unhappier you are. A person who experiences a great gap between these two for an extended period of time will exhibit symptoms of maladjustment: depression, extreme shyness, antagonism toward self and others, self-punishment, and so on.

The handicapped child has special difficulties in adjusting his self-image to his ideal-image because he lives in a world in which people tend to set up ideal-images that are most readily attained by normal or talented individuals. The handicapped tends to accept these same ideals for himself, and because they may be unrealistic for him, he is more often doomed to failure in pursuing them.

It should be remembered that the ego-ideal and the self-concept are not inborn. They are learned by the child as he interacts with his environment, especially with his parents, agemates, and teachers. As he grows older, his ideals are also influenced by people he sees in motion pictures, on television, and in magazines.

It is clear that parents are the most important in forming his self-image and ideals. Their reactions to him serve as a mirror in which he sees himself and defines "Who am I?" When they accept him as a worthy person, he is more likely to be a confident individual. If they do not accept him but reject or overprotect the child, he can rarely accept himself as being worthy.

The importance of this for teachers is fairly clear. They can help the handicapped student choose goals or aspirations which he can more readily attain. It is true that the ego-ideal he can most profitably adopt may not be the typical ideal of his nonhandicapped class-mates. But teachers and counselors can help him learn that there are many alternative ideals toward which people can strive in our society. From among these goals, each of us, handicapped or not, can usually find some that are realistic for our talents.

In addition to aiding the pupil by discussing alternative ambitions that he might adopt, the teacher can help him achieve a more pleas-ing self-concept by treating him in a friendly manner and thus show-ing that he himself accepts the child. The teacher can also promote acceptance by his peers through the techniques discussed earlier.

Furthermore, it is important for the instructor to estimate what kinds of goals the pupil can probably attain and to compare the stu-dent's current efforts to those objectives rather than to some very unlikely ideal. The pupil can then expect to taste success. He can receive compliments for his progress toward realistic objectives. His ego is refueled with confidence to attempt new tasks.

If parents and teachers fail to adjust their expectations to the in-dividual's true potential, serious personality disturbances can re-sult. Wallin (1955:85–87) has illustrated the harm that can be done by teachers who compare a handicapped child to standards that are more appropriate for normal or highly talented ones. In the case he cites, a girl with an undiscovered eye defect was compared invidi-ously with the academic record of her brilliant older brother and sister. The girl later recalled her elementary-school experiences as follows:

My thoughtless teachers never failed to remind me that I was far dif-ferent from my siblings. Instead of mustering up courage to study and prove to them that I was not inferior, I became indifferent to everything. In the fourth grade it was discovered that my right eye was nearly blind and the sight of my other eye was poor. This may have been the reason for my extreme dullness in school. However, from about the third grade through high school, I cared absolutely nothing about any of my school work. At home I would pretend to study while in reality I was daydreaming, making a hero of myself in my school work. I always managed in my dreams to be at the head of the class. Although I thought of superior achievements, I never did one bit of work to help me through school. I would not mingle with other girls or boys because I always felt that they were far better than I was. I would take offense at any word they would say, even if they were only kidding me. As a result of all this, I was graduated from high school extremely low in my class and friendless.[1]

In this case, the girl had the fortune later to attend a college in which her siblings were unknown. She was treated in an understanding, friendly manner and met with success. But in many other cases the ending is not so happy. Too often the handicapped pupil does not receive adult acceptance and encouragement to reach realistic goals, so he struggles through life full of shame, regret, and a desire to punish himself and the world.

Another technique that sometimes aids the handicapped in developing an appropriate self-image and ego-ideal is that of furnishing him opportunities to see how others have handled similar problems. Secondary-school students may gain this vicarious experience through such fictional accounts as the following.[2]

Bristow, *Tomorrow Is Forever* (man wounded in war).

DeLeeuw, *Clay Fingers* (girl with a fractured back).

Felson, *Bertie Comes Through* (fat boy).

Forbes, *Johnny Tremain* (boy with a crippled hand).

Gallico, *Snow Goose* (ugly man with a claw for a hand).

Miers, *The Ivy Years* (college boy with an uncontrollable nervous twitching).

Tunis, *The Kid Comes Back* (baseball player with an injured leg).

The following biographies of handicapped individuals may also prove useful.

Addams, *Twenty Years at Hull House* (a hunchback).

Baker, *Out on a Limb* (girl who lost a leg).

Burgess, *Who Walk Alone* (a leper).

Graham, *Lou Gehrig* (baseball player who was victim of a progressive crippling).

[1] J. E. Wallace Wallin, *Education of Mentally Handicapped Children* (New York: Harper and Brothers, 1955), pp. 85–87.

[2] Isabel V. Eno, "Books for Handicapped Children," *The English Journal,* Vol. 40, No. 5 (May, 1951), p. 277.

Hathaway, *Little Locksmith* (girl with a tubercular disease of the spine).

Keller, *Story of My Life* (woman who was deaf and blind).

Lee, *My Soul More Bent* (young man crippled by polio).

Warfield, *Cotton in My Ears* (girl who was hard of hearing).

When such books are suggested to an exceptional child, it is usually well to ask him to react to them either in the form of a follow-up interview with the teacher or a written book report. To focus the student's attention on important self-adjustment aspects of a book, the teacher may wish to pose such questions as the following at the time the volume is recommended: "While you read, try to decide how the person first found out about his handicap. How did he react to this? Do you think his reaction was a good one? Would it have been better for him if he had reacted differently? How did other people treat him? How did he react to them? Did you like the way the book turned out? Why?"

By focusing on such queries, the student may gain a better insight into ways of adjusting to his own disorder.

WHAT THE HANDICAPPED EXPECTS OF OTHERS

When people have frequently found fault with your behavior in the past, you tend to expect faultfinding in the future. If you have been overindulged for some years, you tend to expect indulgence from new people you meet. If you have sometimes been criticized for the same behavior which at other times is readily accepted by people around you, then you tend to look forward to such inconsistent treatment in the future. And so it is that we face new situations with a psychological set or an expectation based on the ways we have been treated in the past.

Teachers need to keep this in mind when they face handicapped students. Different students bring different expectations to class.

The child who has been encouraged in the past to try suitable tasks and has been complimented for his successes will pose no great psychological adjustment problems when he enters the classroom of a friendly, understanding teacher. This is because the teacher's behavior coincides with the child's expectations.

But many handicapped students have learned to expect treatment other than friendly support. Their past experiences may have taught them to look forward to being rejected, ignored, distrusted, or overindulged. These are the difficult ones, because if the teacher is to be most effective, he must wean them away from the psychological set they hold toward him.

The students who bring marked feelings of inadequacy to class are the ones who need the teacher's continual support. They profit from encouragement to try reasonable tasks which they have learned to fear in the past. To these students the teacher can play the role of an ever-friendly guide.

The overindulged child is also one who needs to learn that the teacher's role differs from what he had expected. This type of pupil is often difficult to work with because the teacher needs to adopt two somewhat conflicting attitudes toward him simultaneously. One attitude is that of enforcer of rules. The teacher is responsible for showing the overindulged pupil that he cannot always ignore other people's rights and simply have his own way. Rather, the student must learn to do his share of the work, wait his turn, and not expect others to cater to his every wish. As teachers assume this role of friendly, firm law enforcer, the student may whine or complain or threaten in order to drive them back into the role he has learned to expect of adults in the past. He may misinterpret the firmness as rejection or dislike. It is at this point that the teacher's second attitude must become evident: that of the encouraging friend. This task of playing dual roles is usually best accomplished when the instructor (1) decides what rules of behavior are reasonable for the student, (2) explains these clearly, (3) explains the consequences that will result if the rules are not followed, (4) enforces the consequences in a calm, matter-of-fact manner, and (5) at the same time freely gives praise and appropriate privileges to the pupil for his academic and social accomplishments.

Students who constantly breach reasonable class rules are sometimes doing so to test the limits of behavior in their environment. They are actually seeking for a sense of lawfulness in their world and a resulting feeling of security. Teachers who consistently enforce fair rules without expressing resentment toward the student can often help bring this sense of stability into his life.

SUMMARY

Despite the fact that students may vary considerably in the kinds of psychophysical disorders they exhibit, all handicapped ones tend to face problems in getting along well with their parents, in adjusting to their agemates, and in accepting themselves as worthy people. Throughout this chapter we have discussed ways in which teachers may be able to help students overcome problems in these areas of adjustment.

SUGGESTED LEARNING ACTIVITIES

1. Read a fictional or biographical account of the life of a person suffering from a psychophysical handicap and (a) describe the social-psychological difficulties he exhibited, (b) tell how he coped with these or how he failed to overcome them, and (c) describe what you believe a teacher might have done to aid in his adjustment during his school years.

2. Interview an elementary- or secondary-school teacher to learn what varieties of handicapped pupils he has dealt with during his years of teaching. Ask about which kinds of social-psychological problems, if any, these students exhibited and what efforts were made to aid them.

SUGGESTED READINGS

CRUICKSHANK, WILLIAM M. (ed.). *Psychology of Exceptional Children and Youth.* Englewood Cliffs: Prentice-Hall, 1955.

———. "The Effect of Physical Disability on Personal Aspiration," *The Quarterly Journal of Child Behavior,* July, 1951, pp. 323–333.

——— and JOHNSON, G. ORVILLE (eds.). *Education of Exceptional Children and Youth.* Englewood Cliffs: Prentice-Hall, 1958.

GARRISON, KARL C., and FORCE, DEWEY G. *The Psychology of Exceptional Children.* New York: The Ronald Press Co., 1959.

KANNER, LEO. "The Emotional Quandaries of Exceptional Children," in *Helping Parents Understand the Exceptional Child.* Langhorne, Pa.: Child Research Clinic of the Woods Schools, 1952. Pp. 21–28.

SMOCK, CHARLES, and CRUICKSHANK, WILLIAM M. "Responses of Handicapped and Normal Children to the Rosenzweig P-F Study," *Quarterly Journal of Child Behavior,* April, 1952, pp. 156–164.

WALLIN, J. E. WALLACE. *Education of Mentally Handicapped Children.* New York: Harper and Brothers, 1955.

CHAPTER 14

Sight

An estimated 20 per cent of children suffer visual defects. So in a typical classroom we can expect that six or seven students will have some trouble seeing properly. It is apparent that at least some of these students are going through school with their difficulties as yet undiscovered. Therefore, it becomes the regular classroom teacher's responsibility to help discover sight problems and to adjust the school program in a manner that minimizes the influence of the visual defect on the student's learning and personality development.

The incidence of defective vision can be understood more precisely when we recognize that in every 10,000 American children:

8,000 have reasonably normal vision.

1,975 have a vision defect which could be corrected, such as with glasses.

Twenty—after as much attempted correction as possible—are still classified as *partially seeing* and thus need the type of teaching and materials provided in *sight-saving* special-education classes. However, surveys show that only 11 per cent of these children are in special classes. The rest attend regular classes and thus have become the responsibility of the regular classroom teacher. (Baker, 1959: 311.)

Five are blind. (Baker, 1959:297.)

DIAGNOSING VISUAL DEFECTS

There are two principal roles the classroom teacher can play in furthering the proper diagnosis of visual defects among his students. First, he can watch in class for symptoms of sight difficulties, and when he identifies students who possibly suffer such a handicap he can refer them to an eye specialist. Second, he can himself carry out some useful simple measurements of visual acuity in cases where eye examinations are not a regular part of the school program.

Identifying Students with Possible Sight Problems

The check list below is intended to help teachers identify symptoms of child behavior and appearance that often signify visual difficulties. A pupil who shows one or more of the symptoms listed here may well warrant referral to the school administration with the recommendation that he be examined by an eye specialist.

CHECK LIST—SYMPTOMS OF POSSIBLE VISUAL DEFECTS

Pupil's Name _____ Date _____

Name of Observer _____

Directions: Check each question which accurately describes this pupil's condition.

I. In his *behavior* does the pupil often:

___A. Frown or scowl?   ___B. Squint?   ___C. Rub his eyes?

___D. Hold books or small objects close to his eyes?

___E. Attempt to brush away a blur?

___F. Have difficulty reading or carrying out other work that requires close use of the eyes?

___G. Shut or cover one eye?

___H. Shade his eyes when he reads or does close work?

___I. Tilt his head or thrust his head forward when looking at either near or distant objects?

___J. Stumble over small objects?

___K. Have trouble participating in games requiring distance vision?

___L. Seem irritable or restless when he is required to do close eye work?

II. Does the pupil *complain* (either voluntarily or when questioned) of:

___A. Experiencing headaches, dizziness, or nausea following close eye work like reading? Or following a movie?

___B. Not seeing clearly?   —C. Blurred vision?

___D. Double vision?   —E. Recurring sties?

___F. Not being able to read what is on the blackboard or the figures on the classroom clock?

___G. The sunlight hurting his eyes?

___H. The lights at home or at school bothering his eyes when he studies?

___I. Itching eyes?   ___J. An eye twitch?

___K. Burning eyes?   ___L. Watering eyes?

___M. Tired eyes after reading or doing close eye work?

___N. Spots before his eyes?

III. Does an *inspection of the child's eyes* reveal:

___A. Scales or crusts on the lids or reddening of lids and loss of eyelashes (possible symptoms of blepharitis)?

___B. Inflamed and watering eyes (symptoms which sometimes indicate conjunctivitis)?

___C. Cloudy or widely dilated pupils, or differences in size of pupils of the two eyes?

___D. Crossed eyes?   ___E. Swollen eyes?   ___F. Sties?

Administering Simple Sight Tests

In addition to watching for symptoms of eye defects and questioning students about their sight, the teacher or school nurse can screen pupils for certain eye defects by using either the Snellen Letter Chart or the "E" Symbol Chart.

The latter is more appropriate for young children who do not yet know their alphabet and for children with marked hearing or speech disorders, because they can respond to the test simply by pointing their arm or finger in the direction of the shafts of the E. Sometimes the examiner will tell the child that the symbol is a three-legged animal, and the child's task is to indicate the direction in which the legs are pointing.

The "E" Symbol Chart is less appropriate for older children who already know their alphabet, because the direction of the E is much easier to guess than the variety of letters on the regular Snellen Letter Chart, which is thus the one to use with older students.

Each of these charts consists of letters of different sizes, ranging from the largest on the top line to the smallest on the bottom. The largest symbol for each chart is the one that can be read by a person with normal vision at a distance of 200 feet, so it is designated the 200 line. In descending order the lines consist of letters of a size that can be seen by a person with normal vision at 100, 70, 50, 40, 30, 20, 15, and 10 feet.

The test is administered in the following manner.

1. The child faces the well-lighted chart at a distance of twenty feet.

2. The pupil himself or the teacher holds a card in front of the left eye to block its vision while the right eye is being tested. If the child is to hold his hand over the eye instead of holding a card, he should be cautioned not to press against the eye, because the pressure might cause the vision of that eye to be blurred when it is later tested.

3. The examiner stands beside the chart and indicates the line or symbol he wishes the pupil to read. In the case of using the "E" chart with young children, the examiner should have a sheet of paper with a square hole the proper size for exposing the "E" he desires the child to see. The paper blocks out the other surrounding symbols and the tester is confident that the child is focusing on the proper one. Or, in order to make the test more of a game for younger children, the examiner may have cut up an "E" symbol card and have made a pack with one "E" of each size. He then can hold up the "E" of an appropriate size for the child to see at the distance of twenty feet, and he can rotate the symbol into different positions.

In using the Snellen Letter Chart with older students, it is usually sufficient for the examiner to point to the letters he wishes the student to read.

Typically the examiner starts with one of the larger symbols near the top of the chart and moves down until he reaches a line that the child sees with great difficulty and responds to with much guessing. The examiner then returns to the line directly above and considers it to be the distance of practical vision of that eye.

4. The examiner records the student's score for the right eye, such as a score of 20/20. The first number in this pair tells the distance of the child from the chart. The second number designates the lowest line that the child could read accurately. In this example, the child could be said to have normal vision, for he read the size symbol that is read at twenty feet by people with normal vision. A child with 20/50 vision is one who can do no better than read at twenty feet what people with normal vision read accurately at a distance of fifty feet.

5. The right eye is covered and the left eye is tested in the same manner. It will be found that the acuity of vision may not be the same for both eyes.

Although the Snellen charts are useful as screening devices, they do not catch all visual defects. For instance, a child may be able to read the chart by straining his eyes for a few seconds as he is tested, but normally he cannot see so accurately. If his better eye is tested first, it is possible that he will remember some letters that he can report when his poorer eye is tested, though he has not actually read them with that eye. And because the eyes are tested separately, the Snellen examination does not measure how well the eyes work together. Therefore it does not reveal cases of muscular imbalance or those in which each eye records an image of a different size.

Telebinocular and Massachusetts Vision Test

The telebinocular, an instrument that is an adaptation of the stereoscope, utilizes a variety of slides and pictures. Because it tests the child's vision with both eyes open, it enables the examiner to determine how the eyes work together. It also indicates fine differences between the two visual images taken by the two eyes. Thus it is useful in identifying children who have reading difficulties caused by their inability to recognize certain words readily because of this difference in the size of the images recorded by each eye.

The Massachusetts Vision Test detects astigmatism and errors of refraction as well as the inadequate fusion of the image received from the two eyes.

Other tests of similar varieties involve the use of such instruments as the Ortho-Rater, Sight-Screener, and Protometer.

Wheel Chart Test

A chart which consists of lines radiating from a center and intersecting with a series of circles of increasing sizes can be used for detecting astigmatism in some children. This disorder is caused by imperfections in the curvature of the lens or the cornea of the eye, causing some parts of the visual field to be clear and other parts blurred. The pupil who has astigmatism sees certain portions of the chart as being shaded differently than other portions, whereas the child with normal sight sees all parts of the chart as being shaded about evenly.

It is recommended that on the basis of such screening tests and teacher observations, children in the following categories be referred for further examination.

a) All children who consistently show any of the symptoms of visual disturbance, regardless of visual acuity (particularly pertinent to the discovery of children whose farsightedness is a handicap and those who have astigmatism).

b) Older children who have visual acuity of 20/30 or less, with or without symptoms.

c) Younger children who, upon rechecking, consistently present a visual acuity of 20/30, with or without symptoms. (Hathaway, 1954:182.)

It should be recognized that when children are screened in the foregoing ways, some who do not suffer from a real visual defect will often be referred to the specialist along with those with defective sight. The eye doctor then determines more precisely which of them need corrective measures and which fall within the normal vision range.

Testing by Vision Experts

The teacher or school administrator often serves as a consultant to parents in choosing the appropriate person to examine a student's eyes. When giving this advice, it is well for the educator to recognize that in many people's minds there exists a confusion about what the term "eye specialist" means. As Baker has pointed out:

Special attention should be given to the terms oculist, ophthalmologist, optometrist, and optician since there are important distinctions between the types of services which they are qualified to give. The terms "oculist" and "ophthalmologist" may be used interchangeably, since both titles refer to registered physicians. They are qualified to examine for general medical conditions of the eyes as well as for refraction and for visual accommodation. While they are properly addressed as "Dr.," they seldom write it in front of their names or put it on their office doors or on their stationery, but have it appear as M.D. after their names.

The term "optometrist" applies to a doctor of optometry who is qualified to examine for refraction and for accommodation of vision but not for diseases of vision. Frequently the optometrist may be associated with the offices of the ophthalmologist where he carries on his professional services. If he has a bona fide degree in optometry he may properly be addressed as "Dr." but he also writes his professional degree of M.D. after his name and omits the "Dr." before it.

Any of these three specialists may write prescriptions for glasses which are to be filled by the *optician* who is a technician for making or dealing in glasses or in filling prescriptions.[1]

MEETING SIGHT PROBLEMS IN THE CLASSROOM

In addition to helping identify pupils with sight difficulties, the teacher needs to know ways to adjust the classroom program to the needs of those with visual defects. The teacher's role includes (1) instituting general practices that promote sight conservation for all students and (2) adopting measures suited to specific eye problems experienced by certain students.

Promoting Good Eye Care

A general vision goal in the classroom is the prevention of eyestrain. This is not because straining the eyes to see in poor light or to read for long periods causes disorders like astigmatism, nearsightedness, or farsightedness. Eyestrain apparently does not even make such defects worse when they already exist. But eyestrain does cause general fatigue, irritability, inefficiency, and dislike for the kinds of schoolwork that bring it about. The teacher can adopt the following measures to lessen this tension and to conserve sight.

At all grade levels, it is obviously desirable to furnish adequate lighting. For a child to read without strain it is usually well to have as much as twelve foot-candles of light on the book. (One foot-candle is the amount of light a standard candle would give at one-foot distance.) A photographic light meter can be used to check the amount of light falling on each desk in different areas of the classroom. In some cases the amount of light will vary from fifty foot-candles near the windows to eight foot-candles in the corners, indi-

---

[1] Harry J. Baker, *Introduction to Exceptional Children* (New York: Macmillan, 1959), pp. 295–296.

cating the need for the use of electric lights in the darker areas of the room. (Dolch, 1948:58.)

When the teacher is talking with the class, he should not stand in front of the windows. If he stands silhouetted against the sunlight, the children's eyes must strain in trying to adjust to both the teacher's dark figure and the bright background.

For children who are working at their desks, it is best to have a diffused light source or to have the light coming from the left and slightly to the rear for the right-handed child and from the right rear (such as over the right shoulder) for the left-handed child. Thus, when the pupil writes, his hand does not cast a shadow over the material he is working on.

Chalkboards, bulletin boards, charts, and demonstrations should be located so they are free from glare. Writing on the chalkboard should be large and done with soft chalk that makes clear, white letters.

It is generally a poor idea to write poems, lengthy tests, or outlines on the chalkboard for students to copy onto paper, because the continual looking up and down from board to paper strains the eyes.

Children should be taught to sit erect while reading and should be cautioned not to read lying down when at home.

If a pupil has been out of school because of illness, it is usually best not to expect him to make up his incomplete work all at once. During the period of recovering from the illness, he is often unable to complete even the regular assignments as efficiently as when he was completely well, much less make up additional work. To play safe, the teacher may excuse the student from certain kinds of close work for a few days. And whenever possible it is best to ask the doctor or school nurse about restrictions that should be placed on school assignments during the student's convalescence.

To prevent eye injuries, pupils should be cautioned not to shoot paper clips, rubber bands, and spitballs at each other or to engage in sword fights with sticks on the playground. They should also be instructed not to rub an eye when a foreign object such as sand has entered it. Rather, they should pull the upper lid down over the lower and allow the tears to wash away the object. Rubbing the eye might cause the particle to scratch the cornea and permanently impair sight.

Aiding Pupils with Defects

In addition to taking precautions to conserve all pupils' vision, the teacher should give particular attention to the way he treats the pupils who suffer visual defects, because different kinds of eye difficulties affect schoolwork in different ways.

The teacher typically has three means of locating those students with vision problems. First, he should look for symptoms of eye defects as outlined on the check list discussed earlier. Second, the school's routine eye examinations, or those supervised by the teacher himself, will bring to his attention other pupils with possible subnormal vision. Third, he should consult the student's health report, which many schools regularly keep as part of their cumulative record about each child. If the pupil wears glasses, the health report will usually tell what the glasses are intended to correct. Sometimes a notation about special cautions regarding the child's activities is included by the eye specialist for the teacher's guidance.

Occasionally a teacher suspects a student of suffering an undiscovered eye defect and therefore refers him to an eye doctor. After the eye examination, it is desirable for the teacher to talk with the doctor to learn what special classroom practices and materials should be provided.

Because it is not always possible for teachers to obtain direct suggestions from the student's doctor, the following are offered as recommendations that are generally sound for aiding students suffering from farsightedness, nearsightedness, astigmatism, muscular imbalance, stereopsis problems, slow accommodation, cataracts, dislocated lens, albinism, and other disorders.

Farsightedness

When the refracted light rays entering the eye come to clearest focus at a distance behind the light-sensitive retina rather than exactly at the retina, the condition is termed farsightedness, or hyperopia. The child who is farsighted finds it easier to look at things at a distance. He finds it difficult to see near objects clearly, for the adjustable lens of the eye must strain to make sufficient accommodation to bring these objects into sharp focus.

It is estimated that half or more children entering first grade are farsighted because their eyeballs are still growing and have yet to reach the size to make perfect accommodation with complete ease. (Dolch, 1948:64.) But this farsightedness apparently does not bother most of them because the lens in the front part of the eye is still very flexible and adjusts readily. For most children, farsightedness is a temporary condition corrected by increased growth of the eyeball. A few, however, find close work like reading and writing tiring, and they come to dislike it. A certain percentage of them will continue to be farsighted throughout their school years and will continue to react negatively to close work.

As may be assumed, the farsighted child is not readily identified simply by use of the Snellen chart. Hence, to locate children who actually suffer from farsightedness, it is important that the teacher watch for other symptoms, such as the child's habitually holding the book at arm's length or his appearing irritable as he does close work. Children should not be required to do close work for extended periods without occasional opportunities to rest their eyes by looking at objects at a greater distance.

The child with marked hyperopia should not be asked to do much outside reading. Efforts should be made to substitute other activities for the heavy load of close map study and reading that other members of the class may be required to carry.

Nearsightedness

When the eyeball is too long from front to back so that the light rays entering the eye come to clearest focus before reaching the light-sensitive retina, the individual is said to be nearsighted or to suffer from myopia. The child who is nearsighted finds it easier to look at objects that are close by. Far-off objects are commonly blurred or not discernible. It is very common eye defect among students.

Unlike many cases of farsightedness in young children, those of nearsightedness do not correct themselves. They tend to get worse with time rather than better. Therefore more serious cases will be found in the upper grades than in the lower ones.

Often nearsightedness that has existed since birth is not discovered until the early grades in school, when it becomes apparent to the teacher that the child cannot make out what is on the blackboard or on charts at the front of the room. Before that time, the child has not realized that trees have individual leaves rather than being only green blurs or that distant houses and cars do not appear to be mere smears to other people as they do to him.

Glasses with a double concave lens provide correction for myopia. But with young children who play roughly, glasses can be dangerous, for they may shatter and injure the eyes. Therefore if it is judged best to provide glasses for the young child, it is important that they be made of unbreakable material.

In cases of pronounced nearsightedness there is often the danger that a sudden jolt or blow to the head will cause the retina to detach itself from the eyeball, rendering the child blind. Therefore the teacher should limit the play of such children so as to minimize the jumping and rough activities that can so seriously endanger their sight.

The nearsighted child should be seated in the front part of the classroom, enabling him to see the chalkboard and teacher demonstrations with the least inconvenience.

Astigmatism

An uneven curvature of the cornea or lens in front of the eye that distorts the image recorded by the retina is termed "astigmatism." Apparently most people have some degree of astigmatism, and when the brain interprets the image it makes a mental adjustment for the distortion. According to Dolch:

> Some persons believe that this mental adjustment to curvature, when it is considerable, causes eye-strain, but it is impossible to be certain whether this is true or not in any particular case. . . . When a person gets glasses, the eye specialist usually includes in them correction for astigmatism. It is another question whether one should wear glasses for astigmatism alone. This is a point of great disagreement. Each person has to be governed by the advice of his eye doctor. It is very doubtful, however, whether children should wear glasses for astigmatism alone. They do not read a great deal. Any glasses are a danger to them.[2]

[2] Edward W. Dolch, *Helping Handicapped Children in School* (Champaign, Ill.: Garrard, 1948), p. 68.

It is often easier for the child with a high degree of astigmatism to do his schoolwork if he is in one of the best-lighted sections of the room.

Muscular Imbalance

Sometimes the muscles controlling movements of the eyeballs fail to make the eyes operate together as a well coordinated unit.

The most common variety of muscular imbalance is strabismus, meaning a failure of the two eyes to direct their gaze at the same object. The child with internal strabismus or esotropia is popularly termed cross-eyed, because one or both eyes point inward toward the nose. The child with external strabismus or exotropia is said to be wall-eyed, because the eyes point outward in different directions. The pupil with slight internal strabismus will have little or no trouble reading. But the one with external strabismus will find it to be a major effort to turn both eyes inward to center on reading matter, so he constantly experiences nervous strain. This may result in a headache, nausea, or a general feeling of discomfort and an unwillingness to do close work.

Because a person cannot long bear two different images reaching his brain for interpretation, the child with serious strabismus comes to pay attention only to the impression from the dominant eye and learns to ignore the other. A child should be treated for this condition as early in life as feasible, because if it continues he may no longer have functional sight in the nondominant eye.

Another form of muscular disorder is termed "nystagmus." It is an involuntary, rapid movement of the eyeball, either in a circular, vertical, or horizontal direction. It may occur while the pupil is studying and constantly forms an unsettling interruption in his work. Possibly nervous tension and fatigue aggravate nystagmus. By observing the pupil over a period of time, the teacher may determine under what conditions the defect is most frequent and can attempt to regulate schoolwork to minimize these conditions.

Stereopsis Problems

Sometimes the right eye records an image of a different size than the left eye, causing a problem of stereopsis or a lack of coordination of the images of the two eyes. Children with this disorder often miscall words in reading because so many look alike to them. They demand much patience on the part of the teacher. They should be taught to ask themselves continually while reading, "Does that word make sense there?" By this constant checking of meaning, these children become much more aware of their errors in mis-seeing words and therefore can look back to the mistaken word and get it correct. They will need this habit of constantly checking the sense of reading all their lives.

Slow Accommodation

The student whose eyes adjust slowly as he changes his gaze from focusing on a close object to focusing on a far object should not be burdened with tasks that require rapid shifting of focus. He should not have much copying from the chalkboard to do or copying from charts at the front of the room.

The teacher, upon recognizing that a pupil suffers from slow accommodation, should not expect him to answer quickly when he must glance from the teacher to his book or paper.

Cataracts

A cataract is any cloudy condition that develops in the lens, progressively dimming the vision. Generally the only method of removing a cataract is by surgery which eliminates the lens. As a result, the child must thereafter wear strong convex glasses (unless he suffers high myopia) because the loss of the lens causes a high degree of farsightedness, usually accompanied by astigmatism. Since he can no longer accommodate to seeing both close and far-off scenes, he may need bifocal glasses.

A student who has undergone surgery for cataracts cannot be expected to carry the reading load and cannot meet the demands to shift focus for different distances that are borne by his classmates with normal vision.

Dislocation of the Lens

The lens in the eye sometimes becomes dislocated through either hereditary or traumatic causes. The dislocation may be complete, so the lens is pushed either far forward or far backward. Or it may be a partial dislocation, resulting in mixed hyperopia, myopia, and astigmatism with a confusing double image being recorded on the retina.

With partial dislocations, suitable glasses may be enough to compensate for the resulting hyperopia. Complete dislocation usually calls for removal of the lens.

Albinism

People who suffer from a hereditary lack of proper skin pigmentation also often suffer disturbing eye defects. They cannot bear bright light, so they need tinted or dark glasses and usually feel more comfortable working in a section of the classroom that is not brightly illuminated. Typically the albino also suffers from nystagmus, myopia, and astigmatism, so it is desirable to reduce the demand for eye work in school. The pupil will find it difficult or impossible to read charts or items written on the distant chalkboard.

Other Disorders

There is a variety of other relatively uncommon vision defects which an occasional regular classroom teacher may encounter among his students. These include:

Infantile glaucoma, in which the eyeball is enlarged from increased pressure within the eye. This often causes blurred vision. The tension should be constantly checked by a doctor and relieved through local medication or a filtering operation. Great care must be taken to avoid a blow to the child's eye.

Retinitis pigmentosa, which involves progressive degeneration of the retina. At first this results in night blindness, then a restricted field of vision, and eventually the child can see only in a small central area.

Coloboma, which is characterized by a congenital lack of some part of the eye structure. If the missing portion is in the lower half of the visual field, the child will bend his head downward to look over the blind area. To compensate for a defect in the upper area, he can hold his head high and peer through the lower portion.

Infections involving different portions of the eye, such as the muscles or the iris.

Aniridia, in which the iris is absent so that the student has the same difficulties experienced by people suffering from albinism.

As has been indicated, in all these cases it is important for the teacher to obtain whatever guidance he can concerning classroom procedures by consulting medical records or talking with an eye specialist. Very often the procedures will include providing special reading materials printed in 18- or 24-point type, placing the child in a section of the classroom best adjusted to his anomaly, and asking other students or parents to read to the pupil materials which he cannot comfortably read alone.

SUMMARY

The classroom teacher can expect about one out of five students to experience some difficulty with vision. Appropriate glasses will correct most of these defects so that the students can proceed with regular schoolwork without much difficulty. Some children will need special treatment in the classroom if they are to make adequate progress. A few of these still will not adjust well to the typical classroom situation and should be assigned instead to sight-saving classes which are provided in larger communities for the partially seeing pupils.

SUGGESTED LEARNING ACTIVITIES

1. Obtain a Snellen chart and administer this examination to several children.

2. Ask the nearest public-school department of special education to demonstrate the use of such sight-screening devices as the telebinocular and Protometer for your university class.

3. Ask the permission of a public school to inspect a series of students' health-record cards. Note the kinds of data about sight recorded on the cards and give your opinion about the usefulness of such reports to the classroom teacher.

4. Visit two classrooms for one period each. During your observation, note the number of pupils wearing glasses. After the class, ask the teacher if any special provisions are required for these students. During the class also observe any symptoms among the pupils which, you believe, might indicate possible undiscovered vision problems. Following the class, ask the teacher if he has noticed any signs in students' appearance or performance which would hint that some were experiencing uncorrected visual defects.

5. Interview a school nurse to learn what types of vision problems most often come to her attention and whether any children in the school suffer serious defects requiring special materials or classroom procedures.

6. If there is a sight-saving class in your community, visit the class to see what materials are provided for the pupils' special needs. Also inquire about the requirements for admission to the class.

SUGGESTED READINGS

ALLEN, H. F. *Make Sure Your Child Has Two Good Eyes*. New York: National Society for the Prevention of Blindness, Publication No. 30, 1956.

BAKER, HARRY J. *Introduction to Exceptional Children*. New York: Macmillan, 1959. Chaps. 18–19.

DOLCH, EDWARD WILLIAM. *Helping Handicapped Children in School*. Champaign, Ill.: Garrard, 1948. Pp. 54–87.

GARRISON, KARL C., and FORCE, DEWEY G. *The Psychology of Exceptional Children*. New York: The Ronald Press Co., 1959. Chap. 9.

HATHAWAY, WINIFRED. *Education and Health of the Partially Seeing Child*. New York: Columbia University Press, 1954.

MICHAL-SMITH, H. (ed.). *Management of the Handicapped Child*. New York: Grune and Stratton, 1957. Chap. 7.

National Society for the Prevention of Blindness. *Helping the Partially Seeing Child in the Regular Classroom* (Pub. No. 156). New York: NSPB.

VAIL, D. *The Truth about Your Eyes*. New York: Farrar, Straus, 1950.

SUGGESTED FILMS

(For rental or sale, consult the National Society for the Prevention of Blindness, 1790 Broadway, New York 19, N.Y.)

Eyes for Tomorrow, 22 minutes, 16-mm. sound. Shows relationship between general health and eyes throughout life.

Johnny's New World, 16 minutes, 16-mm. color, sound. Stresses early detection and treatment of child vision problems.

CHAPTER 15

Hearing

Except in rare cases, the child who is too deaf to understand fairly loud speech is of no real concern to regular classroom teachers, for he will usually be in a special school or special class. But every teacher must deal with children who have a variety of lesser hearing deficiencies. It is hard to say exactly how many hearing-problem cases a typical elementary or high-school teacher will face in a year, because surveys reporting hearing difficulties have used different standards and methods from one investigator to another. Some reports suggest that 5 per cent of the child population suffers from hearing problems,[1] while others place the figure higher.[2] It seems fairly safe to say that in a typical regular classroom, one or two students may well be experiencing trouble in hearing accurately.

Probably the three most important negative effects on the student as a result of hearing loss are those relating to his difficulty in following oral schoolwork, his problem of social adjustment, and the low opinion of himself that he may develop.

The largest number of children and youth with impaired hearing are not those who have been deaf from birth or from an early age but those who experience a progressive hearing loss as they grow up. When this loss is gradual, the individual himself usually does not realize what is happening and so cannot report it to his parents or teachers. Instead, more and more he fails to hear direc-

[1] Warren Gardner, *Report of Committee on Hard-of-Hearing Children of the American Hearing Society,* Reprint 229 of School Health Services Section of the American School Health Association (November, 1955).

[2] Harry J. Baker, *Introduction to Exceptional Children* (New York: Macmillan, 1959), pp. 343–344.

tions clearly, fails to respond when called on in class, and misinterprets what others say to him. As a result, his mistakes in schoolwork increase and he tends to make a poor impression on teachers and classmates. To them he often appears inattentive, odd, self-centered, preoccupied, uninterested, stupid, shy, or careless. As a result, their reactions to him are unfavorable, but he does not understand why.

Even when he realizes what is occurring, the youth who is losing his hearing is liable to be very upset emotionally. As Levine has said:

> The problems of the progressively deafened arise from having to stand helplessly by, as it were, while the bustle of a familiar environment and way of life fade away into stillness. . . .
>
> Countless young hard-of-hearing people live in daily terror at the prospect of being caught in the joshing camaraderie of a hearing group; of being singled out in games; of being called on in class; and, worst of all, of missing the "sweet nothings" whispered into their ears on dates. . . .[3]

To fulfill his responsibilities to aid these pupils, the classroom teacher should be prepared to (1) help diagnose hearing difficulties so that proper aid can be provided, (2) estimate the intellectual potentialities of pupils whose school performance has been affected by hearing loss, and (3) arrange classwork so as to minimize the effect of the disability on the student's school progress, social adjustment, and feelings of self-confidence.

DIAGNOSING HEARING DIFFICULTIES

At first glance, the problem of discovering the hard-of-hearing child might appear fairly simple. All you need to do is to have the class take a standardized hearing test every two or three years and then follow the recommendations given by the hearing expert on how to handle the hard-of-hearing pupil in class. But for several reasons the problem is not so simply solved.

In the first place, most school systems do not appear to make frequent formal checks of each pupil's hearing, so the job of discovering the hard-of-hearing often falls to the regular classroom teacher.

Second, there are many forms of hearing difficulties, not all of

---

[3] Edna Simon Levine, *The Psychology of Deafness* (New York: Columbia University Press, 1960), pp. 61, 63, 65.

which are readily discovered with the typical hearing-test recordings or the pure-tone audiometer which are considered standard instruments for formal hearing tests. When being measured with the pure-tone audiometer, the pupil listens by means of earphones to sequences of pure tones produced at various pitches and varying degrees of loudness. Although this process is valuable and does measure the degree of hearing under these conditions, it does not accurately reveal the problem of the pupil under more normal everyday hearing conditions. It may well miss the student who can understand speech in a quiet room but not in a noisy room. Nor does it reveal the real-life hearing success of the child who has fairly marked hearing loss but who has become very adept at lip reading and therefore in many life situations can function psychologically as if he had much less loss than that measured by the audiometer.

The discovery of the hard-of-hearing child is further complicated in at least two respects.

1. The behavior of a child with hearing loss may not be recognized as arising from this cause, but his deviant behavior may be misinterpreted by parents or teachers as signifying something else, such as feeble-mindedness, a tendency to escape from reality through daydreaming, resistance to adult authority, laziness, malnutrition or subnormal metabolism, or defective speech.

2. Hearing problems are often met in children who have other disabilities as well, so that it is difficult to determine which disability is the most influential in disturbing the child's behavior. For example, feeble-minded children often suffer hearing loss. The same is true of those with epilepsy, thyroid and pituitary disorders, certain kinds of cerebral palsy, impaired vision, and some varieties of emotional disorder. (Meyerson, 1955:128.)

Therefore the assessment of hearing disabilities is not always simple. While keeping this fact in mind, the classroom teacher can still make helpful contributions toward identifying children in the classroom who may be experiencing hearing problems as yet unrecognized and untended by parents and the school staff.

A Classroom Check List

Following is a check list that can help teachers focus attention on observable symptoms of child behavior that often serve as clues to hearing difficulties. A student who exhibits one or (more likely) a combination of the symptoms listed here may well warrant referral by the teacher to the school administration, which can arrange for testing and examination by specialists. A city or county hearing clinic or most eye-ear-nose medical specialists are proper agencies to carry out this examination. (It should be recognized that not all general medical practitioners are qualified to make accurate assessments of hearing loss, so simply sending the child to the neighborhood physician is often an inadequate measure.)

CHECK LIST–SYMPTOMS OF POSSIBLE HEARING DIFFICULTIES

Pupil's name _____ Date _____

List checked by _____

Directions: Check each question that describes this pupil's condition.

I. In his *behavior* does the pupil:

___A. Tilt his head, turn his ear toward the speaker, or cup his hand behind his ear to hear better?

___B. Appear inattentive in class—an apparent daydreamer?

___C. Need to be called on more than once before responding?

___D. Display a blank facial expression when spoken to?

___E. Appear tense while listening?

___F. Closely watch the face and lips of the speaker?

___G. Frequently display confusion about how to do assignments already explained by the teacher?

___H. Have difficulties pronouncing words?

___I. Display peculiar voice qualities, often high-pitched?

___J. Read aloud poorly?

___K. Run words together when speaking?

___L. Usually talk louder than necessary?

___M. Seem to be a mouth breather?

___N. Frequently rub or pick at his ear?

II. Does the pupil *complain* of:

___A. Earaches?

___B. A blocked feeling in his ear or head?

___C. Ringing or buzzing noises?

___D. Nausea or dizziness?

___E. Difficulty in understanding directions?

___F. Headaches in the sinus areas?

___G. Sore throats or a chronic catarrhal condition?

III. Does an *inspection of the child's ears* reveal any:
___A. Discharges from the ears?
___B. Excessive accumulation of wax?
___C. Deformities of the outer ear?

Simple Classroom Hearing Tests

In addition to using a check list such as the foregoing, the teacher can devise a watch-tick test or whisper test that will reveal the cases that should be referred to a specialist for further study.

With the watch-tick test, the pupil is asked to stand close to the blackboard, facing a mark on the board. The pupil holds the palm of his left hand over his left ear and holds his right palm over his right eye so that he cannot see the teacher. The teacher, holding a watch that has a fairly audible tick, stands a few feet to the right of the pupil, who is told to report when he first hears the tick. The watch is moved gradually closer to the pupil's right ear until he signifies he can hear it. A mark is made on the blackboard at the distance of the watch from the pupil when the tick becomes audible. Then the process is repeated for the left ear. By using the same watch in all tests, the teacher can compare the distances at which the tick becomes audible for different children and can thus estimate normal and impaired hearing.

When an appropriate watch is not available, the same type of test can be carried out if the teacher whispers numbers and letters at various distances from the subject.

More Precise Testing

Specialists in diagnosing hearing problems use more precise testing devices.

A common instrument which measures ability to hear speech under controlled conditions is the speech-phonograph audiometer. It may be used with individuals or with as many as forty students, whose sets of earphones are plugged into the audiometer at the same time. The test sounds are on a standard set of phonograph records which contain words or numbers spoken in graded intensities by various kinds of voices, both male and female.

The pure-tone audiometer is a precision electrical instrument that tests the ability to hear pure tones of varied degrees of loudness over a range of six or seven octaves. It may be used for careful diagnosis of individuals' hearing acuity or for screening purposes with groups as large as forty pupils.

Speech-articulation tests are also available. Their purpose is to measure the student's ability to understand the sounds commonly heard in ordinary speech. The testing is done with a standardized list of words and nonsense syllables. Some tests are given against a standard background of noise. These tests are then repeated without background noise to determine the individual's auditory acuity under different hearing conditions.

Descriptions of Hearing Loss

Audiometers permit the measurement of hearing loss in terms of decibels, which are the units used to measure the perceived loudness of a certain sound compared to that of a standard sound. When students have been tested by specialists, the resulting report of hearing acuity is commonly in terms of decibels. Therefore, it is desirable for teachers who read such reports to have some idea of the educational implications of different degrees of loss in terms of decibels. Levine (1960:313–314) has provided the following guide as an aid to educators:

A. Children with slight losses: these children are on the borderline between normal hearing and significant defective hearing. Their loss averages 20 decibels or less in the speech range of the better ear as measured by the pure-tone audiometer. This group usually needs no special considerations other than favorable seating in the classroom.

B. Children with moderate losses: these are the hard-of-hearing children. Their losses average from 25 to 50 decibels in the speech range of the better ear. Generally these children should be able to receive their education in classes for normally hearing children provided they are favorably seated, receive speech training if necessary, and learn speech reading. Those children whose loss is as great as or greater than 35 decibels in the better ear should also be provided with hearing aids and should receive auditory training. Special class services may have to be provided for the more severely hard of hearing in this group if their adjustments are unsatisfactory in the regular classroom.

C. Children with marked losses: these children are on the borderline between the hard of hearing and the deaf. They do not have enough hearing to learn language and speech with the unaided ear, but they have residual hearing that can be utilized in their education. Their losses range from about 55 or 60 to 65 or 75 decibels in the speech range in the better ear. They have sustained their losses from very early childhood or babyhood and do not learn language and speech through the unaided ear. Initially, these children receive their education in schools for the deaf or in special classes from teachers especially trained to develop language and speech. After they have achieved fluency in the use of language and speech, their educational programs may very likely be patterned after those established for hard-of-hearing children.

D. Children with profound losses: these are the deaf children who do not learn speech and language through their ears even with benefit of amplified sound. Their losses range from 70 or 75 decibels to inability to distinguish more than one or two frequencies at the highest measurable level of intensity in the better ear. Such losses, when sustained from birth or very early childhood, typify deaf children who must receive their education from teachers trained to develop the communicative process through very specialized techniques. Educational facilities are provided for these children in schools or classes for the deaf.

JUDGING INTELLECTUAL CAPABILITIES

The hard-of-hearing child—especially the one whose difficulty has not been discovered—typically succeeds in school at a level below his intellectual potential. Likewise, teachers' judgments of the pupil's intellectual abilities are usually inaccurately low, because estimates of the student's potential as revealed by the usual techniques (teacher observation, school marks, verbal-aptitude tests) are adversely affected by his unrecognized and uncorrected hearing disorder.

If the teacher is to suit schoolwork to the pupil's talents, he needs a better evaluation of aptitude than usually results from methods that are suited to the student who hears well.

Generally the testing program for the hard-of-hearing needs to depend heavily on nonverbal and nonlanguage tests which measure the individual's ability to perform some nonoral and nonaural task. Hence, for the preschool child the Randalls Island Performance Series, the Goodenough Draw-A-Man Test, and (for children of kindergarten age) the Columbia Mental Maturity Scale are recommended. If the child's hearing impairment is mild, it is well to include the Revised Stanford-Binet Scale, which will give some idea of the discrepancy between the child's performance on this somewhat verbal test and on the complete performance-type tests mentioned above.

Throughout the elementary grades, the Arthur Point Performance Scales, the Cornell-Coxe Performance Ability Scale, and the Columbia Mental Maturity Scale are useful. The Wechsler Intelligence Scale for Children is a desirable measure, because it has both verbal and performance sections which are scored separately and thus are easily compared. The Stanford-Binet can also be tried as a supplementary measure.

Standardized achievement batteries, such as the Stanford or the Metropolitan, are also appropriate in the elementary grades. They help determine the level at which the child is apparently succeeding in academic schoolwork. The scores on the achievement battery, when compared with the pupil's aptitude scores, give some idea of how nearly the pupil's school success compares with his potential ability.

At the junior-high level, the Wechsler Intelligence Scale for Children and the Stanford-Binet can likewise be given to supplement data from performance tests for pupils having less severe disabilities.

High-school students can be tested with the Wechsler Adult Intelligence Scales or the Wechsler-Bellevue. Such nonlanguage instruments as the Revised Beta and the Nonlanguage Multi-Mental Tests are appropriate for measuring the ability of a hard-of-hearing person whose comprehension of language has been seriously impaired by his auditory disability.

Achievement tests at the secondary levels are also desirable for providing some comparison of apparent ability and current success in academic subjects.

These formal measures should be combined with whatever data are available from observations of psychologists, physicians, parents, or other teachers regarding the pupil's behavior, in order to develop as clear a picture as possible of his abilities.

As already suggested, the hard-of-hearing student runs more risk than the normal-hearing one of experiencing unsatisfactory social relations and of developing an unpleasant picture of himself. As the teacher tries to analyze the pupil's abilities and liabilities, he should also observe the kind of relationship the student has with other pupils and try to discover what opinions the student holds about himself. Hints about his self-image may come from personal talks the teacher has with him, from compositions or stories the student writes as class assignments, and from the amount of confidence he displays in class activities. This information about personal-social adjustment becomes an important element in the teacher's decisions about how to arrange class activities to suit the hearing-handicapped student's needs.

ARRANGING CLASSWORK

We have already discussed the teacher's first responsibility: that of identifying hard-of-hearing children and referring them to a specialist who, after examining the pupil, can provide suggestions about ways to treat the child in school. If the teacher himself talks with the specialist, it is well for him to ask such questions as the following.

How much disability does the pupil suffer? Is his hearing disorder the same for both ears? What are the chances for arresting or improving the hearing? Are there stressful conditions associated with the disability, such as dizziness, imbalance, ringing in the ears, or discharges from the ears? If the child is to wear a hearing aid, how much does it improve his hearing? And what cautions should be observed in the operation and care of this instrument? Are there circumstances in this case that might aggravate deafness, such as emotional disturbance, some general health condition like an allergy, or a condition of the environment, like the presence of dampness, dust, noise, or rapid temperature changes?

With this background of understanding, the teacher can then aid the student by (1) ensuring that he always understands what is going on in class, (2) treating him in a way that will enhance his good adjustment to the disability, and (3) helping his classmates behave in a desirable manner toward him.

Helping the Student Understand Class Activities

The two most important measures for ensuring that the pupil always understands what is going on in class are to seat him where it is easiest for him to hear and to make sure he can see the teacher's and classmates' lips when they speak.

To seat the pupil adequately, the teacher needs to know how much loss there is in each ear so that the better ear can be toward the portion of the classroom from which the teacher usually speaks.

Hard-of-hearing children can become quite adept at lip reading, especially if they receive training in it. Therefore, it is important that the teacher always keep them in mind so that he does not talk while writing on the chalkboard, does not frequently speak from the rear of the room, and does not read from papers that are held so close to the face that they hide his lip movements.

It is also desirable to write assignments on the chalkboard so as to reduce the chances of the hard-of-hearing child's misunderstanding page numbers, questions to be answered, and dates when assignments are due.

Children with rather marked hearing disabilities can usually profit greatly from training in reading speech (i.e., lip movement, facial expression, and gesture). Garrison and Force (1959:270) report:

> In a study of seventeen children who were hard of hearing and who were given instruction in speech reading for from one to three years, 47 percent of the group showed an increase in IQ (test scores), 41 percent showed no change, and 11 percent showed a decrease. Among 76 percent of the group, definite improvements in classroom achievement were noted. Among sixteen children who were hard of hearing but who were not given instruction in lip reading because of lack of parental cooperation, none showed an increase in (tested) IQ during the same period, but 75 percent showed a decrease. Only 18.7 percent made classroom improvement, and all individuals in this group presented definite personality problems.

If possible, this training in speech reading should be given regularly by a specialist in the education of hearing-disabled children. However, if no such aid is available, the teacher may be able to help the child by (1) suggesting he watch himself speak in a mirror at home to become better acquainted with the way the mouth forms different speech sounds, (2) giving lip-reading practice after school hours, and (3) asking the child's parents to practice speech reading with him.

Understanding the Role the Disability Plays

An auditory disorder does not play the same role in the personality of each child. The hearing disability of one pupil may cause him to strive hard to compensate for this shortcoming, and he may therefore win a kind of success in his life that he might never have achieved otherwise. The hearing difficulty of a second pupil may cause him to expect others to serve him and always accord him preferential treatment. And for still another child, the disability may serve as a force that drives him away from the company of his peers and into isolation—perhaps into a world of books or fantasy.

Therefore the teacher should not assume that he should necessarily adopt the identical attitude toward this year's hard-of-hearing student that he successfully used with the one that was in class two years ago. As with all disabilities, the teacher should try to (1) understand the actual limitations that the handicap places on the pupil's performance, (2) reduce the negative effects of the handicap through appropriate classroom procedures, (3) expect enough of the child so that he recognizes he is really one of the regular group and is considered by the teacher and classmates to be a capable person, and (4) recognize how the pupil apparently feels toward his handicap so that through discussions with the teacher the pupil may express his feelings and derive the benefit of the teacher's understanding and counsel.

As recommended in the discussion of other disabilities, the teacher should also talk with the other pupils in the class so that they understand the function of the hearing disorder in their classmate's life and how to treat him so he will make a good adjustment to school.

SUMMARY

The classroom teacher's role in aiding the hard-of-hearing pupil is threefold.

He should help diagnose hearing difficulties so that proper aid can be provided. He should know how to estimate the intellectual potentialities of the hearing-disabled pupil. He should arrange classroom activities so as to minimize the effect of the disability on the student's school progress and on his personal-social adjustment.

SUGGESTED LEARNING ACTIVITIES

1. Test the hearing acuity of several students by using the simple watch-tick or whisper tests described in this chapter.

2. Request the city or county school authorities to allow you and your class to take a group audiometer test, and obtain the results of this test so you can compare the tested hearing acuity of the individuals in the group. On the basis of these records, determine what measures, if any, should be taken by a teacher to adjust classwork to the hearing characteristics of these students.

3. Administer a simple performance test or nonlanguage test to a friend or a school child, trying not to depend on oral directions but using only hand directions and demonstration. This will aid you in understanding the problem of measuring the intellectual aptitudes of someone who is very hard of hearing.

4. Interview three teachers to discover whether they now have, or have had, hard-of-hearing children in their classrooms. Ask them how they discovered that the children were hard of hearing, how the handicap seemed to affect the pupils' personalities, and what classroom measures the teachers adopted to aid the pupils.

5. Interview a school principal, a superintendent, a director of special education, or a curriculum coordinator to learn what measures the school system takes to care for the hearing-handicapped student, that is, what routine testing program is used to discover hearing disorders, what aid is given to the handicapped child (special classes, aid in lip reading, speech training), and what steps are taken to ensure that classroom teachers are informed about the needs of the hard of hearing.

SUGGESTED READINGS

BROWD, VICTOR L. *The New Way to Better Hearing through Hearing Reeducation.* New York: Crown Publishers, 1951.

FRAMPTON, M. E., and GALL, E. D. *Special Education for the Exceptional.* 3 vols. Boston: Porter Sargent, 1955, 1956. See chapters on hearing aids, the hard of hearing, counseling the deafened, and the measurement of hearing.

GARRISON, KARL C., and FORCE, DEWEY G. *The Psychology of Exceptional Children.* New York: The Ronald Press Co., 1959. Chap. 10.

LEVINE, EDNA SIMON. *The Psychology of Deafness.* New York: Columbia University Press, 1960.

MEYERSON, LEE. "A Psychology of Impaired Hearing." In WILLIAM M. CRUICKSHANK (ed.), *Psychology of Exceptional Children and Youth.* Englewood Cliffs: Prentice-Hall, 1955.

MYKLEBUST, HELMER R. *Auditory Disorders in Children: A Manual for Differential Diagnosis.* New York: Grune and Stratton, 1954.

STRENG, HEDGECOCK, *et al. Hearing Therapy for Children.* New York: Grune and Stratton, 1955.

CHAPTER 16

Speech

Since it is one task of the school to help students speak effectively in both formal and informal situations, each classroom teacher finds himself facing problems of encouraging good speech patterns and correcting defective ones.

In clarifying his speech-teaching task, the instructor needs a definition of what defective speech is so that he can recognize which students really need help. Generally a person's speech is considered to be defective if the listener pays at least as much attention to the way he talks as to what he says.

Therefore, a pupil who lisps, omits or substitutes sounds, stutters, grimaces as he speaks, or has a squeaky or harsh voice is considered to have defective speech, provided this individually different way of speaking is noticeable enough to distract the listener from the content of his talk or distort the intended communication or cause the speaker himself to be maladjusted. These problems are labeled "defective speech production." The major part of this chapter is meant to aid teachers with identifying such problems, estimating their causes, and helping students improve.

But even students who enunciate accurately and have pleasing voices can distract the listener or fail to communicate because of the kinds of words or pronunciation or sentence patterns they use. Therefore, matters of usage are also important and will be discussed in the latter portion of the chapter.

DEFECTIVE SPEECH PRODUCTION

How likely is it that pupils with speech-production problems will be found in the typical classroom? It is estimated that from 5 to 10 per cent of the average school population will exhibit difficulties that are serious enough to warrant special attention if they are to be remedied.

The greatest number of these are cases of defective articulation. A lesser number involve stuttering or disturbances of voice. In the following discussion, we shall focus primarily on these three matters. We shall also give some attention to the ways that cleft palate, cerebral palsy, and impaired hearing may affect speech production.

Specialists versus Classroom Teachers

Some speech difficulties are simply a matter of the child's having learned a faulty way of producing some sound when he was small —such as saying "sink" for "think"—which he has not bothered to correct. In many such cases, merely directing his attention to the problem and giving him practice in making the correct sound is sufficient to correct it. In other cases, the defective speech is caused by malformation of the mouth or teeth. Correcting the malformation and retraining the speech in these instances is often rather difficult. Still others involve complex emotional causes which demand psychotherapy if progress toward better speech is to result.

Speech problems can be so varied and can be the result of such a confusing complex of causes that some educators say no correction of speech-production problems should be attempted by a regular classroom teacher. They recommend that if a specialist cannot be obtained to handle the pupil's problem, the classroom teacher should not "meddle."

As reasonable as this argument may at first appear, on closer inspection it becomes obvious that if a pupil with a speech disorder is in a regular classroom the teacher inevitably "meddles." Granted, the teacher may not purposely attempt to correct the fault, but he may try feeding the child words when he stutters in class discussions or may carefully avoid calling on him to recite. Such acts as these are "meddling" because they affect the student's attitude toward himself and toward his problem, and they usually postpone positive corrective steps that might have been taking place during this time. So, in our discussion throughout this chapter, we are not recommending that the teacher try to take over the speech therapist's role when a therapist is available. Rather, we are suggesting that since the classroom instructor's behavior cannot help but affect the child's speech, it is best that the teacher know how to behave properly.

We believe that the regular teacher, without actually being a specialist, can understand basic facts about the common disorders and can make important contributions toward correcting them through (1) helping identify speech problems of children, (2) referring marked problem cases to appropriate specialists if such are available, (3) cooperating with a program recommended by a speech correctionist for the classroom treatment of a child, and (4) giving some time—perhaps at lunch hour or before or after school—to work with an individual child who needs to correct an error that is the result of faulty learning, as is usually the case with the largest body of speech problems: defective articulation.

Some larger school systems have special speech classes or speech correctionists to care for the more obvious deviants. But in most schools, pupils with defective speech must still look to their regular classroom teachers if they are to receive any aid at all. The best way for teachers to be prepared to furnish this help is by taking speech-correction courses or, as a less ambitious measure, by consulting such books as cited at the end of this chapter. The chapter itself serves as an introductory guide to ways of fulfilling this role.

Defective Articulation

About three out of four cases handled by school speech correctionists involve defective articulation. Although children exhibit this in a variety of forms, most errors fall into one of three categories: sound substitutions, sound distortions, and sound omissions.

Sound Substitutions. This means that the pupil replaces the proper sound by an incorrect one. For instance, a *th* sound is substituted for *s* or *z*, so the child says "He thent theven of theeth" for "He sent seven of these." Or he uses *w* for *r*, resulting in "Wun, wun awound the wing" when he means "Run, run around the ring." The *w* sound may also substitute for *l* as in "I wike to wie down" for "I like to lie down." And *f* may replace the voiceless *th* as in "I fink you get free wif a nickel" for "I think you get three with a nickel."

There are many others in addition to these. Usually adolescents who retain a sound substitution in their speech will be rather consistent in using it each time the original proper sound should occur. But among younger children the variety of substitutions is considerably greater and the substitutions may not always be consistent within one child's speech. That is, in some words he may make a correct voiced *th* sound but in others a *v* may be substituted, so he says *uvver* for *other* but correctly says *that* for *that*.

Sound Omissions. This means a pupil commonly leaves out a sound, as when he says "Tand up" and "Top it" for "Stand up" and "Stop it." Like sound substitutions, these will be most frequent among younger children, and they will not always be consistent. The most common form is the omission of final consonants as in "I can' go" for "I can't go." To a lesser degree, consonants in the middle and at the beginning of the word will be left out.

Sound Distortions. Among older children, it is relatively more common to distort sounds than to substitute or omit them. Sound distortions are also frequently found in the speech of younger children.

Among the most commonly distorted sounds are *s* and *z* (which may be hissed too strongly or may sound mushy when air spills over the sides of the tongue), *sh* and *ch*, and others.

Age Differences in Articulatory Defects

The problems of primary-grade teachers differ somewhat from those of upper elementary and secondary teachers. This is true because many more children in the primary grades exhibit articulatory defects, and a large percentage of these defects clear up by Grade 3 or 5 without special speech work.

Girls have generally been found to surpass boys slightly in speech development. Even so, one of the most frequently quoted studies found that not until the age of 6.5 years did as many as 50 percent of the girls studied attain relatively complete mastery of all sounds. And the boys were almost a full year older before as many as 50 percent of them attained the same degree of articulatory skill. (Johnson, 1948:93.)

Therefore the primary teacher should not conclude that every child in the kindergarten or first or second grade is a speech-correction case if he has not mastered all sounds. You can expect him to be still saying such things as "sat" for "that" and "foah" for "four" in these grades. However, this does not mean the primary teacher can ignore speech errors and simply assume they will all clear up "naturally" with time. It does not mean she can wait for the real speech-problem children to be identified by the upper-grade teachers.

Rather, the primary-grade teacher has a dual responsibility: (1) to provide routine daily activities that give all children aid in improving their articulation and (2) to analyze the speech of the children with the most obvious defects and provide special help for them, either through a specialist or by herself if specialists are not available. By catching the real speech-problem cases early, the school can more readily aid them before their defect brings them the unhappiness and maladjustment that so often result for the older child and adult in a society that puts high value on verbal ability.

The upper elementary and secondary teacher will have less difficulty identifying the pupil with a real speech problem but usually will have a more challenging task in trying to correct it, for it now has become a long-established pattern and is likely to be encrusted with psychological defense mechanisms and feelings of inadequacy that are hard to change.

Identifying and Testing for Defects of Articulation

The easiest way to discover speech defects is to follow a teaching procedure that offers frequent opportunities for students to speak, as in class discussions, group work, question-answer sessions, and oral reporting. As the class progresses, the teacher can note articulatory defects among those students who contribute and can also recognize that the very reticent pupils in class may be keeping quiet to hide a speech problem. So that he will not forget the nature of the defects he hears, it is well for the teacher to make a note of them, either as an anecdotal record, or more quickly and conveniently, as a mark on a check list or rating scale which he has prepared in mimeographed form.

As a specific example of such an evaluation device, the following combination check list and rating scale is offered. Note that this is a general type of speech-error sheet providing space not only for articulatory errors but also for stuttering, unfavorable voice quality, distracting mannerisms, and poor organization of the content of the speech.

SPEECH CHECK LIST

Student _____ Grade or Class _____ Date _____

Rated by _____ Position or Title _____

Directions: Mark items that best describe the student's speech, using these symbols:

A = always or almost always
S = sometimes or fairly often
R = rarely or only occasionally

Speech situation observed:
(check one or more)
__Class discussion
__Oral report
__Casual conversation
__Interview with rater
__Summary of various occasions

1. *Articulation*
   __Mumbles   __Distorts sounds (__ for __; __ for __)
   __Tight jaw   __Substitutes sounds (__ for __; __ for __)
   __Satisfactory   __Omits sounds (__, __, __, __)
2. *Voice pitch*
   __High   __Moderate   __Low   __Varies or cracks
3. *Rate*
   __Fast   __Moderate   __Slow   __Alternating or jerky
4. *Volume* (as judged appropriate to the observed situation)
   __Very loud __Loud __Moderate __Somewhat weak __Weak
5. *Fluency or rhythm*
   __Hesitates   __Stutters   __Inserts "uh" or "ah"   __Is smooth
6. *Voice quality*
   __Harsh   __Squeaky   __Thin   __Nasal   __Hoarse
      __Strained   __Breathy   __Pleasant
7. *Vocabulary, usage, pronunciation* (as judged appropriate to age level of speaker, the occasion, and the audience)
   __Rich, very desirable   __Average   __Substandard, poor

8. *Organization of ideas*
   ___Logical, easy to follow   ___Confusing
   ___Moderately logical, fairly easy to follow
9. *Gestures and mannerisms*
   ___Gestures not apparent
   ___Gestures and manner support talk effectively
   ___Mannerisms detract from content of speech (describe such mannerisms below)
10. *General attitude*
    ___Calm and pleasant   ___Sullen
    ___Shy, retiring   ___Blank, impassive
    ___Excited, animated, and pleasant ___Belligerent
11. *Other comments:*

The check list on which classroom observations may be recorded serves as an initial screening device for locating which children have a speech problem and for making a preliminary description of the general nature of the problem. Following this, it is desirable to make a more careful examination of the pupil to determine precisely the characteristics of the problem, its probable cause, and the kind of remedial program that will be most feasible.

Articulatory defects may arise from various causes, often in combination. These include the faulty learning of sounds, deviations in structure of the mouth, substandard hearing, and such others as low general intelligence or an impoverished speech environment. By using a speech-articulation test, inspecting the child's mouth, testing hearing, and testing intelligence, a better estimate can be made of what causes are probably involved in this particular case. The teacher is usually unable to carry out all these examinations alone. But where experts are not available or where the articulatory defect appears to be minor, the classroom teacher is warranted in making the examination.

It is helpful to know that most articulatory defects have resulted from incorrect learning of sounds. So to determine which sounds are faulty and may profit from correct relearning, you can give an articulation test involving these three steps:

1. Carefully observing a controlled sample of the child's connected speech and marking down any articulation errors that occur.

2. Observing the child's speech in less formal conversation to substantiate the observations made in the controlled sample.

3. Having the child try to imitate the sounds which he typically says incorrectly in test words or in connected speech.

Two basic kinds of material are commonly used in carrying out the first two steps in the examination. One consists of test sentences or paragraphs containing a variety of sounds, which the student is asked to read and perhaps discuss. The other, especially useful with younger children, consists of pictures of objects and scenes, which the child is asked to identify and talk about. Sample test materials are furnished in Anderson (1953) and Van Riper (1958).

If test sentences are used, the pupil is asked to read the list of sentences one by one while the examiner notes each error on a record sheet.

To secure evidence about the student's connected speech, the examiner asks him to read a paragraph containing a variety of speech sounds or may engage him in conversation. In this way, the results of the formal testing can be checked and the tester can observe whether the same mistakes show up in both the reading and informal conversation. During this chat an over-all evaluation of the general effect or severity of the articulation problem can be made.

With younger children, many testers prefer using pictures which will elicit the desired words rather than using reading material. The child is furnished a series of colorful scenes which he identifies while the examiner notes sound errors. To elicit an example of connected speech, the examiner may ask the child to make up a story about one of the pictures.

For the third step, the tester has the pupil try to imitate isolated sounds instead of words. Each of the pupil's sound errors should be tested in this manner. To introduce this activity, the examiner says something like the following.

I am going to make a certain sound several times. While I am saying the sound you are to listen very carefully and try to hear exactly how it sounds. You are also to watch my face very carefully and try to see exactly how I make it. Do not say anything until I give you the signal. Just listen and watch carefully. After I have made the sound a number of times, I will nod to you, and you are then to try to say the sound in exactly the same way that I did. You are to try it just once. (Johnson, 1948:109.)

This testing procedure should enable the examiner to answer such questions as: On what sounds does the pupil always make errors? Do some sounds occur as errors only in certain words or in certain positions in a word? Does the child make incorrect sounds during the first two steps of the testing procedure, yet say these same sounds correctly when he conscientiously tries to imitate the teacher's example during the final step of the testing?

By focusing on such questions, the teacher can often identify words in which the child does say the sound correctly, and these words can act as good ones to serve as the bases for a corrective program.

Correcting Physical Disorders

Malformation of teeth and of the mouth (such as a too high or too low roof or hard palate or an extra long or short tongue) can make the task of retraining the child more difficult. A cursory examination by the teacher will suggest whether the mouth formation appears normal. A more thorough check by a medical or dental specialist will give more precise information. Many structural difficulties, such as crooked teeth or tongue-tie, can be relieved. But even where faulty mouth structure occurs, very often the child can learn to say the sounds correctly if he is given proper training.

Retraining to Correct Articulation

After the teacher or speech therapist has tried to have such physical factors as faulty hearing or dental malocclusion corrected, he should plan a retraining program that usually consists of:

1. Providing clear examples of both the error and the correct sound until the pupil can tell them apart. This is called "ear training" or "developing auditory discrimination."

2. Teaching the pupil how to produce the correct sound by itself and to practice until he can say it readily.

3. Using a core of common words in which the sound occurs in order to have the pupil transfer the correct sound into his connected speech.

4. Guiding him to make the sound correctly in all speech, that is, developing the new sound into a speech habit.

Since each individual with a speech problem is different from all others, the exact way the teacher carries out these steps will differ somewhat from one case to another. What kinds of activities or exercises to use and how much time to spend on each must be determined for the individual student, as the teacher judges his needs and attitudes. A sure prescription to fit all cases is not available. However, speech therapists have found that the following types of activities are very often the most useful on which to build a retraining plan.

Discriminating between Correct and Incorrect Sounds

There is an old story of a customer who asked the butcher for "two pounds of kiddlies." The butcher said, "You mean kidneys, don't you?" And the customer answered, "That's what I said, diddle I?"

This customer illustrated an important trait of many people who substitute, omit, or distort sounds. They fail to hear the difference between the way they say a sound and the way other people do. As a first step toward correction, they need training in distinguishing the correct from the incorrect sound. The following activities help develop this skill. Some are for younger children, others for older ones, and some for all ages. From lists like the following the teacher may select those experiences he thinks will best aid a given pupil.

1. The teacher says correctly several times the sound that is causing the pupil difficulty. Then, in order to ensure that the pupil can recognize this sound unit when it appears in words, the teacher reads a list of words, some containing the difficult sound and some not. The child is to raise his hand or to tap with a pencil each time he hears a word containing the sound. Progress can be recorded by scoring one for each correct identification and subtracting one for each miss.

2. The teacher reads aloud a story in which the sound-error words appear many times. The first time through the story, he imitates the pupil's error, cupping his hand behind his ear every time he makes the error. The pupil is asked to do this with him. When the teacher reads the story a second time, he pronounces all words correctly

except for one in which he commits the error. The pupil is asked to cup his ear when he hears the error.

3. A scrapbook of pictures cut from magazines can be made. The pictured objects are ones whose names contain the sound or sounds with which the child is having difficulty. The name of each object is printed below the picture with the problem sound underlined or lettered in a different color. The child is asked to practice saying these words.

4. Pictures of objects, some containing the difficult sound and others not, are given to the child. He is asked to name the objects, then place those containing the difficult sound in one pile and the rest in another pile.

5. The teacher says a word several times, in some cases saying it correctly and in other cases making the student's error. Each time the error is made, the student is to hold up his hand. A second time through the series, the student is to imitate the teacher's error each time it is made.

6. The student is asked to underline all words in a paragraph or in a list that contain the difficult sound.

7. Speaking into a tape recorder, the student along with the teacher reads a list of words. When the student reads a word and makes his usual error, the teacher repeats the same word with the sound made correctly. When the tape is played back, the student is to listen carefully and try to describe the difference between the two productions of each sound.

8. In cases where the child can hear the error in the speech of another child but is not convinced that he himself makes it, the two children can alternate in saying a list of words into a tape recorder. When the tape is played back, the pupil can recognize that he does indeed make the mistake, and he is usually more willing to try to correct it.

9. The student tells a story or recounts an experience. Each time he makes a sound-production error, the teacher taps a pencil or rings a bell to make him aware of it.

10. The student is asked to tell a story, at the same time listening carefully to his own speech and stopping each time he makes an error. He can then imitate the error he has just committed, exaggerating it to impress its occurrence on his mind. (It often surprises

teachers to learn that such apparent negative practice is useful in eradicating the error.)

If the teacher has not recognized it beforehand, he will become convinced as he works with students' speech problems that no progress can be expected unless the student himself strongly wishes to improve. If he does not care to change his faulty habit, working with him will do no good. Therefore one of the purposes of ear training is to convince him that he does make errors.

In summary, the ear training is intended mainly to help the student isolate and identify the sounds that make up speech, to bombard him with a host of examples of the correct sound that he must learn, and to enable him to distinguish between the correct and incorrect sound.

Producing the Correct Sound in Isolation

There are many methods for teaching the pupil the next step: producing the new sound in isolation, apart from its context in familiar words. The more popular of these approaches are the stimulus, the phonetic-placement, and the sound-modification methods. Regular classroom teachers can learn to use these.

Stimulus Method. This is the most common and easiest method. The teacher provides the stimulus by saying the correct sound and asking the pupil to respond by imitating it.

For example, after thorough ear training the teacher may begin: "Roger, you'll now have your first chance to make the new sound. Watch me closely while I say it several times. Then you try. And remember that you aren't to make the old *th-th-th* sound. You are to make the hissing-snake sound like this: *sss, sss, sss, sss*. Now you try it."

If the ear training has been well done, the student usually produces the sound accurately on the first try. When he only approximates the correct sound, the teacher can attempt to demonstrate or explain how it differs from the correct one. Then, after the teacher repeats the simulation sound again several times, he can ask the pupil to try once again. If the correct sound is not produced this time, it would be well to repeat some of the ear-training activities before the student again attempts the sound himself.

Throughout this process, the pupil should not be urged to strain for the sound and become tense, but the entire process should be an easy, leisurely one. The teacher should convey this calmness and lack of pressure in his manner.

During these sessions, it is important that the teacher reward the pupil's efforts so he will feel his work is worth while and will continue trying, but it is wrong to tell him he has succeeded when in reality the sound he has made is still short of the mark. When he has approximated the proper sound but not perfected it, he may well be confused to hear the teacher say only, "Very good" or "Well done." Usually it would be wiser for the teacher to tell him, "That was closer, Roger. It's still not quite a real hissing *sss*. We'll try again a bit later. First, listen to this."

In short, the teacher's remarks are intended not only to reward the pupil's efforts. They also need to define his progress with accuracy. The comments must be honest if the pupil is not to be confused.

Phonetic-Placement Method. When the stimulus method does not work with a pupil, it is well for the teacher to focus his attention on the way the tongue, lips, and jaw are placed for saying the sound correctly. There are various techniques for aiding the student.

One is for the teacher to note the way his own teeth, lips, and jaw move while producing the sound. This movement can be described and perhaps exhibited for the child. "Roger, when you say *sss*, don't let the end of your tongue come between your teeth, but close your teeth and make the tip of your tongue stay against your bottom teeth only. When I open my mouth, see where I keep my tongue to say the *sss*."

Sometimes the teacher and child are side by side in front of a mirror. Or they may hold hand mirrors as they sit beside each other. The child tries to match lip, teeth, and tongue placement with those he sees in the teacher's mirror as they try different sounds.

Diagrams of tongue, jaw, and lip positions for all important sounds are available in certain speech-therapy books, and these can be studied with profit by the teacher or by older students who are trying to correct articulation problems.

In discussing this method, we should recognize that not all people who make a given sound correctly necessarily place tongue and jaw in identical positions. The same correct sound can often be produced in a variety of ways. Thus it is well for the teacher to experiment with various ways of placing the articulatory mechanisms in saying a particular sound. If a pupil cannot succeed with one position, perhaps he can learn another. This experimenting with a variety of patterns is particularly important in cases where the formation of the teeth or jaw is abnormal, making it necessary for the speaker to develop compensatory tongue or lip movements if he is to enunciate correctly.

Sound-Modification Method. This approach involves having the pupil learn the new sound by modifying other sounds which he can already make. The other sounds may be those of speech or ones that imitate noises or such functions as swallowing.

With this method, the student is usually asked to make a certain sound for a short period. As he continues to produce this sound, he moves his lips or teeth or tongue in a specific manner that changes the original sound into one that approximates the one he is trying to learn. He is asked to listen closely to the change that occurs and to note how the movement of the tongue or teeth feels. In this way a tactual, kinesthetic, and auditory image of the new sound is given. Several of the speech-therapy books mentioned at the end of this chapter give specific guides to phonetic-placement aids and also offer activities to help pupils approximate new sounds by modifying old ones. For example, among his suggestions for developing an adequate *sh* sound, Van Riper (1954:243) includes the following:

1. Tell the child to round his lips and flatten his cheeks and "slush" the air out between his teeth.

2. Ask the child to make an *s* sound and pull back the base of the tongue with a pencil stuck between the teeth.

3. Ask child to make a *th,* then to pull back the tongue, shutting the teeth and continuing to blow. . . .

7. If child can say "measure" have him whisper it and prolong the sound.

8. If child can make the *ch* sound, have him "let it leak out," prolonging it rather than releasing it suddenly.

Once the child succeeds in producing the correct sound, it is appropriate to give him a great deal of practice saying it in isolation before he attempts to use it in words. This isolated practice is needed because the incorrect sound has become such a well-established habit that the new sound is not yet able to compete with it effectively in connected speech. He must repeat the new sound persistently enough to produce it without much conscious effort.

To furnish the necessary practice without boring the pupil, the teacher can suggest varied activities. For instance, the student can begin the sound as a whisper, then say it slightly louder with each repetition. He can be asked to concentrate on tongue and lip movements as he says it. He can use the sound in a series of nonsense syllables which the teacher constructs by combining the faulty sound (which is usually a consonant) with vowels and diphthongs. The pupil can keep score of the number of times he repeats each of these syllables.

When the correct articulation is fairly well established, he can be asked to say the new sound and the old incorrect one alternately. This is a form of negative practice which can emphasize for him the difference between the proper and improper forms and, as a result, can strengthen his ability to say the correct one consistently. However, such negative drill should not be used unless the student knows exactly why he is doing it and how it can help him. Thus it is not appropriate for some younger children.

From Words to Connected Speech

After the youngster says the new sound easily and consistently by itself, he is ready to try it in common words, that is, in words he uses daily. If he is old enough to read, the new words can be in the form of a list. The nonreader should be furnished a series of pictures of objects whose names contain the desired sound.

Before the pupil attempts to pronounce one of these words, he first needs to listen and watch closely as the teacher repeats it several times. Then he tries it himself. If he fails to produce the sound accurately in the word, he needs to practice it again in isolation or in nonsense syllables before trying the word once more.

The transfer of the new sound to connected speech should not begin until he can say the sound easily in several commonly used words. These words serve as the nucleus for transposing the correct sound into everyday speech.

Teachers and parents must recognize that at this stage of his retraining, the child should not be expected to say the sound correctly on all occasions. Parents or teachers who, at this stage, stop the pupil each time he makes the error are hurrying the process too much. They end up nagging him. As a result, he may be afraid to try to speak. Or, as sometimes happens, the tension brought on by the nagging causes the errors to multiply rather than diminish.

Therefore the pupil should be assigned only a few situations in which to practice incorporating the new sound into his speaking pattern. For the time being, his casual speech on other occasions is to receive no criticism. As he masters a few of the assigned activities, the variety of practice situations can be increased.

The teacher can think up many appropriate speech situations which will enable the youngster to make this transition. The following examples illustrate the kinds of activities that may be assigned.

1. The child is to tell his parents about a school incident, such as about a ball game or an art lesson or a science field trip. After relating the incident, he is to ask them whether he had said any word wrongly.

2. The student is assigned to tell a joke or anecdote to three or four different classmates during free time. The joke is to contain some words containing the difficult sound, but he is not to let the classmates know he is working on a speech assignment.

3. The pupil is to give an oral report which is part of his regular schoolwork. By planning ahead of time some of the phrases he will use, he is better prepared to say the difficult sounds correctly. During the report to the class, the teacher can record his progress and discuss it with him later.

4. In an individual session with the teacher, the student can assume that he is ordering a meal in a café or buying a bus ticket or meeting an old friend. Each time he makes a sound incorrectly during these spontaneous dramas, he should make a tally mark on a card. This helps him focus attention on speech errors which he is learning to eradicate. If these sessions can be tape-recorded, the student can hear himself when it is played back and can check the number of times he said the sound correctly and incorrectly.

In addition to using the foregoing types of activities, speech therapists often ask the pupil to penalize himself each time he makes the error. The penalty is not something harsh but mild and good-natured, for the purpose is only to increase his awareness of the error, not to punish him in a way that undermines his confidence or makes him resent speech correction. For instance, during an assigned period of time he may carry a pencil and paper so he can make a mark whenever he catches himself in an articulation error. During this same period, he might also have a friend record his errors. Or he may penalize himself by carrying out some silly action whenever he makes a mistake. This could involve patting the top of his head or saying "oh-oh-ah-ah" or touching his right shoelace.

As the pupil succeeds with a greater number of the assigned speech situations in his daily life, he becomes increasingly aware when the old incorrect sound crops up in his speech on occasions other than the assigned ones. Therefore he gradually eliminates his errors in these other situations as well. Eventually the new sound is wholly mastered.

Stuttering

Stuttering has frequently been defined as a disorder of the rhythm of speech characterized by hesitations or the repeating of syllables or words. However, if you listen attentively to the spontaneous conversation of a group of normal youths or adults, you find that this broad definition fits the speech of all of them to some degree. But these people are obviously not all stutterers. Only one school child out of every 100 or 175 is properly diagnosed as a stutterer.

If repetitions and hesitations appear to some extent in everyone's speech, what distinguishes a "normal" lack of fluency from that of the true stutterer?

This can be answered from two viewpoints: that of the listener and that of the speaker. To the listener, stuttering is a disturbance in rhythm so marked that it draws his attention away from what the speaker is saying and focuses attention on the way he stumbles in trying to say it. To the speaker, stuttering is a feeling of anxiety, a fear that comes from his expecting to repeat or block on words he is about to utter. And because of the fear, he does indeed commit the hesitations and repetitions he has dreaded.

How does a person become a stutterer? Speech therapists do not entirely agree upon a cause. A variety of theories have been offered.

(Diehl, 1958.) For example, since a stutterer often has relatives who also suffer from the disorder, some theorists have proposed that the difficulty is biologically inherited. However, the evidence today suggests that the disturbed speech rhythm is learned within the family, not directly inherited.

Another theory has held that stuttering often results when a left-handed child is forced to write with his right hand. But current research suggests that this is rarely if ever true. (Johnson, 1948: 203–204.)

Other theories have focused on chemical composition of the blood, general health, and body shape. But none has proven very convincing or provided much guidance toward correcting the disorder.

Other explanations minimize physiological and biological factors. Instead, they emphasize psychological and social aspects. The most prominent of these theories cites parental mishandling of the child's early speech as the major cause of stuttering. Those who favor this view say that although stuttering sometimes begins in later childhood or adolescence, most cases start between ages two and four. As the young child struggles to master a complex language, it is quite normal for him to repeat syllables or words and to pause frequently. Parents often fail to recognize such faltering as normal. At least, they want him to get over his hesitations as soon as possible. In their impatience they interrupt him, finish his sentences for him, or tell them to "think before you speak" or to "stop repeating like that." If they mistake this normal lack of fluency for real stuttering, parents often try to correct the "problem" by focusing the child's attention on each irregularity in his speaking rhythm. The child, especially if he has a low frustration tolerance, now comes to dread the probability that he may pause or repeat syllables. His dread creates a psychomuscular tension which causes him to do exactly what he has feared he might. In straining to avoid a slight pause, he succeeds only in blocking for a very long moment. In trying not to repeat a *t* sound, he ends up stuttering it several times before getting the whole word out. His speaking life becomes a cycle of anxiety, tension, stuttering, more anxiety, more tension, more stuttering. His is a psychological problem.

While searching for *the* cause of stuttering, some authorities have concluded that the malady may result from different factors in one person's life than in another's. Causes may differ with the biological inheritance and the social environment of the individual. Perhaps the truth lies here.

Despite their disagreement on the etiological factors of stuttering, experts do agree on at least two matters that are of importance to teachers.

1. The symptoms of stuttering differ somewhat from one pupil to another. One student may hesitate only on certain words and only in public-speaking situations. Another may experience major difficulties with all speech experiences. Not only does he stammer and repeat, but his efforts to talk are accompanied by distressing facial grimacing. Some careful observation of a pupil will enable the teacher to discover under what conditions he stutters and how seriously the defect disturbs communication and social relationships.

2. Any conditions which increase the stutterer's fear of not speaking smoothly will increase his stuttering. Therefore, whatever the teacher can do to decrease a pupil's anxiety about the likelihood of stuttering will help decrease the severity of his speech difficulty. For the classroom teacher, this is the most important fact to remember. Treatment of the stutterer should be based on an understanding of this point.

Following are some of the specific things the teacher can do to carry out a program of reducing the student's anxiety about stuttering.

1. *Gain the student's confidence and friendship.* The stuttering child needs, not pity, but frank acceptance as a worth-while person. The teacher can initiate a friendly relationship by showing interest in the student's work and providing him opportunities to talk alone with the instructor. The topic that opens the conversation may be a school assignment, the student's reading interests, or his spare-time activities. Or, if the teacher feels it is appropriate, the talk may be about the pupil's stuttering itself. Whatever the topic, the teacher should indicate by his manner that he is not embarrassed by the pupil's pattern of speaking. The instructor should listen to the pupil with interest and not appear bored or distracted by the clock, by other people in the room, or by papers on his desk. He should not interrupt the student nor feed him a word for which he is obviously struggling. The teacher should not tell him to "take it

easy" or "hurry up" or "get it out" or "take a breath before speaking" or "wait until you've thought it out clearly before you try to talk." The teacher should look at the student, not avoid him, as he stammers his words. The more the teacher accepts the conversation as a normal one, the better the student feels.

The purpose of this friendly, complete acceptance is to give the pupil a confidant to whom he can freely express both positive and negative feelings. As the teacher accepts him more wholeheartedly, the pupil more readily accepts himself. His anxiety about stuttering diminishes. As anxiety diminishes, so does the stuttering.

2. *Encourage the pupil to accept his stuttering and to stutter more easily and more slowly.* Stuttering is a complex psychological problem. It is usually a difficult disorder for the most expert speech therapist to deal with. Even lengthy clinical treatment may often fail to cure it, though such treatment does alleviate the most distressing symptoms. Therefore the classroom teacher cannot expect to cure each stutterer who appears in his classes. Rather, the teacher should be more realistic and should strive only to reduce the symptoms as much as possible and to enable the student to communicate orally despite his stutter.

One step toward this goal is to encourage the pupil to talk about his stuttering problem quite realistically. He should not try to disillusion himself or others about the existence of the problem. It is generally good mental hygiene for him to tell how he feels about speaking to strangers or before a class, about how different people react to him, what his parents have said and done, what he himself has done as a result of this handicap. He also can be encouraged to talk about this problem with his parents, other teachers, and classmates. This self-acceptance of stuttering helps him conquer his anxiety. As a result, it reduces the stuttering itself.

During the teacher's conversation, he can suggest that the student develop a new attitude toward worrying about his malady. If the stutterer is typical, he has heretofore dwelt on the stuttering he has committed in the past. He mulls over a recent incident and wishes he had avoided trying to talk. So he should be encouraged to adopt a different view of these incidents. He should consider each one simply as history which is to be forgotten. When the stuttering has been committed, it is past. It no longer exists. Nothing can be done about it. The student's concern should focus instead on the next interesting idea which he wants to tell someone, and he should tell it in spite of any stutter. If he can adopt such an attitude of acceptance, he will find that the stuttering itself reduces.

Some of the most curious aid for the stutterer comes from his learning to stutter more simply and leisurely. He does not try to avoid stuttering. He merely tries to do it more efficiently and without obstructing mannerisms. There are two facets of this simpler stuttering that warrant particular attention.

The first relates to the grimaces or mannerisms that many times accompany the stammering speech. Often the pupil has developed a habit of turning his head as he struggles on a word, or he may stamp his foot, snap his fingers, twist his mouth, squint his eyes, shut off his breath, slap his thigh, or the like. These subsidiary habits usually develop as a student, by trial and error, has happened upon a mannerism which he fallaciously thinks releases his blocking on words. Once he strikes upon a mannerism and feels it helps him, the habit attaches itself to the stutter and becomes a part of the handicap complex. The set of grimaces is often the most disturbing part of the disorder to the people who see and hear the pupil perform.

In his program of learning to stutter more simply, the student should be encouraged to drop these mannerisms, working on them one by one. In this way he may still stutter, but he does so in a simple, unencumbered way which improves communication and makes a better impression on his listeners. Here is the typical sequence of steps for the teacher to follow in eliminating such odd movements.

(a) Select one specific mannerism to work on, and show the pupil how to watch himself in the mirror to analyze the movements that compose the mannerism.

(b) Have the pupil fake the mannerism or act it out as he talks to the mirror. Even on words which he would not stutter automatically, he should consciously act out the mannerism as if it were a game. In this way he gets conscious control over the way it is performed and can more readily eliminate it.

(c) After much mirror practice, have him fake the stutter and mannerism when talking to parents or close friends.

(*d*) Eventually, have him try in real-life situations to do his stuttering without the accompanying mannerism which he has been working on.

After the student has succeeded in eliminating one movement, he can start work on another specific one which accompanies his stutter. Throughout this process he should *not* have been told to eliminate the stuttering. The stutter he should accept. It is only the accompanying mannerisms he is trying to eliminate.

Stuttering is typically a tense, hurried action. The second part of learning to stutter more simply involves slowing down the stutter pattern. It is important here to recognize that the student is not being told to talk more slowly. Only the stuttering portion should be slowed. "Since you stutter, do it easily and in a relaxed, calm manner. As you slow down your stutter, you'll find it won't be so noticeable. It won't bother you so much."

The two main things the student is encouraged to do are to be slower in initiating the stuttering act and more leisurely in carrying it through. The principal method of teaching this can involve four steps:

(*e*) The teacher demonstrates the difference between hurried and slow stuttering. He shows the difference between starting the stutter quickly and pausing before the stutter is begun. He also shows that once the stutter has begun, it need not be so tense or rapid but can be carried through at a slower pace.

(*f*) The student tries out the teacher's suggestions by first faking his stutter at the usual pace, then trying to say the same phrase with a more leisurely stutter. During this try-out period the teacher should compliment the pupil's successes, should not rebuke any failures, and should clarify any misunderstandings the student has acquired during the earlier explanations.

(*g*) The student adopts a routine of practice before a mirror for five-minute sessions two or three times a day. During this practice he should fake his typical stutter, then try to say the same thing again while stuttering more slowly.

(*h*) When the student has made progress with the leisurely stutter during his own private sessions, he should begin using the slower pace whenever possible with parents and agemates.

Breaking the long-established pattern of rapid stuttering is not an easy task. It takes months, and progress is not steady. Thus patience and encouragement are needed over a long period.

It is appropriate at this point to emphasize that the foregoing suggestions about helping a pupil admit and accept his speech defect are designed for the child who has already recognized that his speech is different from that of others. This recognition has usually been achieved by school-age pupils, at least those above the primary grades. Before he enters your classroom, generally the real stammering child has learned to regard himself as a deviant, a speech-handicap case. But there are other children for whom the foregoing suggestions are *not* appropriate. These are the kindergarten or first-grade pupils whose speech may contain some pauses and repetitions. Parents or friends may have regarded these pauses as stuttering, but the teacher recognizes them as somewhat common at the younger age levels. Though these children lack fluency, they do not feel embarrassed about their speech. They do not exhibit the tenseness and strain about their repetitions that are seen in the real stutterer. So it would be very undesirable for the teacher to bring the hesitations to such a child's attention and risk setting him on a road of self-consciousness that could lead to true stuttering. Instead, the teacher should treat him like a normal speaker. The problem of his speech should not be discussed with him or in front of him. If parents express any concern over his lack of fluency, the teacher should talk with them privately and advise them to treat him like a normal speaker. They should not hurry his expression but should listen with interest to what he tries to say. In this way the child may avoid the traits of a real stutterer.

3. *Provide many speaking opportunities for the student.* As many a stammerer has learned, one way to keep from exposing his defect is to avoid talking. This, of course, is a temporary but specious solution. Especially if he is trying to eliminate grimaces or slow down his stuttering pace, he needs as much practice as possible to establish the new speech habits. Therefore it becomes the teacher's task to furnish speaking situations in which the student can gain practice and confidence in his ability to communicate despite the handicap. Here are a few experiences which have been found useful.

(*a*) Choral reading and singing. (Stutterers often carry out these activities without stumbling on any words.)

(b) Speech games or action games using nonsense or nursery rhymes recited in time to rhythmic movements of the body.

(c) Spontaneous puppet or marionette shows which give the student a chance to speak but afford him some psychological distance from his own personality.

(d) Group projects involving informal discussion or conversation among students rather than formal class presentations which would be more of a threat to the speaker.

(e) Frequent individual oral reading sessions, if the student can read with some degree of skill.

(f) Opportunities to serve as messenger to the office or to other teachers.

(g) Opportunities to volunteer for class discussion or for presenting reports to the class.

When such speech activities are recommended, teachers often ask, "Should the stuttering child be required to take part in them or should he participate only voluntarily?"

It is recalled that anxiety is a major factor in causing stuttering. Thus forcing the frightened student to speak or read aloud only serves to increase his disturbance. He should be given the same chances as his classmates to take part, but he should never be required to do so. The very shy child may be unable to speak at all before the whole class. The teacher needs to start working with him in private conversations where the threat is not so great.

Although the reluctant stutterer should be excused from oral recitations if he desires, he should not be relieved of the volume of schoolwork that the oral presentations represent. That is, if most students have been assigned oral reports, the stutterer who chooses not to talk should be assigned a written report of equal value. In this way he learns that he is regarded by his teacher as an equal of his classmates, capable of doing work of like quality and amount. And perhaps more important, stuttering does not become cherished by the student as a mechanism for escaping work.

In summary, we may conclude that stuttering is a speech defect which usually, if not always, has at its core a fear of not being able to speak fluently. Situations which cause the pupil to doubt his ability and to feel unduly anxious will tend to increase the stutter. When he accepts himself and feels that others accept him despite his stutter, his malady tends to diminish. He can profit from eliminating disturbing mannerisms that have attached themselves to his stutter, and he can learn to stammer in a simpler, more relaxed fashion.

Although the classroom teacher probably will not cure the pupil's disorder, he can go far toward reducing it and helping the pupil communicate despite the handicap.

Voice Disorders

A person is considered to have a good speaking voice if it (1) is loud enough to be heard distinctly but not so loud that it upsets the listeners, (2) has a reasonably pleasant quality—not unduly breathy, hoarse, rasping, nasal, strident, tremulous, or flat, (3) is appropriate in pitch to the age and sex of the speaker, and (4) is expressive, that is, it varies in pitch and loudness in a way that supports the meaning of what is being said.

When a person's voice deviates from these four characteristics to a marked degree, he is said to have a voice disorder. Only 1 or 2 per cent of school children have voice deviations serious enough to warrant attention.

What causes these problems? The fault may be either organic or functional in nature. An organic cause might be the malformation of the mouth, enlarged adenoids which disturb the passage of air between mouth and nasal cavities, or nodules on the vocal cords. It might be defective hearing which leads the pupil to talk too loudly. Therefore when a teacher notices an obvious deviation in voice quality, pitch, or volume in a student, he should ask that a physician make an examination.

However, the majority of children's voice problems are the result of functional rather than organic causes. In some instances a child develops a nasal or growling voice from imitating the voice quality of a parent or sibling. In other cases a pupil's voice is strident and shrill because his father constantly expects him to be superior in all aspects of life or because his mother alternately rejects and overprotects him; these emotional pressures cause tension that displays itself in various symptoms, including the shrill voice. Psychological problems may also cause a child to lack self-confidence and become shy. This shyness may display itself through a weak or flat voice.

The best aid the classroom teacher can give the pupil who has voice problems is to refer him to a speech therapist. However, as noted earlier, therapists are not always available, so if the child is to receive any help at all it must come from the classroom teacher. The following are measures that the regular teacher may try, should he find the time.

1. *Convince the student that the defect exists.* Often the student does not recognize that his voice sounds different from those of his classmates. He will not attempt to correct it unless he becomes convinced it is faulty and should be changed.

The best way to give him a sample of his own speech as others hear it is to tape-record his voice in oral reading, discussion, or conversation. As the teacher and student listen to the tape together, the teacher can point out the ways in which the student's voice differs from the others on the same tape.

2. *Provide ear training.* After the student is convinced his disorder exists, he needs to learn to distinguish between faulty qualities and good voice production. Again the tape recorder will serve to compare his own voice with others. The teacher can further aid him by imitating the voice disorder and then speaking without the fault. This same demonstration sometimes helps the student understand what he is doing with his vocal mechanisms to cause the disorder.

3. *Provide corrective experiences.* Even though one characteristic of voice, such as pitch or nasality, may seem to be the most prominent aspect of the pupil's defect, it is usually desirable for the teacher to work on more than just this one characteristic. He should strive for over-all voice improvement. Thus, if the student cannot completely alter the one most obvious fault, he can still achieve a generally more satisfactory voice by improving other vocal characteristics as well.

It is beyond the scope of our discussion to detail the procedures that can be used for correcting a variety of specific voice deficiencies. For such procedures, the reader is referred to the following readings at the end of the chapter: Fairbanks, 1944; Johnson, 1948; Van Riper, 1958. We shall limit our present discussion to illustrating one of the approaches to aiding pupils who suffer from a common voice problem (improper pitch) and to describing some general procedures that often aid students in over-all improvement of voice quality.

When a pupil's speaking pitch sounds too low or too high for his age and sex, he would probably profit from adopting a more normal pitch. This change is usually desirable for both social and physiological reasons. Socially he will be more acceptable and will suffer less teasing if his voice sounds more like his agemates'. Physiologically his vocal organs will usually be under less strain if he is not continually speaking at too high or too low a level. To help such a student, the teacher can begin by having him sing up and down the scale to determine how well he can reach a more appropriate speaking pitch without straining. When it has been established that he can reach a desirable pitch without strain, he can be asked to sing the tones of the pitch the teacher considers appropriate for him. Then he can sing vowel sounds (*oh, ah, ee, oo*) at this pitch. In further practice sessions he can sing words, phrases, and sentences at the same level, thus committing the new pitch to memory. He can also be asked to read a sentence at the new pitch, then repeat it at the old pitch so he recognizes more surely the difference between the habit he is trying to drop and the one he is learning to adopt. This contrasting of old and new also convinces him that he has the new level within his conscious control. Following a quantity of these types of experiences, the pupil can be encouraged to try the new pitch in certain daily speech situations, such as while talking with the teacher or with his parents. Gradually he increases the number of these situations until all his speaking is done at the new level.

There are numerous ways to help pupils improve general voice quality. For example, a harsh or shrill or excessively loud voice frequently results from an over-all psychological and muscular tension. Thus students can practice relaxing—letting their muscles loosen—and can carry on a discussion or conversation in this consciously relaxed state to note how this affects voice quality.

Most students can profit from ear training. As suggested earlier, they should listen to their own recorded voices. They also can benefit from the negative learning that results from consciously faking the wrong voice quality, pitch, or volume. For instance, an elementary-school teacher may suggest they imitate various voices as they speak into the tape recorder: "Pretend you are an angry witch, then a boy with a bad cold, then a gruff pirate, then a television star who has a most pleasant voice." After trying these roles, they can discuss how they produced each voice.

Periodic reminders to "try during the lunch hour to use the most pleasant, relaxed voice you can" may also aid in drawing attention to voice improvement.

Thus, an awareness of how they sound, and chances to hear themselves when they are speaking in a more appropriate voice, can improve the quality of voice among those students with vocal disorders who have no speech specialist to aid them.

Defective Speech Accompanying Other Handicaps

Speech disorders are often concomitants of such handicaps as cleft lip, cleft palate, cerebral palsy, and impaired hearing. We shall describe each of these briefly so teachers who have students with these handicaps will know what speech problems to expect and what to do about them.

Cleft palate refers to an opening in the roof of the mouth caused by failure of the anteroposterior fissures in the upper mouth to close during the embryonic period. Such improper development may also result in cleft lip, that is, harelip. Either of these disorders makes normal speech extremely difficult or impossible. With cleft palate the plosive sounds of *k*, *g*, *t*, *d*, *p*, and *b* are the most distorted. The student must substitute some other sound when he tries to form these, such as *m* for *b*, *n* for *t*, and *ng* for *k*. Cleft lip typically renders *p* and *b* most difficult to produce. Since *m*, *n*, and *w* are also dependent on proper lip closure, these sounds are likewise somewhat defective when uttered by the pupil with a cleft lip.

The regular classroom teacher cannot be expected to furnish speech therapy for such pupils. The best he can do is to recommend that they have professional medical and speech therapy if they have not already received it. The teacher can, however, aid them in adjusting to school. The suggestions made in Chapter 13 for helping the handicapped student accept himself and be understood by agemates are applicable here. For the classroom instructor, cleft-palate and cleft-lip pupils are candidates more for mental hygiene than for speech therapy.

Cerebral palsy, which is discussed in more detail in Chapter 17, is a term used to describe brain damage which deranges the child's control of his muscles. The symptoms of cerebral palsy may be quite varied, depending on which part of the brain has been damaged. Symptoms can range from only a slight defect in muscle coordination to major bodily rigidity or uncontrollable weaving of legs and arms. Likewise, the muscles governing speech may be affected in varied degrees. One pupil will have no noticeable speech problem, another shows a slurring of certain consonants, and still another may not be able to talk at all. Of the children who suffer from cerebral palsy, perhaps 70 to 80 per cent experience speech problems. (Mecham, 1960:62–63.) Cerebral-palsied children who display the most serious speech disorders will not be found in the regular school but will be treated in clinics and special schools. However, the regular classroom teacher will occasionally have a cerebral-palsied student whose speech is defective to a lesser degree. The teacher is not expected to furnish the basic speech therapy, but he can adopt several measures that will help such students face their speaking responsibilities more adequately.

The pupil's first need is for acceptance from his teacher and classmates. His distorted bodily movements and facial grimacing do not make him naturally attractive to others. Their first tendency is to avoid him or perhaps to mock him. So it often requires extra effort on the teacher's part to accord him the friendship he deserves. One important aspect of making him feel welcome is to accept his way of speaking and allow him to be heard without being rushed or embarrassed. The cerebral-palsied student's speech will often be unclear because he slurs or hesitates or blocks. It is not that he fails to know what to say. He has already thought out his ideas clearly, but he cannot get his muscles to do his bidding. If the listener feels somewhat frustrated by the sound of this halting speech, think of what the speaker himself must experience as he tries so hard to be expressive. He is simply the victim of a body that refuses to do his will. The harder he tries, the worse he becomes. Tension and strong emotion simply increase the lack of control. Hence it behooves classmates and teacher to listen attentively to the palsied pupil and not show impatience with his attempts to talk. If students understand the nature of his condition and know that calm waiting will aid him express his ideas, they usually will cooperate and give him his chance. Patience and understanding are keys to helping the cerebral-palsied speak more adequately.

As already intimated, the more relaxed the palsied pupil feels, the better he can control his muscles. Experiences which encourage relaxation will thus help his speech. In addition to a relaxed classroom atmosphere, there are several direct approaches to relaxation that the teacher may try, not only with the palsied but with other students as well. One is to describe the feeling of loosening and relaxing various groups of muscles, perhaps progressing gradually from those in the fingers to those in the arms, shoulders, chest, throat, face, and so forth. As each group is described slowly, the pupils concentrate on slackening it. Sometimes a general suggestion to become as limp all over as a rag doll or a damp kerchief will effect a loosening of muscle tension. Quiet music, the teacher's oral reading of pleasant stories or verse, and the laughter occasioned by light humor are also relaxing.

Many palsied children have been overprotected by parents. In some cases the child's need to speak is curtailed because parents have habitually foreseen his requirements and fulfilled them without his having to express himself. Further discouragement from speaking is also caused by the frustrations he experiences when he has tried to talk and found it very difficult. Therefore the cerebral-palsied child in school may need extra stimuli to talk more often. The teacher can increase his need for oral communication by giving him responsibilities that require speech, such as asking him to serve on committees and do simple errands. The pupil can be encouraged to try hobbies at which he may succeed, both to give him chances to describe his experiences and to receive recognition from others.

In brief, the cerebral-palsied student usually needs friendship, patience, a lack of pressure when speaking, encouragement to relax, and opportunities to talk with people who understand that he must speak at his own awkward pace without feeling the listener is uninterested or irritated.

Impaired hearing can cause defective speech when the student does not hear either himself or others accurately. The type of speech defect which the child suffers will depend on the nature of his particular hearing problem. A disorder of the inner ear may cause him to speak loudly, to have a monotonous pitch, and perhaps to muffle such sounds as *t, d,* and *n.* Middle-ear troubles may cause him to speak very softly because he hears his own voice much louder than the voices of others. When such symptoms of speech problems are noticed by the teacher, he should first inquire about whether the child's hearing has been tested recently. If not, a test should be requested. When the hearing is indeed faulty, professional therapy may be needed. The classroom teacher himself can be of some aid in correcting faulty articulation by showing the pupil how the tongue or lips are placed to say sounds which the student is not saying correctly. Students who consistently speak too loudly or too softly can be asked to have individual sessions with the instructor. During these sessions, the teacher can have the pupil try different degrees of loudness of speech, thus aiding him in judging more accurately the volumes which are most appropriate for the classroom, the playground, and conversation. Further techniques for helping the hard-of-hearing student are found in Chapter 15.

To summarize our discussion of speech defects found in regular classrooms, we can conclude that the largest number of disorders involve faulty articulation. A smaller percentage of students will stutter or have voice defects. A few will suffer speech problems as a result of cleft lip, cleft palate, cerebral palsy, or faulty hearing. The greatest number of these students have no opportunities for aid from professional speech therapists. Thus, if they are to receive help it must come from their regular classroom teachers.

VARIATIONS OF USAGE

Teachers traditionally have instructed pupils in the *right* sentence patterns, the *correct* vocabulary, and the *proper* grammar to use, naïvely pretending all the while that there was one right or correct or proper form of speech. But in more recent years linguists have directed our attention to a truth about language: there is not one immutable, correct pattern of usage. Rather, the correctness of usage (sentence patterns, pronunciation, enunciation, grammar, vocabulary) depends on the situation, the people involved, and the impression the speaker wishes to make on his listeners.

For example, here are three different ways of expressing the same idea:

"It appears quite obvious that the situation differs markedly from your earlier evaluation of it."

"Oh, no, it's not that way at all."

"Hell, man, tain't dat."

In a certain place and among certain people, each of these furnishes appropriate communication.

Furthermore, it is clear not only that usage differs from one person to another or from one socioeconomic level to another but that each of us adopts somewhat different patterns of speech for different occasions. A secondary-school teacher early one Sunday morning says to his eighteen-month-old daughter, "Does Sandy want Daddy to fix ol' Teddy Bear's lil' ear?" Later at church he ends a prayer with, "Wilt Thou administer to our needs and accept our grateful thanks for Thy goodness and for our salvation." After church he compliments an elderly lady with: "Mrs. Cruickshank, you look spry as a canary with that perky yellow bonnet." On the golf course that afternoon, when he drives a third ball into the pond, he shouts, "Damn, damn, gawd-damn hook." In the evening, on the telephone, he strings together sentence fragments as he talks to the high school's transportation director: "Uh, forty, maybe forty. I don' see how we could, well, we can't get more'n that on a bus, or forty-three at most, forty-three, and that's with some standin', or maybe forty-four, but I don' think so. Forty's it."

To help students handle these varieties of usage most effectively, the teacher appears to have three responsibilities: (1) to teach the patterns of language that are generally acceptable in the business, social, and academic worlds in which the students will probably wish to move, (2) to explain levels of usage to students, and (3) to recommend that pupils tolerate usage differences displayed by other ethnic, regional, and social-class groups.

What Usage to Teach

If many levels of language are found in the speech of Americans, which of these should the school teach?

The usage typically recommended can be termed "educated general American." This is the speech that students hear in conversations between people of considerable schooling, especially in the portion of America outside of New England and north of the Confederacy. It is the usage appropriate to the business world. It is heard on radio and television programs, except, of course, on dramatic shows that feature cowboys, river-boat captains, juvenile delinquents, and rural folk. In such speech the verbs agree with the subjects, the speaker's pronunciation approximates that found in the dictionary, and swear words and vulgarisms are avoided; but terms like "It's me" rather than the stricter "It is I" are permitted.

To decide what constitutes this recommended usage, teachers usually depend on two sources. One is their own speech pattern (or at least what they have been taught is "right"), and the other is books on English-language usage—usually textbooks. In general these sources serve as appropriate guides to acceptable educated American speech. But if the teacher is not native to the community in which he teaches, it is wise for him to utilize a third source as well: the speech patterns common to the moderately well educated people of the district. In the vicinity of Boston, it would be realistic to accept such pronunciations as *idear* for *idea* and *caw* for *car*. In Georgia it would be appropriate to admit *yo-all* as a proper way to address two or more listeners. In Texas it's *y'all*.

Explaining Matters of Usage

Most teachers apparently still follow the tradition of telling students, or at least implying, that there is one correct pattern of usage and that deviations from it are wrong. Therefore, as the teacher instructs pupils in educated general American speech, he should also explain what other kinds of usage exist and under what conditions each is admissible.

He should illustrate the truth that language not only communicates facts and opinions. The style of the words and the sentence patterns and pronunciation in which the facts are couched also tell something about the speaker. In a sense, the speaker's usage brands him. His style of speech helps identify his educational level or socioeconomic class. It may indicate whether he considers himself a peer of the listeners or superior or inferior to them. It may help to show that he is an insider and in the know, as is true with the teen-ager who uses the latest slang or the football player or lumberjack who speaks the cant peculiar to his trade.

A teacher can carry on such a discussion of usage at almost any grade level. After he has opened the discussion with his own illustrations of the way a person's style of speaking varies from one life situation to another, students can furnish examples from their own experience.

Students usually recognize the nonsense contained in teachers' warnings, "You're just not going to get ahead in this world if you don't use correct grammar and pronunciation" ("correct" meaning what the textbook says). Students, especially those from working-class families, daily see adults getting along quite nicely in the world using speech that the teacher would label substandard. These young people recognize that within their own gangs or cliques outside of class it is often desirable to deviate from classroom language in order to be accepted. Pupils' daily experiences corroborate the stand of another type of teacher, the one who says:

You need to fit your style of talk to the group you're with. You not only need to use words that carry your ideas to them clearly. You also need to use a style of speech which makes listeners accept you the way you wish to be accepted. So if you want to be welcomed by the gang playing stickball in the vacant lot, you talk in a style of which they approve. If you want to impress a teacher with your academic ability, you use more complex words, make verbs and subjects agree, and enunciate clearly. The trick is to know each style and when to use it. The trouble with some students is that they only know one style—the kind acceptable to their companions outside school. They don't realize that *ain't* and *he don't know nothin'* and swear words are not acceptable speech in such situations as selling goods in a store or applying for a job in an office or giving a talk before a class in school. We aren't trying to eliminate the way you already talk. We are trying to help you add more speech skills—to know more than one style of speech. Then it is up to you to recognize in what situations it is best to use this style learned in school and in what situations it is better to use some other style.

An Attitude of Tolerance

As the teacher shows the class that there is no single correct usage in America, he also has an opportunity to suggest a tolerant attitude toward language styles different from those of the local community. Pupils can learn to regard with interest speech patterns which differ from their own without branding these deviations as necessarily undesirable. So those in Iowa can recognize that the southern drawl of the new enrollee at school is normal speech in his native state of Louisiana, and it should not be scorned. They can appreciate that their own parents' speech may differ in some respects from that recommended at school, but within their parents' social and occupational circles their usage is quite normal. And perhaps pupils can learn that certain aspects of their own speech would need to be tolerated by the majority of other Americans because the local usage is somewhat unique (the New Englander's "ay-up" for "yes" or the Indianan's "wait on me" instead of "wait for me" or the Pennsylvania-Dutch reversal of "leave" and "let").

SUMMARY

Most teachers are apparently capable of furnishing discussion and speech opportunities in class and at least a modicum of suggestions about how to improve the common shortcomings students may exhibit in speaking. However, fewer classroom teachers command the specialized techniques for dealing with the more deviant speakers—that 5 to 10 per cent of students who suffer speech disorders that warrant particular attention if they are to be alleviated. Recommendations have been given in this chapter for aiding such pupils within the regular classroom.

In addition, suggestions have been offered for bringing students' attention to focus on the variety of language styles or usage found in a typical community. We believe that students profit from understanding that usage patterns are not completely standardized, but a person's style of speech needs to be adjusted somewhat to the varied situations in which he finds himself.

SUGGESTED LEARNING ACTIVITIES

1. To gain practice in evaluating speech, use the Speech Check List in this chapter for recording your analysis of (a) a pupil giving a report to a class in school, (b) a young child describing a television program he

has seen or an experience he has had during the past week, (c) a teacher or a public lecturer speaking before a group.

2. Interview a speech therapist or school psychologist to learn what he believes are (a) the main errors teachers make in cases of speech-handicapped pupils and (b) the best ways that regular classroom teachers can aid such students.

3. In a speech-therapy book such as those in the suggested readings, locate the description of a case of a speech-handicapped pupil. Write a résumé of the principal symptoms the pupil exhibited, the apparent causes of his difficulty, the types of therapy attempted, and the success of the therapy. Indicate also what principles or information from this case study are of value to a regular classroom teacher who sometime might face a similarly handicapped pupil.

4. To gain experience in recognizing different levels of usage, listen to the speech of people in several different walks of life or in several different situations, such as those shopping in the supermarket, viewing a ball game, playing cards, or visiting at a snack bar. During your observations, jot down vocabulary, sentence patterns, examples of pronunciation and enunciation, and gestures which were used in these situations but which would not typically be appropriate to a classroom situation.

SUGGESTED READINGS

ANDERSON, VIRGIL A. *Improving the Child's Speech.* New York: Oxford University Press, 1953. A book for classroom teachers and parents.

DIEHL, CHARLES F. *A Compendium of Research and Theory on Stuttering.* Springfield, Ill.: Charles C Thomas, 1958. Clear summaries of 193 studies and articles.

FAIRBANKS, GRANT. *Voice and Articulation Drillbook.* New York: Harper and Brothers, 1944. Practice exercises for voice and articulation.

FROESCHELS, EMIL. *Twentieth Century Speech and Voice Correction.* New York: Philosophical Library, 1948. Experts discuss a series of serious speech defects.

JOHNSON, WENDELL; BROWN, SPENCER F.; CURTIS, JAMES F.; EDNEY, CLARENCE W.; and KEASTER, JACQUELINE. *Speech Handicapped School Children.* New York: Harper and Brothers, 1948. The most helpful book for classroom teachers.

MECHAM, MERLIN J.; BERKO, MARTIN J.; and BERKO, FRANCIS GIDEN. *Speech Therapy in Cerebral Palsy.* Springfield, Ill.: Charles C Thomas, 1960.

PRONOVOST, WILBERT. *The Teaching of Speaking and Listening in the Elementary School.* New York: Longmans, Green, 1959.

RASMUSSEN, CARRIE. *Speech Methods in the Elementary School.* New York: The Ronald Press Co., 1962.

VAN RIPER, CHARLES. *Speech Correction: Principles and Methods.* Englewood Cliffs: Prentice-Hall, 1954. Specific procedures for teachers.

———. *Speech Therapy: A Book of Readings.* Englewood Cliffs: Prentice-Hall, 1953.

———, and BUTLER, KATHARINE G. *Speech in the Elementary Classroom.* New York: Harper and Brothers, 1955.

———, and IRWIN, JOHN V. *Voice and Articulation.* Englewood Cliffs: Prentice-Hall, 1958. Methods for diagnosing and treating voice and articulation defects.

WEST, ROBERT; ANSBERRY, MERLE; and CARR, ANNA. *The Rehabilitation of Speech.* New York: Harper and Brothers, 1957. Pathology of speech and corrective measures.

CHAPTER 17

Physical Handicaps and
Other Disorders

Although sight, hearing, and speech difficulties are the most common psychophysical defects met in the regular classroom, teachers must also deal occasionally with some less common ones: orthopedic or crippling handicaps, cerebral palsy, epilepsy, heart conditions, disfigurements, malnutrition, allergies, tuberculosis, and diabetes.

ORTHOPEDIC OR CRIPPLING HANDICAPS

Orthopedic handicaps are defects that cause interference with the normal use of bones, muscles, or joints. Children suffering from such defects are often called "cripples." Although the term "cripple" is sometimes used to include children with heart conditions or cerebral palsy, we shall limit its use here to other more precisely orthopedic problems, such as the case of the child made lame by poliomyelitis, the one born with a twisted back, or the one who is disabled through tuberculosis of the bones of the arm.

The exact percentage of children suffering orthopedic handicaps is not known, partly because different investigators have used different definitions of crippling conditions. Estimates have ranged from one child per thousand to ten per thousand. (Garrison, 1959:309.) These estimates appear to focus on the more serious conditions, so if we include slighter degrees of lameness or deformity the incidence may be higher.

When the child's movement is quite seriously impaired, he is frequently cared for in a special school so that he is not the responsibility of a regular classroom teacher. But the bulk of crippled children will be found in regular classrooms where it becomes the teacher's task to adjust the program to the defects of the child and at the same time to involve him as much as possible in typical activities so as to maximize the pupil's own self-esteem and also his acceptance by age-mates.

In judging how to alter the regular program to suit the cripple, the teacher will receive his best guidance from the medical report on the child furnished by the doctor who has attended the pupil. Often there are restrictions on such pupils' physical activities or special instructions needed for manipulating orthopedic equipment the student uses, like a back brace or crutches. Sometimes periodic exercises should be performed by the pupil. Therefore, when a student of this type enters the class in the fall, the teacher should consult the school's medical record as soon as possible and, if feasible, talk over the handicap condition with the school nurse, the attending physician, and the parents.

Psychological Considerations

As with all easily observable personal defects, crippling conditions are accompanied by the kinds of psychological and social problems discussed in the Introduction to Part IV. Thus it is desirable for the teacher to try to estimate the attitude of the child's parents toward his condition, the child's own opinion of himself, and the extent to which the child adjusts well to his classmates.

This information will be gathered from the pupil's cumulative-record folder, from last year's teacher, from the parents, from personal conferences with the child during the routine of classwork, and from observations of the pupil in class and in recreational activities. On the basis of this information, the teacher forms a picture of the pupil's personality and thus can better answer such questions as the following.

Has he been rejected by others so that he needs extra affection and encouragement in order to accept himself? Or has he been overprotected so that I should expect him to begin doing more things by himself and to take more responsibility?

Does he need to develop some special skill or hobby that might gain admiration from classmates and heighten his self-regard?

Does he seem to have no one who will listen to his personal thoughts and confidences, so that he needs an interested and non-censoring friend or counselor to talk with?

Does he have unrealistic vocational or academic goals, so that he needs special guidance in setting up objectives to which he can realistically aspire?

What kinds of groups can I have him work with in the classroom so that he will have the best chance for developing friendships?

How should I talk with his parents? Should I emphasize the pupil's potentialities that they have failed to recognize? Or point out the pupil's limitations that the parents have not accepted? Suggest extra work he may do at home to aid his school progress? Suggest that the student and the parents read about the lives of other cripples who have faced and conquered similar problems?

Through these types of inquiry the teacher can often hit upon measures that fit the class program better to the needs of the crippled student.

CEREBRAL PALSY

"Cerebral" refers to the brain. "Palsy" or "paralysis" means that the control of movements in some area of the body is defective because part of the nervous system does not function properly. Cerebral palsy, as distinguished from other types of paralysis, such as spinal palsy resulting from poliomyelitis in the spine, means that the disturbance of body movement has been caused by an interference in the centers of the brain which control body movements.

Although cerebral palsy can appear at any time in life, it is most likely to occur before or during birth or within a few weeks after birth. It can be caused by anything that injures the brain areas that control movement. The most common causes include developmental defects occurring before birth; Rh incompatibility of the blood of mother and father; premature birth, resulting in the rupture of underdeveloped blood vessels in the baby's brain; birth difficulties such as prolonged labor or the use of forceps in delivery; illness during the first few weeks after birth; and encephalitis (inflammation of the brain) brought on by such children's diseases as measles and mumps. Injuries to the head from a blow or fall, resulting in brain hemorrhages, can lead to cerebral palsy at any time during life. (Phelps, 1958:3–7.)

Types of Cerebral Palsy

There are five main types of cerebral palsy: spastic, athetoid, rigidity, ataxic, and tremor. These sometimes occur in combination.

The most common variety is the spastic type. The child suffering from this moves in the direction he intends but only slowly, stiffly, and a little at a time. This is because when he attempts to bend a joint the opposing muscles contract and block the movement. His ability to enunciate words may also be affected.

The next most common is the athetoid type. It is the opposite of the spastic. The child is always in motion, even when he does not wish to be. He has difficulty controlling speech, arm, or leg muscles.

Children with the rigidity type move slowly because their muscles are partially contracted all the time. In some cases the child is only intermittently rigid. At other times he moves about at will.

The child with the best chance for complete recovery is the one with the ataxic type. The nerve centers controlling his sense of weight and position in space are defective, so that he lacks a proper sense of balance, and his walking and talking may be delayed.

The least frequent variety is the true tremor type or shaking palsy in which the hands, arms, or neck shake in a rhythmical fashion. "Many such children have attended high school and college and are completely independent, but they have to use a typewriter for practically all their writing. Indeed it is difficult to teach them to do more with their hands than sign their names for legal purposes." (Phelps, 1958:11.)

Other psychophysical defects often accompany the palsied condition. In one study of more than 1,300 cerebral-palsied children, 68 per cent had speech disorders; 25 per cent, defective vision; and 12 per cent, defective hearing.[1] Seizures—that is, fits, spells, convul-

[1] Thomas W. Hopkins, Harry V. Bice, and Kathryn C. Colton, *Evaluation and Education of the Cerebral Palsied Child: New Jersey Study* (Washington, D.C.: International Council for Exceptional Children, 1954).

sions, or spasms—occur in perhaps a quarter to a third of the cases.

Mental retardation is sometimes a further complicating condition. But frequently it is hard to know just what the mental ability of cerebral-palsied children is because they are the most difficult of all handicapped children to test. Their inability to control speech and limb muscles often prevents them from expressing to the psychologist what they are thinking. In discussing the lack of a specific intelligence scale for the cerebral-palsied, Newland has written:

> . . . in the absence of individual devices suitable for use with the cerebral palsied, a "cafeteria" approach generally has been used. Depending upon the condition of the particular child, certain items from one scale are used in connection with other items lifted from other scales on the assumption that all such items, taken together, psychologically rather than additively, would give at least a general idea of the mental level at which the child was functioning, or could function.[2]

It should be obvious that such a pick-and-choose procedure can have value only when used by a very experienced psychometrist, and even then it yields only a rough estimate.

Educating the Cerebral-Palsied

Although the cerebral-palsied can often be aided in adjusting to their handicap, they can seldom hope for a real cure. Educationally their future is not particularly bright.

The hard fact is that many cannot meet the academic goals established for normal children. The majority can succeed in meeting the academic standards of the elementary school at the normal age or later; a much smaller number is able to complete high school on a basis of equality with the regular high-school population; and a very limited number can succeed in college. A few children with normal or superior intelligence are unable to attend school because of severe physical handicaps. This group is provided with educational facilities largely through home instruction, but some are cared for in special private institutions.[3]

---

[2] William M. Cruickshank (ed.), *Psychology of Exceptional Children and Youth* (Englewood Cliffs: Prentice-Hall, 1955), p. 86.

[3] Winthrop M. Phelps, Thomas W. Hopkins, and Robert Cousins, *The Cerebral-Palsied Child: A Guide for Parents* (New York: Simon and Schuster, 1958), pp. 144–145.

Specific methods for teaching the cerebral-palsied pupil cannot be discussed with any completeness here, for the problems are often great and the techniques can be complex in cases where other defects, as of sight and hearing, accompany the palsy. The writings of Cruickshank (1951), Phelps (1958), and Strauss (1948) in the selected readings at the end of this chapter provide specific guides to teaching.

We can, however, present the following points to orient the regular classroom instructor to measures that should be taken if a cerebral-palsied child is enrolled in the class.

1. A complete physical-psychological examination must be made by competent physicians and psychologists to establish the exact nature of the disability and possible accompanying defects, such as mental retardation and speech, vision, or hearing impairment. On the basis of this diagnosis, an estimate should be made concerning the advisability of leaving the child in the regular classroom or transferring him to some other educational facility, such as to a special class in the public school, a special school for the cerebral-palsied, or home teaching. In determining the child's placement, it should be recognized that the following difficulties typically must be faced if the child is kept in the regular classroom:

(a) The regular teacher usually fears for the child's safety. He lacks confidence in his own ability to include the cerebral-palsied child safely in class activities involving movement. He often lacks confidence in the child's ability to take part in speech work and to engage in physical activities. So the child becomes a bystander whose difference is further emphasized by his lack of opportunity to participate.

(b) The regular teacher seldom has training in the special techniques and materials needed by the cerebral-palsied. Teaching the cerebral-palsied can be more time-consuming than teaching any other kind of special case if a sight defect (such as nystagmus) or speech disorder is also present. The typical teacher does not have this time to spend on the individual. So the cerebral-palsied pupil is often left to shift for himself.

Because of these conditions, the regular classroom is very frequently a poor place to educate these children. Special classes in the public school or special schools are more suitable, because they (i) remove pupils from intellectual and physical competition which they cannot match in regular classes, (ii) are smaller and permit more individualized teaching by people who are expert in special education, and (iii) make special equipment and a more realistic curriculum possible.

2. If the cerebral-palsied child is kept in the regular classroom, a report from the medical specialist who has examined him should be available to the teacher, describing the limitations for his activities and the special kinds of aid or equipment he requires.

The aid the cerebral-palsied child needs includes much teacher patience with his very slow writing and speech and a friendly, relaxed classroom atmosphere to minimize the tensions that can aggravate his condition. The cerebral-palsied student who perhaps has a hearing defect becomes much more fatigued than the normal student, because he must be extra alert every moment to follow the lesson. The tension resulting from this constant concentration demands release through some kind of intermittent relaxing activity. So the teacher should pace the child's work and relaxation with this in mind.

Sometimes special equipment is needed. For the child with a sight defect, it may be desirable to obtain one of the modern basal-reading series printed in extra large type. At both elementary and secondary levels, large-type materials are also available in science, other language arts, mathematics, and social studies. After the student has studied with these books and has done much blackboard reading for a prolonged period, he may be able to change to the regular textbooks his classmates use. Other materials may include bright crayons for desk work and colored chalks for blackboard work, for these often aid the brain-injured child to learn more readily.

3. It is important for the teacher to recognize that the cerebral-palsied, like children with other kinds of central nervous system injuries, have problems of perception not experienced by the normal child. For instance:

(a) They have trouble discriminating background from foreground stimuli, such as distinguishing the teacher's voice from other noises or voices in the room or distinguishing certain kinds of figures on a page.

(*b*) They exhibit perseveration, that is, they repeat words or actions in a meaningless manner. When the teacher asks, "Is this the right book?" the child may answer, "Right book . . . right book . . . right book."

(*c*) They often write numbers and letters backward or upside down. Although this tendency is frequently found among normal children who are in the primary grades, it is more marked and persistent among brain-damaged children.

(*d*) They may experience dissociation, which is an inability to bring objects close together; for instance, a child may not be able to move two pencils closer together on the table when asked to do so.

(*e*) They may have defective perception of size, shape, and distance. Therefore they have difficulty learning reading and writing as taught by the usual techniques. (Cruickshank, 1951; Phelps, 1958:175–176.)

When we consider these difficulties faced by the cerebral-palsied pupil, it is not surprising to learn that quite frequently he is retarded in his school progress. Under the best conditions, he makes only slow gains. And when he is in the regular classroom, he is usually not in ideal surroundings for his optimum development. To give him his chance, the classroom teacher should try to dedicate more individual time to him and to enlist the aid of classmates in this task.

EPILEPSY

Epilepsy is a disorder long known to man, principally because in its most conspicuous form it manifests itself in violent seizures or convulsions. Although in past centuries it was often thought to be caused by strange spirits inhabiting the victim's body, it is now recognized as resulting from a disturbance of the normal activity of the brain.

The number of people suffering from epilepsy is not known for certain; but an analysis of World War I and World War II draft figures suggests that out of one thousand people in the general population, six or seven are epileptic. (Hoch, 1947:46.)

Generally the intellectual ability of epileptics is about the same as that of unselected nonepileptics. Unlike cerebral-palsied children, the epileptic ones do not necessarily suffer other disorders that complicate their adjustment to a regular school program, such as speech and vision defects. And since medical treatment today can frequently control the seizures, most epileptic children and youth will be found in the public schools and as such are the responsibility of the regular teacher.

The things most important for the classroom teacher to know are (1) the nature of epilepsy and its symptoms, (2) how to deal with a child who may suffer or is suffering a seizure, and (3) how to deal with parents and with other students in the class, such as ones who witness a seizure and thus recognize that they have an epileptic classmate.

The Nature of Epilepsy

Epilepsy is perhaps best defined as consisting of repeated attacks of loss of consciousness, with or without observable muscular tension or spasms and accompanied by changes in the electrical potentials of the brain.

The disorder shows itself in a variety of degrees of violence. It ranges from the type involving a series of intense convulsions that lasts perhaps half an hour to the type characterized by only a momentary loss of consciousness which is seen by an observer as nothing more than a blinking of the eyes.

There is a great variety of forms the seizures may take. But the majority of cases may be placed in one of the following five groups:

Type 1: Petit mal. This is the mildest form. Three variations of petit mal have been distinguished:

(*a*) Petit mal or pycnoepilepsy involves no convulsion. Rather it is characterized by a loss of consciousness for a few moments.

The child stands still or may even continue walking during the episode. Motor activity is minimal but may be present as flickering movements of the eyelids and face or mild rhythmical jerkings of the hands and arms. The seizure begins and ends abruptly, and after it is over the trend of conversation is resumed by the child as if nothing had happened. . . . It is more frequently found in children than in adults. Attacks range in frequency from one to 200 a day. (Broida *in* Cruickshank, 1955:350.)

(*b*) Akinetic epilepsy involves a sudden collapse of muscles. If only upper body muscles are involved, a nodding of the head results. If the collapse is a general one of all muscles, the child falls. Such attacks may be frequent.

(c) Myoclonic jerks are single jerks of arm or body muscles, apparently without loss of consciousness.

Type 2: Grand mal. This is the most violent form, involving the most generalized convulsions. It may take various forms in different persons and may vary somewhat from time to time in the life of a single person. But in general it is as Strecker has described it.

He goes down as though sandbagged, wherever he happens to be, and may seriously injure himself in fall. There may be the epileptic cry. He convulses first with stiffening (tonus) and then writhing and twisting (clonus) of the limbs. He may froth at the mouth and if he bites his tongue, as often happens, the froth is bloody. The patient is blue in the face, the breathing is labored, the eyes are apt to roll upward and their pupils do not react to light. Often control of bladder and bowels is lost.[4]

Type 3: Jacksonian. This appears to be a modified grand mal. It begins with numbness or tingling or twitching of one arm or leg or of one side of the trunk and spreads (in what is called the "march") to include more of the body. The person usually retains consciousness unless it spreads to the other side of the body and turns into a grand mal. In Jacksonian epilepsy, the patient sees and feels the beginning jerks and numbness spread from the extremity but is unable to stop it.

Type 4: Convulsive seizure with localizing symptoms. This type involves seizures or sensations in a localized part of the body without the spread or march. The most common seizure is a turning of the hand and eyes to one side. The attack may start with a jerking of the face muscles or of the affected arm or leg. The patient may experience strange sensations of vision, taste, or smell.

Type 5: Psychomotor. The main characteristic of this variety is a period of amnesia, that is, loss of memory of what is occurring, although the patient may appear to be conscious. Contortions of the trunk muscles may or may not occur. During the attack he may act automatically but appear confused or stupid. He may sit still, may make chewing motions, or may become violent if physical restraint is attempted. Since psychomotor attacks vary so much from one per-

---

[4] E. A. Strecker, *Basic Psychiatry* (New York: Random House, 1952), p. 103.

son to another, it is the most difficult type to diagnose and is sometimes mistaken for hysteria.

The causes of epilepsy are varied, complex, and not completely understood. But there is considerable evidence to show that heredity plays a part. Disturbances in the chemistry of the body through glandular disorders and toxic conditions (like kidney disease) are frequently involved as causes. In some cases, brain injury before or during birth or damage resulting from infection after diseases like sleeping sickness or meningitis brings on epilepsy. A severe head injury or tumor may also be a cause.

Dealing with an Epileptic Pupil

Epilepsy usually begins during childhood or adolescence. It is possible that a child's or youth's first seizure may occur in or near school. Therefore it is important that teachers understand something of its nature so they can care for the child calmly and efficiently and allay the fears and shock of those who may witness it.

People who are accustomed to handling epileptic seizures do not become excited by the convulsions but let them run their course. Most attacks will terminate themselves harmlessly regardless of what you do or do not do. What is important is that you remain calm and that, if the seizure is of the grand mal variety, the patient be prevented from biting his tongue as the jaws convulse. This may be done by placing on the tongue a protective pad made from a folded cloth or handkerchief or a piece of wood as a wedge between the teeth. This will also prevent him from sucking in vomited matter as he breathes hard in his labored, hissing fashion.

About one-half of epileptic patients experience an aura or warning before the convulsion occurs. Apparently an aura is more common among adults than among children. It may take a variety of forms, such as tingling or burning sensations, visual or auditory sensations. This premonition is usually experienced only a moment before the person loses consciousness. But this is often enough to enable the patient or those nearby to prepare for the seizure. Therefore the teacher or classmates may prevent the child from falling in a dangerous spot, such as against the sharp corner of a table or on the stairs.

Usually, however, the attack is not of the grand mal type and little is required of the teacher other than calm understanding of what is occurring.

When the child recovers, it is usually well for the teacher not to display undue concern or appear too sympathetic, for this may embarrass the pupil. A kind but businesslike attitude and a resumption of regular activities without further ado is usually most successful. If the pupil appears to be all right after an attack of a mild variety, he can continue with his schoolwork. If the condition appears more serious, arrangements should be made for him to be taken home.

It is fairly clear that psychological events may precipitate the seizures in many epileptics. Studies have shown that strong emotions of fear and frustration, hostile impulses arising from disturbed interpersonal relationships, and sexual stimulation without adequate discharge are among the psychological conditions that may initiate an attack. (Garrison, 1959:399.)

The kind of psychological state or event that may precipitate seizures varies from one patient to another. Therefore it is desirable for the teacher to inquire of parents or an attending physician concerning what emotional situations may be crucial for a given epileptic child who may be enrolled in his class. Or the teacher can try to see what conditions seem to precede or accompany the attacks that may occur in school. In this way some control may be exercised over the psychological pressures the pupil faces.

The proper therapy for epileptic children involves three kinds of treatment: medical, psychological, and social. Attacks can often be controlled medically through administering drugs, through improving diet and general health, and, in certain cases, through neurosurgery. But the success of such medical measures will usually be affected strongly by the nature of—or the lack of—psychological therapy to accompany them.

Broida (Cruickshank, 1955:378) has written:

Some form of psychologic treatment, whether it be intensive or supportive psychotherapy, guidance, or counseling, is indicated for all children suffering from epilepsy. The form or intensity of such treatment will vary from one individual to another consistent with the varying degrees of personality disturbances epileptic children exhibit. Of utmost importance is recognition that failure to institute psychological treatment, other therapeutic endeavors notwithstanding, often results in the perpetuation or exacerbation of the handicap.

Bridge (1949:420) has emphasized that "In a proportion of children, particularly at the age of adolescence or beyond, the emotional disturbance may be the dominant causative factor, and in psychotherapy lies the best possibility of cure."

The regular classroom teacher cannot expect to be a therapist, but he can take certain steps that will contribute to improved mental hygiene for the epileptic. First, he can try to understand the problems faced by the epileptic and be a friendly listener to problems the child may wish to discuss. Second, if no psychological therapy is being provided at present for the child, the teacher can stress the desirability of this to school authorities and, perhaps, in talks with the parents so that efforts are made to secure this aid along with medical help. Third, the teacher can try to minimize the stressful psychological situations the child must face in school. Fourth, if the child is receiving psychological therapy, the teacher can ask the therapists what part he can play in aiding the child.

The Epileptic's Social Environment

From the teacher's standpoint, the most important people in the epileptic pupil's social environment are parents and schoolmates.

Epilepsy is different from other handicaps in that the person is apparently very normal in intelligence and behavior until the unexpected moment when a seizure occurs and he quite loses control of himself. In addition, there is a long tradition of believing that epileptics are people possessed of strange—probably evil—spirits. Hence awe, shame, and disgrace are often associated with the handicap. These are hard things for parents to accept. So it is usually important for parents of epileptics to have opportunities to talk through with a counselor their relationships to their child and their attitudes toward his disorder. When it is apparent to the teacher that parents' attitudes are not realistic or desirable, he may wish to suggest they consult with the school's guidance counselors, the county child-guidance clinicians, or a physician who specializes in this area. In this way they can better visualize the child's present and future.

Sometimes, however, professional aid is not available for the parents, and this task of counseling falls to the teacher. In his role as counselor, the teacher should recognize that it is not enough simply to tell the parents not to worry about the problem, that it will work out all right. Rather, the parents need a sympathetic listener who recognizes their problems but who can, at the same time, realistically discuss the outlook for the child in light of the facts in his individual case. Bridge's (1949:495) helpful inspection of this counseling relationship, though aimed primarily at physicians, can be studied with profit by a teacher who has an epileptic's parents to deal with.

Apparently the normal pupil in the class can more easily understand the problems and personality needs of a lame child or one with poor vision than he can an epileptic's. This is because the epileptic's disorder remains hidden most of the time behind a normal façade. It is therefore especially important that the teacher use such approaches as suggested in Chapter 13 in aiding classmates to understand the feelings and needs of a person suffering from this handicap.

Today it is clear that as medical and psychological therapy improve and as the people in the epileptic patient's environment come to take a more accepting attitude toward his defect, the chances for the epileptic's living a good life are increasing. Most can get along quite well in the regular school program with proper medical treatment and with understanding teachers and classmates. A New York City study reported that only a very small percentage of children experienced seizures so severe that they disrupted the class unduly.[5] Home study was recommended for the serious cases which needed to be excluded from the regular school program.

Thus, for most epileptics the outlook is increasingly good.

HEART CONDITIONS

In general, heart disease in children is the result of either congenital defects of the heart or damage done by rheumatic fever. The frequency of heart disease among children is not accurately known. Estimates range from less than 1 per cent to 6 per cent or more.

[5] Board of Education, *Epileptic Children* (New York: Board of Education, New York City, 1941), p. 59.

(Garrison, 1959:417.) The frequency is apparently greater in cold, wet, higher-altitude areas, which have a larger incidence of rheumatic fever than warmer, drier regions. Rheumatic fever is also more common among children living in poorer, crowded conditions than among those of the well-to-do sections of a community.

The cause of rheumatic fever is not really understood, but it is known that a streptococcal infection is very frequently present at the onset of the disease. The original rheumatic infection usually begins between ages four and fifteen, with the height of onset between seven and eight years. During recovery from the infection, the heart is often damaged. The child who has suffered one attack is susceptible to subsequent attacks, and if the heart is not damaged the first time it may be later. Each new attack can bring increased damage. A specific, generally effective cure for rheumatic fever has not yet been established. The most common treatment is bed rest, often for extended periods of time, so that the child may miss a great deal of school as a result of this illness.

The Heart-Disease Pupil at School

The typical heart-disease pupil may be expected to have a somewhat different psychological view of himself and his world from that of other children suffering from crippling conditions. The heart-disease child's attitudes toward family and self tend to be more similar to the attitudes of normal children than to the attitudes of other handicapped children. Investigators have suggested that this difference is due to the hidden nature of the cardiac patient's handicap.

From an external point of view nothing in the visible picture serves to set this child apart from others. Insofar as society is concerned, the child is seen as normal in every sense of the word. Society accepts him as a normal member. The child does not have to feel different due to any barrier which his culture establishes. Thus he operates as a normal individual. It is only when the defect becomes a visible one that the handicap per se begins to have a serious impact on the adjustment process. (Cruickshank, 1955:317.)

Although in the self-adjustment sense the hidden nature of the disability is an advantage, at the same time it poses some problems for teachers and parents. Children with serious heart conditions must have restrictions placed on their physical exertions. At school, this task of policing falls to the teacher. Because the student looks and feels no different from normal pupils, he can be expected to resent teacher-imposed or parent-imposed limitations that curtail his chances of enjoying the active companionship of his agemates. Teachers therefore can look for fewer problems of low self-esteem among cardiac pupils but can expect some show of resentment at the limits imposed on their activity.

The teacher should seek a specific description from the child's health record or attending physician concerning the amount of physical exercise the pupil should be allowed. Too often parents and teachers are unduly cautious, so that the child with congenital heart disease may suffer from too much restriction rather than too much freedom. The teacher should always, however, be alert to signs of marked overfatigue or illness and should report these to the school nurse or the home so a proper physical checkup can be made.

DISFIGUREMENTS

Some students have healthy, efficient bodies and brains but they suffer the social-psychological handicap of a physical disfigurement. By "disfigurement" we mean anything about the person's appearance that is sufficiently different from the ideals or norms of his society to make him an object of dislike, distaste, or ridicule. This definition would, therefore, include such a variety of things as a large birthmark on the face, advanced acne, a harelip that does not affect speech but distorts appearance, extreme shortness of stature or (in the case of girls) tallness, unusual body proportions, or facial features considered by most people to be very unattractive.

For the teacher, these cases entail no physical danger or special teaching methods. Rather, they involve the pupil's adjustment to himself and to other people. One difficulty is in telling who is "suffering" from an apparent disfigurement and who is not. The importance of a blemish to the child himself is often quite different from that attached to it by people he meets daily. The adolescent who has newly acquired the acne common to his stage of growth may spend agonized hours with his nose close to the mirror, seeing his minor skin eruptions as major disfigurements that will repel all those (especially of the other sex) whom he would like as friends. So he is miserable all out of proportion to what his teachers might guess.

By use of the techniques of observation and sociometrics suggested in Chapter 13, the teacher can make an estimate of which pupils with disfigurements need aid in personal-social adjustment and which do not. Even when the teacher decides that a pupil could use help, it is often very difficult to know what, if anything, can be done. The approaches suggested in Chapter 13 are possibilities the teacher can consider trying.

MALNUTRITION

In a nation where the principal farm problem is enormous food surpluses, there are still many children and youth experiencing some degree of malnutrition. Sometimes this involves the intake of an insufficient quantity of food. The person goes hungry. This is a major problem today in underdeveloped nations. But a person who eats a sufficient bulk of food is still considered malnourished if his diet lacks a balance of the different types of nutrient necessary for optimum health. This variety of malnutrition is the more common in a country of plenty like the United States.

The fact that there are malnourished school children in districts which have the ability to support an adequate standard of living has been demonstrated by numerous diet studies. One such study was conducted by Eppright and Roderuck in Iowa. From one week of dietary records of 1,188 school children at elementary and secondary levels, the investigators estimated what proportion of children were receiving food-energy value and nutrients which were less than two-thirds of the amount recommended by the National Research Council as being sufficient. Generally the girls' diets, especially during adolescence, were poorer than the boys'. An example of the percentages of children with diets below two-thirds the recommended amount for four of the nutrient areas studied is given in Table 17–1.

There are several reasons why malnutrition exists in children whose families could provide adequate diets. Perhaps the most important is the lack of understanding or real concern on the part of mothers about what constitutes a balanced diet. Another is that children sometimes choose to eat only what tastes sweetest to them and neglect other more healthful foods. In other cases, children have strong aversions to certain foods or are allergic to them.

TABLE 17–1

PERCENTAGE OF CHILDREN WITH BELOW–STANDARD INTAKE OF FOUR FOOD ELEMENTS *

		6–8 years	9–11 years	12–14 years	15 years
Food-energy value	Girls	2.1	4.4	4.2	4.3
	Boys	0.0	2.4	5.1	4.9
Protein	Girls	2.1	3.3	7.9	9.6
	Boys	0.0	2.4	1.7	1.9
Calcium	Girls	19.8	25.2	29.7	45.6
	Boys	10.9	14.7	29.7	20.7
Iron	Girls	4.9	6.0	16.3	31.5
	Boys	2.0	3.7	6.2	2.9

* Adapted from Ercel S. Eppright and Charlotte Roderuck, "Diet and Nutritional Status of Iowa School Children," *American Journal of Public Health,* Vol. 45 (1955), pp. 464–471.

If the dietary deficiency is slight, the pupil may experience only fatigue and greater irritability than usual. More critical malnutrition results in restlessness, inattention, forgetfulness, a low tolerance for frustration, or symptoms suggesting mental retardation. Physical symptoms may include an abnormal intolerance to light, inflammation of the eyelids, peeling or cracked lips, inflamed gums, and dental caries. In the most serious cases, there is retardation of growth and a susceptibility to a variety of illnesses.

Children's ability to succeed in school, both academically and in personal-social relations, is affected by nutrition. That is, retarded school progress may be caused by low energy or lack of alertness resulting from a chronically poor diet. And irritability in social relations may cause the child to lose friends.

Such symptoms as these can suggest to the teacher that the difficulties a pupil is experiencing may be seated in food deficiencies. A child suspected of having substandard nutrition should be referred to the school nurse or doctor, especially in instances where the teacher believes the parents' eating practices may be at fault and that they would resent the teacher's suggesting to them directly that diet might be the child's trouble. In other cases, where there is no school nurse or doctor readily available, the teacher may wish to have the child write down a week's record of his meals. With the aid of a nutrition book on desirable food values, the teacher himself may analyze these diets and make an estimate of their adequacy before talking over this possibility with the mother of the pupil.

Teachers in science and health education carry a major responsibility for convincing pupils that a properly balanced diet is necessary and for making sure students know how to determine what a balanced diet is. Student projects can support this learning. For instance, pupils may analyze the food value of the typical lunches eaten in the school cafeteria. They can plan a week's menus of nutrient-rich meals. They can analyze the contents of the meals they normally eat during the week. They can organize exhibits on balanced diets and can prepare bulletin-board displays showing drawings of the results of deficiencies of different nutrients. They can create posters illustrating balanced meals and post these in the school lunchroom.

If midmorning milk or fruit juice and crackers are not a part of the routine in the elementary grades, it would be well for teachers and administrators to support a drive to establish this as a practice, at least for the primary level.

Through such measures, teachers can improve the health, the disposition, and the efficiency of many of their pupils.

ALLERGIES

An allergy is a hypersensitiveness to certain things, such as pollens, specific foods, or medicines. Or an allergy may result from a negative psychological reaction to some person with whom the child has strong emotional ties that are accompanied by strong feelings of resentment or dislike.

The symptoms of this hypersensitiveness or emotional reaction can range from simple sneezing to the severe pains of a migraine headache. Or the allergy can bring on such reactions as itching, breaking out in a rash, swelling of the face so that the eyes nearly close, or the suffocating gasping of asthma.

An estimated twenty million people suffer from allergies. Therefore teachers can expect to meet a quantity of children who experience some kind of allergic reaction.

There is not a great deal that the teacher can do to prevent the development of allergies and asthma, because the causes usually lie in the family background or home experiences of the child. There may very well be a hereditary tendency to allergies. The feeding of new or special foods to an excess during convalescence from an illness may start an allergic reaction to these foods. The development of asthma, with the breathing difficulties it entails, apparently has a close connection with conflicts the child experiences with one or both parents.

The teacher can, however, try to observe any conditions in the classroom that set off or aggravate an allergy. When a child begins sneezing and his eyes water, although he seems not to have a cold, the bouquet of sunflowers on the teacher's desk may be at fault. An analysis of conditions existing in the classroom (such as a difficult test or a visit from the child's mother) shortly before an asthma attack occurs may alert the teacher to what situations apparently precipitate the allergic reaction in the pupil. Such information can then be passed on to the school nurse or guidance counselors for consideration as they discuss a plan for aiding the child. In addition, if foods to which a child may be allergic are written in the health report, teachers can be aware of things the child should not eat at school parties or in the lunchroom.

OTHER HANDICAPS

The types of handicap conditions discussed so far in this chapter do not exhaust all kinds the regular classroom teacher may meet, but they do include the most common.

Basic suggestions for aiding students with such handicaps as heart conditions are also true of chronic ailments like kidney diseases and other disorders of internal organs.

Tuberculosis, though not the killer it once was, is still a debilitating disease that strikes young people, usually those in very poor economic circumstances. The teacher can be of most aid by cooperating in the support of X-ray programs and by teaching good personal hygiene.

Diabetes will be found in some school children. In diabetes the body does not effectively use food substances, especially sugar. Since the insulin important to the utilization of sugar is not properly secreted by the pancreas, insulin must be injected into the body. Teachers can be helpful to the diabetic child by watching for symptoms of persisting fatigue, which is caused by the unavailability of sugars and, secondarily, of fats. The teacher can also cooperate with the doctor's schedule for insulin shots and with his cautions about the child's activity and diet limitations.

SUMMARY

Occasionally teachers must work with students who suffer from some physical disorder such as a crippling condition, cerebral palsy, epilepsy, heart disease, a disfigurement, malnutrition, an allergy, tuberculosis, or diabetes.

If pupils are to gain the most from school, they require the teacher's aid in (1) minimizing the physical effect of their handicap in adjusting to a regular school program, (2) protecting them from injury or from overtaxing their energy, and (3) minimizing the adverse psychological and social effects of their handicap.

SUGGESTED LEARNING ACTIVITIES

1. Invite a school nurse to talk to your group about (a) the kinds of physical handicaps certain children in her school are suffering, (b) the kinds of medical records routinely kept on such children, and (c) the kinds of special aid given to these children by the school.

2. Invite a school psychologist or guidance counselor to describe to your group (a) any cases he has handled of pupils whose school adjustment has been adversely affected by a physical handicap, (b) the factors, such as parental attitude or inadequate school provisions, that tended to aggravate the pupils' adjustment problem, and (c) what the counselor and/or the teachers did to try to improve the pupils' condition.

3. Collect from the city or county school superintendent's office information about how the following types of pupils are handled in this particu-

lar school district: (a) crippled children, (b) cerebral-palsied pupils, (c) epileptics, (d) rheumatic-fever and heart patients, and (e) others suffering from chronic disorders.

4. In such periodicals as *Exceptional Children, Child Development, The American Journal of Diseases of Children, Nervous Child, The Journal of Pediatrics*, or more general journals in psychology and education, locate one article about one of the topics discussed in this chapter. Summarize the main points of this article for your classmates and give your analysis of the importance the findings in the article might have for teachers or parents of handicapped children.

5. Ask an experienced teacher whether he or she remembers having taught a student suffering from one of the disorders discussed in this chapter. Ask the teacher to describe (a) the problems this pupil faced in doing his schoolwork, (b) any problems the pupil might have had in personal-social relations, (c) the pupil's apparent general attitude toward his school life, (d) his relationship to the teacher, such as his exhibiting antagonism, apathy, or overdependency, (e) what special provisions, if any, the teacher needed to make for the student, (f) what contact the teacher had with the parents and what their attitude toward the child seemed to be, and (g) what additional knowledge or training the teacher felt he or she needed in order to work most successfully with the pupil.

SUGGESTED READINGS

BAKER, HARRY J. *Introduction to Exceptional Children.* New York: Macmillan, 1959. Chaps. 8, 27.

BRIDGE, E. M. *Epilepsy and Convulsive Disorders in Children.* New York: McGraw-Hill, 1949.

CRUICKSHANK, WILLIAM M. (ed.). *Psychology of Exceptional Children and Youth.* Englewood Cliffs: Prentice-Hall, 1955. Chaps. 6–8.

———— and DOLPHIN, JANE E. "The Educational Implications of Psychological Studies of Cerebral-Palsied Children," *Journal of the International Council for Exceptional Children,* October, 1951.

FRAMPTON, M. E., and GALL, E. D. (eds.). *Special Education for the Exceptional.* Boston: Porter Sargent, 1955. Vol. II.

GARRISON, KARL C., and FORCE, DEWEY G. *The Psychology of Exceptional Children.* New York: The Ronald Press Co., 1959. Chaps. 12–17.

GOODENOUGH, FLORENCE L. *Exceptional Children.* New York: Appleton-Century-Crofts, 1956. Chaps. 26–30.

HECK, ARCH O. *The Education of Exceptional Children.* New York: McGraw-Hill, 1953. Chaps. 9–11, 22.

HOCH, P. H., and KNIGHT, R. P. (eds.). *Epilepsy: Psychiatric Aspects of Convulsive Disorders.* New York: Grune and Stratton, 1947.

MICHAL-SMITH, H. (ed.). *Management of the Handicapped Child.* New York: Grune and Stratton, 1957. Chaps. 9–12.

PHELPS, WINTHROP M.; HOPKINS, THOMAS W.; and COUSINS, ROBERT. *The Cerebral-Palsied Child: A Guide for Parents.* New York: Simon and Schuster, 1958.

STRAUSS, ALFRED A., and LEHTINEN, LAURA E. *Psychopathology and Education of the Brain-Injured Child.* New York: Grune and Stratton, 1947.

Author Index

Subject Index